FILMED BOOKS AND PLAYS

For Referen

Not to be taken from this room

FILMED BOOKS AND PLAYS

A list of Books and Plays from which
Films have been made, 1928-1969

A. G. S. Enser, FLA, FRSA
(*Borough Librarian of Eastbourne*)

Revised and with a supplementary list
for 1968 and 1969

SEMINAR PRESS NEW YORK
A GRAFTON BOOK

FIRST PUBLISHED 1968 BY
ANDRE DEUTSCH LIMITED
105 GREAT RUSSELL STREET
LONDON WC1

REVISED EDITION PUBLISHED 1971
SECOND IMPRESSION OF REVISED EDITION 1972
COPYRIGHT © 1968, 1971 BY A. G. S. ENSER
ALL RIGHTS RESERVED
PRINTED IN GREAT BRITAIN
ISBN 0–12–827050–5
LIBRARY OF CONGRESS CATALOG CARD NUMBER 70–149483
PUBLISHED IN THE WESTERN HEMISPHERE BY
SEMINAR PRESS, INC.
111 FIFTH AVENUE NEW YORK,
NEW YORK 10003

CONTENTS

PREFACE

SCOPE

This list of films made from books or plays covers films produced between 1928 and 1967. It is a cumulated list comprising FILMED BOOKS AND PLAYS, 1928–1949; SUPPLEMENT I, 1950–1951; SUPPLEMENT II, 1952–1954; SUPPLEMENT III, 1955–1957; and SUPPLEMENT IV, 1958–1960; together with additions 1961–1967.

The commencing date 1928 was chosen because from that year onwards most films produced for public viewing were talking pictures.

Nearly all the films listed are either British or American in origin.

It is not claimed that the list is completely exhaustive, and I should be pleased to be informed of omissions.

ARRANGEMENT

There are three indexes, namely:

(a) Film Title Index
(b) Author Index
(c) Change of Original Title Index

The articles 'The', 'A' or 'An' are placed at the end of the title instead of at the beginning, and are ignored in alphabetical arrangement.

THE FILM TITLE INDEX is arranged alphabetically under the title of the film. Underneath is shown the name of the maker or distributing company (usually in abbreviation) and the year the film was registered.

Opposite is shown the name of the author of the book from which the film was made, and underneath, the name of the publisher. Where another title, in italics, follows the name of the author, this signifies that the film company changed the title of the book from the original shown in italics to that printed opposite. Where (P) is found, this signifies that the book is in play form.

THE AUTHOR INDEX is arranged alphabetically under the names of authors with further alphabetical arrangement under each author of his works which have been filmed. Underneath the title of the work filmed is shown the name of the publisher. Opposite is shown the name of the maker of the film or distributing company. Should a title in italics follow, this signifies the title under which the film was presented. It will be noted that in this author index liberty has been taken to use an author's pseudonym, where employed, in preference to his real name. Reference in such cases is made from the real name to the pseudonym used, e.g.,

STURE-VASA, Mary *see* O'HARA, Mary. *pseud.*

In the case of dual authors, the author entry is made under the name of the first mentioned on the title page. The second author's name is also listed but reference given to the name of the first author, under which the entry will be found, e.g.,

SIMON, S. J. *jt. author* See BRAHMS, C.

THE CHANGE OF ORIGINAL TITLE INDEX is an alphabetical arrangement of the original book titles differing from their film titles. Underneath the original book title is found the name of the author. Opposite is found the title of the film, with underneath the name of the maker or distributing company and the year the film was registered.

HOW TO USE THE INDEXES

If the name of the film is known but not the name of the author of the book, refer to the FILM TITLE INDEX. Ignore any article 'The', 'A' or 'An'.

If the name of the author is known but not that of the book nor film, refer to the AUTHOR INDEX where, under the author's name, will be found in alphabetical arrangement the titles of his works which have been filmed.

If it is desired to know what works of a particular author have been filmed, refer to the AUTHOR INDEX.

If the original title of the book is known but not that given to the film, nor the author's name refer to the CHANGE OF ORIGINAL TITLE INDEX.

THE INDEXES ARE INTENDED FOR THE USE OF:

Information services in public and special libraries, as well as film societies and all concerned with the film industry.

ACKNOWLEDGMENTS

In the compilation of this cumulated list, I am very grateful for all the help given me by Miss W. V. Baulcomb and my wife.

A. G. S. ENSER

EASTBOURNE, April 1968

INTRODUCTION TO SUPPLEMENT AND REVISED EDITION

As stated in the PREFACE to the previous edition, I invited notification of omissions between 1928–1967. I am, therefore, very grateful both to reviewers and personal correspondents who have pointed out errors and omissions. In particular, I wish to thank Mr. H. A. Thevenet of Buenos Aires who has been especially helpful.

For any compiler of such a book as this, there are many pitfalls, and what was correct at one period of time can be incorrect later. Both film companies and publishers create difficulties for the bibliographer. The former may announce a film using the original title of the author from which the book is taken, then present the film under an entirely different title. Or, they announce a film using a different title from that chosen by the author, but on presentation may revert to the author's title or even use another title altogether. Then, the film title as well as the book title may vary in different countries. Publishers too, as a film tie-in, may republish the book using a title chosen by the film company.

Once again, it is not claimed that the list is completely exhaustive, and I shall be pleased to be informed of omissions and errors.

A. G. S. ENSER

EASTBOURNE, September 1970

LIST OF ABBREVIATIONS

AA	Anglo-Amalgamated Film Company
AB	Associated British Film Distributors
ABP	Associated British and Pathe Film Distributors
ALL	Alliance Productions Ltd
ARC	The Archers Film Productions Ltd
AUT	Auten Films
BD	British and Dominion Films Ltd
BI	British International Films
BL	British Lion Films Ltd
BN	British National Films Ltd
CFF	Children's Film Foundation
CIN	Cineguild Incorporated
COL	Columbia Productions Ltd
CONT	Continental Films Ltd
EAL	Ealing Studios Ltd
EL	Eagle Lion Distributors Ltd
FOX	Fox and Twentieth Century Fox Ltd
GB	Gaumont British Ltd
GFD	General Film Distributors Ltd
ID	First Division Films
IN	International Motion Pictures
t. author	joint author
LF	London Films
MGM	Metro-Goldwyn-Mayer Ltd
MON	Monogram Films
OLY	Olympic Films
PAR	Paramount Productions Ltd
pseud	pseudonym
PRC	Producers' Releasing Corporation
RANK	J. Arthur Rank Film Distribution

11

FILM-TITLE INDEX

A

ABE LINCOLN IN ILLINOIS
RKO 1940

Sherwood, R. E. (*Abe Lincoln of . . .*) (P)
Scribner, N.Y.

ABOUT FACE
WAR 1952

Monks, J. *and* Finklehoffe, F. F. (*Brother rat*) (P)
Random House, N.Y.

ABOUT MRS LESLIE
PAR 1954

Delmar, V.
Hale

ABOVE SUSPICION
MGM 1943

McInnes, H.
Harrap

ABOVE US THE WAVES
GFD 1954

Warren, C. E. T. *and* Benson, J.
Harrap

ACCENT ON YOUTH
PAR 1935

Raphaelson, S. (P)
French

ACCOUNT RENDERED
RANK 1957

Barrington, P.
Barker

ACCUSED, THE
PAR 1949

Truesdell, J. (*Be still my love*)
Boardman

ACCUSED OF MURDER
REP 1956

Burnett, W. R. (*Vanity Row*)
Corgi

ACROSS THE BRIDGE
RANK 1957

Greene, G.
Heinemann

ACROSS THE WIDE MISSOURI
MGM 1951

De Voto, B.
Eyre & Spottiswoode

ACTION FOR SLANDER
UA 1938

Borden, M.
Heinemann

ACTION IN THE NORTH ATLANTIC
WAR 1943

Gilpatric, G.
Dutton, N.Y.

ACT OF LOVE
UA 1954

Hayes, A. (*Girl on the Via Flaminia, The*)
Gollancz

ACT OF MURDER, AN
UN 1948

Lothar, E. (*Mills of God, The*)
Secker

ACTRESS, THE
MGM 1953

Gordon, R. (*Leading lady*) (P)
Dramatists, N.Y.

ADA DALLAS
MGM 1960

Williams, W.
Muller

ADAM HAD FOUR SONS
COL 1941

Bonner, C. (*Nor perfume nor wine*)
Cassell

ADDRESS UNKNOWN
COL 1944

Taylor, K.
Hamilton

ADMIRABLE CRICHTON, THE
COL 1957

Barrie, *Sir* J. M. (P)
Hodder & Stoughton

ADVENTURE
MGM 1945

Davis, C. B. (*Anointed, The*)
Barker

ADVENTURE IN IRAQ
WAR 1943

Archer, W. (*Green goddess, The*) (P)
Heinemann

ADVENTURE IN THE HOPFIELDS
ABP 1954

Lavin, N, *and* Thorp, M. (*Hop dog, The*)
Oxford U.P.

ADVENTURE ISLAND
PAR 1947

Stevenson, R. L. (*Ebb tide*)
Various

ADVENTURES OF HAJJI BABA, THE
FOX 1954

Morier, J. J. (*Adventures of Hajji Baba of Ispahan*)
Modern Library, N.Y.

ADVENTURES OF HUCKLEBERRY FINN, THE
MGM 1939
MGM 1960

Twain, M. (*Huckleberry Finn*)
Various

ADVENTURES OF MARTIN EDEN, THE
COL 1942

London, J. (*Martin Eden*)
Heinemann

ADVENTURES OF QUENTIN DURWARD
MGM 1955

Scott, *Sir* W. (*Quentin Durward*)
Various

ADVENTURES OF ROBINSON CRUSOE, THE
UA 1954

Defoe, D.
Various

ADVENTURES OF TOM SAWYER, THE
UA 1938

Twain, M. (*Tom Sawyer*)
Various

ADVISE AND CONSENT
BL 1962

Drury, A.
Collins

AFFAIR AT THE VILLA FIORITA, THE
WAR 1964

Godden, R. (*Battle of the Villa Fiorita*)
Macmillan

AFFAIRS OF CAPPY RICKS, THE
REP 1937

Kyne, P. B. (*Cappy Ricks*)
Hodder & Stoughton

AFFAIRS OF CELLINI
UA 1934

Mayer, E. J. (*Firebrand, The*) (P)
French

16

AFRICAN FURY
ABP 1955

Michael, G.
Joseph

AFRICAN QUEEN, THE
ROMULUS 1951

Forester, C. S.
Joseph

AFTER OFFICE HOURS
BI 1932

Druten, J. van. (*London Wall*) (P
Gollancz

AFTER THE BALL
BL 1957

De Frece, *Lady* (*Recollections of Vesta Tilly*)
Hutchinson

AGE OF INNOCENCE
RKO 1934

Wharton, *Mrs* E.
Appleton-Century, N.Y.

AGONY AND THE ECSTACY, THE
FOX 1964

Stone, I.
Collins

AH WILDERNESS
MGM 1935

O'Neill, E. G.
Cape

AIN'T LIFE WONDERFUL
ABP 1953

Williams, B. (*Uncle Willie and the bicycle shop*)
Harrap

ALFIE
PAR 1965

Naughton, B. (P)
French

ALFIE
PAR 1965

Naughton, B.
MacGibbon & Kee

ALIBI, THE
WAR 1935

Lardner, R.
Garden City, N.Y.

ALICE ADAMS
RKO 1935

Tarkington, B.
Odyssey Press, N.Y.

ALICE IN WONDERLAND
PAR 1933
RKO 1951

Carroll, L.
Various

ALLEGHENY UPRISING
RKO 1939

Swanson, N. H. (*First rebel, The*)
Grosset, N.Y.

ALL FALL DOWN
MGM 1961

Herlihy, J. L.
Dutton, N.Y.

ALLIGATOR NAMED DAISY, AN
RANK 1955

Terrot, C.
Collins

ALL MEN ARE ENEMIES
FOX 1934

Aldington, R.
Heinemann

ALL OVER THE TOWN
WESSEX 1948

Delderfield, R. F. (P)
French

**ALL QUIET ON THE WESTERN
FRONT**
UN 1930

Remarque, E. M.
Putnam

ALL THAT MONEY CAN BUY RKO 1941	Benet, S. V. (*Devil and Daniel Webster, The*) Oxford U.P.
ALL THE FINE YOUNG CANNIBALS MGM 1960	Marshall, R. (*Brixby girls, The*) Heinemann
ALL THE KING'S MEN COL 1949	Warren, R. P. Eyre & Spottiswoode
ALL THE WAY HOME PAR 1963	Agee, J. (*Death in the family, A*) Gollancz
ALL THIS AND HEAVEN TOO WAR 1940	Field, R. Collins
ALL THIS AND MONEY TOO UA 1963	Hardy, L. (*Grand Duke and Mr Pimm, The*) Cape
ALMOST MARRIED FOX 1932	Soutar, A. (*Devil's triangle*) Hutchinson
ALONG CAME JONES RKO 1945	LeMay, A. (*Useless cowboy, The*) Collins
ALPHABET MURDERS, THE MGM 1966	Christie, A. (*ABC murders, The*) Collins
AMATEUR GENTLEMAN, THE UA 1936	Farnol, J. Sampson Low
AMAZING DR CLITTERHOUSE, THE WAR 1938	Lyndon, B. (P) Hamilton
AMAZING QUEST, THE KLEMENT 1936	Oppenheim, E. P. (*Amazing quest of Mr Ernest Bliss, The*) Hodder & Stoughton
AMBUSH MGM 1950	Short, L. Collins
AMERICANIZATION OF EMILY, THE MGM 1963	Huie, W. B. Allen
AMOROUS ADVENTURES OF MOLL FLANDERS, THE PAR 1964	Defoe, D. (*Moll Flanders*) Various
AMOROUS PRAWN, THE BL 1962	Kimmins, A. (P) French
ANASTASIA FOX 1956	Bolton, G. (P) French
ANATOLIAN SMILE, THE WAR 1964	Kazan, E. (*America, America*) Collins

TITLE OF FILM	AUTHOR AND PUBLISHER
ANATOMY OF A MURDER COL 1959	Traver, R. Faber
ANDERSONVILLE COL 1959	Kantor, M. W. H. Allen
AND NOW TOMORROW PAR 1944	Field, R. Collins
AND ONE WAS WONDERFUL MGM 1940	Miller, A. D. Methuen
ANDROCLES AND THE LION RKO 1952	Shaw, G. B. (P) Constable
ANGEL BABY CONT DIS 1961	Barber, E. O. (*Jenny Angel*) Putnam
ANGEL WHO PAWNED HER HARP, THE BL 1954	Terrot, C. Collins
ANGEL WITH THE TRUMPET BL 1950	Lothar, E. Harrap
ANGRY HILLS, THE MGM 1959	Uris, L. Wingate
ANIMAL FARM ABP 1954	Orwell, G. Secker & Warburg
ANIMAL KINGDOM, THE RKO 1932	Barry, L. (P) French, N.Y.
ANNA AND THE KING OF SIAM FOX 1946	Landon, M. Harrap
ANNA CHRISTIE MGM 1930	O'Neill, E. G. (P) Random House, N.Y.
ANNA KARENINA MGM 1935 BL 1948	Tolstoy, L. N. Various
ANNA LUCASTA COL 1948	Yordon, P. Random House, N.Y.
ANNE OF GREEN GABLES RKO 1934	Montgomery, L. M. Harrap
ANNE OF WINDY POPLARS RKO 1940	Montgomery, L. M. (*Anne of Windy Willows*) Harrap
ANN VICKERS RKO 1933	Lewis, S. Cape

ANOTHER PART OF THE FOREST
UN 1948

Hellman, L. F. (P)
Viking, N.Y.

ANOTHER TIME, ANOTHER PLACE
PAR 1958

Coffee, L. (*Weep no more*)
Cassell

ANTHONY ADVERSE
WAR 1936

Allen, H.
Gollancz

ANY WEDNESDAY
WAR 1966

Resnik, M. (*Son of any Wednesday*) (P)
Stein & Day, N.Y.

ANYTHING CAN HAPPEN
PAR 1952

Papashvily, G. *and* Papashvily, H.
Heinemann

APACHE
UA 1954

Wellman, P. I. (*Bronco Apache*)
News of the World

APACHE TERRITORY
COL 1958

L'Amour, L. (*Burning hills*)
Jason Press, N.Y.

APPOINTMENT WITH VENUS
GFD 1951

Tickell, J.
Hodder & Stoughton

ARCH OF TRIUMPH
UA 1948

Remarque, E. M.
Hutchinson

ARE HUSBANDS NECESSARY
PAR 1942

Rorick, I. S. (*Mr and Mrs Cugat*)
Jarrolds

AREN'T MEN BEASTS
AB 1937

Sylvaine, V. (P)
French

AREN'T MEN BEASTS
AB 1937

Sylvaine, V.
Jenkins

AREN'T WE ALL
PAR 1932

Lonsdale, F. (P)
Heinemann

ARIZONA
COL 1940

Kelland, C. B.
Harper, N.Y.

ARKANSAS JUDGE
REP 1941

Stone, I. (*False witness*)
Doubleday, N.Y.

ARMS AND THE MAN
GB 1940

Shaw, G. B. (P)
Various

ARMY BRAT
MGM 1946

Waddleton, T. D. (*Little Mr Jim*)
Coward-McCann, N.Y.

AROUND THE WORLD IN EIGHTY DAYS
UA 1957

Verne, J.
Various

ARRIVEDERCI, BABY!
PAR 1967

Deming, R. (*Careful man, The*)
W. H. Allen

TITLE OF FILM	AUTHOR AND PUBLISHER
ARROWHEAD PAR 1953	Burnett, W. R. (*Adobe walls*) Knopf, N.Y.
ARROW IN THE DUST ABP 1954	Foreman, L. L. (*Road to San Jacinto*) Dutton, N.Y.
ARROWSMITH UA 1931	Lewis, S. (*Martin Arrowsmith*) Cape
ARSENE LUPIN MGM 1932	LeBlanc, M. Newnes
ARSENIC AND OLD LACE WAR 1944	Kesselring, J. O. (P) Random House, N.Y.
ARTURO'S ISLAND GALA 1963	Morante, E. Collins
AS HUSBANDS GO FOX 1934	Crothers, R. (P) French
ASK ANY GIRL MGM 1959	Wolfe, W. Hammond
AS LONG AS THEY'RE HAPPY GFD 1954	Sylvaine, V. (P) French
ASPHALT JUNGLE, THE MGM 1950	Burnett, W. R. Heinemann
ASSAULT ON A QUEEN PAR 1966	Finney, J. Eyre & Spottiswoode
ASSIGNMENT IN BRITTANY MGM 1943	MacInnes, H. Harrap
ASSIGNMENT – PARIS COL 1952	Gallico, P. (*Trial by terror*) Joseph
AS THE EARTH TURNS WAR 1934	Carroll, G. Macmillan
ASTONISHED HEART, THE GFD 1949	Coward, N. (P) Heinemann
AS YOU DESIRE ME MGM 1932	Frank, L. (*Carl and Anna*) Davis
AS YOU LIKE IT FOX 1933	Shakespeare, W. (P) Various
ATLANTIC BI 1930	Raymond, E. (*Berg, The*) (P) Benn
ATTEMPTS TO KILL AA 1961	Wallace, E. (*Lone house mystery, The*) Collins

AT THE VILLA ROSE
AB 1940

Mason, A. E. W.
   Hodder & Stoughton

AT WAR WITH THE ARMY
PAR 1951

Allardice, J. (P)
   French, N.Y.

AUNT CLARA
BL 1954

Streatfeild, N.
   Collins

AUNTIE MAME
WAR 1958

Dennis, P.
   Vanguard, N.Y.

AUNTIE MAME
WAR 1958

Lawrence, J. *and* Lee, R. E. (P)
   Vanguard, N. Y.

AUTUMN CROCUS
BI 1930

Anthony, C. L. (P)
   Gollancz

AVALANCHE
PRC 1946

Boyle, K.
   Faber

AVENGERS, THE
REP 1950

Beach, R. E. (*Don Careless*)
   Hutchinson

AWAY ALL BOATS
UI 1955

Dodson, K.
   Angus and Robertson

B

BABBIT
IN 1934

Lewis, S.
   Cape

BABY AND THE BATTLESHIP, THE
BL 1956

Thorne, A.
   Heinemann

BABY DOLL
WAR 1956

Williams,, T. (P)
   Secker & Warburg

BABY, THE RAIN MUST FALL
COL 1965

Foote, H. (*Travelling lady, The*) (P)
   Dramatists, N.Y.

BACHELOR IN PARADISE
MGM 1961

Caspary, V.
   Pan

BACHELOR'S FOLLY
WW 1932

Wallace, E. (*Calendar, The*) (P)
   Collins

BACK FROM THE DEAD
FOX 1957

Turney, C. (*Other one, The*)
   Holt, N.Y.

BACKGROUND
ABP 1953

Chetham-Strode, W. (P)
   French

BACKGROUND TO DANGER
WAR 1943

Ambler, E. (*Uncommon danger*)
   Hodder & Stoughton

BACK STREET
UN 1931
UN 1941
UN 1961

Hurst, F.
Cape

BACK TO GOD'S COUNTRY
GFD 1953

Curwood, J. O.
Triangle Bks, N.Y.

BAD DAY AT BLACK ROCK
MGM 1955

Niall, M.
Muller

BAD SEED, THE
WAR 1956

March, W.
Hamilton

BADGER'S GREEN
HIGHBURY 1949

Sherriff, R. C. (P)
Gollancz

BAD MEN OF TOMBSTONE
ABP 1949

Monoghan, J. (*Last of the badmen*)
Bobbs-Merrill, Indianapolis

BAD SEED
War 1956

March W.
Hamilton

BAHAMA PASSAGE
PAR 1941

Hayes, N. (*Dido Cay*)
Davies

BALCONY, THE
BL 1963

Genet, J. (P)
Faber

BAMBI
RKO 1942

Salten, F.
Cape

BANANA RIDE
ABP 1941

Travers, B. (P)
French

BAND OF ANGELS
WAR 1956

Warren, R. P.
Eyre & Spottiswoode

BARABBAS
COL 1962

Lagerkvist, P.
Four Square Bks

BAREFOOT IN THE PARK
PAR 1967

Simon, N. (P)
French, N.Y.

BAREFOOT MAILMAN, THE
COL 1951

Pratt, T.
Cassell

**BARRETTS OF WIMPOLE STREET,
THE**
MGM 1934
MGM 1956

Besier, R. (P)
Gollancz

**BARRETTS OF WIMPOLE STREET,
THE**
MGM 1934
MGM 1956

Besier, R.
Gollancz

BAR 20
UA 1943

Mulford, C. E.
Hodder & Stoughton

BAR 20 RIDES AGAIN
PAR 1935

Mulford, C. E.
Hodder & Stoughton

BAT, THE
WAR 1959

Rinehart, M. R. (P)
French

BATTLE CRY
WAR 1954

Uris, L.
Wingate

BATTLE HYMN
UI 1956

Hess, D. E.
Davies

BATTLE OF THE BULGE
CINERAMA 1965

Merriam, R. E.
Panther

BATTLE OF THE RIVER PLATE, THE
RANK 1956

Powell, M. (*Graf Spee*)
Hodder & Stoughton

BAT WHISPERS, THE
UA 1931

Rinehart, M. R. (*Bat, The*)
Cassell

BEACHCOMBER
GFD 1954

Maugham, W. S. (*Vessel of wrath*)
Heinemann

BEACHHEAD
UA 1953

Hubler, R. G. (*I've got mine*)
Putnam, N.Y.

BEAST WITH FIVE FINGERS
WAR 1946

Harvey, W. F.
Dent

BEAT THE DEVIL
ROMULUS 1953

Helvick, J.
Boardman

BEAU BRUMMELL
MGM 1954

Fitch, C. (P)
Lane, N.Y.

BEAU GESTE
PAR 1939
UI 1966

Wren, P. C.
Murray

BEAU IDEAL
RKO 1931

Wren, P. C.
Murray

BEAU JAMES
PAR 1957

Fowler, G.
Viking, N.Y.

BEAU SABREUR
PAR 1928

Wren, P. C.
Murray

BEAUTY FOR SALE
MGM 1933

Baldwin, F. (*Beauty*)
Sampson Low

24

TITLE OF FILM	AUTHOR AND PUBLISHER
BEAUTY'S DAUGHTER FOX 1935	Norris, K. Murray
BECAUSE THEY'RE YOUNG COL 1960	Farris, J. (*Harrison High*) Gollancz
BECKET PAR 1963	Anouilh, J. (P) Methuen
BECKY SHARP RKO 1935	Thackeray, W. M. (*Vanity Fair*) Various
BEDELIA GFD 1946	Caspary, V. Eyre & Spottiswoode
BEDFORD INCIDENT, THE BL 1964	Rascovich, M. Secker & Warburg
BEFORE I WAKE GN 1955	Debrett, H. Dodd, N.Y.
BEGGARS OF LIFE PAR 1928	Tully, J. Chatto & Windus
BEGGAR'S OPERA, THE BL 1953	Gay, J. (P) French
BEHIND THAT CURTAIN FOX 1930	Biggers, E. D. Harrap
BEHIND THE HEADLINES RANK 1956	Chapman, R. Laurie
BEHIND THE MASK BL 1958	Wilson, J. R. (*Mask, The*) Heinemann
BEHOLD A PALE HORSE COL 1964	Pressburger, E. (*Killing a mouse on Sunday*) Harcourt, N.Y.
BEHOLD MY WIFE PAR 1935	Parker, G. (*Translations of a savage*) Methuen
BELLA DONNA OLY 1935 UN 1945	Hichens, R. Heinemann
BELL, BOOK AND CANDLE COL 1958	Druten, J. van (P) French
BELLE OF NEW YORK, THE MGM 1952	McLellan, C. M. S. (P) French
BELL FOR ADANO, A FOX 1945	Hersey, J. R. Gollancz
BELLS ARE RINGING MGM 1960	Comden, B. *and* Green, A. (P) Random House, N.Y.

BELLS GO DOWN, THE
EAL 1943 — Methuen

BELLS ON THEIR TOES
FOX 1952 — Gilbreth, F. B. *and* Carey, E.
Heinemann

BELOVED INFIDEL
FOX 1959 — Graham, S. *and* Frank, G.
Cassell

BELOVED VAGABOND, THE
COL 1937 — Locke, W. J.
Lane

BEN HUR
MGM 1931
MGM 1959 — Wallace, L.
Various

BENSON MURDER CASE, THE
PAR 1930 — Dine, S. S. van
Benn

BERNARDINE
FOX 1957 — Chase, M. (P)
Oxford U.P.

BEST MAN WINS, THE
COL 1948 — Twain, M. (*Celebrated jumping frog of Calaveras, The*)
Various

BEST OF EVERYTHING, THE
FOX 1959 — Jaffé, R.
Cape

BEST YEARS OF OUR LIVES, THE
RKO 1946 — Kantor, M. (*Glory for me*)
Coward-McCann, N.Y.

BETRAYAL FROM THE EAST
RKO 1945 — Hynd, A.
McBride, N.Y.

BETWEEN HEAVEN AND HELL
FOX 1956 — Gwaltney, F. I. (*Day the century ended, The*)
Secker & Warburg

BETWEEN TWO WORLDS
WAR 1944 — Vane, S. (*Outward bound*) (P)
Chatto & Windus

BEWARE MY LOVELY
RKO 1952 — Dineli, M. (*Man, The*) (P)
Dramatists, N.Y.

BEWARE OF PITY
TC 1946 — Zweig, S.
Cassell

BEYOND THE CURTAIN
RANK 1960 — Wallis, A. J. *and* Blair, C. E. (*Thunder above*)
Jarrolds

BEYOND THE FOREST WAR 1951	Engstrand, S. D. Cape
BEYOND THE RIVER FOX 1955	Simenon, G. (*Bottom of the bottle*) Doubleday, N.Y.
BEYOND THIS PLACE REN 1959	Cronin, A. J. Gollancz
BHOWANI JUNCTION MGM 1955	Masters, J. Joseph
BICYCLE THIEVES MGM 1949	Bartolini, L. Joseph
BIG BANKROLL WAR 1961	Katcher, L. Gollancz
BIG CLOCK, THE PAR 1948	Fearing, K. Lane
BIG COUNTRY, THE UA 1958	Hamilton, D. Wingate
BIG FISHERMAN, THE DISNEY 1959	Douglas, L. C. Davies
BIG HEAT, THE COL 1953	McGivern, W. P. Hamilton
BIG HOUSE, THE MGM 1930	Robinson, L. Macmillan
BIG JACK MGM 1949	Flexner, J. T. (*Doctors on horseback*) Heinemann
BIG KNIFE, THE UA 1955	Odets, C. (P) Random House, N.Y.
BIG NIGHT, THE UA 1951	Ellin, S. (*Dreadful summit*) Simon & Schuster, N.Y.
BIG RED DISNEY 1962	Kjelgaard, J. A. Grosset, N.Y.
BIG SKY, THE RKO 1952	Guthrie, A. B. Boardman
BIG SLEEP, THE WAR 1946	Chandler, R. Hamilton
BIG SNATCH, THE GALA 1963	Trinian, J. (*Big grab, The*) Pyramid Bks.
BILLIE UA 1965	Alexander, R. (*Time out for Ginger*) (P) Dramatists, N.Y.

BILL OF DIVORCEMENT, A
RKO 1932
RKO 1940

Dane, C. (P)
Heinemann

BILLY BUDD
ANGLO-ALLIED 1962

Melville, H.
Various

BILLY BUDD
ANGLO-ALLIED 1962

Coxe, L. O. *and* Chapman, R. H. (P)
Hill and Wang, N.Y.

BILLY LIAR
WAR 1962

Waterhouse, K.
Joseph

BILLY LIAR
WAR 1962

Waterhouse, K. *and* Hall, W. (P)
Joseph

BILLY THE KID
MGM 1941

Burns, W. N. (*Saga of Billy the Kid*)
Grosset, N.Y.

**BIOGRAPHY OF A BACHELOR
GIRL**
MGM 1935

Behrman, S. N. (*Biography*) (P)
French

BIRD MAN OF ALCATRAZ
UA 1962

Gaddis, T. E.
Four Square Bks

BIRDS, THE
RANK 1963

Du Maurier, D.
Gollancz

BISHOP MURDER CASE, THE
MGM 1930

Dine, S. S. van.
Cassell

BISHOP'S WIFE, THE
RKO 1947

Nathan, R. (*In Barley fields*)
Constable

BITTER HARVEST
RANK 1962

Hamilton, P. (*Twenty thousand streets under the sky*)
Constable

BITTER SWEET
MGM 1940

Coward, N. (P)
Heinemann

**BITTER TEA OF GENERAL YEN,
THE**
COL 1933

Stone, *Mrs*. G.
Bobbs-Merrill, Indianapolis

BLACK ACES
UN 1937

Payne, S.
Wright & Brown

BLACK ANGEL
UN 1946

Woolrich, C.
Doubleday, N.Y.

BLACK ARROW
COL 1948

Stevenson, R. L.
Various

BLACK BEAUTY
FOX 1946

Sewell, A.
Various

TITLE OF FILM	AUTHOR AND PUBLISHER
BLACKBOARD JUNGLE MGM 1954	Hunter, E. Constable
BLACK CAMEL FOX 1931	Biggers, E. D. Cassell
BLACK EAGLE COL 1948	Henry, O. (*Passing of Black Eagle*) Various
BLACK LIMELIGHT ALL 1939	Sherry, G. (P) French
BLACK MAGIC UA 1949	Dumas, A. (*Memoirs of a physician*) Routledge
BLACKMAILER GFD 1951	Myers, E. (*Mrs Christopher*) Chapman & Hall
BLACK NARCISSUS ARC 1947	Godden, R. Davies
BLACK ROSE, THE FOX 1949	Costain, T. B. Staples
BLACK SHIELD OF FALWORTH, THE UI 1954	Pyle, H. (*Men of iron*) Various
BLACK SWAN, THE FOX 1942	Sabatini, R. Hutchinson
BLACK TULIP, THE CINERAMA 1965	Dumas, A. Various
BLACK WIDOW FOX 1954	Quentin, P. Simon & Schuster, N.Y.
BLANCHE FURY CIN 1948	Shearing, J. Heinemann
BLAZE AT NOON PAR 1947	Gann, E. K. Aldor
BLAZE OF THE SUN PAR 1959	Hougron, J. Hurst & Blackett
BLIND DATE RANK 1959	Howard, L. Longmans
BLINDFOLD UI 1965	Fletcher, L. Eyre & Spottiswoode
BLIND GODDESS, THE FOX 1948	Hastings, *Sir* P. (P) French

BLITHE SPIRIT CIN 1945	Coward, N. (P) Heinemann
BLOCKADE RKO 1928	Chatterton, E. K. (*'Q' ships and their story*) Sidgwick & Jackson
BLOOD ALLEY WAR 1955	Fleischman, A. S. Corgi Bks
BLOOD AND SAND FOX 1941	Ibanez, V. B. Grosset, N.Y.
BLOODHOUNDS OF BROADWAY FOX 1952	Runyon, D. Various
BLOOD ON MY HANDS UI 1949	Butler, G. (*Kiss the blood off my hands*) Jarrolds
BLUE ANGEL, THE PAR 1930 FOX 1959	Mann, H. Jarrolds
BLUE BIRD THE FOX 1940	Maeterlinck, M. (P) Various
BLUE JEANS FOX 1959	Herlihy, J. L. *and* Noble, W. (*Blue denim*) (P) Random House, N.Y.
BLUE LAGOON INDIVIDUAL 1949	Stacpoole, H. de V. Various
BLUE MAX, THE FOX 1965	Hunter, J. D. Muller
BOBO, THE WAR 1967	Cole, B. (*Olimpia*) W. H. Allen
BODY SNATCHER, THE RKO 1945	Stevenson, R. L. Various
BOMBAY MAIL UN 1934	Blochman, L. G. Collins
BONAVENTURE GFD 1951	Hastings, C. (P) French
BONJOUR TRISTESSE COL 1957	Sagan, F. Murray
BON VOYAGE DISNEY 1962	Hayes, M. *and* Hayes, J. A. Deutsch
BORDER LEGION PAR 1930	Grey, Z. Hodder & Stoughton
BORDERLINES UA 1965	Telfer, D. (*Caretakers, The*) Macdonald

BORN FREE BL 1965	Adamson, J. Collins
BORN RECKLESS FOX 1930	Clarke, D. H. (*Louis Beretti*) Long
BORN TO BE BAD RKO 1950	Parrish, A. (*All kneeling*) Benn
BORN TO KILL RKO 1947	Gunn, J. E. (*Deadlier than the male*) World, N.Y.
BORN YESTERDAY COL 1951	Kanin, G. (P) Viking, N.Y.
BOTANY BAY PAR 1952	Nordhoff, C. *and* Hall, J. N. Chapman & Hall
BOUGHT WAR 1931	Henry, H. (*Jackdaws strut*) Paul
BOYD'S SHOP RANK 1960	Ervine, St. J. G. (P) Allen & Unwin
BOY ON A DOLPHIN, THE FOX 1957	Divine, D. Murray
BOYS IN BROWN GFD 1949	Beckwith, R. (P) Marshall
BRAMBLE BUSH WAR 1959	Mergendahl, C. Muller
BRANDED PAR 1950	Evans, E. Various
BRANDY FOR THE PARSON MGM 1952	Household, G. Joseph
BRASHER DOUBLOON, THE MGM 1947	Chandler, R. (*High window, The*) Hamilton
BRASS BOTTLE, THE RANK 1964	Anstey, F. Murray
BRAT FARRAR HAMMER 1950	Tey, J. Davies
BRAVADOS, THE FOX 1958	O'Rourke, F. Heinemann
BRAVE BULLS, THE COL 1950	Lea, T. Heinemann
BREAKFAST AT TIFFANYS PAR 1961	Capote, T. Hamilton

31

BREAKING POINT
WAR 1950

Hemingway, E. (*To have and to have not*)
Cape

BREAKING POINT, THE
BUTCHER 1960

Meynell, L.
Collins

BREAK IN THE CIRCLE
EXCLUSIVE 1954

Loraine, P.
Hodder & Stoughton

BREATH OF SCANDAL, A
PAR 1960

Molnar F. (*Olympia*) (P)
Brentano, N.Y.

BREWSTER'S MILLIONS
UA 1945

McCutcheon, G. B.
Various

BRIDAL PATH, THE
BL 1959

Tranter, N.
Hodder & Stoughton

BRIDES ARE LIKE THAT
IN 1936

Conners, B. (*Applesauce*) (P)
French, N.Y.

BRIDGE OF SAN LUIS RAY, THE
MGM 1929
UA 1944

Wilder, T.
Longmans

BRIDGE ON THE RIVER KWAI, THE
COL 1957

Boulle, P.
Fontana

BRIDGES AT TOKO-RI, THE
PAR 1954

Michener, J. A.
Secker & Warburg

BRIDGE TO THE SUN
MGM 1961

Terasaki, G.
Joseph

BRIEF ENCOUNTER
CIN 1946

Coward, N. (*Still life*) (P)
French

BRIGADOON
MGM 1954

Lerner, A. J. (P)
Theatre Arts

BRIGHT LEAF
WAR 1950

Fitz-Simons, F.
Rinehart, N.Y.

BRIGHTON ROCK
AB 1948

Greene, G.
Heinemann

BRIGHT VICTORY
UI 1951

Kendrick, B. H. (*Lights out*)
W. H. Allen

BRITANNIA OF BILLINGSGATE
GB 1933

Jope-Slade, C. *and* Stokes, S. (P)
French

BRITISH AGENT
IN 1934

Lockhart, *Sir* R. H. B. (*Memoirs of a . . .*)
Putnam

BROKEN ARROW
FOX 1950

Arnold, E. (*Blood brother*)
Collins

32

BROTHER ORCHID WAR 1940	Connell, R. E. (P) French, N.Y.
BROTHER RAT FOX 1938	Monks, J. *and* Finklehoffe, F. R. (P) Random House, N.Y.
BROTHERS, THE FOX 1947	Strong, L. A. G. Gollancz
BROTHERS IN LAW BL 1956	Cecil, H. Joseph
BROTHERS KARAMAZOV, THE MGM 1957	Dostoevski, F. Various
BROTHERS RICO COL 1957	Simenon, G. Doubleday, N.Y.
BROWNING VERSION, THE GFD 1951	Rattigan, T. (P) French
BROWN ON 'RESOLUTION' GB 1933	Forester, C. S. Lane
BUCCANEER, THE PAR 1938	Saxon, L. (*LaFitte the pirate*) Appleton-Century, N.Y.
BUGLES IN THE AFTERNOON WAR 1952	Haycox, E. Hodder & Stoughton
BUILD MY GALLOWS HIGH RKO 1947	Homes, G. Grosset, N.Y.
BULLDOG DRUMMOND AT BAY REP 1937	'Sapper' Hodder & Stoughton
BULLDOG DRUMMOND COMES BACK PAR 1937	'Sapper' (*Female of the species, The*) Hodder & Stoughton
BULLDOG DRUMMOND IN AFRICA PAR 1938	'Sapper' (*Challenge, The*) Hodder & Stoughton
BULLDOG DRUMMOND'S PERIL PAR 1938	'Sapper' (*Third round, The*) Hodder & Stoughton
BULLDOG DRUMMOND'S SECRET POLICE PAR 1939	'Sapper' (*Temple Tower*) Hodder & Stoughton
BUNKER BEAN RKO 1936	Wilson, H. L. Lane
BUNNY LAKE IS MISSING COL 1965	Piper, E. Secker & Warburg
BURN 'EM UP O'CONNOR MGM 1939	Campbell, *Sir* M. (*Salute to the gods*) Cassell

BUSMAN'S HOLIDAY
MGM 1940

Sayers, D. L. (*Busman's honeymoon*)
Gollancz

BUSMAN'S HOLIDAY
MGM 1940

Sayers, D. L. and Byrne, M. St. C.
(*Busman's honeymoon*) (P)
Harcourt, N.Y.

BUT NOT FOR ME
PAR 1959

Raphaelson, S. (*Accent on youth*) (P)
Gollancz

BUTTERFIELD 8
MGM 1960

O'Hara, J.
Cresset Press

BUT THE FLESH IS WEAK
MGM 1932

Novello, I. (*Truth game, The*) (P)
French, N.Y.

BY LOVE POSSESSED
UA 1961

Cozzens, J. G.
Longmans

**BY THE LIGHT OF THE SILVERY
MOON**
WAR 1953

Tarkington, B. (*Penrod*)
Hodder & Stoughton

C

CAESAR AND CLEOPATRA
PASCAL 1945

Shaw, G. B. (P)
Various

CAINE MUTINY, THE
COL 1954

Wouk, H.
Cape

CAIRO
MGM 1963

Burnett, W. R. (*Asphalt jungle, The*)
Corgi Bks

CALENDAR, THE
GFD 1932
GFD 1948

Wallace, E. (P)
French, N.Y.

CALL HER SAVAGE
FOX 1932

Thayer, T.
Long

CALLING BULLDOG DRUMMOND
MGM 1951

Fairlie, G.
Hodder & Stoughton

CALLING PHILO VANCE
WAR 1940

Dine, S. S. van (*Kennel murder case, The*)
Cassell

CALL IT A DAY
WAR 1937

Smith, D. (P)
Gollancz

CALL OF THE WILD, THE
UA 1935

London, J.
Heinemann

CALLING DR. KILDARE
MGM 1935

Brand, M.
Hodder & Stoughton

CALLING OF DAN MATTHEWS, THE
COL 1946

Wright, H. B.
Hodder & Stoughton

CALYPSO
BL 1956

Poe, E. A. (*Gold bug, The and Telltale heart, The*)
Various

CAMELOT
WAR 1967

White, T. H. (*Once and future king, The*)
Collins

CAMILLE
MGM 1936

Dumas, A. *fils* (*La Dame aux Camélias*)
Various

CAMPBELL'S KINGDOM
RANK 1957

Innes, H.
Collins

CANARY MURDER CASE, THE
PAR 1929

Dine, S. S. van
Benn

CANTERVILLE GHOST, THE
MGM 1944

Wilde, O.
Collins

CANYON PASSAGE
UN 1946

Haycox, E.
Hodder & Stoughton

CAPE FEAR
UI 1962

Macdonald, J. D. (*Executioners, The*)
Hale

CAPPY RICKS RETURNS
REP 1935

Kyne, P. B. (*Cappy Ricks comes back*)
Hodder & Stoughton

CAPTAIN BLOOD
WAR 1936

Sabatini, R.
Hutchinson

CAPTAIN BLOOD, FUGITIVE
COL 1952

Sabatini, R. (*Captain Blood returns*)
Hutchinson

CAPTAIN BOYCOTT
INDIVIDUAL 1947

Rooney, P.
Talbot Press

CAPTAIN CAUTION
UA 1940

Roberts, K.
Collins

CAPTAIN FROM CASTILLE
FOX 1948

Shellabarger, S.
Macmillan

CAPTAIN HORATIO HORNBLOWER, R.N.
WAR 1951

Forester, C. S. (*Captain Hornblower, R.N.*)
Joseph

CAPTAIN IS A LADY, THE
MGM 1940

Crothers, R. (*Old lady* 31) (P)
Various

CAPTAIN LIGHTFOOT
UI 1954

Burnett, W. R.
Macdonald

CAPTAIN NEWMAN, M.D.
UI 1963

Rosten, L.
Gollancz

CAPTAINS COURAGEOUS
MGM 1937

Kipling, R.
Macmillan

CAPTAIN'S TABLE, THE
RANK 1958

Gordon, R.
Joseph

CAPTIVE CITY, THE
WAR 1965

Appleby, J.
Hodder & Stoughton

CARAVAN
FOX 1934
BL 1947

Smith, *Lady* E.
Hutchinson

CARD, THE
GFD 1951

Bennett, A.
Methuen

CARDINAL, THE
COL 1963

Robinson, H. M.
Macdonald

CAREER
PAR 1959

Lee, J. (P)
Random House, N.Y.

CAREER
RKO 1939

Strong, P. D.
Grosset, N.Y.

CARETAKER, THE
BL 1963

Pinter, H. (P)
Methuen

CARNIVAL
COL 1935
TC 1946

Mackenzie, *Sir* C.
Various

CARPETBAGGERS, THE
PAR 1963

Robbins, H.
Blond

CARRIE
PAR 1950

Dreiser, T. (*Sister Carrie*)
Constable

CARRINGTON, V.C.
INDEPENDENT 1954

Christie, D. *and* Christie, C. (P)
Heinemann

CARRY ON, ADMIRAL
REN 1957

Hay, I. *and* King-Hall, S. (*Off the record*) (P)
French

CARVE HER NAME WITH PRIDE
RANK 1957

Minney, R. J.
Newnes

CASE AGAINST MRS AMES, THE
PAR 1936

Roche, A. S.
Melrose

CASE OF ELINOR NORTON, THE
FOX 1935

Rinehart, M. R.
Cassell

CASE OF SERGEANT GRISCHA, THE
RKO 1930

Zweig, A.
Secker

CASE OF THE BLACK CAT, THE
IN 1936

Gardner, E. S. (*Case of the caretaker's cat, The*)
Cassell

CASE OF THE CURIOUS BRIDE, THE
IN 1935

Gardner, E. S.
Cassell

CASE OF THE HOWLING DOG, THE
WAR 1934

Gardner, E. S.
Grosset, N.Y.

CASE OF THE LUCKY LEGS, THE
WAR 1935

Gardner, E. S.
Cassell

**CASE OF THE STUTTERING
BISHOP, THE**
WAR 1937

Gardner, E. S.
Cassell

CASE OF THE VELVET CLAWS, THE
IN 1936

Gardner, E. S.
Cassell

CASH McCALL
WAR 1959

Hawley, C.
Hammond

CASINO MURDER CASE, THE
MGM 1935

Dine, S. S. van
Cassell

CASINO ROYALE
COL 1966

Fleming, I.
Cape

CAST A DARK SHADOW
EROS 1955

Green, J. (*Murder mistaken*) (P)
Evans

CAST A GIANT SHADOW
UA 1965

Berkman, T.
Doubleday, N.Y.

CAST A LONG SHADOW
UA 1959

Overholster, W. D.
Ward Lock

CASTAWAYS, THE
DISNEY 1961

Verne, J.
Various

CASTLE IN THE AIR
ABP 1952

Melville, A. (P)
French

CAT AND MOUSE
EROS 1958

Halliday, M.
Hodder & Stoughton

CAT BALLOU
COL 1965

Chansler, R. (*Ballad of Cat Ballou, The*)
Little Brown, Boston

CAT CREEPS, THE
UN 1930

Willard, J. (*Cat and the canary, The*)
Hudson

CAT ON A HOT TIN ROOF MGM 1958	Williams, T. (P) Secker & Warburg
CAUGHT MGM 1948	Block, L. (*Wild calendar*) World, N.Y.
CAVALCADE FOX 1933 FOX 1955	Coward, N. (P) Heinemann
CELL 2455, DEATH ROW COL 1955	Chessman, C. Longmans
CENTENNIAL SUMMER FOX 1946	Idell, A. E. Sampson Low
CERTAIN SMILE, A FOX 1958	Sagan, F. Murray
CHAD HANNA FOX 1940	Edmonds, W. D. Collins
CHAIN, THE COL 1952	Wellman, P. I. Laurie
CHALK GARDEN, THE RANK 1963	Bagnold, E. (P) French
CHALLENGE TO LASSIE MGM 1949	Atkinson, E. (*Greyfriar's Bobby*) Hamilton
CHAPMAN REPORT, THE WAR 1962	Wallace, I. Cassell
CHARGE IS MURDER, THE MGM 1963	Dewlen, A. Longmans
CHARLEY MOON BL 1956	Arkell, R. Joseph
CHARLEY'S AUNT COL 1930 FOX 1941	Thomas, B. (P) French, N.Y.
CHARLIE CHAN CARRIES ON FOX 1931	Biggers, E. D. Cassell
CHASE, THE COL 1965	Foote, H. (P) Dramatists, N.Y.
CHASING YESTERDAY RKO 1935	France, A. (*Crime of Silvester Bonnard, The*) Collins
CHEAPER BY THE DOZEN FOX 1950	Gilbreth, F. B. *and* Carey, E. G. Heinemann

CHEERS FOR MISS BISHOP
UA 1941

Aldrich, *Mrs* B. (*Miss Bishop*)
Hodder & Stoughton

CHEYENNE AUTUMN
WAR 1964

Sandoz, M.
McGraw-Hill, N.Y.

CHICKEN EVERY SUNDAY
FOX 1948

Taylor, R.
Methuen

CHICKEN-WAGON FAMILY
FOX 1935

Benefield, B.
Triangle Bks, N.Y.

CHILD IN THE HOUSE
EROS 1956

McNeill, J.
Hodder & Stoughton

CHILD IS BORN, A
WAR 1940

Axelson, *Mrs* M. M.
Cladwell, Idaho

CHILD OF DIVORCE
RKO 1946

Atlas, L. (*Wednesday's child*) (P)
French, N.Y.

CHILDREN'S HOUR
UA 1962

Hellman, L. (P)
Dramatists, N.Y.

CHILTERN HUNDREDS, THE
TC 1949

Home, W. D. (P)
French

CHINA SEAS
MGM 1935

Garstin, C.
Chatto & Windus

CHINA SKY
RKO 1945

Buck, P.
Blue Ribbon Bks, N.Y.

CHIP OF THE FLYING U
UN 1940

Bower, B. M.
Grosset, N.Y.

CHIPS ARE DOWN, THE
LOPERT 1949

Sartre, J-P.
Rider

CHOCOLATE SOLDIER, THE
MGM 1941

Molnar, F. (*Guardsman, The*) (P)
Macey-Masius, N.Y.

CHRISTMAS CAROL
MGM 1938

Dickens, C.
Various

CHRISTMAS HOLIDAY
UN 1944

Maugham, W. S.
Heinemann

CHRISTOPHER BEAN
MGM 1933
FOX 1956

Fauchois, R. (*Late Christopher Bean, The*)
(P)
Gollancz

CHRISTOPHER COLUMBUS
GFD 1949

Sabatini, R. (*Columbus*)
Hutchinson

CHUKA PAR 1967	Jessup, R. Jenkins
CIMARRON RKO 1931 MGM 1960	Ferber, E. Heinemann
CINCINNATI KID, THE MGM 1965	Jessup, R. Gollancz
CIRCLE OF DECEPTION FOX 1960	Waugh, A. (*Guy Renton*) Consul Bks
CIRCUS QUEEN MURDER COL 1933	Abbot, A. (*Murder of the circus queen, The*) Collins
CITADEL, THE MGM 1938	Cronin, A. J. Gollancz
CITY ACROSS THE RIVER UI 1949	Shulman, I. (*Amboy Dukes, The*) Doubleday, N.Y.
CITY FOR CONQUEST WAR 1940	Kandel, A. Joseph
CITY JUNGLE, THE WAR 1959	Powell, R. (*Philadelphian, The*) Hodder & Stoughton
CLAIRVOYANT, THE GB 1935	Lothar, E. Secker
CLARENCE PAR 1937	Tarkington, B. (P) French, N.Y.
CLASH BY NIGHT RKO 1952	Odets, C. (P) Random House, N.Y.
CLAUDIA FOX 1943	Franken, R. W. H. Allen
CLAUDIA FOX 1943	Franken, R. (P) French, N.Y.
CLAUDIA AND DAVID FOX 1946	Franken, R. W. H. Allen
CLIVE OF INDIA UA 1935	Lipscombe, W. P. *and* Minney R.J. (P) Gollancz
CLOCHEMERLE BLUE RIBBON 1951	Chevalier, G. Secker & Warburg
CLUE OF THE TWISTED CANDLE, THE AA 1960	Wallace, E. Newnes

TITLE OF FILM	AUTHOR AND PUBLISHER
CLUNY BROWN FOX 1946	Sharpe, M. Collins
CODE OF THE WEST RKO 1947	Grey, Z. Hodder & Stoughton
COLDITZ STORY, THE BL 1954	Reid, P. R. Hodder & Stoughton
COLLECTOR, THE BL 1964	Fowles, J. Cape
COLONEL EFFINGHAM'S RAID FOX 1945	Fleming, B. Various
COMANCHEROS, THE FOX 1961	Wellman, P. I. Doubleday, N.Y.
COME AND GET IT UA 1936	Ferber, E. Heinemann
COME BACK, LITTLE SHEBA PAR 1952	Inge, W. M. (P) Random House, N.Y.
COME BLOW YOUR HORN PAR 1963	Simon, N. (P) Doubleday, N.Y.
COMEDIANS, THE MGM 1967	Greene, G. Bodley Head
COMEDY MAN, THE BL 1964	Hayes, D. Abelard-Schuman
COME FLY WITH ME MGM 1963	Glemser, B. (*Girl on a wing*) Macdonald
COMMAND DECISION MGM 1948	Haines, W. W. Cassell
COMMAND DECISION MGM 1948	Haines, W. W. (P) Random House, N.Y.
COMPULSION FOX 1959	Levin, M. Muller
CONDEMNED UA 1939	Niles, B. (*Condemned to Devil's Island*) Cape
CONDEMNED OF ALTONA, THE FOX 1964	Sartre, J–P. (*Loser wins*) (P) Hamilton
CONE OF SILENCE BL 1959	Beatty, D. Secker & Warburg
CONFESSIONS OF A COUNTER-SPY RANK 1960	Morros, B. (*My ten years as a counter-spy*) Laurie

TITLE OF FILM	AUTHOR AND PUBLISHER
CONFIDENTIAL AGENT WAR 1945	Greene, G. Heinemann
CONFIDENTIAL REPORT WAR 1955	Welles, O. (*Mr Arkadin*) W. H. Allen
CONFLICT OF WINGS BL 1954	Sharp, D. Putnam, N.Y.
CONGO MAISIE MGM 1940	Collinson, W. (*Congo landing*) McBride, N.Y.
CONQUERING HORDE PAR 1931	Hough, E. (*North of 36*) Appleton-Century, N.Y.
CONQUEROR, THE RKO 1955	Clou, J. (*Caravan to Carnal, A.*) Redman
CONQUEST OF SPACE PAR 1955	Bonestell, C. *and* Ley, W. Sidgwick
CONSPIRATOR MGM 1949	Slater, H. Lehmann
CONSPIRATORS, THE WAR 1944	Prokosch, F. Chatto & Windus
CONSTANT NYMPH, THE FOX 1934 WAR 1943	Kennedy, M. Heinemann
CONSTANT NYMPH, THE FOX 1934 WAR 1943	Kennedy, M. (P) Doubleday, N.Y.
CONVICTED COL 1950	Flavin, M. (*One way out*) (P) French, N.Y.
CORN IS GREEN, THE WAR 1945	Williams, E. (P) Heinemann
CORONER CREEK COL 1948	Short, L. Collins
CORRIDOR OF MIRRORS GFD 1948	Massie, C. Faber
COTTAGE TO LET GFD 1941	Kerr, G. (P) French
COUNSELLOR AT LAW UN 1933	Rice, E. (P) Gollancz
COUNTERFEIT TRAITOR, THE PAR 1962	Klein, A. (*Double dealers*) Faber

COUNT 5 AND DIE FOX 1957	Wynne, B. Souvenir Press
COUNTRY GIRL, THE PAR 1954	Odets, C. (*Winter journey*) (P) Viking Press, N.Y.
COUNT OF MONTE CRISTO, THE UA 1934	Dumas, A. Various
COUNT YOUR BLESSINGS MGM 1959	Mitford, N. (*Blessing, The*) Hamilton
COURTSHIP OF EDDIES' FATHER, THE MGM 1963	Toby, M. Gibbs & Phillips
COVENANT WITH DEATH, A WAR 1966	Becker, S. Hamilton
COWBOY COL 1957	Harris, F. (*On the Trail*) Lane
COW COUNTRY ABP 1953	Bishop, C. (*Shadow Range*) Macmillan, N.Y.
CRACK IN THE MIRROR FOX 1960	Haedrich, M. W. H. Allen
CRAIG'S WIFE COL 1936	Kelly, G. (P) French
CRASHING THRU' MON 1939	Erskine, L. Y. (*Renfrew rides the Range*) Appleton-Century, N.Y.
CRIME AND PUNISHMENT COL 1935 WAR 1958	Dostoevski, F. M. Various
CRIME BY NIGHT WAR 1946	Homes, G. (*Forty whacks*) Grosset, N.Y.
CRIMSON CIRCLE, THE NEW ERA 1930	Wallace, E. Hodder & Stoughton
CRISS CROSS UI 1949	Tracy, D. Constable
CRITIC'S CHOICE WAR 1962	Levin, I. (P) Random House, N.Y.
CROSSFIRE RKO 1947	Brooks, R. (*Brick foxhole, The*) Harper, N.Y.
CROSSWINDS PAR 1951	Burtis, T. (*New Guinea gold*) Doubleday, N.Y.

CROUCHING BEAST, THE
OLY 1936

Williams, V. (*Clubfoot*)
Hodder & Stoughton

CROWDED SKY, THE
WAR 1960

Searls, H.
Harper, N.Y.

CRUEL SEA, THE
GFD 1952

Monsarrat, N.
Cassell

CRY FOR HAPPY
COL 1960

Campbell, G.
Harcourt, N.Y.

CRY FROM THE STREETS, A
EROS 1958

Coxhead, E. (*Friend in need, A*)
Collins

CRY HAVOC
MGM 1943

Kenward, A. R. (P)
French

CRY IN THE NIGHT, A
WAR 1956

Masterson, W. (*All through the night*)
W. H. Allen

CRY OF BATTLE
WAR 1964

Appel B. (*Fortress in the rice*)
Bobbs-Merrill, Indianapolis

CRY OF THE CITY
FOX 1948

Helseth, H. E. (*Chair for Martin Rome, The*)
Dodd, N.Y.

CRY, THE BELOVED COUNTRY
BL 1951

Paton, A.
Cape

CRY, THE BELOVED COUNTRY
BL 1951

Anderson, M. (*Lost in the stars*) (P)
Sloane, N.Y.

CRY TOUGH
UA 1959

Shulman, I. (*Children of the dark*)
Holt, N.Y.

CRY WOLF
WAR 1947

Carleton, *Mrs* M.C.
Sun Dial, N.Y.

CUCKOO IN THE NEST
GB 1938

Travers, B. (P)
Bickers

CUCKOO IN THE NEST
GB 1938

Travers, B.
Lane

CURE FOR LOVE, THE
BL 1949

Greenwood, W. (P)
French

CURSE OF FRANKENSTEIN, THE
WAR 1957

Shelley, *Mrs* M. W. (*Frankenstein*)
Various

CURSE OF THE WEREWOLF, THE
RANK 1960

Endore, G. (*Werewolf of Paris, The*)
Long

CURTAIN FALLS, THE
BL 1964

Druon, M.
Hart-Davis

CURTAIN UP
GFD 1952

King, P. (*On Monday next*) (P)
French

CYNARA
UA 1932

Harwood, H. M. *and* Brown, R. G.
Benn

D

DADDY LONG LEGS
FOX 1931
FOX 1955

Webster, J.
Hodder & Stoughton

DAISY KENYON
FOX 1947

Janeway, *Mrs* E.
Doubleday, N.Y.

DAMAGED LIVES
PAR 1935

Eustace, C. J.
Putnam, N.Y.

DAMSEL IN DISTRESS, A
RKO 1937

Wodehouse, P. G.
Jenkins

DAM BUSTERS, THE
ABP 1954

Brickhill, P.
Evans

DAMES DON'T CARE
FANCEY 1954

Cheyney, P.
Collins

DAMNED, THE
BL 1963

Lawrence, H. L. (*Children of the light*)
Macdonald

DANCE PRETTY LADY
BI 1931

Mackenzie, *Sir* C. (*Carnival*)
Various

DANGER AHEAD
MON 1940

Erskine, L. Y. (*Renfrew's long trail*)
Grossett, N.Y.

DANGEROUS CORNER
RKO 1934

Priestley, J. B. (P)
Heinemann

DANGEROUS EXILE
RANK 1957

Wilkins, V. (*King reluctant, A*)
Cape

DANGEROUS PARADISE
PAR 1930

Conrad, J. (*Victory*)
Various

DANGER SIGNAL
WAR 1945

Bottome, P. (*Murder in the bud*)
Faber

DANGER WITHIN
BL 1958

Gilbert, M. (*Death in Captivity*)
Pan

DARK AT THE TOP OF THE STAIRS, THE
WAR 1960

Inge, W. M. (P)
Random House, N.Y.

DARK COMMAND
REP 1940

Burnett, W. R.
Heinemann

DARK MAN, THE
GFD 1951

Dell, J. (*Nobody ordered wolves*)
Heinemann

DARK PAGE, THE
COL 1952

Fuller, S.
Duell, N.Y.

DARK PASSAGE
WAR 1947

Goodis, D.
World, N.Y.

DARK VICTORY
WAR 1939

Brewer, G. E. *and* Bloch, B. (P)
Dramatists, N.Y.

DARK WATERS
UA 1944

Cockrell, F. M. *and* Cockrell, M.
World, N.Y.

DAUGHTER OF DARKNESS
PAR 1948

Catto, M. (*They walk alone*) (P)
Secker & Warburg

DAUGHTER OF THE DRAGON
PAR 1931

Rohmer, S. (*Daughter of Fu Manchu*)
Cassell

DAVID AND LISA
BL 1963

Rubin, T. I. (*Lisa and David*)
Macmillan

DAVID COPPERFIELD
MGM 1935

Dickens, C.
Various

DAWN PATROL, THE
IN 1930
WAR 1938

Saunders, J. M.
Queensway Press

DAY OF THE OUTLAW
UA 1959

Wells, L. E.
Hale

DAY OF THE TRIFFIDS, THE
RANK 1962

Wyndham, J.
Joseph

**DAY THEY ROBBED THE BANK OF
ENGLAND, THE**
MGM 1959

Brophy, J.
Fontana

DAY TO REMEMBER, A
GFD 1953

Tickell, J. (*Hand and the flower, The*)
Hodder & Stoughton

D DAY SIXTH OF JUNE
FOX 1956

Shapiro, L. (*Sixth of June, The*)
Collins

DEAD END
UA 1937

Kingsley, S. (P)
Dramatists, N.Y.

DEADLINE AT DAWN
RKO 1946

Irish, W.
Lippincott, Philadelphia

DEADLY AFFAIR, THE
BL 1966

Le Carré, J. (*Call for the dead*)
Gollancz

TITLE OF FILM	AUTHOR AND PUBLISHER
DEADLY IS THE FEMALE UA 1949	Kantor, M. Coward-McCann, N.Y.
DEADLY COMPANIONS, THE WAR 1961	Fleischman, A. S. (*Yellowleg*) Muller
DEADLY DUO, THE UA 1962	Jessup, R. Boardman
DEADLY RECORD AA 1959	Hooke, N. W. Hale
DEAD MEN TELL NO TALES ALL 1939	Beeding, F. (*Norwich victims, The*) Hodder & Stoughton
DEAR AND GLORIOUS PHYSICIAN PAR 1963	Caldwell, T. Collins
DEAR BRIGITTE FOX 1965	Haase, J. (*Erasmus with freckles*) Simon & Schuster, N.Y.
DEAR HEART WAR 1964	Mosel, T. (P) Obolensky, N.Y.
DEAR MR PROHACK GFD 1949	Bennett, A. (*Mr Prohack*) Various
DEAR OCTOPUS GFD 1943	Smith, D. (P) Heinemann
DEAR RUTH PAR 1947	Krasna, N. (P) Gollancz
DEATH AT BROADCASTING HOUSE PHOENIX 1935	Gielgud, V. H. Rich & Cowan
DEATH OF A SALESMAN COL 1951	Miller, A. (P) Cresset Press
DEATH ON THE DIAMOND MGM 1934	Fitzsimmons, C. Grosset, N.Y.
DECAMERON NIGHTS EROS 1953	Boccaccio, G. (*Decameron, The*) Various
DECISION BEFORE DAWN FOX 1951	Howe, G. L. (*Call it treason*) Hart-Davis
DECISION OF CHRISTOPHER **BLAKE, THE** WAR 1948	Hart, M. (*Christopher Blake*) (P) Random House, N.Y.
DEEP BLUE SEA, THE FOX 1955	Rattigan, T. (P) Hamilton
DEEP IN MY HEART MGM 1954	Arnold, E. Duell, N.Y.

DEEP SIX, THE
WAR 1957

Dibner, M.
Cassell

DEEP VALLEY
WAR 1947

Totheroh, D.
Hutchinson

DEEP WATERS
FOX 1948

Moore, R. (*Spoonhandle*)
Grosset, N.Y.

DEERSLAYER
REP 1943
FOX 1957

Cooper, F. J.
Various

DELAVINE AFFAIR, THE
MON 1954

Chapman, R. (*Winter wears a shroud*)
Laurie

DELUGE, THE
RKO 1933

Wright, S. F.
Allied Press

DENTIST IN THE CHAIR
REN 1960

Finch, M.
Ace Bks

DESERT FURY
PAR 1947

Stewart, R.
World, N.Y.

DESERT GOLD
PAR 1936

Grey, Z.
Nelson

DESERT PURSUIT
ABP 1952

Perkins, K. (*Desert voices*)
Wright & Brown

DESERT SAND
UA 1955

Robb, J. (*Punitive action*)
Hamilton

DESIGN FOR LIVING
PAR 1933

Coward, N. (P)
Heinemann

DESIRÉE
FOX 1954

Selinko, A.
Heinemann

DESIRE ME
MGM 1947

Frank, L. (*Carl and Anna*)
Davies

DESIRE UNDER THE ELMS
PAR 1958

O'Neill, E. G. (P)
Cape

DESPERATE HOURS, THE
PAR 1954

Hayes, J.
Deutsch

DESPERATE HOURS, THE
PAR 1954

Hayes, J. (P)
Random House, N.Y.

DESPERATE MAN, THE
AA 1959

Somers, P. (*Beginners luck*)
Collins

DESPERATE MOMENT
GFD 1953

Albrand, M.
Chatto & Windus

48

DESPERATE SEARCH MGM 1952	Mayse, A. Harrap
DESTINATION TOKYO WAR 1943	Fisher, S. G. Appleton-Century, N.Y.
DESTRY UI 1954	Brand, M. (*Destry rides again*) Hodder & Stoughton
DESTRY RIDES AGAIN UN 1932 UN 1939	Brand, M. Hodder & Stoughton
DETECTIVE STORY PAR 1951	Kingsley, P. (P) Random House, N.Y.
DETOUR PRC 1946	Goldsmith, M. M. Hurst & Blackett
DEVIL AT 4 O'CLOCK, THE COL 1961	Catto, M. Pan
DEVIL-DOLL, THE MGM 1936	Merritt, A. (*Burn, witch, burn*) Methuen
DEVIL MAKES THREE, THE MGM 1952	Bachmann, L. (*Kiss of death*) Knopf, N.Y.
DEVIL NEVER SLEEPS, THE FOX 1962	Buck, P. Pan
DEVIL'S DAFFODIL, THE BL 1961	Wallace, E. (*Daffodil mystery*) Ward Lock
DEVIL'S DISCIPLE, THE UA 1959	Shaw, G.B. (P) Constable
DIAL 'M' FOR MURDER WAR 1954	Knott, F. (P) Random House, N.Y.
DIAL 999 AA 1955	Graeme, B. (*Way out, The*) Hutchinson
DIAMOND HEAD COL 1962	Gilman, P. Joseph
DIAMOND JIM UN 1935	Morell, P. Hurst & Blackett
DIARY OF A COUNTRY PRIEST, THE GGT 1950	Bernanos, G. Lane
DIARY OF ANNE FRANK, THE FOX 1959	Frank, A. Gollancz
DIARY OF ANNE FRANK, THE FOX 1959	Goodrich, F. *and* Hackett, A. (P) French

DIARY OF MAJOR THOMPSON
GALA 1957

Daninos, P.
Cape

DINNER AT EIGHT
MGM 1933

Kaufman, G. S. *and* Ferber, E. (P)
Heinemann

DIPLOMATIC COURIER
FOX 1952

Cheyney, P. (*Sinister errand*)
Collins

DIRTY DOZEN, THE
MGM 1966

Nathanson, E. M.
Barker

DISPUTED PASSAGE
PAR 1939

Douglas, L. C.
Davies

DISTANT TRUMPET, A
WAR 1964

Horgan, P.
Macmillan

DOCK BRIEF, THE
MGM 1962

Mortimer, J. (P)
Elek

DOCTOR AND THE GIRL, THE
MGM 1949

Meersch, M. van der. (*Bodies and souls*)
Pilot Press

DOCTOR AT LARGE
RANK 1957

Gordon, R.
Joseph

DOCTOR AT SEA
BFD 1955

Gordon, R.
Joseph

DOCTOR BULL
FOX 1933

Cozzens, J. G. (*Cure of the flesh*)
Longmans

DOCTOR DOLITTLE
FOX 1966

Lofting. H.
Cape

DOCTOR IN CLOVER
RANK 1965

Gordon, R.
Joseph

DOCTOR IN LOVE
RANK 1959

Gordon, R.
Joseph

DOCTOR IN THE HOUSE
GFD 1954

Gordon, R.
Joseph

DOCTOR'S DILEMMA, THE
MGM 1958

Shaw, G. B. (P)
Constable

DOCTOR ZHIVAGO
MGM 1965

Pasternak, B.
Collins

DODSWORTH
UA 1936

Lewis, S.
Cape

DODSWORTH
UA 1936

Howard, S. C. (P)
Harcourt, N.Y.

DOG OF FLANDERS, A
RKO 1935
FOX 1959

Ouida
Chatto & Windus

DOMINANT SEX, THE
AB 1937

Egan, M. (P)
Gollancz

DON CHICAGO
BN 1945

Roberts, C. E. B.
Jarrolds

DON'T BOTHER TO KNOCK
FOX 1952

Armstrong, C. (*Mischief*)
Davies

DON'T BOTHER TO KNOCK
WAR 1961

Hanley, C. (*Love from everybody*)
Hutchinson

DON'T GO NEAR THE WATER
MGM 1957

Brinkley, W.
Cape

DON'T MAKE WAVES
MGM 1966

Wallach, I. (*Muscle beach*)
Gollancz

DON'T RAISE THE BRIDGE, LOWER THE RIVER
BL 1967

Wilk, M.
Heinemann

DOOR IN THE WALL
ABP 1956

Wells, H. G.
Benn

DOUBLE CONFESSION
ABP 1950

Garden, J. (*All on a summer's day*)
Joseph

DOUBLE IMAGE
FOX 1959

MacDougall, R. *and* Allan, E. (P)
French

DOUBLE INDEMNITY
PAR 1944

Cain, J. M.
Hale

DOUBLE MAN, THE
WAR 1966

Maxfield, H. S. (*Legacy of a spy*)
Heinemann

DOUBTING THOMAS
FOX 1935

Kelly, G. (*Torch-bearers*) (P)
French, N.Y.

DOUGHGIRLS, THE
WAR 1944

Fields, J. (P)
Random House, N.Y.

DOWN 3 DARK STREETS
UA 1954

Gordon, *Mrs* M. *and* Gordon, G. (*Case file F.B.I.*)
Doubleday, N.Y.

DRACULA
UN 1931
UI 1957

Stoker, B. (P)
Rider

TITLE OF FILM	AUTHOR AND PUBLISHER
DRAGONWYCK FOX 1946	Seton, A. Hodder & Stoughton
DRAGON SEED MGM 1944	Buck, P. Methuen
DREAM GIRL PAR 1947	Rice, E. (P) Coward-McCann, N.Y.
DR FAUSTUS BL 1966	Marlowe, C. (P) Various
DRIFT FENCE PAR 1935	Grey, Z. Hodder & Stoughton
DR JEKYLL AND MR HYDE PAR 1932 MGM 1941	Stevenson, R. L. Various
DR KILDARE'S CRISIS MGM 1940	Brand, M. Hodder & Stoughton
DR NO UA 1962	Fleming, I. Cape
DR STRANGELOVE; OR HOW I LEARNED TO STOP WORRYING AND LOVE THE BOMB COL 1963	George, P. (*Two hours to doom*) Corgi
DR SYN GB 1937 DISNEY 1963	Thorndike, R. Various
DRUMS UA 1938	Mason, A. E. W. (*Drum, The*) Hodder & Stoughton
DRUMS ALONG THE MOHAWK FOX 1939	Edmonds, W. D. Jarrolds
DRUMS IN THE DEEP SOUTH RKO 1952	Noble, H. (*Woman with a sword*) Doubleday, N.Y.
DRUMS OF DESTINY NEW REALM 1962	Michael, G. (*Michaels in Africa, The*) Muller
DRUMS OF FU MANCHU REP 1943	Rohmer, S. Cassell
DRY ROT BL 1956	Chapman, J. (P) English Theatre Guild

DUEL AT DIABLO
UA 1966

Albert, M. (*Apache rising*)
Muller

DUEL IN THE SUN
MGM 1946

Busch, N.
W. H. Allen

DULCY
MGM 1940

Kaufman, G. S. *and* Connelly, M. (P)
Various

DUNKIRK
MGM 1958

Trevor, E. (*Big pick-up*)
Heinemann

DUST IN THE SUN
WAR 1958

Cleary, J. (*Justin Bayard*)
Collins

DUSTY ERMINE
TWICKENHAM 1936

Grant, N. (P)
French

E

EACH DAWN I DIE
WAR 1939

Odlum, J.
Various

EARL OF CHICAGO
MGM 1940

Williams, B.
Harrap

EARTH V. THE FLYING SAUCERS
COL 1956

Keyhoe, D. E. (*Flying saucers from outer space*)
Hutchinson

EASIEST WAY, THE
MGM 1931

Walter, E. (P)
Dodd, N.Y.

EAST LYNNE
FOX 1931

Wood, *Mrs* H.
Various

EAST OF EDEN
WAR 1954

Steinbeck, J.
Heinemann

EAST RIVER
MGM 1949

Asch, S.
Macdonald

EAST SIDE, WEST SIDE
MGM 1950

Davenport, M.
Collins

EASY COME, EASY GO
PAR 1947

McNulty, J. L. (*Third Avenue, New York*)
Little Brown, Boston

EASY LIVING
PAR 1937

Caspary, V.
Longmans

ECHO OF BARBARA
RANK 1960

Burke, J.
Long

EDGE OF DARKNESS
WAR 1943

Woods, W. H.
Grosset, N.Y.

EDGE OF DOOM
RKO 1950

Brady, L.
Cresset Press

EDGE OF FURY
UA 1958

Coates, R. M. (*Wisteria Cottage*)
Gollancz

EDWARD, MY SON
MGM 1949

Morley, R. *and* Langley, N. (P)
French

EGG AND I, THE
UN 1947

Macdonald, B.
Hammond

EGYPTIAN, THE
FOX 1954

Waltari, M. (*Sinuhe the Egyptian*)
Putnam

EIGHT IRON MEN
COL 1952

Brown, H. (*Sound of hunting, A*)
Knopf, N.Y.

80,000 SUSPECTS
RANK 1963

Trevor, E. (*Pillars of midnight, The*)
Heinemann

EL DORADO
PAR 1967

Brown, H. (*Stars in their courses, The*)
Cape

ELECTRA
UA 1963

Euripedes (P)
Various

ELEPHANT BOY
UA 1937

Kipling, R. (*Toomai of the elephants*)
Macmillan

ELEPHANT WALK
PAR 1954

Standish, R.
Davies

**ELLERY QUEEN AND THE
PENTHOUSE MYSTERY**
COL 1941

Queen, E. (*Penthouse mystery*)
Grosset, N.Y.

**ELLERY QUEEN AND THE PERFECT
CRIME**
COL 1941

Queen, E. (*Perfect crime, The*)
Grosset, N.Y.

**ELLERY QUEEN, MASTER
DETECTIVE**
COL 1940

Queen, E.
Grosset, N.Y.

ELMER GANTRY
UA 1959

Lewis, S.
Cape

ELUSIVE PIMPERNEL, THE
BL 1950

Orczy, *Baroness* E.
Hutchinson

EMIL AND THE DETECTIVES
UFA 1931
DISNEY 1964

Kastner, E.
Cape

EMPEROR JONES UA 1933	O'Neill, E. G. (P) Cape
EMPEROR'S CANDLESTICKS, THE MGM 1937	Orczy, *Baroness* E. Hodder & Stoughton
EMPTY SADDLES UN 1936	Wilson, C. Ward Lock
ENCHANTED APRIL RKO 1935	'Elizabeth' Macmillan
ENCHANTED COTTAGE, THE RKO 1945	Pinero, *Sir* A. W. (P) Heinemann
ENCHANTED ISLAND WAR 1958	Melville, H. (*Typee*) Dent
ENCHANTMENT RKO 1949	Godden, R. (*Fugue in time*) Joseph
ENCORE GFD 1951	Maugham, W. S. Heinemann
END AS A MAN COL 1957	Willingham, C. Barker
END AS A MAN COL 1957	Willingham, C. (*Strange one, The*) (P) Grosset, N.Y.
END OF THE AFFAIR, THE COL 1954	Greene, G. Heinemann
END OF THE RIVER, THE ARCHERS 1947	Holdridge, D. (*Death of a common man*) Hale
ENEMY BELOW, THE FOX 1957	Rayner, D. A. (*Escort*) Kimber
ENTERTAINER, THE BL 1960	Osborne, J. (P) Evans
ESCAPADE EROS 1955	McDougall, R. (P) Heinemann
ESCAPADE IN FLORENCE DISNEY 1963	Fenton, E. (*Mystery in Florence*) Constable
ESCAPE RKO 1930 FOX 1948	Galsworthy, J. (P) Duckworth
ESCAPE MGM 1940	Vance, E. Collins

TITLE OF FILM	AUTHOR AND PUBLISHER
ESCAPE FROM ZAHREIN PAR 1962	Barrett, M. (*Appointment in Zahrein*) Pan
ESCAPE IN THE DESERT WAR 1945	Sherwood, R. E. (*Petrified forest, The*) (P) Scribner, N.Y.
ESCAPE ME NEVER UA 1935	Kennedy, M. (P) Heinemann
ESCAPE ME NEVER UA 1935	Kennedy, M. Heinemann
ESTHER WATERS WESSEX 1948	Moore, G. (P) Heinemann
ESTHER WATERS WESSEX 1948	Moore, G. Various
EVE GALA 1963	Chase, J. H. Panther
EVE OF ST. MARK, THE FOX 1944	Anderson, M. (P) Lane
EVERYTHING IS THUNDER GB 1936	Hardy, J. L. Lane
EXECUTIVE SUITE MGM 1954	Hawley, C. Hammond
EX-FLAME TIFFANY 1931	Wood, *Mrs* H. (*East Lynne*) Various
EXODUS UA 1960	Uris, L. Wingate
EXPERIMENT PERILOUS RKO 1944	Carpenter, M. Harrap
EXPERT, THE WAR 1932	Ferber, E. (*Old man Minick*) Doubleday, N.Y.
EXTRAORDINARY SEAMAN MGM 1967	Rock, P. Souvenir Press
EYES IN THE NIGHT MGM 1942	Kendrick, B. H. (*Odour of violets*) Methuen

F

FABIAN OF THE YARD EROS 1954	Fabian, R. Naldrett Press
FABIOLA BL 1951	Wiseman, N. P. S. (*Cardinal*) Various

TITLE OF FILM	AUTHOR AND PUBLISHER
FACE IN THE CROWD, A WAR 1957	Schulberg, B. W. (*Some faces in the crowd*) Lane
FACE IN THE NIGHT GN 1956	Graeme, B. (*Suspense*) Hutchinson
FACE TO FACE RKO 1952	Crane, S. (*Bride comes to Yellow Sky, The*) Knopf, N.Y.
FAHRENHEIT 451 UI 1966	Bradbury, R. Hart-Davis
FAIL SAFE BL 1963	Burdick, E. *and* Wheeler, H. Hutchinson
FAIR WARNING FOX 1931	Brand, M. (*Untamed, The*) Hodder & Stoughton
FAIR WIND TO JAVA REP 1953	Roark, G. Falcon Press
FAITHFUL HEART, THE GFD 1932	Hoffe, M. (P) Heinemann
FALCON TAKES OVER, THE RKO 1942	Chandler, R. (*Farewell, my lovely*) Hamilton
FALLEN ANGEL FOX 1945	Holland, M. Dutton, N.Y.
FALLEN IDOL, THE FOX 1948	Greene, G. (*Basement room, The*) Cresset Press
FALLEN SPARROW, THE RKO 1943	Hughes, D. B. Nicholson & Watson
FALL OF THE HOUSE OF USHER, THE AA 1960	Poe, E. A. Various
FAME IS THE SPUR TC 1947	Spring, H. Collins
FAMILY DOCTOR FOX 1957	Fleming, J. (*Deeds of Mr Deadcert, The*) Hutchinson
FAMILY HONEYMOON UN 1949	Croy, H. Hurst & Blackett
FANATIC COL 1965	Blaisdell, A. (*Nightmare*) Gollancz
FANNY WAR 1960	Behrman, S. N. *and* Logan, J. (P) Random House, N.Y.
FANNY BY GAS LIGHT GFD 1944	Sadleir, M. Constable

TITLE OF FILM	AUTHOR AND PUBLISHER
FANNY HILL GALA 1965	Cleland, J. Luxor Press
FAREWELL, MY LOVELY RKO 1944	Chandler, R. Hamilton
FAREWELL TO ARMS, A PAR 1932 FOX 1957	Hemingway, E. Cape
FAR FROM THE MADDING CROWD WAR 1966	Hardy, T. Macmillan
FAR HORIZONS, THE PAR 1955	Emmons, D. G. (*Sacajawea of the Shoshones*) Binfords, Portland, Oregon
FARMER TAKES A WIFE, THE FOX 1953	Edmonds, W. D. (*Rome haul*) Triangle Bks, N.Y.
FARMER'S WIFE, THE AB 1940	Phillpotts, E. (P) French
FAST AND LOOSE MGM 1939	Page, M. (*Fast company*) Heinemann
FATE IS THE HUNTER FOX 1964	Gann, E. K. Hodder & Stoughton
FATHER BROWN COL 1954	Chesterton, G. K. (*Father Brown stories*) Cassell
FATHER BROWN, DETECTIVE PAR 1935	Chesterton, G. K. (*Wisdom of Father Brown, The*) Cassell
FATHER OF THE BRIDE MGM 1950	Streeter, E. Hamilton
FATHER'S DOING FINE ABP 1952	Langley, N. (*Little lambs eat ivy*) (P) French
FBI STORY, THE WAR 1958	Whitehead, D. Panther
FEMININE TOUCH, THE RANK 1956	Russell, S. M. (*Lamp is heavy, A*) Angus & Robertson
FERRY TO HONG KONG RANK 1959	Kent, S. Hutchinson
FEVER IN THE BLOOD WAR 1960	Pearson, W. Macmillan
FIERCEST HEART, THE FOX 1960	Cloete, S. Collins

TITLE OF FILM	AUTHOR AND PUBLISHER
55 DAYS AT PEKING RANK 1962	Edwards, S. Bantam Bks, N.Y.
FIGHTER, THE UA 1952	London, J. (*Mexican, The*) Appleton-Century, N.Y.
FIGHTING CARAVANS PAR 1931	Grey, Z. Hodder & Stoughton
FIGHTING GUARDSMAN, THE COL 1945	Dumas, A. (*Companions of Jehu, The*) Dent
FIGHTING MAD MON 1939	Erskine, L. Y. (*Renfrew rides again*) Appleton-Century, N.Y.
FINE MADNESS, A WAR 1965	Baker, E. Joseph
FINN AND HATTIE PAR 1931	Stewart, D. O. (*Mr and Mrs Haddock abroad*) Doran, N.Y.
FIRE DOWN BELOW COL 1957	Kent, S. Hutchinson
FIRE OVER ENGLAND UA 1937	Mason, A. E. W. Hodder & Stoughton
FIRST COMES COURAGE COL 1943	Arnold, E. (*Commandos, The*) Rich & Cowan
FIRST GENTLEMAN, THE COL 1948	Ginsbury, N. (P) Hammond
FIRST LEGION, THE UA 1951	Lavery, E. G. (P) French, N.Y.
FIRST MEN IN THE MOON, THE COL 1963	Wells, H. G. Various
FIRST MRS FRASER, THE STERLING 1932	Ervine, St. J. (P) Chatto & Windus
FIVE AND TEN MGM 1931	Hurst, F. Cape
FIVE FINGER EXERCISE COL 1962	Shaffer, P. (P) French
FIVE FINGERS FOX 1952	Moyzisch, L. C. (*Operation Cicero*) Wingate
FIVE LITTLE PEPPERS AND HOW THEY GREW COL 1939	Sidley, M. Various

TITLE OF FILM	AUTHOR AND PUBLISHER
FIVE ON A TREASURE ISLAND BL 1957	Blyton, E. Hodder & Stoughton
FIVE WEEKS IN A BALLOON FOX 1962	Verne, J. Various
FLAME IN THE STREETS RANK 1961	Willis, T. (*Hot summer night*) (P) French
FLAMINGO ROAD WAR 1949	Wilder, R. Grosset, N.Y.
FLAMING STAR FOX 1960	Huffaker, C. (*Flaming lance*) Simon & Schuster, N.Y.
FLAT TWO AA 1962	Wallace, E. Long
FLESH AND BLOOD BL 1951	Bridie, J. (*Sleeping clergyman, A*) (P) French
FLESH AND FANTASY UN 1943	Wilde, O. (*Lord Arthur Savile's crime*) Various
FLESH IS WEAK, THE EROS 1957	Miller, G. Corgi
FLIGHT FROM ASHIYA UA 1963	Arnold, E. Muller
FLIGHT OF THE PHOENIX, THE FOX 1965	Trevor, E. Heinemann
FLIGHT OF THE WHITE STALLION, THE DISNEY 1963	Podhajsky, A. (*White stallions of Vienna, The*) Harrap
FLIM-FLAM MAN, THE FOX 1966	Owen, G. (*Ballad of the flim-flam man*) Macmillan, N.Y.
FLOATING DUTCHMAN, THE AA 1953	Bentley, N. Joseph
FLOODS OF FEAR RANK 1958	Hawkins, J. *and* Hawkins, W. Eyre & Spottiswoode
FLORIAN MGM 1940	Salten, F. Cape
FLORENTINE DAGGER, THE WAR 1935	Hecht, B. Harrap
FLOWER DRUM SONG UI 1961	Lee, C. Y. Gollancz

FLY AWAY PETER GFD 1948	Dearsley, A. P. (P) French
FOLLOW ME BOYS! DISNEY 1967	Kantor, M. (*God and my country*) World, N.Y.
FOLLOW THAT DREAM UA 1962	Powell, R. (*Pioneer go home*) Hodder & Stoughton
FOLLOW THAT HORSE WAR 1959	Mason, H. (*Photo finish*) Joseph
FOLLY TO BE WISE BL 1952	Bridie, J. (*It depends what you mean*) (P) Constable
FOOLS RUSH IN PINEWOOD 1949	Horn, K. (P) French
FOOTSTEPS IN THE FOG COL 1955	Jacobs, W. W. (*Interruption, The*) Methuen
FOOTSTEPS IN THE NIGHT AUTEN 1932	Simpson, *Mrs* C. F. Methuen
FOR BEAUTY'S SAKE FOX 1941	Kelland, C. B. (*Skin deep*) Various
FOR BETTER, FOR WORSE ABP 1954	Watkyn, A. (P) Elek
FORBIDDEN FRUIT CAMEO-POLY 1952	Simenon, G. (*Act of Passion*) Routledge
FORBIDDEN TERRITORY HOFFBERG 1938	Wheatley, D. Hutchinson
FORBIDDEN VALLEY UN 1938	Hardy, S. Macaulay, N.Y.
FORCE OF EVIL MGM 1949	Wolfert, I. (*Tucker's people*) Gollancz
FOREVER AMBER FOX 1947	Winsor, K. Macdonald
FOREVER FEMALE PAR 1953	Barrie, *Sir* J. M. (*Rosalind*) (P) Hodder & Stoughton
FORGOTTEN VILLAGE, THE MGM 1941	Steinbeck, J. Viking Press, N.Y.
FORLORN RIVER PAR 1937	Grey, Z. Hodder & Stoughton
FORSYTE SAGA, THE MGM 1950	Galsworthy, J. (*Man of property, The*) Heinemann

FOR THEM THAT TRESPASS ABP 1949	Raymond, E. Cassell
FORTUNE IS A WOMAN COL 1957	Graham, W. Hodder & Stoughton
FORTUNES OF CAPTAIN BLOOD, **THE** COL 1950	Sabatini, R. Hutchinson
FOR WHOM THE BELL TOLLS PAR 1943	Hemingway, E. Cape
FOUNTAIN, THE RKO 1934	Morgan, C. Macmillan
FOUNTAINHEAD WAR 1949	Rand, A. Cassell
FOUR DAYS WONDER UN 1937	Milne, A. A. Methuen
FOUR FACES WEST UA 1948	Rhodes, E. M. (*Paso por acqui*) Houghton Mifflin, Boston
FOUR FEATHERS, THE PAR 1930 UA 1939	Mason, A. E. W. Murray
FOUR HORSEMEN OF THE **APOCALYPSE, THE** MGM 1961	Blasco-Ibanez, C. Various
FOUR HOURS TO KILL PAR 1935	Krasna, N. (*Small miracle*) (P) French, N.Y.
FOUR JUST MEN, THE EALING 1939	Wallace, E. Various
FOUR POSTER, THE COL 1952	Hartog, J. de. (P) Sampson Low
FOUR-SIDED TRIANGLE EXCLUSIVE 1952	Temple, W. F. Long
FOXES OF HARROW, THE FOX 1947	Yerby, F. Heinemann
FOXFIRE UI 1954	Seton, A. Hodder & Stoughton
FOXHOLE IN CAIRO BL 1960	Mosley, L. (*Cat and the mice, The*) Barker
FRANCHISE AFFAIR, THE ABP 1951	Tey, J. Davies

FRANCIS UI 1949	Stern, D. Farrar, N.Y.
FRANKENSTEIN UN 1931	Shelley, *Mrs.* M. W. Dent
FRAULEIN FOX 1957	McGovern, J. Calder
FRECKLES FOX 1960	Porter, G. S. Hodder & Stoughton
FRENCH ARE A FUNNY RACE, THE CONTINENTAL 1957	Daninos, P. (*Major Thompson lives in France*) Cape
FRENCH LEAVE AB 1937	Berkeley, R. (P) French
FRENCH MISTRESS, A BL 1960	Monro, R. (P) French
FRENCH WITHOUT TEARS PAR 1940	Rattigan, T. (P) French
FRENCHMAN'S CREEK PAR 1944	Du Maurier, D. Gollancz
FRIEDA EALING 1947	Millar, R. (P) English Theatre Guild
FRIENDLY PERSUASION MGM 1956	West, J. Hodder & Stoughton
FRIENDS AND LOVERS RKO 1931	Dekobra, M. (*Sphinx has spoken, The*) Laurie
FRIGHTENED LADY, THE BL 1941	Wallace, E. (P) French, N.Y.
FRIGHTENED LADY, THE BL 1932 BL 1941	Wallace, E. (*Case of the frightened lady, The*) Hodder & Stoughton
FROM HERE TO ETERNITY COL 1953	Jones, J. Collins
FROM RUSSIA WITH LOVE UA 1963	Fleming, I. Cape
FROM THE EARTH TO THE MOON WAR 1958	Verne, J. Various
FROM THE TERRACE FOX 1960	O'Hara, J. Cresset Press

FROM THIS DAY FORWARD
RKO 1946

Bell, T. (*All brides are beautiful*)
Grosset, N.Y.

FRONTIER RANGERS
MGM 1959

Roberts, K. (*North-west passage*)
Collins

FRONT PAGE, THE
UA 1931

Hecht, B. *and* MacArthur, C. C. (P)
Covici, N.Y.

FRONT PAGE STORY
BL 1953

Gaines, R. (*Final night*)
Heinemann

FRONTIER MARSHAL
FOX 1939

Lake, S. (*Wyatt Earp*)
Various

FUGITIVE, THE
RKO 1947

Greene, G. (*Power and the glory, The*)
Heinemann

FUGITIVE KIND, THE
UA 1960

Williams, T. (*Orpheus descending*) (P)
Secker & Warburg

FULL HOUSE
FOX 1952

Henry, O.
Hodder & Stoughton

FULL OF LIFE
COL 1957

Fante, J.
Little Brown, Boston

FULL TREATMENT, THE
COL 1960

Thorn, R. S.
Heinemann

FUMED OAK
GFD 1952

Coward, N. (P)
Heinemann

FUNERAL IN BERLIN
PAR 1966

Deighton, L.
Cape

FURIES, THE
PAR 1950

Busch, N.
W. H. Allen

FUZZY PINK NIGHTGOWN, THE
UA 1957

Tate, S.
Harper, N.Y.

G

GABY
MGM 1955

Sherwood, R. E. (*Waterloo Bridge*) (P)
Scribner, N.Y.

GAMBIT
UI 1966

Lane, K.
Hodder & Stoughton

GAME FOR THREE LOSERS
WAR 1965

Lustgarten, E.
Museum Press

GAME IS OVER, THE
COL 1967

Zola, E. (*Kill, The*)
Arrow Bks

GARDEN MURDER CASE, THE
MGM 1936

Dine, S. S. van.
  Cassell

GARDEN OF ALLAH, THE
UA 1936

Hichens, R.
  Methuen

GASLIGHT
BN 1940
MGM 1944

Hamilton, P. (P)
  French

GAUNT WOMAN, THE
RKO 1950

Gilligan, E.
  Scribner, N.Y.

GAY CABALLERO
FOX 1932

Gill, T. (*Gay bandit of the border*)
  Collins

GENERAL CRACK
WAR 1930

Preedy, G.
  Lane

GENERAL DIED AT DAWN, THE
PAR 1936

Booth, C. G.
  Bell

GENTLE ANNIE
MGM 1944

Kantor, M.
  Various

GENTLE GUNMAN, THE
GFD 1952

Macdougall, R. (P)
  Elek

GENTLE JULIA
FOX 1936

Tarkington, B.
  Grosset, N.Y.

GENTLEMEN MARRY BRUNETTES
UA 1955

Loos, A. (*But . . .*)
  Brentano, N.Y.

GENTLEMEN PREFER BLONDES
FOX 1953

Loos, A.
  Cape

GENTLEMEN'S AGREEMENT
FOX 1947

Hobson, *Mrs.* L.
  Cassell

GEORDIE
BL 1955

Walker, D.
  Collins

GEORGE AND MARGARET
WAR 1940

Savory, G. (P)
  French, N.Y.

GEORGE WASHINGTON SLEPT HERE
WAR 1942

Kaufman, G. S. *and* Hart, M. (P)
  Random House, N.Y.

GEORGY GIRL
COL 1966

Forster, M.
  Secker & Warburg

GHOST AND MRS MUIR, THE
FOX 1947

Dick, R. A.
  Harrap

c

GHOST TRAIN, THE
GFD 1931
GFD 1941

Ridley, A. (P)
French, N.Y.

GHOSTS OF BERKELEY SQUARE, THE
BN 1947

Brahms, C. *and* Simon, S. J. (*No nightingales*)
Joseph

GIANT
WAR 1956

Ferber, E.
Gollancz

GIDEON'S DAY
COL 1958

Marric, J. J.
Hodder & Stoughton

GIDGET
COL 1959

Kohner, F.
Joseph

GIFT FROM THE BOYS, A
COL 1959

Buchwald, A.
Harper, N.Y.

GIGI
MGM 1958

Colette
Secker & Warburg

GIRL FROM ALASKA, THE
REP 1942

Case, R. O. (*Golden portage, The*)
Jarrolds

GIRL FROM MANDALAY
REP 1936

Campbell, R. (*Death in Tiger Valley*)
Hodder & Stoughton

GIRL HE LEFT BEHIND, THE
WAR 1957

Hargrove, M.
Viking Press, N.Y.

GIRL HUNTERS, THE
FOX 1964

Spillane, M.
Barker

GIRL IN THE HEADLINES, THE
BL 1963

Payne, L. (*Nose on my face, The*)
Hodder & Stoughton

GIRL IN THE NEWS
FOX 1941

Vickers, R.
Jenkins

GIRL IN WHITE, THE
MGM 1952

Barringer, E. D. (*Bowery to Bellevue*)
Norton, N.Y.

GIRL MUST LIVE, A
UN 1941

Bonett, E.
Miles

GIRL NAMED TAMIKO, A
PAR 1963

Kirkbride, R.
Pan Bks

GIRL OF THE LIMBERLOST, A
MON 1934

Porter, G. S.
Hodder & Stoughton

GIRL OF THE NIGHT
WAR 1960

Greenwald, H. (*Call girl, The*)
Elek

GIRL ON THE BOAT, THE
UA 1962

Wodehouse, P. G.
Jenkins

GIRLS OF PLEASURE ISLAND, THE
PAR 1953

Maier, W. (*Pleasure Island*)
Wingate

GIRLS OF SUMMER
PAR 1959

Nash, N. R. (P)
French, N.Y.

GIRL WHO COULDN'T QUITE, THE
MON 1949

Marks, L. (P)
French

GIRL WHO DARED, THE
REP 1944

Field, M. (*Blood on her shoe*)
Jarrolds

GIRL WITH GREEN EYES
UA 1964

O'Brien, E. (*Lonely girl, The*)
Cape

GIVE ME YOUR HEART
WAR 1936

Mallory, J. (*Sweet aloes*)
Cassell

GIVE US THE MOON
GFD 1944

Brahms, C. *and* Simon, S. J. (*Elephant in white, The*)
Joseph

GIVE US THIS DAY
GFD 1949

Di Donato, P. (*Christ in concrete*)
World, N.Y.

GLAD TIDINGS
EROS 1953

Delderfield, R. F. (P)
Rylee

GLASS CAGE, THE
EXCLUSIVE 1955

Martin, A. E. (*Curious crime*)
Muller

GLASS KEY, THE
PAR 1935
PAR 1942

Hammett, D.
Cassell

GLASS MENAGERIE
WAR 1950

Williams, T. (P)
Lehmann

GNOMOBILE
DISNEY 1966

Stern, G. B.
Laurie

GOD IS MY CO-PILOT
WAR 1945

Scott, R. L.
Hodder & Stoughton

GOD'S LITTLE ACRE
UA 1958

Caldwell, E.
Heinemann

GOLD BUG, THE
BL 1956

Poe, E. A.
Various

GOLDEN BOY
COL 1938

Odets, C. (P)
Gollancz

GOLDEN EAR-RINGS
PAR 1947

Foldes, Y.
Hale

TITLE OF FILM	AUTHOR AND PUBLISHER
GOLDEN HAWK, THE COL 1952	Yerby, F. Heinemann
GOLDEN HEAD, THE CINERAMA 1965	Pilkington, R. (*Nepomuk of the river*) Macmillan
GOLDEN SALAMANDER GFD 1949	Canning, V. Hodder & Stoughton
GOLDFINGER UA 1963	Fleming, I. Cape
GOLD FOR THE CAESARS MGM 1963	Seward, F. A. Redman
GOLD OF THE SEVEN SAINTS WAR 1961	Frazee, S. (*Desert guns*) World, N.Y.
GO NAKED IN THE WORLD MGM 1960	Chamales, T. Deutsch
GONE TO EARTH BL 1950	Webb, M. Cape
GONE WITH THE WIND MGM 1939	Mitchell, M. Macmillan
GOODBYE AGAIN UA 1961	Sagan, F. (*Aimez-vous Brahms*) Murray
GOODBYE CHARLIE FOX 1965	Axelrod, G. (P) French, N.Y.
GOODBYE, MY FANCY WAR 1951	Kanin, F. (P) French, N.Y.
GOODBYE, MY LADY WAR 1956	Street, J. H. Invincible Press
GOOD COMPANIONS, THE FOX 1933 ABP 1957	Priestley, J. B. Heinemann
GOOD COMPANIONS, THE FOX 1933 ABP 1957	Priestley, J. B. *and* Knoblock, E. (P) French, N.Y.
GOODBYE MR. CHIPS MGM 1939	Hilton, J. Hodder & Stoughton
GOODBYE MR. CHIPS MGM 1939	Hilton, J. *and* Burnham, B. (P) French, N.Y.
GOOD EARTH, THE MGM 1937	Buck, P. Methuen

GOOD MORNING, MISS DOVE FOX 1955	Patton, F. G. Gollancz
GOOD NEIGHBOUR SAM COL 1965	Finney, J. Eyre & Spottiswoode
GOOD-TIME GIRL GFD 1948	La Bern, A. J. (*Night darkens the streets*) Nicholson & Watson
GRACIE ALLEN MURDER CASE, THE PAR 1939	Dine, S. S. van. Cassell
GRAND CANARY FOX 1934	Cronin, A. J. Gollancz
GRAND CENTRAL MURDER MGM 1942	McVeigh, S. Houghton Mifflin, Boston
GRAND HOTEL MGM 1932	Baum, V. Bles
GRAND NATIONAL NIGHT REN 1953	Christie, D. *and* Christie, C. (P) French
GRAPES OF WRATH, THE FOX 1940	Steinbeck, J. Heinemann
GRASS IS GREENER, THE UI 1960	Williams, H. *and* Williams, M. (P) Gollancz
GREAT DAY IN THE MORNING RKO 1955	Andrew, R. H. Lane
GREAT DIVIDE, THE IN 1930	Moody, W. V. (P) Macmillan
GREAT ESCAPE, THE UA 1963	Brickhill, P. Faber
GREATEST STORY EVER TOLD, THE UA 1965	Oursler, F. Worlds Work
GREAT EXPECTATIONS UN 1934 CINEGUILD 1946	Dickens, C. Various
GREAT GAME, THE ADELPHI 1953	Thomas, B. (*Shooting star*) (P) Deane
GREAT GATSBY, THE PAR 1949	Fitzgerald, F. S. K. Grey Walls Press
GREAT IMPERSONATION, THE UN 1936 UN 1942	Oppenheim, E. P. Hodder & Stoughton

TITLE OF FILM	AUTHOR AND PUBLISHER
GREAT IMPOSTER, THE UI 1960	Crichton, R. Gollancz
GREAT MAN, THE UI 1956	Morgan, A. Dutton, N.Y.
GREAT MEADOW, THE MGM 1931	Roberts, E. M. Cape
GREAT SINNER, THE MGM 1949	Dostoevski, F. M. (*Great gambler*) Macmillan
GREEN DOLPHIN STREET MGM 1947	Goudge, E. Hodder & Stoughton
GREEN EYES CHESTERFIELD 1934	Ashbrook, H. (*Murder of Stephen Kester*) Eyre & Spottiswoode
GREEN FINGERS BN 1947	Arundel, E. (*Persistent warrior, The*) Jenkins
GREEN FOR DANGER INDIVIDUAL 1947	Brand, C. Lane
GREENGAGE SUMMER, THE RANK 1960	Godden, R. Macmillan
GREEN GODDESS, THE WAR 1930	Archer, W. (P) Heinemann
GREEN GRASS OF WYOMING FOX 1949	O'Hara, M. Eyre & Spottiswoode
GREEN GROW THE RUSHES BL 1951	Clewes, H. Lane
GREEN HELL UN 1940	Duguid, J. Various
GREEN HELMET, THE MGM 1960	Cleary, J. Collins
GREEN LIGHT, THE WAR 1937	Douglas, L. C. Davies
GREEN MAN, THE BL 1956	Maunder, F. *and* Gilliat, S. (*Meet a body*) (P) French
GREEN MANSIONS MGM 1958	Hudson, W. H. Various
GREEN PACK, THE BL 1936	Wallace, E. (P) French

GREEN PACK, THE
BL 1936

Wallace, E. *and* Curtis, R. G.
Hutchinson

GREEN PASTURES
WAR 1936

Connelly, M. (P)
Gollancz

GREEN SCARF, THE
BL 1954

Cars, G. des. (*Brute, The*)
Wingate

GREEN YEARS, THE
MGM 1946

Cronin, A. J.
Gollancz

GRIP OF FEAR, THE
COL 1962

Gordons, The. (*Operation terror*)
Macdonald

GROUP, THE
UA 1965

McCarthy, M.
Weidenfeld & Nicolson

GUADACANAL DIARY
FOX 1943

Tregaskis, R. W.
Wells & Gardner

GUARDSMAN, THE
MGM 1931

Molnar, F. (P)
Macy-Masius, N.Y.

GUEST IN THE HOUSE
UA 1944

Wilde, H. *and* Eunson, D. (*Dear Evelyn*) (P)
French

GUILT IS MY SHADOW
ABP 1950

Curtis, P. (*You're best alone*)
Macdonald

GUILTY?
GN 1956

Gilbert, M. (*Death has deep roots*)
Pan Bks

GUINEA PIG, THE
PILGRIM-PATHE 1949

Strode, W. S. (P)
Sampson Low

GULLIVER'S TRAVELS
PAR 1939

Swift, J.
Various

GUNFIGHTERS
COL 1947

Grey, Z. (*Twin sombreros*)
Hodder & Stoughton

GUN FURY
COL 1954

Granger, K. R. G. (*Ten against Caesar*)
Houghton, Mifflin, Boston

GUN GLORY
MGM 1957

Yordan, P. (*Man of the West*)
Deutsch

GUNS AT BATASI
FOX 1964

Holles, R. (*Siege of Battersea, The*)
Joseph

GUNSMOKE
GFD 1952

Fox, N. A. (*Roughshod*)
Dodd, N.Y.

GUNS OF AUGUST, THE RANK 1964	Tuchman, R. (*August* 1914) Constable
GUNS OF DARKNESS WAR 1964	Clifford, F. (*Act of mercy*) Hamilton
GUNS OF DIABLO MGM 1964	Taylor, R. L. (*Travels of Jaimie McPheeters, The*) Macdonald
GUNS OF NAVARONE, THE COL 1959	MacLean, A. Collins
GUNS OF THE TIMBERLANDS WAR 1959	L'Amour, L. Jason Press, N.Y.
GUY NAMED JOE, A MGM 1943	Cairn, J. Hollywood Pubns
GYPSY WAR 1962	Lee, G. R. Pan Bks
GYPSY AND THE GENTLEMAN, THE RANK 1957	Hooke, N. W. (*Darkness I leave you*) Hale

H

HAIRY APE, THE UA 1944	O'Neill, E. G. (P) Cape
HALLELUJAH TRAIL, THE UA 1965	Gullick, B. Doubleday, N.Y.
HAMLET TC 1948	Shakespeare, W. (P) Various
HAMMER THE TOFF BUTCHER 1952	Creasey, J. Long
HANGING TREE, THE WAR 1958	Johnson, D. M. Deutsch
HANGMEN ALSO DIE UA 1943	Habe, H. (*Thousand shall fall, A*) Harrap
HANSEL AND GRETEL RKO 1954	Grimm, J. K. *and* Grimm, W. K. Various
HAPPENING, THE PAR 1967	Curry, E. Corgi
HAPPIEST DAYS OF YOUR LIFE, THE BL 1949	Dighton, J. (P) Elek

HAPPINESS OF THREE WOMEN, THE ADELPHI 1954	Evans, E. (*Wishing well*) (P) French
HAPPY ANNIVERSARY UA 1959	Fields, J. *and* Chodorov, J. (*Anniversary waltz*) (P) Random House, N.Y.
HAPPY FAMILY, THE APEX 1952	Hutton, M. G. (P) Deane
HAPPY LAND FOX 1943	Kantor, M. Longmans
HAPPY THIEVES, THE UA 1961	Condon, R. (*Oldest confession, The*) Longmans
HAPPY TIME, THE COL 1952	Fontaine, R. L. Hamilton
HAPPY TIME, THE COL 1952	Taylor, S. A. (P) Dramatists, N.Y.
HARDER THEY FALL COL 1956	Schulberg, B. W. Lane
HARD MAN, THE COL 1957	Katcher, L. Macmillan, N.Y.
HARLOW PAR 1964	Shulman, I. Mayflower
HARPER WAR 1967	Macdonald, R. (*Moving target, The*) Pan
HARRIET CRAIG COL 1950	Kelly, G. (*Craig's wife*) (P) French
HARRY BLACK FOX 1958	Walker, D. Collins
HARVESTER, THE REP 1936	Porter, G. S. Hodder & Stoughton
HARVEY GFD 1950	Chase, M. (P) Dramatists, N.Y.
HATE SHIP BI 1930	Graeme, B. Hutchinson
HATFUL OF RAIN, A FOX 1957	Gazzo, M. V. (P) Random House, N.Y.
HATTER'S CASTLE PAR 1942	Cronin, A. J. Gollancz

HAUNTING, THE MGM 1963	Jackson, S. (*Haunting of Hill House, The*) Joseph
HAVING WONDERFUL CRIME RKO 1945	Rice, E. Nicholson & Watson
HAVING WONDERFUL TIME RKO 1938	Kober, A. (P) Dramatists, N.Y.
HAWAII UA 1965	Michener, J. A. Secker & Warburg
HAZARD PAR 1948	Chanslor, R. Various
HEART OF A CHILD RANK 1958	Bottome, P. Faber
HEART OF THE MATTER BL 1953	Greene, G. Heinemann
HEAT LIGHTING WAR 1934	Hull, H. R. Cobden Sanderson
HEAVEN CAN WAIT FOX 1943	Ackland, R. (*Birthday*) (P) French, N.Y.
HEAVEN KNOWS MR. ALLISON FOX 1957	Shaw, C. Muller
HEFFERAN FAMILY, THE FOX 1956	Taylor, R. (*Chicken every Sunday*) Methuen
HEIDI FOX 1937 UA 1954	Spyri, J. Various
HEIRESS, THE PAR 1949	Goetz, R. *and* Goetz, A. (P) Reinhardt & Evans
HEIRESS, THE PAR 1949	James, H. (*Washington Square*) Macmillan
HE KNEW WOMEN RKO 1930	Behrman, S. N. (*Second man*) (P) Various
HELL BELOW ZERO COL 1953	Innes, H. (*White South, The*) Collins
HELLCATS OF THE NAVY COL 1957	Lockwood, C. A. *and* Adamson, H. C. (*Hellcats of the sea*) Greenberg, N.Y.
HELLER IN PINK TIGHTS PAR 1960	L'Amour, L. (*Heller with a gun*) Muller

HELL IS A CITY WAR 1959	Procter, M. Hutchinson
HELL IS FOR HEROES PAR 1962	Anders, C. Corgi Bks
HELL IS SOLD OUT EROS 1951	Dekobra, M. Laurie
HELL ON FRISCO BAY WAR 1955	McGivern, W. P. (*Darkest hour*) Collins
HELL'S HEROES UN 1930	Kyne, P. B. (*Three godfathers, The*) Various
HELL'S OUTPOST REP 1954	Short, L. (*Silver Rock*) Collins
HENRY V TC 1945	Shakespeare, W. (P) Various
HE RAN ALL THE WAY UA 1951	Ross, S. Farrar, N.Y.
HERE COME THE HUGGETTS GFD 1948	Constanduros, M. *and* Constanduros, D. Sampson Low
HERE COMES MR. JORDAN COL 1941	Segall, H. (*Halfway to heaven*) (P) French
HERE WE GO ROUND THE MULBERRY BUSH UA 1967	Davies, H. Pan
HER FIRST ROMANCE MON 1940	Porter, G. S. (*Her father's daughter*) Murray
HERITAGE OF THE DESERT PAR 1933 PAR 1939	Grey, Z. Nelson
HEROES OF THE TELEMARK RANK 1965	Drummond, J. D. (*But for these men*) W. H. Allen
HER SISTER'S SECRET PRC 1946	Kaus, G. (*Dark angel*) Cassell
HER STRANGE DESIRE POWERS 1932	Middleton, E. (*Potiphar's wife*) Laurie
HER TWELVE MEN MGM 1954	Baker, L. McGraw-Hill, N.Y.
HER WONDERFUL LIFE COL 1950	Moss, A. *and* Marvel, E. (*Legend of the Latin Quarter*) W. H. Allen

HIAWATHA
ABP 1952

Longfellow, H. W. (Poem)
Various

HIDDEN HOMICIDE
RANK 1958

Capon, P. (*Death at Shinglestrand*)
Ward Lock

HIGH AND THE MIGHTY, THE
WAR 1954

Gann, E. K.
Hodder & Stoughton

HIGH BARBAREE, THE
MGM 1947

Nordhoff, C. B. *and* Hall, J. N.
Faber

HIGH BRIGHT SUN, THE
RANK 1964

Black, I. S.
Hutchinson

HIGH HELL
PAR 1958

Frazee, S. (*High cage*)
Macmillan, N.Y.

HIGH SIERRA
WAR 1941

Burnett, W. R.
Heinemann

HIGH SOCIETY
MGM 1956

Barry, P. (*Philadelphia story, The*) (P)
French

HIGH VERMILION
PAR 1951

Short, L.
Collins

HIGH WIND IN JAMAICA, A
FOX 1964

Hughes, R.
Chatto & Windus

HIGH WINDOW, THE
FOX 1947

Chandler, R.
Hamilton

HILDA CRANE
FOX 1956

Raphaelson, S. (P)
Random House, N.Y.

HILL IN KOREA, A
BL 1956

Catto, M.
Hutchinson

HILLS OF OLD WYOMING
PAR 1937

Mulford, C. E. (*Round-up, The*)
Hodder & Stoughton

HINDLE WAKES
GB 1932
MON 1952

Houghton, S. (P)
Various

HIS DOUBLE LIFE
PAR 1933

Bennett, A. (*Great adventure*)
Methuen

HIS EXCELLENCY
GFD 1951

Arlington, A.
Chatto & Windus

HIS EXCELLENCY
GFD 1951

Christie, D. *and* Christie, P. (P)
Elek

HIS GIRL FRIDAY
COL 1940

Hecht, B. *and* MacArthur, C. C. (*Front page, The*) (P)
Covici, N.Y.

HIS MAJESTY O'KEEFE
WAR 1954

Klingman, L. *and* Green, G.
Hale

HIS WOMAN
PAR 1931

Collins, D. (*Sentimentalists*)
Little Brown, Boston

HISTORY OF MR. POLLY
TC 1949

Wells, H. G.
Various

HITLER'S CHILDREN
RKO 1943

Ziemer, G. (*Education for death*)
Constable

HIT THE DECK
MGM 1954

Osborne, H. (*Shore leave*) (P)
French, N.Y.

H. M. PULHAM, Esq
MGM 1941

Marquand, J. P.
Hale

H.M.S. DEFIANT
COL 1962

Tilsley, F. (*Mutiny*)
Eyre & Spottiswoode

HOBSON'S CHOICE
BI. 1931
BL 1953

Brighouse, H. (P)
French

HOLD BACK THE DAWN
PAR 1941

Frings, *Mrs.* K.
Duell, N.Y.

HOLD BACK THE NIGHT
ABP 1956

Frank, P.
Hamilton

HOLE IN THE HEAD, A
UA 1959

Schulman, A. (P)
Random House, N.Y.

HOLLOW TRIUMPH
EL 1948

Forbes, M.
Martin

HOLLY AND THE IVY, THE
BL 1952

Browne, W. (P)
Elek

HOMBRE
FOX 1966

Leonard, E.
Hale

HOME AT SEVEN
BL 1951

Sherriff, R. C. (P)
Gollancz

HOME BEFORE DARK
WAR 1958

Bassing, E.
Longmans

HOME FROM THE HILL
MGM 1959

Humphrey, W.
Pan Bks

TITLE OF FILM	AUTHOR AND PUBLISHER
HOME IS THE HERO BL 1959	Macken, W. (P) Macmillan
HOME ON THE RANGE PAR 1935	Grey, Z. (*Code of the West*) Hodder & Stoughton
HOME SWEET HOMICIDE FOX 1946	Rice, C. World, N.Y.
HONEYMOON FOR THREE WAR 1941	Scott, A. *and* Haight, G. (*Goodbye again*) (P) French, N.Y.
HONEYMOON MACHINE MGM 1961	Semple, L. (*Golden fleecing, The*) (P) French, N.Y.
HOP-ALONG-CASSIDY PAR 1935	Mulford, C. E. Hodder & Stoughton
HOP-ALONG-CASSIDY RETURNS PAR 1936	Mulford, C. E. Hodder & Stoughton
HORIZONTAL LIEUTENANT, THE MGM 1962	Cotler, G. (*Bottletop affair, The*) Panther Bks
HORSE'S MOUTH, THE UA 1958	Cary, J. Joseph
HORSE SOLDIERS, THE UA 1959	Sinclair, H. Muller
HORSE WITHOUT A HEAD, THE DISNEY 1963	Berna, P. (*Hundred million frames, A*) Penguin Bks
HOSTAGES PAR 1943	Heym, S. Putnam
HOTEL WAR 1966	Hailey, A. Pan
HOTEL BERLIN WAR 1945	Baum, V. (*Berlin Hotel*) Joseph
HOTEL RESERVE RKO 1944	Ambler, E. (*Epitaph for a spy*) Hodder & Stoughton
HOT ENOUGH FOR JUNE RANK 1963	Davidson, L. (*Night of Wenceslas*) Gollancz
HOUDINI PAR 1953	Kellock, H. Heinemann
HOUND DOG MAN FOX 1959	Gipson, F. B. (*Circles round the wagon*) Joseph

HOUND OF THE BASKERVILLES,   Doyle, *Sir* A. C.
  THE   Murray
  ID 1932
  FOX 1939
  UA 1959

HOUR BEFORE DAWN   Maugham, W. S.
  PAR 1944   Doubleday, N.Y.

HOUSE ACROSS THE LAKE, THE   Hughes, K. (*High Wray*)
  ABP 1954   Gifford

HOUSE BY THE RIVER, THE   Herbert, *Sir* A. P.
  REP 1950   Methuen

HOUSE DIVIDED, A   Buck, P.
  UN 1932   Methuen

HOUSE IN MARSH ROAD, THE   Meynell, L.
  GN 1960   Collins

HOUSE IN THE SQUARE, THE   Balderston, J. L. (*Berkeley Square*) (P)
  FOX 1951   French

HOUSE IS NOT A HOME, A   Adler, P.
  PAR 1964   Heinemann

HOUSE OF A THOUSAND CANDLES,   Nicolson, M.
  THE   Hale
  REP 1936

HOUSE OF FEAR   Doyle, *Sir* A. C. (*Adventure of the five*
  UN 1945   *orange pips*)
                                      Murray

HOUSE OF NUMBERS   Finney, J.
  MGM 1957   Eyre & Spottiswoode

HOUSE OF SECRETS, THE   Noel, S.
  RANK 1956   Deutsch

HOUSE OF THE ARROW   Mason, A. E. W.
  AB 1940   Hodder & Stoughton
  ABP 1953

HOUSE OF THE SEVEN GABLES,   Hawthorne, N.
  THE   Various
  UN 1940

HOUSE OF THE SEVEN HAWKS,   Canning, V. (*House of the seven flies, The*)
  THE   Hodder & Stoughton
  MGM 1959

HOUSE OF THE SPANIARD, THE   Behrend, A.
  GB 1936   Heinemann

79

HOUSE ON TELEGRAPH HILL, THE
FOX 1951

Lyon, D. (*Tentacles*)
Harper, N.Y.

HOUSEKEEPER'S DAUGHTER, THE
UA 1939

Clarke, D. H.
Laurie

HOUSEMASTER
ALL 1939

Hay, I.
Hodder & Stoughton

HOUSEMASTER
ALL 1939

Hay, I. (P)
French

HOWARDS OF VIRGINIA, THE
COL 1940

Page, E. (*Tree of liberty*)
Collins

HOW GREEN WAS MY VALLEY
FOX 1941

Llewellyn, R.
Joseph

HOW I WON THE WAR
UA 1967

Ryan, P.
Muller

HOW TO SUCCEED IN BUSINESS WITHOUT REALLY TRYING
UA 1966

Mead. J.
Macdonald

HUCKSTERS, THE
MGM 1947

Wakeman, F.
Falcon Press

HUD
PAR 1963

McMurty, L. (*Horseman, pass by*)
Hamilton

HUGGETTS ABROAD, THE
HGF 1949

Constanduros, M. *and* Constanduros, D.
Sampson Low

HUMAN COMEDY, THE
MGM 1943

Saroyan, W.
Faber

HUMAN DESIRE
COL 1954

Zola, E. (*La Bête humaine*)
Various

HUMORESQUE
WAR 1946

Hurst, F.
Smith, N.Y.

HUNCHBACK OF NOTRE DAME, THE
RKO 1939
RANK 1957

Hugo, V.
Various

HUNGRY HILL
TC 1947

Du Maurier, D.
Gollancz

HUNTERS, THE
FOX 1958

Salter, J.
Heinemann

HUNTINGTOWER
PAR 1928

Buchan, J.
Hodder & Stoughton

TITLE OF FILM	AUTHOR AND PUBLISHER
HURRICANE UA 1937	Nordhoff, C. B. *and* Hall, J. N. Chapman & Hall
HURRY SUNDOWN PAR 1966	Gilden, K. B. Heinemann
HUSBAND'S HOLIDAY PAR 1931	Pascal, E. (*Marriage bed, The*) Allen & Unwin
HUSTLER, THE FOX 1961	Tevis, W. Joseph

I

I AM A CAMERA BL 1955	Druten, J. van. (P) Random House, N.Y.
I AM A FUGITIVE WAR 1932	Burns, R. E. (*I am a fugitive from the chain gang*) Paul
I BELIEVE IN YOU EALING 1953	Stokes, S. (*Court circular*) Joseph
ICE COLD IN ALEX ABP 1957	Landon, C. Heinemann
ICE PALACE WAR 1960	Ferber, E. Gollancz
IDEAL HUSBAND, AN BL 1948	Wilde, O. (P) Methuen
I DIED A THOUSAND TIMES WAR 1955	Burnett, W. R. (*High Sierra*) Various
IDIOT'S DELIGHT MGM 1939	Sherwood, R. E. (P) Heinemann
IDLE ON PARADE COL 1959	Camp, W. MacGibbon
IDLE RICH MGM 1929	Ellis, E. (*White collars*) (P) French, N.Y.
IF A MAN ANSWERS RANK 1962	Wolfe, W. Hammond
IF I HAD A MILLION PAR 1932	Andrews, R. H. Hurst & Blackett
IF I WERE FREE RKO 1933	Druten, J. van. (*Behold we live*) (P) Gollancz

IF WINTER COMES
MGM 1947

Hutchinson, A.S.M.
Hodder & Stoughton

I KILLED THE COUNT
GN 1939

Coppel, A. (P)
Heinemann

I LIVED WITH YOU
GB 1935

Novello, I. (P)
Methuen

I'LL CRY TOMORROW
MGM 1955

Roth, L.
Gollancz

I'LL GET YOU FOR THIS
BL 1951

Chase, J. H.
Jarrolds

ILL MET BY MOONLIGHT
RANK 1956

Moss, W. S.
Corgi Bks

I LOVE TROUBLE
COL 1948

Huggins, R. (*Double take*)
Grosset, N.Y.

I'M ALRIGHT JACK
BL 1959

Hackney, A. (*Private life*)
Gollancz

I MARRIED A DOCTOR
IN 1936

Lewis, S. (*Main Street*)
Cape

I MARRIED ADVENTURE
COL 1940

Johnson, O. H.
Hutchinson

I'M FROM MISSOURI
PAR 1939

Croy, H. (*Sixteen hands*)
Hamilton

IMITATION GENERAL
MGM 1958

Chamberlain, W. (*Trumpets of Company K*)
Ballantine, N.Y.

IMITATION OF LIFE
UN 1934
RANK 1959

Hurst, F. (*Anatomy of me*)
Cape

IMMORTAL SERGEANT, THE
FOX 1943

Brophy, J.
Collins

IMPATIENT MAIDEN
UN 1932

Clarke, D. H. (*Impatient virgin*)
Long

**IMPORTANCE OF BEING EARNEST,
THE**
GFD 1952

Wilde, O. (P)
Heinemann

IN A LONELY PLACE
COL 1950

Hughes, D. B.
Duell, N.Y.

INCREDIBLE JOURNEY, THE
DISNEY 1962

Burnford, S.
Hodder & Stoughton

INCREDIBLE SHRINKING MAN, THE RANK 1957	Matherson, R. Chamberlain Press, Philadelphia
INDISCREET WAR 1958	Krasna, N. (*Kind sir*) (P) Dramatists, N.Y.
INFORMER, THE RKO 1935	O'Flaherty, L. Cape
INFORMERS, THE RANK 1963	Warner, D. (*Death of a snout*) Cassell
IN HARM'S WAY COL 1965	Bassett, J. (*Harm's way*) Heinemann
INHERIT THE WIND UA 1960	Lawrence, J. *and* Lee, R. E. (P) Random House, N.Y.
IN HIS STEPS GN 1936	Sheldon, C. M. Warne
IN LOVE AND WAR FOX 1958	Myrer, A. (*Big war, The*) Hamilton
IN NAME ONLY RKO 1939	Breuer, B. (*Memory of love*) Rich & Cowan
INNOCENTS, THE FOX 1961	James, H. (*Turn of the screw, The*) Dent
INNOCENT SINNERS RANK 1957	Godden, R. (*Episode of sparrows, An*) Macmillan
INN OF THE SIXTH HAPPINESS, THE FOX 1958	Burgess, A. (*Small woman, The*) Evans
IN SEARCH OF THE CASTAWAYS DISNEY 1962	Verne, J. (*Captain Grant's children*) Various
INSIDE DAISY CLOVER WAR 1965	Lambert, G. Hamilton
INSIDE THE LINES RKO 1930	Biggers, E. D. (P) French, N.Y.
INSPECTOR, THE FOX 1962	Hartog, J. de. Hamilton
INSPECTOR CALLS, AN BL 1954	Priestley, J. B. (P) French
INSPECTOR GENERAL, THE WAR 1949	Gogol, N. V. (P) French, N.Y.

INTENT TO KILL
FOX 1958

Bryan, M.
Eyre & Spottiswoode

INTERNS, THE
COL 1962

Frede, R.
Corgi Bks

INTERPOL
COL 1957

Forrest, A. J.
Wingate

IN THE CHINESE ROOM
FOX 1959

Connell, V. (*Chinese Room, The*)
Secker & Warburg

IN THE COOL OF THE DAY
MGM 1963

Ertz, S.
Collins

IN THE DOGHOUSE
RANK 1961

Duncan, A. (*It's a vet's life*)
Joseph

IN THE FRENCH STYLE
COL 1963

Shaw, I.
Cape

IN THE HEAT OF THE NIGHT
UA 1967

Ball, J.
Joseph

IN THE WAKE OF A STRANGER
BUTCHER 1959

Black, I. S.
Dakers

IN THIS OUR LIFE
WAR 1942

Glasgow, E.
Cape

INTRUDER, THE
BL 1953

Maugham, R. (*Line on Ginger*)
Chapman & Hall

INTRUDER IN THE DUST
MGM 1949

Faulkner, W.
Random House, N.Y.

**INVASION OF THE BODY
SNATCHERS, THE**
COL 1956

Finney, J. (*Body snatchers, The*)
Eyre & Spottiswoode

INVISIBLE MAN, THE
UN 1933

Wells, H. G.
Various

I PASSED FOR WHITE
WAR 1960

Bradley, M. H.
Davies

IPCRESS FILE, THE
RANK 1964

Deighton, L.
Hodder & Stoughton

I REMEMBER MAMMA
RKO 1948

Druten, J. van. (P)
Dramatists, N.Y.

IRENE
ARGYLE 1950

Marsh, R. J.
Chatto & Windus

I RING DOORBELLS
PRC 1946

Birdwells, R.
  Messner, N.Y.

IRON CURTAIN
FOX 1948

Gouzenko, I. (*This was my choice*)
  Dent

IRON DUKE, THE
GB 1935

Lindsay, P.
  Queensway Press

IRON MAN
UI 1951

Burnett, W. R.
  Heinemann

IRON MISTRESS, THE
WAR 1952

Wellman, P. I.
  Laurie

I SHALL RETURN
FOX 1950

Wolfert. I. (*American guerilla in the
  Philippines*)
  Gollancz

ISLAND IN THE SKY
WAR 1953

Gann, E. K.
  Joseph

ISLAND IN THE SUN
FOX 1957

Waugh, A.
  Cassell

ISLAND OF LOST SOULS
EROS 1959

Wells, H. G. (*Island of Dr Moreau, The*)
  Heinemann

ISLAND OF THE BLUE DOLPHINS
RANK 1964

O'Dell, S.
  Constable

ISLE OF SINNERS
REGENT 1952

Quefflec, H.
  Verschoyle

ISN'T IT ROMANTIC
PAR 1948

Nolan, J. (*Gather ye rosebuds*)
  Appleton-Century, N.Y.

IS PARIS BURNING?
PAR 1965

Collins, L. *and* Lapierre, D.
  Gollancz

**IS YOUR HONEYMOON REALLY
NECESSARY?**
ADELPHI 1953

Tidmarsh, E. V. (P)
  Deane

I TAKE THIS WOMAN
PAR 1931

Rinehart, M. R. (*Lost ecstasy*)
  Doran, N.Y.

IT ALL CAME TRUE
WAR 1940

Bromfield, L. (*Better than life*)
  Cassell

IT ALWAYS RAINS ON SUNDAYS
EALING 1948

La Bern, A. J.
  Nicholson & Watson

I THANK A FOOL
MGM 1962

Lindop, A. E.
  Collins

IT HAPPENED ONE NIGHT COL 1934	Adams, S. H. (*Night bus*) Longmans
IT HAPPENS EVERY SPRING FOX 1950	Davies, V. Farrar, N.Y.
IT HAPPENS EVERY THURSDAY GFD 1953	McIlvaine, J. McRae-Smith
I, THE JURY UA 1953	Spillane, M. Barker
IT'S A DOG'S LIFE MGM 1955	Davis, R. H. (*Bar sinister, The*) Scribner, N.Y.
IT'S NEVER TOO LATE ABP 1956	Douglas, F. (P) Evans
IT STARTED IN TOKYO WAR 1961	Gruber, F. (*Twenty plus two*) Boardman
IT'S TOUGH TO BE FAMOUS IN 1932	McCall, M. (*Gold fish bowl, The*) Paul
IVANHOE MGM 1951	Scott, *Sir* W. Various
IVY UI 1947	Lowndes, *Mrs.* M. B. (*Story of Ivy*) Eyre & Spottiswoode
I WANT TO LIVE UA 1958	Rawson, T. Muller
I WAS A SPY FOX 1934	McKenna, M. Jarrolds
I WAS MONTY'S DOUBLE ABP 1958	James, M. E. C. Rider
I WOULDN'T BE IN YOUR SHOES MON 1948	Irish, W. Lippincott, Philadelphia

J

JALNA RKO 1935	Roche, M. de la. Macmillan
JAMAICA INN PAR 1939	Du Maurier, D. Gollancz
JANE EYRE MON 1934 FOX 1944	Bronte, C. Various

JANIE WAR 1944	Bentham, J. *and* Williams, H. V. (P) French, N.Y.
JASSY GFD 1947	Lofts, N. Joseph
JAVA HEAD ID 1935	Hergesheimer, J. Heinemann
JEANNIE TANSA 1942	Stuart, A. (P) Hamilton
JENNIE GERHARDT PAR 1933	Dreiser, T. Constable
JESSICA UA 1961	Sandstrom, F. (*Midwife of Pont Clery, The*) Ace Bks
JEW SÜSS GB 1935	Feutchwanger, L. (P) Hutchinson
JEW SÜSS GB 1935	Feutchwanger L. Hutchinson
JEZEBEL WAR 1938	Frankau, P. Rich & Cowan
JIGSAW BL 1962	Waugh, H. (*Sleep long my love*) Gollancz
JOAN OF ARC RKO 1948	Anderson, M. (*Joan of Lorraine*) (P) Anderson House, N.Y.
JOEY BOY BL 1965	Chapman, E. Cassell
JOHN LOVES MARY WAR 1949	Krasna, N. (P) Dramatists, N.Y.
JOHNNY ANGEL RKO 1945	Booth, C. G. (*Mr. Angel comes aboard*) Doubleday, N.Y.
JOHNNY COOL UA 1964	McPartland, J. (*Kingdom of Johnny Cool, The*) Muller
JOHNNY GUITAR REP 1954	Chanslor, R. Hale
JOHNNY ONE-EYE UA 1950	Runyon, D. Constable

JOHNNY ON THE SPOT
FANCY 1954

Cronin, M. (*Paid in full*)
Museum Press

JOHNNY TREMAIN
DISNEY 1957

Forbes, E.
Constable

JOHNNY VAGABOND
UA 1943

Bromfield, L. (*McLeod's folly*)
Cassell

JOKER IS WILD
PAR 1957

Cohn, A.
Random House, N.Y.

JOLLY BAD FELLOW, A
BL 1964

Vulliamy, C. E. (*Don among the dead men*)
Joseph

JOSEPH AND HIS BRETHREN
COL 1954

Parker, L. N. (P)
Bodley Head

JOURNEY FOR MARGARET
MGM 1942

White, W. L.
Hurst & Blackett

JOURNEY INTO FEAR
RKO 1942

Ambler, E.
Hodder & Stoughton

JOURNEY'S END
TIFFANY 1930

Sherriff, R. C. (P)
Gollancz

JOURNEY'S END
TIFFANY 1930

Sherriff, R. C. *and* Bartlett, V.
Gollancz

**JOURNEY TO THE CENTRE OF THE
EARTH**
FOX 1959

Verne, J.
Various

JOY IN THE MORNING
MGM 1965

Smith, B.
Heinemann

JUAREZ
WAR 1939

Harding, B. (*Phantom crown*)
Harrap

JUBAL
COL 1956

Wellman, P. I. (*Jubal Troop*)
Grosset, N.Y.

JUBILEE TRAIL
REP 1954

Bristow, G.
Eyre & Spottiswoode

JUGGLER, THE
COL 1953

Blankfort, M.
Dobson

JULIA MISBEHAVES
MGM 1948

Sharp, M. (*Nutmeg tree*)
Various

JULIUS CAESAR
MGM 1953

Shakespeare, W. (P)
Various

TITLE OF FILM	AUTHOR AND PUBLISHER
JUNGLE BOOK, THE DISNEY 1966	Kipling, R. Macmillan
JUNIOR MISS FOX 1945	Benson, *Mrs*. S. Sun Dial, N.Y.
JUNIOR MISS FOX 1945	Chodorov, J. *and* Fields, J. (P) Dramatists, N.Y.
JUNO AND THE PAYCOCK BI 1930	O'Casey, S. (P) Macmillan
JUPITER'S DARLING MGM 1954	Sherwood, R. E. (*Road to Rome, The*) (P) French, N.Y.
JUST FOR YOU PAR 1952	Benet, S. V. (*Famous*) Farrar, N.Y.
JUSTINE FOX 1969	Durrell, L. (*Alexandria quartet*) Faber
JUST WILLIAM AB 1940	Crompton, R. Newnes

K

KATE PLUS TEN WAINWRIGHT 1938	Wallace, E. Ward Lock
KAZAN, THE WOLF DOG COL 1949	Curwood, J. O. Grosset, N.Y.
KEEPER OF THE BEES MON 1935	Porter, G. S. Hutchinson
KEEPER OF THE FLAME MGM 1942	Wylie, I. A. R. Cassell
KEEPERS OF YOUTH POWERS 1932	Ridley, A. Benn
KENNEL MURDER CASE, THE WAR 1933	Dine, S. S. van. Cassell
KENTUCKIAN, THE UA 1955	Holt, F. (*Gabriel Horn*) Various
KENTUCKY FOX 1938	Foote, J. T. (*Look of eagles*) Appleton-Century, N.Y.
KEY, THE COL 1958	Hartog, J. de. (*Stella*) Hamilton
KEY LARGO WAR 1948	Anderson, M. (P) Random House, N.Y.

KEYS OF THE KINGDOM
FOX 1944

Cronin, A. J.
Gollancz

KHARTOUM
CINERAMA 1966

Caillou, A.
W. H. Allen

KID FOR TWO FARTHINGS, A
INDEPENDENT 1954

Mankowitz, W.
Deutsch

KID GALAHAD
WAR 1937
UA 1962

Wallace, F.
Hale

KIDNAPPED
FOX 1938
MON 1949
DISNEY 1959

Stevenson, R. L.
Various

KILLERS, THE
UN 1946
RANK 1964

Hemingway, E.
Cape

KILLERS OF KILIMANJARO
COL 1959

Hunter, J. A. (*African bush adventures*)
Various

KILLER WALKS, A
GN 1952

Barton, R. (*Envy my simplicity*)
Chapman & Hall

KILLING, THE
UA 1956

White, L. (*Clean break*)
Boardman

KIM
MGM 1949

Kipling, R.
Macmillan

KIND LADY
MGM 1935
MGM 1951

Chodorov, E. (P)
French

KIND OF LOVING, A
AA 1962

Barstow, S.
Joseph

KING AND COUNTRY
WAR 1965

Hodson, J. L. (*Return to woods*)
Gollancz

KING AND COUNTRY
WAR 1965

Wilson, J. (*Hamp*) (P)
Evans

KING AND I, THE
FOX 1956

Landon, M. (*Anna and the King of Siam*)
Harrap

KING CREOLE
PAR 1958

Robbins, H. (*Stone for Danny Fisher, A*)
Hale

KING IN SHADOW
BL 1959

Neumann, R. (*Queen's doctor, The*)
Gollancz

90

TITLE OF FILM	AUTHOR AND PUBLISHER
KING OF THE KHYBER RIFLES FOX 1954	Mundy, T. Hutchinson
KING RAT BL 1965	Clavell, J. Joseph
KING RICHARD AND THE CRUSADERS WAR 1954	Scott, *Sir* W. (*Talisman, The*) Various
KINGS GO FORTH UA 1958	Brown, J. D. Cassell
KING SOLOMON'S MINES GB 1937 MGM 1950	Haggard, *Sir* R. H. Cassell
KING'S ROW WAR 1941	Bellamann, H. Cape
KIPPS FOX 1941	Wells, H. G. Various
KISMET IN 1931 MGM 1955	Knoblock, E. (P) Methuen
KISS AND TELL COL 1945	Herbert, F. H. (P) Longmans
KISS BEFORE DYING, A UA 1956	Levin, I. Joseph
KISS ME DEADLY UA 1954	Spillane, M. Barker
KISS OF FIRE GFD 1955	Lauritzen, J. (*Rose and the flame, The*) Hurst & Blackett
KISS THE BOYS GOODBYE PAR 1941	Boothe, C. (P) Various
KISS THEM FOR ME FOX 1957	Wakeman, F. (*Shore leave*) Farrar, N.Y.
KISS TOMORROW GOODBYE WAR 1950	McCoy, H. Barker,
KITCHEN, THE BL 1961	Wesker, A. (P) Faber
KITTY PAR 1945	Marshall, *Mrs.* R. Collins
KITTY FOYLE RKO 1940	Morley, C. D. Lippincott, Philadelphia

TITLE OF FILM	AUTHOR AND PUBLISHER
KNACK, THE UA 1965	Jellicoe, A. (P) Dell, N.Y.
KNAVE OF HEARTS ABP 1954	Hemon, L. (*M. Ripois and his Nemesis*) Allen & Unwin
KNIGHTS OF THE ROUND TABLE MGM 1954	Malory, *Sir* T. (*Morte d'Arthur, Le*) Various
KNIGHT WITHOUT ARMOUR UA 1937	Hilton, J. Macmillan
KNIGHTS OF THE RANGE PAR 1940	Grey, Z. Hodder & Stoughton
KNOCK ON ANY DOOR COL 1949	Motley, W. Collins
KON-TIKI RKO 1951	Heyerdahl, T. (*Kontiki expedition*) Allen & Unwin

L

LABURNUM GROVE ABP 1935	Priestley, J. B. (P) Heinemann
LADDIE RKO 1935	Porter, G. S. Murray
LADIES IN RETIREMENT COL 1941	Percy, E. *and* Denham, R. (P) Random House, N.Y.
LADY AND THE TRAMP, THE DISNEY 1955	Greene, W. Simon & Schuster, N.Y.
LADY CHATTERLEY'S LOVER COL 1956	Lawrence, D. H. Heinemann
LADY IN THE DARK, THE PAR 1944	Pryce, M. Lane
LADY IN THE LAKE MGM 1946	Chandler, R. Hamilton
LADY IN THE MORGUE UN 1938	Latimer, J. Methuen
LADY L MGM 1965	Gary, R. Joseph
LADY MISLAID, A ABP 1958	Horne, K. (P) English Theatre Guild
LADY OF SCANDAL, THE MGM 1930	Lonsdale, F. (*High road, The*) (P) Collins

LADY POSSESSED, A REP 1951	Kellino, P. (*Del Palma*) Hale
LADY SURRENDERS, A UN 1930	Erskine, J. (*Experiment in sincerity*) Putnam
LADY TO LOVE, A MGM 1930	Howard, S. (*They knew what they wanted*) (P) Chatto & Windus
LADY VANISHES, THE MGM 1938	White, E. L. (*Wheel spins, The*) Collins
LADY WINDERMERE'S FAN FOX 1949	Wilde, O. (P) Methuen
LADY WITH A LAMP, THE BL 1951	Berkeley, R. (P) Gollancz
LAMP STILL BURNS, THE TC 1943	Dickens, M. (*One pair of feet*) Joseph
LANDFALL AB 1948	Shute, N. Heinemann
LA RONDE BL 1964	Schnitzler, A. Ace Bks
LA RONDE COMMERCIAL 1951	Schnitzler, A. (*Merry go round*) Weidenfeld & Nicolson
LASH, THE IN 1931	Bartlett, L. *and* Bartlett, V. S. (*Adios*) Murray
LASSIE COME HOME MGM 1943	Knight, E. M. Cassell
LAST ANGRY MAN, THE COL 1959	Greene, G, Pan Bks
LAST CHANCE, THE MGM 1945	Schweizer, R. Drummond & Secker
LAST FRONTIER, THE COL 1955	Roberts, R. E. (*Gilded rooster, The*) Laurie
LAST HUNT, THE MGM 1955	Lott, M. Houghton Mifflin, Boston
LAST HURRAH, THE COL 1958	O'Connor, E. Pan Bks
LAST MAN TO HANG COL 1956	Bullett, G. (*Jury, The*) Dent
LAST OF MRS CHEYNEY, THE MGM 1937	Lonsdale, F. (P) Collins

LAST OF THE MOHICANS, THE UA 1936	Cooper, J. F. Various
LAST OF THE REDSKINS COL 1949	Cooper, J. F. (*Last of the Mohicans, The*) Various
LAST PAGE, THE EXCLUSIVE 1952	Chase, J. H. (P) French
LAST ROUND UP, THE PAR 1934	Grey, Z. (*Border Legion, The*) Hodder & Stoughton
LAST TIME I SAW PARIS, THE MGM 1954	Fitzgerald, F. S. (*Babylon revisited*) Scribner, N.Y.
LAST TRAIL, THE FOX 1933	Grey, Z. Hodder & Stoughton
LAST WARNING, THE UN 1939	Latimer, J. (*Dead don't care, The*) Methuen
LATE EDWINA BLACK, THE GFD 1951	Dinner, W. *and* Morum, W. (P) French
LATE GEORGE APLEY, THE FOX 1947	Marquand, J. P. Hale
LAURA FOX 1944	Caspary, V. Eyre & Spottiswoode
LAURA FOX 1944	Caspary, V. *and* Sklar, G. (P) Dramatists, N.Y.
LAUGHING ANNE REP 1953	Conrad, J. (*Within the tides*) Dent
LAW AND DISORDER BL 1957	Roberts, D. (*Smugglers' circuit*) Methuen
LAW AND ORDER UN 1932	Burnett, W. R. ('*Saint Johnson*') Heinemann
LAW AND THE LADY, THE MGM 1951	Lonsdale, F. (*Last of Mrs Cheyney, The*) (P) Collins
LAWLESS EIGHTIES, THE BL 1957	Smith, A. J. (*Brother Van*) Various
LAW OF THE TROPICS WAR 1941	Hobart, A. T. (*Oil for the lamps of China*) Cassell
LAWRENCE OF ARABIA BL 1962	Lawrence, T. E. (*Seven pillars of wisdom*) Cape
LAXDALE HALL ABP 1953	Linklater, E. Cape

LEAGUE OF FRIGHTENED MEN, THE Stout, R.
COL 1937   Cassell

LEAGUE OF GENTLEMEN, THE   Boland, J.
RANK 1960   Boardman

LEASE OF LIFE   Baker, F.
EALING 1954   Angus & Robertson

LEATHER BOYS, THE   George, E.
BL 1962   Blond

LEATHER BURNERS, THE   Lomax, B.
UA 1943   Muller

LEAVE HER TO HEAVEN   Williams, B. A.
FOX 1945   Hale

LEFT HAND OF GOD, THE   Barrett, W. E.
FOX 1955   Corgi Bks

LEGEND OF LOBO, THE   Seton, E. T. (*Lobo and other stories*)
DISNEY 1962   Hodder & Stoughton

LEMON DROP KID, THE   Runyon, D.
PAR 1951   Lippincott, N.Y.

LEOPARD, THE   Lampedusa, G. di.
FOX 1962   Collins

LEOPARD MAN, THE   Woolrich, C. (*Black alibi*)
RKO 1943   Simon & Schuster, N.Y.

LES MISERABLES   Hugo V.
UA 1935   Various
FOX 1952

LET NO MAN WRITE MY EPITAPH   Motley, W.
COL 1960   Collins

LET'S BE HAPPY   Stuart, A. (*Jeannie*) (P)
ABP 1957   French, N.Y.

LET'S DO IT AGAIN   Richman, A. (*Not so long ago*) (P)
COL 1953   French, N.Y.

LET'S KILL UNCLE   O'Grady, R.
UI 1967   Longmans

LET THE PEOPLE SING   Priestley, J. B.
BN 1942   Heinemann

LETTER, THE   Maugham, W. S. (P)
PAR 1929   Heinemann
WAR 1940

95

LETTER FROM AN UNKNOWN WOMAN, A
UI 1948

Zweig, S.
Cassell

LETTER TO THREE WIVES
FOX 1948

Klemper, J. (*Letter to five wives*)
Scribner, N.Y.

LETTY LYNTON
MGM 1932

Lowdnes, *Mrs.* M. B.
Benn

LIBEL
MGM 1959

Wooll, E. (P)
French

LIFE FOR RUTH
RANK 1962

Drummond, W.
Corgi Bks

LIFE WITH FATHER
WAR 1947

Day, C.
Chatto & Windus

LIGHT IN THE FOREST, THE
DISNEY 1958

Richter, C.
Gollancz

LIGHT IN THE PIAZZA
MGM 1962

Spencer, E.
Heinemann

LIGHTNING STRIKES TWICE
WAR 1951

Echard, M. (*Dark fantastic*)
Invincible Press

LIGHT OF HEART, THE
FOX 1942

Williams, E. (P)
Heinemann

LIGHT OF WESTERN STARS, THE
PAR 1930
PAR 1940

Grey, Z.
Nelson

LIGHT THAT FAILED, THE
PAR 1939

Kipling, R.
Macmillan

LIGHT UP THE SKY
BRYANSTON 1960

Storey, R. (*Touch it light*) (P)
French

LILIES OF THE FIELD, THE
UA 1963

Barrett, W. E.
Heinemann

LILITH
BL 1965

Salamanca, J. R.
Heinemann

LILY CHRISTINE
PAR 1932

Arlen, M.
Collins

LION, THE
FOX 1962

Kessell, J.
Hart-Davis

LION AND THE LAMB
COL 1931

Oppenheim, E. P.
Hodder & Stoughton

LION IN THE STREETS, A   Langley, A. L.
WAR 1953   McGraw-Hill, N.Y.

LIQUIDATOR, THE   Gardner, J.
MGM 1965   Muller

LIST OF ADRIAN MESSENGER   Macdonald, P.
UI 1963   Penguin

LITTLE BOY LOST   Laski, M.
PAR 1953   Cresset Press

LITTLE CAESAR   Burnett, W. R.
IN 1930   Cape

LITTLE COLONEL   Johnston, A. F.
FOX 1935   Various

LITTLE FOXES, THE   Hellman, L. F. (P)
RKO 1941   Hamilton

LITTLE HUT, THE   Roussin, A.
MGM 1957   Random House, N.Y.

LITTLE LORD FAUNTLEROY   Burnett, F. H.
UA 1936   Warne

LITTLE MAN, WHAT NOW?   Fallada, H.
UN 1934   Putnam

LITTLE MEN   Alcott, L. M.
RKO 1940   Various

LITTLE MINISTER, THE   Barrie, *Sir* J. M.
RKO 1934   Cassell

LITTLE ORVIE   Tarkington, B.
RKO 1940   Heinemann

LITTLE PRINCESS, THE   Burnett, F. H.
FOX 1939   Various

LITTLE SHEPHERD OF KINGDOM   Fox, J.
   COME, THE   Scribner, N.Y.
FOX 1961

LITTLE WOMEN   Alcott, L. M.
RKO 1933   Various
MGM 1948

LITTLE WORLD OF DON CAMILLO,   Guareschi, G.
   THE   Gollancz
LF 1952

LIVE NOW, PAY LATER   Story, J. T.
REGAL 1962   Secker & Warburg

D   97

LIVES OF A BENGAL LANCER, THE PAR 1935	Brown, F. Y. (*Bengal Lancer*) Gollancz
LIZZIE MGM 1957	Jackson, S. (*Bird's nest, The*) Farrar, N.Y.
LODGER, THE FOX 1944	Lowndes, *Mrs.* M. B. Benn
LOLITA MGM 1962	Nabokov, K. Corgi Bks
LONDON BELONGS TO ME UN 1948	Collins, N. Collins
LONELINESS OF THE LONG DISTANCE RUNNER, THE BL 1962	Sillitoe, A W. H. Allen
LONELY ARE THE BRAVE UI 1962	Abbey, E. (*Brave cowboy, The*) Eyre & Spottiswoode
LONELYHEARTS UA 1959	West, N. (*Miss Lonelyhearts*) Grey Walls Press
LONE STAR RANGER FOX 1930 FOX 1942	Grey, Z. Harper
LONE WOLF RETURNS COL 1936	Vance, J. L. Grosset, N.Y.
LONG AND THE SHORT AND THE TALL, THE WAR 1960	Hall, W. (P) Heinemann
LONG DAY'S JOURNEY INTO NIGHT FOX 1962	O'Neill, E. G. (P) Cape
LONGEST DAY, THE FOX 1962	Ryan, C. Gollancz
LONG GRAY LINE COL 1954	Maher, M. *and* Campion, N. R. (*Bringing up the brass*) McKay, N.Y.
LONG HAUL, THE COL 1957	Mills, M. Pan Bks
LONG, HOT SUMMER, THE FOX 1957	Faulkner, W. (*Hamlet, The*) Chatto & Windus
LONG KNIFE, THE AA 1958	Truss, S. (*Long night, The*) Hodder & Stoughton

LONG, LONG TRAILER, THE MGM 1954	Twiss, C. Crowell, N.Y.
LONG MEMORY, THE GFD 1953	Clewes, H. Macmillan
LONG SHIPS, THE BL 1963	Bengtsson, F. Collins
LONG VOYAGE HOME, THE UA 1940	O'Neill, E. G. (P) Cape
LONG WAIT, THE UA 1954	Spillane, M. Barker
LOOK BACK IN ANGER ABP 1959	Osborne, J. (P) Faber
LOOKING FORWARD MGM 1933	Anthony, C. L. (*Service*) (P) French
LORD BABS GFD 1932	Howard, K. Benn
LORD JIM COL 1964	Conrad, J. Dent
LORD LOVE A DUCK UA 1965	Hine, A. Atheneum Press, N.Y.
LORD OF THE FLIES BL 1963	Golding, W. Faber
LORNA DOONE ATP 1935 COL 1951	Blackmore, R. D. Various
LOSER TAKES ALL BL 1956	Greene, G. Heinemann
LOST COMMAND COL 1966	Larteguy, J. (*Centurians, The*) Hutchinson
LOST HORIZON COL 1937	Hilton, J. Macmillan
LOST MOMENT, THE UN 1947	James, H. (*Aspern papers, The*) Macmillan
LOST PATROL RKO 1934	Macdonald, P. (*Patrol*) Collins
LOST PEOPLE, THE GFD 1949	Boland, B. (*Cockpit*) (P) Elek

LOST STAGE VALLEY
COL 1951

Bonham, F.
Simon & Schuster, N.Y.

LOST WEEK-END, THE
PAR 1945

Jackson, C.
Lane

LOST WORLD, THE
FOX 1960

Doyle, *Sir* A. C.
Murray

LOUDEST WHISPER, THE
UA 1962

Hellman, L. (*Children's hour, The*) (P)
Dramatists, N.Y.

LOVE BEGINS AT TWENTY
IN 1936

Flavin, M. (*Broken dishes*) (P)
French, N.Y.

LOVE CAGE, THE
MGM 1965

Keene, D. (*Joy house*)
Consul Bks

LOVED ONE, THE
MGM 1965

Waugh, E.
Chapman & Hall

LOVE FROM A STRANGER
UA 1937

Vosper, F. (P)
French

**LOVE IS A MANY SPLENDOURED
THING**
FOX 1955

Han Suyin, (*Many splendoured thing, A*)
Cape

LOVE LETTERS
PAR 1945

Massie, C. (*Pity my simplicity*)
Faber

LOVE LETTERS OF A STAR
UN 1936

King, R. (*Case of the constant god*)
Methuen

LOVELY TO LOOK AT
MGM 1952

Miller, A. D. (*Gowns by Roberta*)
Various

LOVE ON THE DOLE
UA 1941

Greenwood, W.
Cape

LOVE ON THE DOLE
UA 1941

Gow, R. *and* Greenwood, W. (P)
French

LOVERS MUST LEARN
WAR 1962

Fineman, I. (*These our lovers*)
Long

LOVES OF JOANNA GODDEN, THE
GFD 1947

Smith, S. K. (*Joanna Godden*)
Cassell

LOYALTIES
AUT 1934

Galsworthy, J. (P)
Duckworth

L SHAPED ROOM, THE
BL 1962

Banks, L. R.
Chatto & Windus

LUCK OF GINGER COFFEY, THE
BL 1965

Moore, B.
Deutsch

LUCK OF THE IRISH
FOX 1948

Jones, G. P. *and* Jones, C. B.
Random House, N.Y.

LUCKY JIM
BL 1957

Amis, K.
Gollancz

LUCKY STIFF, THE
UA 1948

Rice, C.
World, N.Y.

LUMMOX
UA 1930

Hurst, F.
Cape

LUST FOR LIFE
MGM 1956

Stone, I.
Bodley Head

LUV
BL 1966

Schisgal, M. (P)
Coward-McCann, N.Y.

LUXURY LINER
PAR 1933

Kaus, G.
Cassell

LYDIA BAILEY
FOX 1952

Roberts, K.
Collins

M

MACABRE
ABP 1957

Durrant, T. (*Marble forest*)
Wingate

MACBETH
REP 1948
BL 1960

Shakespeare, W. (P)
Various

MACOMBER AFFAIR, THE
UA 1947

Hemingway, E.
Cape

MADAME BOVARY
MGM 1949

Flaubert, G.
Cape

MADAME CURIE
MGM 1943

Curie, E.
Heinemann

MADISON AVENUE
FOX 1960

Kirk, J. (*Build-up boys, The*)
Hart-Davis

MADNESS OF THE HEART
TC 1949

Sandstrom, F.
Cassel

MADONNA OF THE SEVEN MOONS
GFD 1945

Lawrence, M.
Hurst & Blackett

MADONNA OF THE STREETS
COL 1930

Maxwell, W. B. (*Ragged messenger, The*)
Butterworth

101

'MAGGIE, THE' EALING 1954	White, J. D. Heinemann
MAGIC BOW GFD 1946	Komroff, M. Heinemann
MAGIC BOX, THE BL 1951	Allister, R. (*Friese-Greene*) Marsland
MAGIC FIRE REP 1956	Harding, B. Harrap
MAGNIFICENT AMBERSONS, THE RKO 1942	Tarkington, B. Grosset, N.Y.
MAGNIFICENT OBSESSION UN 1935 UI 1954	Douglas, L. C. Allen & Unwin
MAGNIFICENT YANKEE, THE MGM 1950	Biddle, F. (*Mr. Justice Holmes*) Scribner, N.Y.
MAJORITY OF ONE, A WAR 1961	Spigelgass, L. (P) French, N.Y.
MAJOR BARBARA PASCAL 1941	Shaw, G. B. (P) Various
MAKE HASTE TO LIVE REP 1954	Gordon, M. *and* Gordon, G. Doubleday, N.Y.
MAKE ME AN OFFER BL 1954	Mankowitz, W. Deutsch
MAKE ME A STAR PAR 1932	Wilson, H. L. (*Merton of the movies*) Cape
MAKE MINE MINK RANK 1960	Coke, P. (*Breath of Spring*) (P) French
MAKE WAY FOR A LADY RKO 1936	Jordan, E. G. (*Daddy and I*) Grosset, N.Y.
MALPAS MYSTERY, THE AA 1960	Wallace, E. (*Face in the night*) Long
MALTESE FALCON, THE WAR 1941	Hammett, D. Cassell
MAN ABOUT THE HOUSE, A LF 1947	Young, F. B. Heinemann
MAN ABOUT THE HOUSE, A LF 1947	Young, F. B. (P) Heinemann

TITLE OF FILM	AUTHOR AND PUBLISHER
MAN ABOUT TOWN FOX 1932	Clift, D. Long
MAN AT THE CARLTON TOWER AA 1961	Wallace, E. (*Man at the Carlton*) Hodder & Stoughton
MAN CALLED PETER, A FOX 1954	Marshall, C. (*Story of Peter Marshall, The*) Davies
MANCHURIAN CANDIDATE UA 1962	Condon, R. Pan Bks
MAN DETAINED AA 1961	Wallace, E. (*Debt discharged, A*) Ward Lock
MANDY GFD 1952	Lewis, H. (*Day is ours, The*) Macdonald
MAN FOR ALL SEASONS, A COL 1966	Bolt, R. (P) French
MAN FROM BITTER RIDGE, THE GFD 1955	Raine, W. M. (*Rawhide justice*) Hodder & Stoughton
MAN FROM DAKOTA, THE MGM 1940	Kantor, M. (*Arouse and beware*) Gollancz
MANHUNT FOX 1958	Locke, C. O. (*Road to Socorro, The*) Hutchinson
MAN IN GREY, THE GFD 1943	Smith, *Lady* E. Hutchinson
MAN IN HALF-MOON STREET PAR 1944	Lyndon, B. (P) Hamilton
MAN INSIDE, THE COL 1958	Chaber, M. E. Eyre & Spottiswoode
MAN IN THE ATTIC, THE FOX 1953	Lowndes, *Mrs.* M. B. (*Lodger, The*) Benn
MAN IN THE GREY FLANNEL SUIT, THE FOX 1956	Wilson, S. Cassell
MAN IN THE IRON MASK, THE UA 1939	Dumas, A. Collins
MAN IN THE MIDDLE FOX 1963	Fast, H. (*Winston affair, The*) Methuen
MAN IN THE NET, THE UA 1958	Quentin, P. Gollancz

MAN IN THE ROAD, THE GN 1956	Armstrong, A. (*He was found in the road*) Methuen
MAN IN THE VAULT RKO 1957	Gruber, F. (*Lock and the key, The*) Worlds Work
MAN OF ARAN GB 1934	Mullen, P. Faber
MAN OF THE FOREST PAR 1935	Grey, Z. Hodder & Stoughton
MAN ON THE EIFFEL TOWER, THE BL 1950	Simenon, G. (*Battle of nerves, A*) Routledge
MAN THEY COULDN'T ARREST, THE GB 1933	'Seamark' Hodder & Stoughton
MAN TRAP EXCLUSIVE 1953	Trevor, E. (*Queen in danger*) Boardman
MAN TRAP PAR 1961	Macdonald, J. P. (*Restless*) Pan Bks
MANUELA BL 1957	Woods, W. Hart-Davis
MAN WHO CAME TO DINNER, THE WAR 1941	Kaufman, G. S. *and* Hart, M. (P) Random House, N.Y.
MAN WHO COULD CHEAT DEATH, THE PAR 1959	Lyndon, B. (*Man in Half-Moon Street, The*) (P) Hamilton
MAN WHO COULD WORK MIRACLES, THE UA 1937	Wells, H. G. Cresset Press
MAN WHO LOVED REDHEADS, THE BL 1954	Rattigan, T. (*Who is Sylvia?*) (P) Hamilton
MAN WHO NEVER WAS, THE FOX 1955	Montague, E. E. S. Evans
MAN WHO UNDERSTOOD WOMEN FOX 1959	Gary, R. (*Colours of the day, The*) Joseph
MAN WHO WAS NOBODY, THE AA 1960	Wallace, E. Ward Lock
MAN WHO WATCHED THE TRAINS GO BY, THE EROS 1952	Simenon, G. Routledge

MAN WHO WOULDN'T DIE, THE FOX 1942	Rawson, C. (*No coffin for the corpse*) Little Brown, Boston
MAN WITHIN, THE FOX 1947	Greene, G. Heinemann
MAN WITH MY FACE, THE UA 1951	Taylor, S. W. Hodder & Stoughton
MAN WITHOUT A STAR UI 1955	Linford, D. Morrow, N.Y.
MAN WITH THE GOLDEN ARM, THE UA 1955	Algren, N. Doubleday, N.Y.
MAN WITH THE TWISTED LIP, THE GN 1951	Doyle, *Sir* A. C. Murray
MAN WITH THIRTY SONS, THE MGM 1952	Bowen, C. D. (*Yankee from Olympus*) Benn
MANHUNT FOX 1941	Household, G. (*Rogue male*) Chatto & Windus
MAN-PROOF MGM 1938	Lea, F. H. (*Four Marys*) Nicholson & Watson
MANSLAUGHTER PAR 1930	Miller, A. D. Dodd, N.Y.
MARACAIBO PAR 1958	Silliphant, S. Farrar, N.Y.
MARAUDERS, THE WAR 1962	Ogburn, C. (*Merrill's marauders*) Hodder & Stoughton
MARCHING ALONG FOX 1952	Sousa, J. P. Hale
MARGIN FOR ERROR FOX 1943	Boothe, C. (P) Hamilton
MARIE ANTOINETTE MGM 1938	Zweig, S. Cassell
MARJORIE MORNINGSTAR WAR 1957	Wouk, H. Cape
MARK OF CAIN, THE TC 1948	Shearing, J. (*Airing in a closed carriage*) Hutchinson
MARK OF THE RENEGADE UI 1951	McCulley, J. (*Mark of Zorro*) Grosset, N.Y.
MARK OF ZORRO, THE FOX 1940	McCulley, J. Grosset, N.Y.

MARNIE
UI 1964

Graham, W.
Hodder & Stoughton

MARRIAGE IS A PRIVATE AFFAIR
MGM 1944

Kelly, J.
Cassell

MARRIAGE OF CONVENIENCE
AA 1960

Wallace, E. (*Three oak mystery, The*)
Ward Lock

MARY, MARY
WAR 1963

Kerr, J. (P)
Doubleday, N.Y.

MARY POPPINS
DISNEY 1964

Travers, P. L.
Penguin

MASK OF DIMITRIOS, THE
WAR 1944

Ambler, E.
Hodder & Stoughton

MASK OF DOUBT
EXCLUSIVE 1954

White, J. E. M. (*Mask of dust*)
Hodder & Stoughton

MASQUE OF THE RED DEATH, THE
AA 1964

Poe, E. A.
Various

MASQUERADE
UA 1965

Canning, V. (*Castle Minerva*)
Hodder & Stoughton

MASTER OF BALLANTRAE, THE
WAR 1953

Stevenson, R. L.
Various

MASTER OF BANKDAM, THE
ALL 1947

Armstrong, T. (*Crowthers of Bankdam, The*)
Collins

MASTER OF THE WORLD
AA 1961

Verne, J.
Sampson Low

MASTER SPY
GN 1962

Jennings, D. K. (*They also serve*)
Badger Bks

MATCHMAKER, THE
PAR 1958

Wilder, T. (P)
French

MATING GAME, THE
MGM 1959

Bates, H. E. (*Darling buds of May, The*)
Joseph

MAVERICK QUEEN, THE
REP 1956

Grey, Z.
Hodder & Stoughton

MAYBE IT'S LOVE
WAR 1934

Anderson, M. (*Saturday's children*) (P)
Longmans, N.Y.

MEDAL FOR THE GENERAL, A
BN 1944

Ronald, J.
Hodder & Stoughton

MEET ME IN ST LOUIS
MGM 1944

Benson, *Mrs.* S.
Random House, N.Y.

MEET ME TONIGHT GFD 1952	Coward, N. (P) Heinemann
MEET MR. CALLAGHAN EROS 1954	Cheyney, P. (*Urgent hangman, The*) Collins
MEET MR. CALLAGHAN EROS 1954	Verner, G. (P) French
MEET MR. LUCIFER GFD 1953	Ridley, A. (*Beggar my neighbour*) (P) Evans
MEET NERO WOLFE COL 1936	Stout, R. (*Fer de lance*) Cassell
MELVILLE GOODWIN, USA WAR 1956	Marquand, J. P. Hale
MEMBER OF THE WEDDING, THE COL 1952	McCullers, C. Cresset Press
MEN AGAINST SPEED FOX 1958	Ruesch, H. (*Racer, The*) Hurst & Blackett
MEN ARE SUCH FOOLS WAR 1938	Baldwin, F. Sampson Low
MEN BEHIND BARS ABP 1954	Duffy, C. *and* Kenning, D. (*San Quentin*) Davies
MEN IN HER LIFE COL 1941	Smith, *Lady* E. (*Ballerina*) Gollancz
MEN IN WAR UA 1957	Praag, V. V. (*Day without end*) Sloane, N.Y.
MEN IN WHITE MGM 1934	Kingsley, S. Gollancz
MEN OF TOMORROW MUNDUS 1935	Gibbs, A. H. (*Young Apollo, The*) Hutchinson
MENACE, THE COL 1932	Wallace, E. (*Feathered serpent*) Hodder & Stoughton
MERTON OF THE MOVIES MGM 1947	Wilson, H. L. Cape
MESSAGE TO GARCIA FOX 1936	Hubbard, E. Lothian, N.Y.
MICHAEL AND MARY UN 1932	Milne, A. A. (P) Chatto & Windus
MICHAEL O'HALLORAN REP 1937 MON 1949	Porter, G. S. Murray

TITLE OF FILM	AUTHOR AND PUBLISHER
MICHAEL STROGOFF RKO 1937	Verne, J. Various
MICKY EL 1948	Goodin, P. (*Clementine*) Dutton, N.Y.
MIDDLE OF THE NIGHT COL 1959	Chayefsky, P. (P) Random House, N.Y.
MIDDLE WATCH BI 1930 AB 1940	Hay, I. *and* Hall, S. K. (P) French
MIDNIGHT EPISODE COL 1951	Simenon, G. (*Monsieur La Souris*) Gallimard, Paris
MIDSHIPMAID, THE GB 1932	Hay, I. *and* Hall, S. K. (P) French
MIDSHIPMAN EASY ATP 1935	Marryat, F. (*Mr. Midshipman Easy*) Various
MIDSUMMER NIGHT'S DREAM, A WAR 1935	Shakespeare, W. (P) Various
MIGHTY TREVE, THE UN 1937	Terhune, A. P. (*Treve*) Grosset, N. Y.
MIKADO, THE UN 1939	Gilbert, *Sir* W. S. (P) Macmillan
MILDRED PIERCE WAR 1945	Cain, J. M. Hale
MILLIE RKO 1931	Clarke, D. H. Long
MILLIE'S DAUGHTER COL 1947	Clarke, D. H. Laurie
MILLIONAIRESS, THE FOX 1960	Shaw, G. B. (P) Constable
MILLION POUND NOTE, THE GFD 1953	Twain, M. Harper, N.Y.
MILL ON THE FLOSS, THE STANDARD 1939	Eliot, G. Various
MILL ON THE PO LUX 1950	Bacchelli, R. Hutchinson
MIND BENDERS, THE AA 1963	Kennaway, J. Pan Bks

TITLE OF FILM	AUTHOR AND PUBLISHER
MIND OF MR. REEDER, THE RAYMOND 1939	Wallace, E. (*Mind of Mr. J. G. Reeder, The*) Hodder & Stoughton
MINE OWN EXECUTIONER BL 1948	Balchin, N. Collins
MINE WITH THE IRON DOOR, THE COL 1936	Wright, H. B. Appleton-Century, N.Y.
MINISTRY OF FEAR PAR 1944	Greene, G. Heinemann
MIRACLE IN THE RAIN WAR 1956	Hecht, B. Knopf, N.Y.
MIRACLE OF THE BELLS PAR 1944	Janney, R. W. H. Allen
MIRACLE ON 34TH STREET FOX 1948 FOX 1956	Davies, V. Harcourt, N.Y.
MIRACLE WORKER, THE UA 1962	Gibson, W. (P) Knopf, N.Y.
MISSION OF DANGER MGM 1959	Roberts, K. (*North-west passage*) Collins
MISSION TO MOSCOW WAR 1943	Davies, J. E. Gollancz
MISS JULIE LF 1951	Strindberg, J. A. (P) Dent
MISSOURI TRAVELLER, THE DISNEY 1958	Burress, J. Vanguard, N.Y.
MISS SADIE THOMPSON COL 1954	Maugham, W. S. (*Rain*) (P) French
MISS SUSIE SLAGLE'S PAR 1945	Tucker, A. Grosset, N.Y.
MISTER BUDDWING MGM 1967	Hunter, E. (*Buddwing*) Constable
MISTER ROBERTS WAR 1955	Heggen, T. Nicholson
MISTER ROBERTS WAR 1955	Heggen, T. *and* Logan, J. (P) Random House, N.Y.
MISTER SCOUTMASTER FOX 1953	Cochran, R. E. (*Be prepared*) Sloane, N.Y.

MISTY FOX 1961	Henry, M. (*Misty of Chincoteague*) Collins
MIX ME A PERSON BL 1962	Story, J. T. Corgi Bks
MOBY DICK WAR 1930 WAR 1954	Melville, H. Various
MODESTY BLAISE FOX 1965	O'Donnell, P. Souvenir Press
MOGAMBO MGM 1953	Collison, W. (*Farewell to women*) McBride, N. Y.
MOLL FLANDERS FOX 1954	Defoe, D. Various
MOMENT OF DANGER ABP 1959	Mackenzie, D. Pan Bks
MONEY FROM HOME PAR 1953	Runyon, D. Various
MONEY TRAP, THE MGM 1965	White, L. Boardman
MONKEY ON MY BACK UA 1957	Brown, W. Elek
MONKEY'S PAW, THE RKO 1932 BUTCHER 1948	Jacobs, W. W. *and* Parker, L. N. (P) Harrap
MONSIEUR BEAUCAIRE PAR 1946	Tarkington, B. Grosset, N.Y.
MOON AND SIXPENCE, THE UA 1942	Maugham, W. S. Heinemann
MOONFLEET MGM 1955	Faulkner, J. M. Little Brown, Boston
MOON IS BLUE, THE UA 1953	Herbert F. H. (P) Random House, N.Y.
MOON IS DOWN, THE FOX 1943	Steinbeck, J. (P) Viking Press, N.Y.
MOON IS DOWN, THE FOX 1943	Steinbeck, J. Heinemann
MOON'S OUR HOME, THE PAR 1936	Baldwin, F. Sampson Low

MOONSPINNERS, THE
DISNEY 1964

Stewart, M.
Hodder & Stoughton

MOONSTONE, THE
MON 1934

Collins, W.
Various

MOONTIDE
FOX 1942

Robertson, W.
Hamilton

MORALS OF MARCUS, THE
GB 1935

Locke, W. J. (*Morals of Marcus Ordeyne, The*)
Lane

MORGAN—A SUITABLE CASE FOR TREATMENT
BL 1966

Mercer, D. (P)
Calder

MORNING DEPARTURE
GFD 1950

Woollard, K. (P)
French

MORTAL STORM, THE
MGM 1940

Bottome, P.
Faber

MOSS ROSE
FOX 1947

Shearing, J.
Heinemann

MOTHER DIDN'T TELL ME
FOX 1950

Bard, M. (*Doctor wears three faces, The*)
Hammond

MOULIN ROUGE
UA 1952

La Mure, P.
Collins

MOUNTAIN, THE
PAR 1956

Troyat, H.
Allen & Unwin

MOUNTAIN IS YOUNG, THE
PAR 1959

Han Suyin
Cape

MOUNTAIN ROAD, THE
COL 1959

White, T. H.
Cassell

MOURNING BECOMES ELECTRA
RKO 1948

O'Neill, E. G. (P)
Cape

MOUSE ON THE MOON
UA 1962

Wibberly, L. (*Mouse that roared, The*)
Hale

MOUSE THAT ROARED, THE
COL 1959

Wibberly, L. (*Wrath of grapes*)
Hale

MR. AND MRS. NORTH
MGM 1941

Davis, O. (P)
French, N.Y.

MR. BELVEDERE RINGS THE BELL
FOX 1951

McEnroe, R. E. (*Silver whistle, The*) (P)
Theatre Arts

MR. BLANDINGS BUILDS HIS DREAM HOUSE RKO 1948	Hodgins, E. Joseph
MR. DEEDS GOES TO TOWN COL 1936	Kelland, C. B. Barker
MR. DENNING DRIVES NORTH BL 1951	Coppel, A. Harrap
MR. DODDS TAKES THE AIR WAR 1937	Kelland, C. B. (*Great crooner, The*) Barker
MR. EMMANUEL TC 1944	Golding, L. Rich & Cowan
MR. HOBBS TAKES A VACATION FOX 1962	Streeter, E. (*Mr. Hobbs' holiday*) Hamilton
MR. MOSES UA 1965	Catto, M. (*Mister Moses*) Heinemann
MR. PEABODY AND THE MERMAID UN 1948	Jones, G. P. *and* Jones, C. B. (*Peabody's mermaid*) Joseph
MR. PERRIN AND MR. TRAILL TC 1948	Walpole, H. Various
MR. ROBERTS WAR 1954	Heggen, T. *and* Logan, J. (P) Random House, N.Y.
MRS. GIBBONS' BOYS BL 1962	Clickman, W. *and* Stein, J. (P) French, N.Y.
MR. SKEFFINGTON WAR 1944	'Elizabeth' Heinemann
MR. SMITH GOES TO WASHINGTON COL 1939	Landery, C. Dent
MRS. MIKE UA 1950	Freedman, B. *and* Freedman, N. Hamilton
MRS. MINIVER MGM 1942	Struther, J. Chatto & Windus
MRS. PARKINGTON MGM 1944	Bromfield, L. Cassell
MRS. WIGGS OF THE CABBAGE PATCH PAR 1934	Rice, A. C. Grosset, N.Y.
MR. WINKLE GOES TO WAR COL 1944	Pratt, T. Duell, N.Y.

MUDLARK, THE
FOX 1950

Bonnet, T.
W. H. Allen

MURDER
BI 1930

Dane, C. *and* Simpson, H. de G.
Hodder & Stoughton

MURDER AT THE GALLOP
MGM 1963

Christie, A. (*After the funeral*)
Collins

MURDER BY PROXY
EXCLUSIVE 1954

Nielson, H.
Gollancz

MURDERER'S ROW
BL 1966

Hamilton, D.
Muller

MURDER INC.
WAR 1952

Eastwood, J.
Dakers

MURDER, INCORPORATED
FOX 1960

Turkus, B. *and* Feder, S.
Gollancz

MURDER IN THE CATHEDRAL
FILM TRADERS 1951

Eliot, T. S. (P)
Faber

MURDER IN THE PRIVATE CAR
MGM 1934

Rose, E. E. (*Rear car*) (P)
French, N.Y.

MURDER IN THORNTON SQUARE
MGM 1944

Hamilton, P. (*Gaslight*) (P)
French

MURDER IS MY BUSINESS
PRC 1946

Halliday, B.
Dodd, N.Y.

MURDER MOST FOUL
MGM 1963

Christie, A. (*Mrs. McGinty's dead*)
Collins

MURDER OF DR. HARRIGAN
IN 1936

Eberhart, M. G. (*From this dark stairway*)
Heinemann

MURDER ON A BRIDLE PATH
RKO 1936

Palmer, S. (*Puzzle of the briar pipe*)
Collins

MURDER ON A HONEYMOON
RKO 1935

Palmer, S. (*Puzzle of the pepper tree*)
Jarrolds

MURDER ON DIAMOND ROW
UA 1937

Wallace, E. (*Squeaker, The*)
Hodder & Stoughton

MURDER ON THE SECOND FLOOR,
THE
WAR 1941

Vosper, F. (P)
French

MURDER REPORTED
COL 1957

Chapman, R. (*Murder for the millions*)
Laurie

MURDER SHE SAID
MGM 1961

Christie A. (*4.50 from Paddington*)
Collins

MURDERS IN THE RUE MORGUE
UN 1932

Poe, E. A.
Various

MURDER WITHOUT CRIME
ABP 1950

Thompson, J. L. (P)
French

MURDER WITH PICTURES
PAR 1936

Coxe, G. H.
Heinemann

MUTINY ON THE BOUNTY
MGM 1935
MGM 1962

Nordhoff, J. N. *and* Hall, C.
Chapman & Hall

MY BROTHER JONATHAN
AB 1948

Young, F. B.
Heinemann

MY COUSIN RACHEL
FOX 1952

Du Maurier, D.
Gollancz

MY DAUGHTER JOY
BL 1950

Nemirowsky, I. (*David Golden*)
Constable

MY DEATH IS A MOCKERY
ADELPHI 1952

Baber, D.
Heinemann

MY FAIR LADY
WAR 1964

Shaw, G. B. (*Pygmalion*) (P)
Constable

MY FORBIDDEN PAST
RKO 1951

Banks, P. (*Carriage entrance*)
Putnam, N.Y.

MY FRIEND FLICKA
FOX 1943

O'Hara, M.
Eyre & Spottiswoode

MY GLORIOUS BROTHERS
UA 1959

Fast, H.
Panther Bks

MY GUN IS QUICK
UA 1957

Spillane, M.
Barker

MY MAN GODFREY
UN 1936
UI 1957

Hatch, E.
Barker

MY NAME IS JULIA ROSS
COL 1945

Gilbert, A. (*Woman in red, The*)
Collins

MY OWN TRUE LOVE
PAR 1948

Foldes, Y. (*Make you a fine wife*)
Hutchinson

MY REPUTATION
WAR 1946

Jaynes, C.
World, N.Y.

MY SISTER AND I
GFD 1948

Bonett, E. (*High pavement*)
Heinemann

MY SISTER EILEEN
COL 1942
COL 1955

Fields, J. and Chodorov, J. (P)
Macmillan

MY SISTER EILEEN
COL 1942
COL 1955

McKenney, R.
Chatto & Windus

MY SIX CONVICTS
COL 1952

Wilson, D. P.
Hamilton

MY SON, MY SON
UA 1940

Spring, H.
Collins

MYSTERIOUS DR. FU MANCHU
PAR 1929

Rohmer, S. (*Mystery of Dr. Fu Manchu, The*)
Methuen

MYSTERIOUS ISLAND
COL 1962

Verne, J.
Dent

MYSTERIOUS RIDER THE
PAR 1933
PAR 1938

Grey, Z.
Hodder & Stoughton

MYSTERY HOUSE
WAR 1938

Eberhart, M. G. (*Mystery of Hunting's End*)
Lane

MYSTERY OF EDWIN DROOD
UN 1935

Dickens, C.
Various

MYSTERY OF MARIE ROGET
UN 1942

Poe, E. A.
Various

MYSTERY OF ROOM 13
ALL 1941

Wallace, E. (*Room* 13)
Allied Press

MY WIFE'S FAMILY
ABP 1956

Duprez, F. (P)
French

N

NAKED AND DEAD, THE
WAR 1958

Mailer, N.
Wingate

NAKED EDGE, THE
UA 1961

Ehrlich, M. (*First train to Babylon*)
Gollancz

NAKED HEART, THE
BL 1950

Hemon, L. (*Maria Chapdelaine*)
Macmillan

NAKED HOURS, THE
COMPTON 1965

Moravia, A. (*Appointment at the beach*)
Secker & Warburg

NAKED IN THE SUN RKO 1956	Slaughter, F. G. (*Warrior, The*) Doubleday, N.Y.
NAKED JUNGLE, THE PAR 1953	Stephenson, C. (*Leiningen versus the ants*) Barker
NAKED RUNNER, THE WAR 1966	Clifford, F. Hodder & Stoughton
NANA MGM 1933 GALA 1955	Zola, E. Various
NANNY, THE WAR 1965	Piper, E. Secker & Warburg
NARROW CORNER WAR 1933	Maugham, W. S. Heinemann
NARROWING CIRCLE, THE EROS 1955	Symons, J. Gollancz
NATIONAL VELVET MGM 1944	Bagnold, E. (P) Heinemann
NATIVE SON CLASSIC 1951	Wright, R. Gollancz
NATIVE SON CLASSIC 1951	Green, P. *and* Wright, P. (P) Harper, N.Y.
NET, THE GFD 1952	Pudney, J. Joseph
NEVADA PAR 1935	Grey, Z. Hodder & Stoughton
NEVADA SMITH PAR 1963	Robbins, H. (*Carpetbaggers, The*) Blond
NEVER A DULL MOMENT RKO 1950	Swift, K. (*Who could ask for anything more*) Simon & Schuster, N.Y.
NEVER BACK LOSERS AA 1962	Wallace, E. (*Green ribbon, The*) Hutchinson
NEVER LET ME GO MGM 1953	Bax, R. (*Come the dawn*) Hutchinson
NEVER LOVE A STRANGER ABP 1957	Robbins, H. Corgi Bks
NEVER SO FEW MGM 1959	Chamales, T. Pan Bks

NEVER TAKE NO FOR AN ANSWER INDEPENDENT 1951	Gallico, P. W. (*Small miracle, The*) Joseph
NEVER THE TWAIN SHALL MEET MGM 1931	Kyne, P. B. Various
NEVER TOO LATE WAR 1965	Long, S. A. (P) French, N.Y.
NEW MORALS FOR OLD MGM 1932	Druten, J. van. (*After all*) (P) Gollancz
NICHOLAS NICKLEBY EALING 1947	Dickens, C. Various
NIGHT AND THE CITY FOX 1950	Kersh, G. Heinemann
NIGHTCOMERS RANK 1959	Ambler, E. Hodder & Stoughton
NIGHT COMES TOO SOON BUTCHER 1947	Lytton, B. (*Haunted and the haunters, The*) (P) Various
NIGHT GAMES GALA 1966	Zetterling, M. Constable
NIGHT HAS A THOUSAND EYES PAR 1948	Hopley, G. Oxford U.P.
NIGHT HAS EYES, THE ANGLO-AMERICAN 1952	Kennington, A. Jarrolds
NIGHT IN HAVANA UA 1957	Sylvester, R. (*Big boodle, The*) Random House, N.Y.
NIGHT IN NEW ORLEANS, A PAR 1942	Langham, J. R. (*Sing a song of murder*) Hale
NIGHT LIFE OF THE GODS UN 1935	Smith, T. Methuen
NIGHTMARE ALLEY FOX 1947	Gresham, W. Heinemann
NIGHTMARE IN DUBLIN RANK 1957	Loraine, P. (*Dublin nightmare*) Hodder & Stoughton
NIGHT MUST FALL MGM 1937 MGM 1964	Williams, E. (P) Gollancz
NIGHT OF JANUARY 16TH PAR 1941	Rand, A. (P) Longmans

117

NIGHT OF THE DEMON
COL 1957

James, M. R. (*Casting the runes*)
Arnold

NIGHT OF THE GENERALS, THE
BL 1966

Kirst, H. H.
Collins

NIGHT OF THE HUNTER, THE
UA 1955

Grubb, D.
Hamilton

NIGHT OF THE IGUANA, THE
MGM 1963

Williams, T. (P)
Secker & Warburg

NIGHT OF THE QUARTER MOON
MGM 1959

Coen, F.
Corgi Bks

NIGHT TO REMEMBER, A
RANK 1957

Lord, W.
Longmans

NIGHT UNTO NIGHT
WAR 1949

Wylie, P.
Farrar, N.Y.

NIGHT WAS OUR FRIEND
MONARCH 1951

Pertwee, M. (P)
English Theatre Guild

NIGHT WITHOUT STARS
GFD 1951

Graham, W.
Hodder & Stoughton

NIKKI, WILD DOG OF THE NORTH
DISNEY 1961

Curwood, J. O. (*Nomads of the North*)
Nelson

NINE HOURS TO RAMA
FOX 1962

Wolpert, S.
Hamilton

1984
ABP 1956

Orwell, G.
Gollancz

NINE TILL SIX
ATP 1932

Stuart, A. *and* Stuart, P. (P)
French, N.Y.

NOBODY LIVES FOREVER
WAR 1946

Burnett, W. R.
World, N.Y.

NO DOWN PAYMENT
FOX 1957

McPartland, J.
Macdonald

NO HANDS ON THE CLOCK
PAR 1941

Homes, G.
Various

NO HIGHWAY
FOX 1951

Shute, N.
Heinemann

NO KIDDING
AA 1960

Anderson, V. (*Beware of children*)
Hart-Davis

NO LOVE FOR JOHNNIE
RANK 1960

Fienburgh, W.
Hutchinson

118

NO MAN OF HER OWN
PAR 1950

Irish, W. (*I married a dead man*)
Lippincott, Philadelphia

NO MORE ORCHIDS
COL 1932

Perkins, G.
Wright & Brown

NONE BUT THE LONELY HEART
RKO 1944

Llewellyn, R.
Joseph

NO ONE MAN
PAR 1932

Hughes, R.
Jarrolds

NO ORCHIDS FOR MISS BLANDISH
ALL 1948

Chase, J. H.
Jarrolds

NOOSE FOR A LADY
AA 1953

Verner, G. (*Whispering woman*)
Wright & Brown

NO PLACE FOR JENNIFER
ABP 1949

Hambledon, P. (*No difference to me*)
Sampson Low

NO RESTING PLACE
ABP 1951

Niall, I.
Heinemann

NO ROAD BACK
RKO 1956

Cary, F. L. *and* Weathers, P. (*Madam Tic-Tac*) (P)
French

NO ROOM AT THE INN
BN 1948

Temple, J. (P)
Sampson Low

NO ROOM FOR THE GROOM
UI 1952

Teilhet, D. L. (*My true love*)
Gollancz

NOR THE MOON BY NIGHT
RANK 1958

Packer, J.
Eyre & Spottiswoode

NORTHERN PATROL
ABP 1954

Curwood, J. O. (*Nomads of the North*)
Various

NORTH OF THE RIO GRANDE
PAR 1937

Mulford, C. E. (*Cottonwood Gulch*)
Hodder & Stoughton

NORTH STAR
RKO 1933

Hellman, L. F.
Macmillan

NORTH-WEST MOUNTED POLICE
PAR 1940

Fetherstonhaugh, R. C. (*Royal Canadian mounted police*)
Various

NORTH-WEST PASSAGE
MGM 1940

Roberts, K.
Collins

NO SAD SONGS FOR ME
COL 1950

Southard, R.
Doubleday, N.Y.

NOT AS A STRANGER
UA 1955

Thompson, M.
Joseph

NOT FOR HONOUR AND GLORY
COL 1965

Larteguy, J. (*Yellow fever*)
Hutchinson

NO TIME FOR COMEDY
WAR 1940

Behrman, S. N. (P)
Random House, N.Y.

NO TIME FOR SERGEANTS
WAR 1958

Hyman, M.
Dent

NO TIME FOR SERGEANTS
WAR 1958

Levin, I. *and* Hyman, M. (P)
Random House, N.Y.

NOTORIOUS LANDLADY, THE
COL 1962

Shulman, I.
Gold Medal Bks

NOW AND FOREVER
ABP 1955

Delderfield, R. F. (*Orchard walls, The*) (P)
French

NOW BARRABAS WAS A ROBBER
WAR 1949

Home, W. D. (*Now Barrabas*)
Longmans

NOWHERE TO GO
MGM 1958

Mackenzie, D.
Elek

NOW, VOYAGER
WAR 1949

Prouty, O.
Hodder & Stoughton

NUN'S STORY, THE
WAR 1958

Hulme, K.
Muller

NURSE ON WHEELS
WAR 1963

Jones, J. (*Nurse is a neighbour*)
Joseph

NURSE'S SECRET, THE
WAR 1941

Rinehart, M. R. (*Miss Pinkerton*)
Various

O

OBSESSION
GFD 1949

Coppel, A. (*Man about a dog, A*)
Harrap

ODD MAN OUT
TC 1947

Green, F. L.
Joseph

ODDS AGAINST TOMORROW
UA 1959

McGivern, W.
Fontana

ODETTE, G. C.
BL 1950

Tickell, J.
Chapman & Hall

OEDIPUS REX
OEDIPUS REX 1956

Sophocles (P)
Various

OFFICE WIFE
WAR 1930

Baldwin, F.
Sampson Low

OF HUMAN BONDAGE
RKO 1934
WAR 1946
MGM 1963

Maugham, W. S.
Heinemann

OF MICE AND MEN
UA 1939

Steinbeck, J.
Heinemann

OF MICE AND MEN
UA 1939

Steinbeck, J. (P)
Covici, N.Y.

OH DAD, POOR DAD
PAR 1966

Kopit, A. (. . . *Mama's hung you in the closet and I'm feeling so sad*) (P)
Methuen

OH! FOR A MAN!
FOX 1957

Axelrod, G. (*Will success spoil Rock Hunter ?*) (P)
Random House, N.Y.

OH! MEN! OH! WOMEN!
FOX 1957

Chodorov, E. (P)
French

OH! SAILOR BEHAVE!
WAR 1931

Rice, E. (*See Naples and die*) (P)
French, N.Y.

OIL FOR THE LAMPS OF CHINA
WAR 1935

Hobart, *Mrs*. A. T.
Cassell

OLD ACQUAINTANCE
WAR 1943

Druten, J. van. (P)
Random House, N.Y.

OLD DARK HOUSE, THE
UN 1932
BL 1963

Priestley, J. B. (*Benighted*)
Heinemann

OLD ENGLISH
WAR 1930

Galsworthy, J. (P)
Duckworth

OLD FASHIONED GIRL, AN
EL 1948

Alcott, L. M.
Sampson Low

OLD MAID, THE
WAR 1939

Wharton, *Mrs*. E. N.
Grosset, N.Y.

OLD MAN AND THE SEA
WAR 1957

Hemingway, E.
Cape

OLD YELLER
DISNEY 1958

Gipson, F. B.
Harper, N.Y.

OLIVER TWIST
MON 1933
CINEGUILD 1948

Dickens, C.
Various

OLIVIA
FDF 1950

'Olivia'
Hogarth Press

ON APPROVAL
BOX 1944

Lonsdale, F. (P)
Collins

ON BORROWED TIME
MGM 1939

Watkins, L. E.
Davies

ON BORROWED TIME
MGM 1939

Osborne, P. (P)
Dramatists, N.Y.

ONCE A JOLLY SWAGMAN
WESSEX 1949

Slater, M.
Lane

ONCE MORE MY DARLING
UI 1949

Davis, *Mrs.* L. (*Come be my love*)
Doubleday, N.Y.

ONCE MORE, WITH FEELING
COL 1959

Kurnitz, H. (P)
Random House, N.Y.

ONE DESIRE
UI 1955

Richter, C. (*Tracy Cromwell*)
Knopf, N.Y.

ONE EYED JACKS
PAR 1960

Neider, C. (*Authentic death of Hendry Jones, The*)
Harper, N.Y.

ONE FOOT IN HEAVEN
WAR 1941

Spence, H.
Harrap

ONE HUNDRED AND ONE
DALMATIANS
DISNEY 1960

Smith, D.
Heinemann

ONE JUMP AHEAD
GFD 1955

Chapman, R.
Laurie

ONE MORE SPRING
FOX 1950

Nathan, R.
Cassell

ONE MORE TOMORROW
WAR 1946

Barry, P. (*Animal kingdom*) (P)
French, N.Y.

ONE NIGHT IN LISBON
PAR 1941

Druten, J. van. (*There's always Juliet*) (P)
French, N.Y.

ONE ROMANTIC NIGHT
UA 1930

Molnar, F. (*Swan, The*) (P)
Longmans, N.Y.

ONE SUNDAY AFTERNOON
PAR 1933
WAR 1948

Hagan, P. (P)
French, N.Y.

ONE THAT GOT AWAY, THE
RANK 1957

Burt, K. *and* Leasor, J.
Collins *and* Joseph

ONE THIRD OF A NATION PAR 1939	Arent, A. *ed.* Random House, N.Y.
ONE TOUCH OF VENUS UN 1948	Perelman, S. J. *and* Nash, O. (P) Little Brown, Boston
ONE WAY PENDULUM UA 1964	Simpson, N. F. (P) Methuen
ONE WILD OAT EROS 1951	Sylvaine, V. (P) French
ON FRIDAY AT 11 BL 1961	Chase, J. H. (*World in my pocket, The*) Pan Bks
ONIONHEAD WAR 1958	Hill, W. Deutsch
ONLY THE VALIANT WAR 1950	Warren, C. M. Macmillan, N.Y.
ONLY TWO CAN PLAY BL 1961	Amis, K. (*That uncertain feeling*) Gollancz
ON THE BEACH UA 1959	Shute, N. Heinemann
ON THE FIDDLE AA 1961	Delderfield, R. F. (*Stop at a winner*) Hodder & Stoughton
ON THE NIGHT OF THE FIRE SOMLO 1939	Green, F. L. Joseph
OPERATION AMSTERDAM RANK 1958	Walker, D. E. (*Adventure in diamonds*) Evans
OPERATION MADBALL COL 1962	Carter, A. (P) French, N.Y.
OPPOSITE SEX, THE MGM 1956	Booth, C. (*Women, The*) (P) Dramatists Play Service
ORDERS ARE ORDERS BL 1954	Hay, I. *and* Armstrong, A. (P) French
OREGON PASSAGE ABP 1957	Shirrefs, G. D. (*Trails end*) Avalon, N.Y.
OSCAR, THE PAR 1965	Sale, R. Cassell
OTHELLO UA 1956 EAGLE FILMS 1966	Shakespeare, W. (P) Various

OUR BETTERS
RKO 1933

Maugham, W. S. (P)
Heinemann

OUR HEARTS WERE YOUNG AND GAY
PAR 1944

Skinner, C. O. *and* Kimbrugh, E.
Constable

OUR MAN IN HAVANA
COL 1959

Greene, G.
Heinemann

OUR MOTHER'S HOUSE
MGM 1967

Gloag, J.
Pan

OUR TOWN
UA 1940

Wilder, T. N. (P)
Coward-McCann, N.Y.

OUR VINES HAVE TENDER GRAPES
MGM 1945

Martin, G. V. (*For . . .*)
Joseph

OUTCAST OF THE ISLANDS, AN
LF 1951

Conrad, J.
Various

OUTCASTS OF POKER FLAT
RKO 1937
FOX 1952

Harte, B.
Various

OUT OF THE FOG
GN 1962

Graeme, B. (*Fog for a killer*)
Hutchinson

OUT OF THE FOG
WAR 1941

Shaw, I. (*Gentle people, The*) (P)
Dramatists, N.Y.

OUTWARD BOUND
WAR 1930

Vane, S. (P)
Boni, N.Y.

OVER 21
COL 1945

Gordon, R. (P)
Dramatists, N.Y.

OVERLANDERS, THE
EALING 1946

Butler, D.
World Film Pubns

OWD BOB
BG 1937

Olivant, A
Various

OX-BOW INCIDENT, THE
FOX 1956

Clark, W. van T.
Gollancz

P

PACIFIC DESTINY
BL 1956

Grimble, *Sir* A. (*Pattern of islands*)
Murray

PAD, THE (AND HOW TO USE IT)
UI 1967

Shaffer, P. (*Private ear, The*) (P)
French

PADDY THE NEXT BEST THING
FOX 1933

Page, G.
Hurst & Blackett

PAINTED HILLS MGM 1951	Hull, A. (*Shep of the painted hills*) Chapman & Hall
PAINTED VEIL, THE MGM 1934	Maugham, W. S. Heinemann
PAIR OF BRIEFS RANK 1961	Brooke, H. *and* Bannerman, K. (*How say you?*) (P) Evans
PAJAMA GAME WAR 1957	Bissell, R. P. (*7½ cents*) Little Brown, Boston
PAJAMA GAME WAR 1957	Abbott, G. *and* Bissell, R. P. (P) Random House, N.Y.
PAL JOEY COL 1957	O'Hara, J. Cresset Press
PANTHER'S MOON GFD 1950	Canning, V. Hodder & Stoughton
PAPER ORCHID COL 1949	La Bern, A. J. Marlowe
PARADINE CASE, THE BI 1949	Hichens, R. Convoy Bks
PARADISE FOR THREE MGM 1938	Kastner, E. (*Three men in the snow*) Cape
PARENT TRAP, THE DISNEY 1961	Kastner, E. (*Lottie and Lisa*) Cape
PARIS BLUES UA 1961	Flender, H. Panther Bks
PARIS-UNDERGROUND UA 1945	Shiber, *Mrs.* E. Harrap
PARNELL MGM 1937	Schauffler, E. (P) Gollancz
PAROLE FIXER PAR 1940	Hoover, J. E. (*Persons in hiding*) Dent
PARRISH WAR 1960	Savage, M. Longmans
PARSON OF PANAMINT, THE PAR 1941	Kyne, P. B. Grosset, N.Y.
PARTNERS IN CRIME AA 1960	Wallace, E. (*Man who knew, The*) Newnes

125

PASSAGE FROM HONG KONG
WAR 1941

Biggers, E. D. (*Agony Column*)
Bobbs-Merrill, Indianapolis

PASSAGE HOME
GFD 1955

Armstrong, R.
Dent

**PASSING OF THE THIRD FLOOR
BACK, THE**
GB 1936

Jerome, J. K.
Hurst & Blackett

PASSIONATE SUMMER, THE
RANK 1958

Mason, R. (*Shadow and the peak, The*)
Collins

PASSION FLOWER
MGM 1930

Norris, K.
Murray

PASSIONATE FRIENDS, THE
CINEGUILD 1949

Wells, H. G.
Benn

PASSPORT TO TREASON
EROS 1956

O'Brine, M.
Hammond

PASSWORD IS COURAGE, THE
MGM 1962

Castle, J.
Souvenir Press

PASTOR HALL
UA 1940

Toller, E. (P)
Lane

PATCH OF BLUE, A
MGM 1966

Kata, E. (*Be ready with bells and drums*)
Penguin

PATHFINDER, THE
COL 1953

Cooper, J. F.
Various

PATHS OF GLORY
UA 1957

Cobb, H.
Heinemann

PATIENT IN ROOM 18, THE
WAR 1938

Eberhart, M. G.
Heinemann

PAWNBROKER, THE
PAR 1964

Wallant, E. L.
Gollancz

PAYMENT DEFERRED
MGM 1932

Forester, C. S.
Lane

PAYMENT DEFERRED
MGM 1932

Forester, C. S. (P)
Lane

PAYROLL
AA 1960

Bickerton, D.
Eyre & Spottiswoode

PEARL, THE
RKO 1948

Steinbeck, J.
Heinemann

TITLE OF FILM	AUTHOR AND PUBLISHER
PEARL OF DEATH UN 1944	Doyle, *Sir* A. C. (*Six Napoleons*) Murray
PENELOPE MGM 1966	Cunningham, E. V. Deutsch
PENROD AND SAM IN 1931 WAR 1937	Tarkington, B. (*Penrod*) Hodder & Stoughton
PEOPLE AGAINST O'HARA, THE MGM 1951	Lipsky, E. Wingate
PEOPLE VERSUS DR. KILDARE, THE MGM 1941	Brand, M. (*Dr. Kildare's trial*) Dodd, N.Y.
PERFECT ALIBI, THE RKO 1931	Milne, A. A. (P) Putnam, N.Y.
PERFECT MARRIAGE, THE PAR 1946	Raphaelson, S. (P) Dramatists, N.Y.
PERIL FOR THE GUY BL 1956	Kennett, J. Brockhampton
PERILOUS JOURNEY, A REP 1953	Roe, V. (*Golden tide, The*) Cassell
PERIOD OF ADJUSTMENT MGM 1962	Williams, T. (P) Secker & Warburg
PERRI DISNEY 1957	Salten, F. Cape
PERSONAL PROPERTY MGM 1937	Harwood, H. M. (*Man in possession*) (P) Benn
PERSONS IN HIDING PAR 1939	Hoover, J. E. Dent
PETER IBBETSON PAR 1935	Du Maurier, G. Various
PETER PAN RKO 1953	Barrie, *Sir* J. M. (P) Hodder & Stoughton
PETRIFIED FOREST, THE WAR 1936	Sherwood, R. E. (P) Scribner, N.Y.
PEYTON PLACE FOX 1957	Metalious, G. Muller
PHANTOM FRIEND, THE OLY 1935	Lowndes, *Mrs.* M. B. (*Lodger, The*) Methuen

TITLE OF FILM	AUTHOR AND PUBLISHER
PHANTOM LADY UN 1944	Irish, W. Lippincott, Philadelphia
PHANTOM OF THE OPERA, THE UN 1943 UI 1962	Leroux, G. Various
PHANTOM OF THE RUE MORGUE WAR 1954	Poe, E. A. (*Murder in the Rue Morgue*) Various
PHANTOM STRIKES, THE MON 1939	Wallace, E. (*Ringer, The*) (P) Hodder & Stoughton
PHILADELPHIA STORY MGM 1940	Barry, P. (P) French
PICCADILLY JIM MGM 1936	Wodehouse, P. G. Jenkins
PICKWICK PAPERS, THE REN 1952	Dickens, C. Various
PICNIC COL 1955	Inge, W. (P) Random House, N.Y.
PICTURE OF DORIAN GRAY, THE MGM 1945	Wilde, O. Various
PIED PIPER FOX 1942	Shute, N. Heinemann
PIGEON THAT TOOK ROME, THE PAR 1962	Downes, D. (*Easter dinner, The*) Rinehart, N.Y.
PIGEON THAT WORKED A MIRACLE DISNEY 1958	Liggett, T. (*Pigeon fly home*) Holiday, N.Y.
PILGRIMAGE FOX 1933	Wylie, I. A. R. Cassell
PINK STRING AND SEALING WAX EALING 1946	Pertwee, R. (P) English Theatre Guild
PINKY FOX 1949	Sumner, *Mrs.* C. R. (*Quality*) Dymock
PIRATE, THE MGM 1948	Behrman, S. N. (P) Random House, N.Y.
PIT AND THE PENDULUM, THE AA 1961	Poe, E. A. Various
PITFALL UA 1948	Dratler, J. Oxford U.P.
PIT OF DARKNESS BUTCHER 1961	McCutcheon, H. (*To duty death*) Long

128

TITLE OF FILM	AUTHOR AND PUBLISHER

PLACE IN THE SUN, A
PAR 1951

Dreiser, T. (*American tragedy, An*)
Various

PLACE OF ONE'S OWN, A
GFD 1945

Sitwell, *Sir* O.
Macmillan

PLACE TO GO, A
BL 1964

Fisher, M. (*Bethnal Green*)
Cassell

PLAINSMAN, THE
PAR 1936

Wilstach, F. (*Wild Bill Hickok*)
Sun Dial, N.Y.

PLEASE DON'T EAT THE DAISIES
MGM 1960

Kerr, J.
Heinemann

PLEASE TURN OVER
AA 1959

Thomas, B. (*Book of the month*) (P)
French

PLEASURE OF HIS COMPANY, THE
PAR 1959

Taylor, S. A. *and* Skinner, C. O. (P)
Heinemann

PLOUGH AND THE STARS, THE
RKO 1936

O'Casey, S. (P)
Macmillan

PLUNDER
WILCOX 1937

Travers, B. (P)
Bickers

PLUNDER OF THE SUN
WAR 1953

Dodge, D.
Random House, N.Y.

PLYMOUTH ADVENTURE, THE
MGM 1952

Gebler, E.
Cassell

POET'S PUB
AQUILA 1949

Linklater, E.
Cape

POISON PEN
AB 1940

Llewellyn, R. (P)
French

POLLYANNA
DISNEY 1960

Porter, G. S.
Harrap

POLLY FULTON
MGM 1949

Marquand, J. P.
Hale

PORK CHOP HILL
UA 1959

Marshall, S. L. A.
Panther Bks

PORT AFRIQUE
COL 1956

Dryer, B. V.
Cassell

PORTRAIT OF CLARE
ABP 1949

Young, F. B.
Heinemann

TITLE OF FILM	AUTHOR AND PUBLISHER
POSTMAN ALWAYS RINGS TWICE, THE MGM 1946	Cain, J. M. Cape
POWDERSMOKE RANGE RKO 1935	Macdonald, W. C. Collins
POWER AND THE GLORY, THE PAR 1962	Greene, G. Heinemann
POWER AND THE PRIZE, THE MGM 1956	Swiggett, H. Hodder & Stoughton
PRELUDE TO FAME GFD 1950	Huxley, A. L. (*Young Archimedes*) Chatto & Windus
PREMATURE BURIAL, THE AA 1962	Poe, E. A. Various
PRESIDENT'S LADY, THE FOX 1953	Stone, I. (*Immortal wife*) Invincible Press
PRESS FOR TIME JARFID 1966	McGill, A. (*Yea, yea, yea*) Secker & Warburg
PRESSURE POINT UA 1963	Lindner, R. (*Fifty minute hour, The*) Corgi Bks
PRICE OF SILENCE, THE GN 1959	Meynell, L. (*One step from murder*) Collins
PRIDE AND PREJUDICE MGM 1940	Austen, J. Various
PRIDE AND THE PASSION, THE UA 1957	Forester, C. S. (*Gun, The*) Joseph
PRIDE OF THE MARINES WAR 1945	Butterfield, R. P. (*Al Schmid, Marine*) Norton, N.Y.
PRINCE AND THE PAUPER WAR 1937 DISNEY 1961	Twain, M. Chatto & Windus
PRINCE OF FOXES FOX 1949	Shellabarger, S. Macmillan
PRINCE OF PLAYERS FOX 1954	Ruggles, E. Davies
PRINCE WHO WAS A THIEF, THE GFD 1951	Dreiser, T. World, N.Y.
PRISONER, THE COL 1955	Boland, B. (P) Elek

PRISONER OF ZENDA
UA 1937
MGM 1952

Hope, A.
Harrap

PRIVATE AFFAIRS OF BEL AMI, THE
UA 1947

De Maupassant, G. (*Bel Ami*)
Various

PRIVATE ANGELO
ABP 1949

Linklater, E.
Cape

PRIVATE LIVES
MGM 1931

Coward, N. (P)
Heinemann

PRIVATE LIVES OF ELIZABETH AND ESSEX, THE
WAR 1939

Anderson, M. (*Elizabeth the Queen*) (P)
Longmans, N.Y.

PRIVATE'S PROGRESS, A
BL 1956

Hackney, A.
Gollancz

PRIVATE WORLDS
PAR 1935

Bottome, P.
Lane

PRIZE, THE
MGM 1963

Wallace, I.
Cassell

PRIZE OF GOLD, A
COL 1954

Catto, M.
Heinemann

PROFESSIONALS, THE
COL 1966

O'Rourke, F. (*Mule for the Marquesa, A*)
Fontana

PROFESSOR TIM
RKO 1957

Sheils, G. (P)
Macmillan

PROUD AND PROFANE
PAR 1956

Crockett, L. H. (*Magnificent devils*)
Dymock

PROUD ONES
FOX 1956

Athanas, V.
Rich & Cowan

PSYCHE 59
BL 1964

Ligneris, F. (*Psyche 63*)
Spearman

PSYCHO
PAR 1960

Block, R.
Hale

PT 109
WAR 1963

Donovan, R. J. (*Wartime adventures of President John Kennedy, The*)
Panther Bks

PUBLIC DEFENDER
RKO 1931

Goodchild, G. (*Splendid crime, The*)
Hodder & Stoughton

PUMPKIN EATER, THE
BL 1963

Mortimer, P.
Penguin

PURPLE NOON
HILLCREST 1961

Highsmith, P. (*Talented Mr. Ripley, The*)
Pan Bks

PURPLE PLAIN, THE
GFD 1954

Bates, H. E.
Joseph

PYGMALION
MGM 1938

Shaw, G. B. (P)
Constable

Q

QUALITY STREET
RKO 1937

Barrie, *Sir* J. M. (P)
Hodder & Stoughton

QUARE FELLOW, THE
BL 1962

Behan, B. (P)
Methuen

QUARTETTE
GFD 1949

Maugham, W. S.
Heinemann

QUEEN BEE
COL 1955

Lee, E.
Hurst & Blackett

QUEEN OF SPADES, THE
AB 1949

Pushkin, A. S.
Various

QUEEN OF THE MOB
PAR 1940

Hoover, J. E. (*Persons in hiding*)
Dent

QUIET AMERICAN, THE
UA 1957

Greene, G.
Heinemann

QUIET FLOWS THE DON
GALA 1958

Sholokhov, M. (*And quiet flows the Don*)
Putnam

QUIET MAN, THE
REP 1952

Walsh, M.
Angus & Robertson

QUIET WEDDING
PAR 1941

MacCracken, E. (P)
French

QUIET WEEK END
AB 1946

MacCracken, E. (P)
French

QUILLER MEMORANDUM, THE
JARFID 1966

Hall, A. (*Berlin memorandum, The*)
Collins

QUO VADIS?
IN 1929
MGM 1949

Sienkiewicz, H.
Various

R

RACERS, THE
FOX 1954

Ruesch, H. (*Racer, The*)
Hurst & Blackett

TITLE OF FILM	AUTHOR AND PUBLISHER
RACKET, THE RKO 1952	Cormack, B. (P) French, N.Y.
RAFFLES UA 1930 UA 1940	Hornung, E. W. Grayson
RAGE IN HEAVEN MGM 1941	Hilton, J. (*Dawn of reckoning*) Butterworth
RAGE TO LIVE, A UA 1964	O'Hara, J. Cresset Press
RAGING TIDE, THE UI 1951	Gann, E. K. (*Fiddler's green*) Sloane, N.Y.
RAIN UA 1932	Maugham, W. S. (P) Heinemann
RAINBOW TRAIL FOX 1932	Grey, Z. Harper
RAINMAKER, THE PAR 1956	Nash, N. R. (P) Random House, N.Y.
RAINS CAME, THE FOX 1939	Bromfield, L. Cassell
RAINS OF RANCHIPUR, THE FOX 1955	Bromfield, L. (*Rains came, The*) Cassell
RAINTREE COUNTRY MGM 1957	Lockridge, R. Macdonald
RAISING A RIOT BL 1954	Toombs, A. Hammond
RAISIN IN THE SUN, A COL 1960	Hansberry, L. (P) Methuen
'RALLY ROUND THE FLAG, BOYS' FOX 1958	Shulman, M. Heinemann
RAMONA FOX 1936	Jackson, *Mrs*. H. M. Sampson Low
RAMPAGE WAR 1963	Caillou, A. Davies
RAMROD UA 1947	Short, L. Collins
RANDOM HARVEST MGM 1942	Hilton, J. Macmillan

RAPTURE
FOX 1964

Hastings, P. (*Rapture in my rags*)
Dent

RAT, THE
RKO 1938

Bottome, P.
Allan

RAT RACE, THE
PAR 1960

Kanin, G. (P)
Dramatists, N.Y.

RATTLE OF A SIMPLE MAN
WAR 1964

Dyer, C. (P)
French

RAWHIDE YEARS, THE
UI 1955

Fox, N. A.
Collins

RAZOR'S EDGE, THE
FOX 1946

Maugham, W. S.
Heinemann

REACH FOR GLORY
GALA 1962

Rae, J. (*Custard boys*, *The*)
Hart-Davis

REACH FOR THE SKY
RANK 1956

Brickhill, P.
Collins

REACH FOR TOMORROW
COL 1959

Motley, W. (*Let no man write my epitaph*)
Longmans

REACHING FOR THE SUN
PAR 1941

Smitter, W. (*F.O.B. Detroit*)
Dent

REAL GLORY, THE
UA 1939

Clifford, C. L.
Heinemann

REAP THE WILD WIND
PAR 1942

Strabel, T.
Collins

REBECCA
UA 1940

Du Maurier, D.
Gollancz

REBECCA OF SUNNYBROOK FARM
FOX 1932
FOX 1938

Wiggins, *Mrs.* K. D.
Various

REBEL WITHOUT A CAUSE, A
WAR 1955

Schulman, I. (*Children of the dark*)
World, N.Y.

RECKLESS MOMENT, THE
COL 1949

Holding, *Mrs.* E. (*Blank wall*)
Simon & Schuster, N.Y.

RED BADGE OF COURAGE, THE
MGM 1951

Crane, S.
Various

RED BERET, THE
COL 1953

Saunders, H. St. J.
Joseph

RED CANYON
UN 1949

Grey, Z. (*Wildfire*)
Hodder & Stoughton

RED DANUBE MGM 1949	Marshall, B. Constable
RED HOUSE, THE UA 1947	Jerusalem, E. Laurie
RED PEPPERS GFD 1952	Coward, N. (P) Heinemann
RED PONY, THE BL 1949	Steinbeck, J. Viking Press, N.Y.
RED WAGON ALL 1935	Smith, *Lady E.* Gollancz
REFLECTIONS IN A GOLDEN EYE WAR 1966	McCullers, C. Cresset Press
RELUCTANT DEBUTANTE, THE MGM 1958	Home, W. D. (P) French
RELUCTANT HEROES ABP 1951	Morris, C. (P) English Theatre Guild
RELUCTANT WIDOW, THE GFD 1950	Heyer, G. Heinemann
REMAINS TO BE SEEN MGM 1953	Lindsay, H. *and* Crouse, R. (P) Dramatists, N.Y.
REMEMBER THAT FACE COL 1951	Findley, F. Reinhardt & Evans
RENEGADE CANYON COL 1953	Dawson, P. Collins
RENDEZVOUS PAR 1950	Barrie, *Sir* J. M. (*Alice sit by the fire*) (P) Hodder & Stoughton
RENDEZVOUS MGM 1935	Yardley, H. O. (*American black chamber, The*) Faber
REPRIEVE WAR 1962	Resko, J. MacGibbon
REPRISAL COL 1956	Gordon, A. Hamilton
RESPECTABLE PROSTITUTE, THE GALA 1955	Sartre, J-P. (P) Penguin

RESURRECTION
UN 1931

Tolstoy, L. N.
Various

RETURN FROM THE ASHES
UA 1965

Monteilhet, H.
Panther Bks

RETURN OF DON CAMILLO, THE
MIRACLE FILMS 1954

Guareschi, G. (*Don Camillo and the prodigal son*)
Gollancz

RETURN OF DR. FU MANCHU
PAR 1930

Rohmer, S.
Hurst & Blackett

RETURN OF SHERLOCK HOLMES
PAR 1929

Doyle, *Sir* A. C.
Murray

RETURN TO PARADISE
UA 1953

Michener, J. A.
Random House, N.Y.

RETURN TO PEYTON PLACE
FOX 1960

Metalious, G.
Muller

REUNION IN VIENNA
MGM 1933

Sherwood, R. E. (P)
Scribner, N.Y.

REVOLT OF MAMIE STOVER, THE
FOX 1956

Huie, W. B.
W. H. Allen

RHAPSODY
MGM 1954

Richardson, H. H. (*Maurice Guest*)
Heinemann

RHODES
GB 1936

Millin, S. G.
Chatto & Windus

RHUBARB
PAR 1951

Smith, H. A.
Barker

RICHARD III
BL 1955

Shakespeare, W. (P)
Various

RICH MAN, POOR GIRL
MGM 1938

Ellis, E. (*White collars*) (P)
French, N.Y.

RICH MAN'S FOLLY
PAR 1931

Dickens, C. (*Dombey and son*)
Various

RIDE BEYOND VENGEANCE
COL 1966

Dewlen, A. (*Night of the Tiger, The*)
Longmans

RIDE THE PINK HORSE
UI 1947

Hughes, D. B.
Duell, N.Y.

RIDERS OF THE PURPLE SAGE
FOX 1931
FOX 1941

Grey, Z.
Harper, N.Y.

RIGHT TO LIVE
WAR 1935

Maugham, W. S. (*Sacred flame, The*) (P)
Heinemann

RING, THE
UA 1953

Shulman, I. (*Cry tough*)
Dial Press, N.Y.

RINGER, THE
ID 1932
REGENT 1952

Wallace, E.
Hodder & Stoughton

RINGER, THE
ID 1932
REGENT 1952

Wallace, E. (P)
Hodder & Stoughton

RIO CONCHOS
FOX 1964

Huffaker, C. (*Guns of the Rio Conchos*)
Muller

RISE AND SHINE
FOX 1941

Thurber, J. (*My life and hard times*)
Hamilton

RIVER, THE
UA 1951

Godden, R.
Joseph

RIVER LADY
UN 1948

Brach, H. *and* Water, F.
Cassell

RIVER'S END
WAR 1930
WAR 1940

Curwood, J. O.
Grosset, N.Y.

ROAD BACK
UN 1937

Remarque, E. M.
Putnam

ROAD TO SINGAPORE
WAR 1931

Pertwee, R. (*Heat wave*) (P)
French, N.Y.

ROARIN' LEAD
REP 1937

Macdonald, W. C.
Collins

ROBBER'S ROOST
FOX 1933
UA 1955

Grey, Z.
Hodder & Stoughton

ROBBERY UNDER ARMS
RANK 1957

Boldrewood, R.
Macmillan

ROBE, THE
FOX 1953

Douglas, L. C.
Davies

ROBERTA
RKO 1935

Miller, A. D. (*Gowns by Roberta*)
Various

ROCKETS GALORE
RANK 1958

Mackenzie, *Sir* C.
Chatto & Windus

137

TITLE OF FILM	AUTHOR AND PUBLISHER
ROCKETS IN THE DUNES RANK 1960	Lamplugh, L. Cape
ROCKING HORSE WINNER, THE TC 1949	Lawrence, D. H. Heinemann
ROGUE COP MGM 1954	McGivern, W. P. Collins
ROMANOFF AND JULIET RANK 1961	Ustinov, P. (P) Heinemann Educational
ROMEO AND JULIET MGM 1936 GFD 1954 GALA 1956	Shakespeare, W. (P) Various
ROMMEL-DESERT FOX FOX 1951	Young, D. (*Rommel*) Collins
ROOKERY NOOK MGM 1930	Travers, B. Lane
ROOKERY NOOK MGM 1930	Travers, B. (P) Bickers
ROOM AT THE TOP BL 1958	Braine, J. Eyre & Spottiswoode
ROOM FOR ONE MORE WAR 1952	Rose, A. P. Houghton Mifflin, Boston
ROOM IN THE HOUSE MON 1955	Evans, E. E. (*Bless this house*) (P) French
ROONEY RANK 1958	Cookson, C. Macdonald
ROOTS OF HEAVEN, THE FOX 1958	Gary, R. Joseph
ROPE WAR 1948	Hamilton, P. (P) French
ROSEANNA McCOY RKO 1951	Bannum, A. Holt, N.Y.
ROSES OF PICARDY, THE EXCELLENT 1930	Mottram, R. H. (*Spanish Farm, The*) Chatto & Windus
ROSE TATTOO PAR 1954	Williams, T. (P) Secker & Warburg
ROUGH AND THE SMOOTH, THE MGM 1959	Maugham, R. Chapman & Hall

ROUGH COMPANY COL 1954	Hamilton, D. Wingate
ROUGHLY SPEAKING WAR 1945	Pierson, *Mrs.* L. Simon & Schuster, N.Y.
ROUGH SHOOT UA 1953	Household, G. Joseph
ROUNDERS, THE MGM 1965	Evans, M. Macmillan, N.Y.
ROYAL BED RKO 1931	Sherwood, R. E. (*Queen's husband, The*) (P) Scribner, N.Y.
ROYAL FAMILY OF BROADWAY PAR 1930	Kaufman, G. S. *and* Ferber, E. (*Royal family, The*) (P) French, N.Y.
RUGGLES OF RED GAP PAR 1935	Wilson, H. L. Various
RUMBLES ON THE DOCKS COL 1957	Paley, F. Crown, N.Y.
RUNNING MAN, THE COL 1963	Smith, S. (*Ballad of the running man*) Hamilton
RUNNING OF THE TIDE MGM 1949	Forbes, E. Houghton Mifflin, Boston
RUN SILENT, RUN DEEP UA 1958	Beach, E. L. Wingate
RUSSIANS ARE COMING—THE RUSSIANS ARE COMING UA 1966	Benchley, N. (*Off islanders, The*) Penguin
RUTHLESS EL 1948	Stoddart, D. (*Prelude to night*) Coward-McCann, N.Y.

S

SABOTAGE GB 1936	Conrad, J. (*Secret agent, The*) Various
SABRINA FAIR PAR 1954	Taylor, S. (P) Random House, N.Y.
SACRED FLAME, THE WAR 1939	Maugham, W. S. (P) Heinemann
SAIL A CROOKED SHIP COL 1961	Benchley, N. Hutchinson

TITLE OF FILM	AUTHOR AND PUBLISHER
SAILOR, BEWARE! BL 1956	King, P. *and* Cary, F. L. (P) Elek
SAILOR FROM GIBRALTAR, THE UA 1967	Duras, M. Calder
SAINT IN NEW YORK, THE RKO 1938	Charteris, L. Hodder & Stoughton
SAINT JOAN UA 1957	Shaw, G. B. (P) Constable
SAINT MEETS THE TIGER, THE REP 1943	Charteris, L. (*Meet the Tiger*) Ward Lock
SAINT'S VACATION, THE RKO 1941	Charteris, L. (*Getaway*) Hodder & Stoughton
SALAAMBO FOX 1959	Flaubert, G. Dent
SALLY IN OUR ALLEY ABP 1932	McEvoy, C. (*Likes of 'er, The*) Harrap
SAL OF SINGAPORE PATHE 1929	Collins, D. (*Sentimentalists*) Little Brown, Boston
SALOON BAR EALING 1942	Harvey, J. *Jun.* (P) French
SALUTE JOHN CITIZEN BN 1942	Greenwood, R. (*Mr. Bunting at war*) Dent
SALUTE THE TOFF BUTCHER 1951	Creasey, J. Long
SAMMY GOING SOUTH BL 1962	Canaway, W. H. Hutchinson
SAN ANTONE REP 1952	Carroll, C. (*Golden herd*) Morrow, N.Y.
SANCTUARY FOX 1960	Faulkner, W. Chatto & Windus
SANCTUARY FOX 1960	Faulkner, W. (*Requiem for a nun*) Chatto & Windus
SAND FOX 1949	James, W. Cassell
SANDERS OF THE RIVER UA 1935	Wallace, E. Ward Lock
SAND PEBBLES, THE FOX 1966	McKenna, R. Gollancz

TITLE OF FILM	AUTHOR AND PUBLISHER
SANDS OF THE KALAHARI PAR 1965	Mulvihill, W. Longmans
SAN FRANCISCO STORY, THE WAR 1952	Summers, R. A. (*Vigilante*) Duell, N.Y.
SANGAREE PAR 1933	Slaughter, F. G. Jarrolds
SANTE FE COL 1951	Marshall, J. L. Random House, N.Y.
SAPPHIRE RANK 1959	Cousins, E. G. Panther Bks
SARABAND FOR DEAD LOVERS EL 1949	Simpson, H. Heinemann
SARACEN BLADE, THE COL 1954	Yerby, F. Heinemann
SARATOGA TRUNK WAR 1945	Ferber, E. Heinemann
SATURDAY ISLAND RKO 1951	Brooke, H. Heinemann
SATURDAY NIGHT AND SUNDAY MORNING BL 1960	Sillitoe, A. W. H. Allen
SATURDAY'S CHILDREN WAR 1940	Anderson, M. (P) Longmans, N.Y.
SATURDAY'S HERO COL 1950	Lampell, M. (*Hero, The*) Messner, N.Y.
SAVAGE, THE PAR 1952	Foreman, L. L. (*Don Desperado*) Cassell
SAVAGE SAM DISNEY 1963	Gipson, F. Hodder & Stoughton
SAXON CHARM, THE UI 1948	Wakeman, F. Rinehart, N.Y.
SAYONARA WAR 1957	Michener, J. A. Secker & Warburg
SCAPEGOAT, THE MGM 1958	Du Maurier, D. Gollancz
SCAR, THE ABP 1949	Holding, C. H. Eerdmans, Grand Rapids
SCARAMOUCHE MGM 1952	Sabatini, R. Hutchinson
SCARFACE UA 1932	Trail, A. Long

SCARFACE MOB, THE
WAR 1959

Ness, E. *and* Fraley, O. (*Untouchables, The*)
Messner, N.Y.

SCARLET LETTER, THE
MAJESTIC 1934

Hawthorne, N.
Various

SCARLET PIMPERNEL, THE
UA 1935

Orczy, *Baroness* E.
Hodder & Stoughton

SCATTERGOOD BAINES
RKO 1941

Kelland, C. B.
Hodder & Stoughton

SCHOOL FOR SCOUNDRELS
WAR 1960

Potter, S. (*Gamesmanship, Oneupmanship, Lifemanship*)
Hart-Davis

SCREAMING MIMI
COL 1957

Brown, F.
Boardman

SCROOGE
PAR 1935
REN 1951

Dickens, C. (*Christmas carol, A*)
Various

SCUDDA HOO! SCUDDA HAY!
FOX 1948

Chamberlain, G. A.
Grosset, N.Y.

SEA AROUND US, THE
RKO 1953

Carson, R. L.
Staples

SEA CHASE, THE
WAR 1954

Geer, A.
Collins

SEA GOD, THE
PAR 1930

Russell, J. (*Where the pavement ends*)
Butterworth

SEAGULLS OVER SORRENTO
MGM 1954

Hastings, H. (P)
Elek

SEA HAWK, THE
WAR 1940

Sabatini, R.
Various

SEANCE ON A WET AFTERNOON
RANK 1964

McShane, M.
Cassell

SEA OF GRASS
MGM 1947

Ritchter, C. M.
Constable

SEARCHERS, THE
WAR 1956

LeMay, A.
Collins

SEARCH FOR BRIDEY MURPHY, THE
PAR 1956

Bernstein, M.
Hutchinson

TITLE OF FILM	AUTHOR AND PUBLISHER
SEA SHALL NOT HAVE THEM, THE EROS 1954	Harris, J. Hurst & Blackett
SEA WALL RANK 1957	Duras, M. (*Sea of troubles*) Methuen
SEA-WIFE FOX 1957	Scott, J. D. (*Sea Wyf and Biscuit*) Heinemann
SEA WOLF, THE FOX 1930 WAR 1941	London, J. Heinemann
SEALED VERDICT PAR 1948	Shapiro, L. Doubleday, N.Y.
SEARCHING WIND, THE PAR 1946	Hellman, L. F. (P) Viking Press, N.Y.
SECOND HAND WIFE FOX 1933	Norris, K. Murray
SECOND HONEYMOON CONT 1931	Ayres, R. M. Hodder & Stoughton
SECOND MRS. TANQUERAY, THE VANDYKE 1952	Pinero, *Sir* A. W. (P) Heinemann
SECONDS PAR 1965	Ely, D. Deutsch
SECOND TIME ROUND FOX 1961	Roberts, R. E. (*Star in the West*) Pocket Bks
SECRET AGENT GB 1936	Maugham, W. S. (*Ashenden*) Heinemann
SECRET BEYOND THE DOOR, THE UI 1948	King, R. Various
SECRET FOUR, THE MON 1940	Wallace, E. (*Four just men, The*) Various
SECRET GARDEN, THE MGM 1949	Burnett, F. H. Heinemann
SECRET INTERLUDE FOX 1955	Basso, H. (*View from Pompey's Head*) Collins
SECRET LIFE OF WALTER MITTY RKO 1949	Thurber, J. World, N.Y.
SECRET OF DR. KILDARE, THE MGM 1939	Brand, M. Hodder & Stoughton

SECRET OF STAMBOUL, THE HOB 1939	Wheatley, D. (*Eunuch of Stamboul, The*) Hutchinson
SECRET OF ST. IVES, THE COL 1949	Stevenson, R. L. (*St. Ives*) Various
SECRET TENT BL 1956	Addyman, E. (P) English Theatre Guild
SECRETS OF THE PURPLE REEF, THE FOX 1960	Cottrell, D. (*Silent Reef*) Hodder & Stoughton
SECRET WAYS, THE RANK 1960	McLean, A. (*Last frontier*) Collins
SEED UN 1931	Norris, C. G. Heinemann
SEE HERE, PRIVATE HARGROVE MGM 1944	Hargrove, M. Hodder & Stoughton
SEE HOW THEY RUN BL 1955	King, P. (P) French
SEE YOU IN HELL, DARLING WAR 1966	Mailer, N. (*American dream, An*) Deutsch
SEMINOLE UPRISING EROS 1955	Brandon, C. (*Bugle's wake*) Dutton, N.Y.
SEPARATE BEDS MGM 1964	Goodman, G. J. W. (*Wheeler-dealers, The*) Doubleday, N.Y.
SEPARATE TABLES UA 1958	Rattigan, T. (P) French
SEQUOIA MGM 1934	Hoyt, V. J. Grosset, N.Y.
SERENADE WAR 1956	Cain, J. M. Penguin
SERGEANT YORK WAR 1941	Cowan, S. K. (*Sergeant York and his people*) Various
SERIOUS CHARGE EROS 1959	King, P. (P) French
SERVANT, THE WAR 1963	Maugham, R. Heinemann
SEVEN BRIDES FOR SEVEN BROTHERS MGM 1954	Benet, S. V. (*Sobbin' women, The*) Heinemann

TITLE OF FILM	AUTHOR AND PUBLISHER
SEVEN CITIES OF GOLD FOX 1955	Ziegler, I. G. (*Nine days of Father Serra*) Longmans
SEVEN DAYS IN MAY PAR 1963	Knebel, F. *and* Bailey, C. W. Corgi Bks
SEVEN DAYS' LEAVE PAR 1930	Barrie, *Sir* J. M. (*Old lady shows her medals, The*) (P) Hodder & Stoughton
SEVEN KEYS TO BALDPATE RKO 1930 RKO 1935 RKO 1947	Biggers, E. D. Grosset, N.Y.
SEVENTEEN PAR 1940	Tarkington, B. (P) French, N.Y.
SEVENTH CROSS, THE MGM 1944	Seghers, A. Hamilton
7TH DAWN UA 1964	Keon, M. (*Durian tree, The*) Hamilton
SEVENTH HEAVEN, THE FOX 1937	Strong, A. (P) French, N.Y.
SEVEN THIEVES FOX 1960	Catto, M. (*Lions at the kill*) Hutchinson
SEVENTH SIN, THE MGM 1957	Maugham, W. S. (*Painted veil, The*) Heinemann
SEVEN THUNDERS RANK 1957	Croft-Cooke, R. Macmillan
SEVEN WAYS FROM SUNDOWN UI 1960	Huffaker, C. Muller
SEVEN YEAR ITCH, THE FOX 1954	Axelrod, G. (P) Random House, N.Y.
SEVEN YEARS IN TIBET CURZON 1956	Harrer, H. Hart-Davis
SEX AND THE SINGLE GIRL WAR 1964	Brown, H. G. Muller
SHADOW, THE GLOBE 1936	Stuart, D. Wright & Brown
SHADOW OF A WOMAN WAR 1946	Perdue, V. (*He fell down dead*) Doubleday, N.Y.
SHAKE HANDS WITH THE DEVIL UA 1959	Conner, R. Dent

SHANE PAR 1953	Schaefer, J. W. Deutsch
SHARE OUT, THE AA 1962	Wallace, E. (*Jack O'Judgement*) Ward Lock
SHE RKO 1935 WAR 1964	Haggard, *Sir* H. R. Macdonald
SHE DIDN'T SAY NO! ABP 1958	Troy, U. (*We are seven*) Heinemann
SHEPHERD OF THE HILLS, THE PAR 1941	Wright, H. B. Grosset, N.Y.
SHERLOCK HOLMES AND THE VOICE OF TERROR UN 1942	Doyle, *Sir* A. C. (*His last bow*) Various
SHE SHALL HAVE MURDER BL 1950	Ames, D. Hodder & Stoughton
SHE'S WORKING HER WAY THROUGH COLLEGE WAR 1952	Thurber, J. *and* Nugent, E. (*Male animal, The*) (P) Random House, N.Y.
SHETLAND BUS, THE FORLONG 1954	Howarth, D. Nelson
SHIELD FOR MURDER UA 1954	McGivern, W. P. Dodd, N.Y.
SHINING HOUR, THE MGM 1938	Winter, K. (P) Heinemann
SHINING VICTORY WAR 1941	Cronin, A. J. (*Jupiter laughs*) (P) Gollancz
SHIPBUILDERS, THE BN 1944	Blake, G. Faber
SHIP FROM SHANGHAI MGM 1930	Collins, D. (*Ordeal, The*) Allan
SHIP OF FOOLS COL 1964	Porter, K. A. Secker & Warburg
SHIRALEE, THE MGM 1957	Niland, D'A. Angus & Robertson
SHOCK TREATMENT FOX 1964	Van Atta, W. Doubleday, N.Y.
SHORT CUT TO HELL PAR 1957	Greene, G. (*Gun for sale, A*) Heinemann

SHORT GRASS
ABP 1951

Blackburn, T. W.
Sampson Low

SHOW BOAT
UN 1929
UN 1936
MGM 1951

Ferber, E.
Heinemann

SHOP AT SLY CORNER, THE
BL 1946

Percy, E. (P)
French

SHRIKE, THE
UI 1955

Kramm, J. (P)
Random House, N.Y.

SIDE SHOW OF LIFE
WAR 1931

Locke, W. J. (*Mounteback*)
Lane

SIERRA BARON
FOX 1958

Blackburn, T. W.
Random House, N.Y.

SIGN OF FOUR
WW 1932

Doyle, *Sir* A. C.
Various

SIGN OF THE RAM, THE
COL 1949

Ferguson, M.
Hale

SIGN OF THE CROSS, THE
PAR 1932
PAR 1944

Barrett, W.
Various

SIGNPOST TO MURDER
MGM 1965

Doyle, M. (P)
French

SILENCERS, THE
COL 1965

Hamilton, D.
Hodder & Stoughton

SILENT DUST
ABP 1952

Pertwee, R. *and* Pertwee, M. (*Paragon, The*) (P)
English Theatre Guild

SILENT ENEMY, THE
ROMULUS 1958

Pugh, M. (*Commander Crabb*)
Macmillan

SILENT WORLD, THE
RANK 1955

Cousteau, J.
Hamilton

SILVER CHALICE, THE
WAR 1954

Costain, T. B.
Hodder & Stoughton

SILVER DARLINGS, THE
ALL 1947

Gunn, N. M.
Faber

SILVER HORDE, THE
RKO 1930

Beach, R.
Hodder & Stoughton

SILVER WHIP, THE
FOX 1953

Schaefer, J. W. (*Big Range*)
Deutsch

SIMON AND LAURA RANK 1955	Melville, A. (P) French
SINGER NOT THE SONG, THE RANK 1960	Lindop, A. E. Heinemann
SINGLE HANDED FOX 1952	Forester, C. S. (*Brown on 'Resolution'*) Lane
SINISTER MAN, THE AA 1961	Wallace, E. Hodder & Stoughton
SINK THE BISMARCK FOX 1960	Forester, C. S. (*Hunting the Bismarck*) Joseph
SIN OF MADELON CLAUDET MGM 1931	Knoblock, E. (*Lullaby, The*) (P) Putnam
SINCE YOU WENT AWAY UA 1944	Wilder, M. A. McGraw-Hill, N.Y.
SING SING NIGHTS MON 1934	Keeler, H. S. Ward Lock
SINNER TAKES ALL MGM 1936	Chambers, W. (*Murder for a wanton*) Melrose
SINS OF RACHEL CADE, THE WAR 1960	Mercer, C. (*Rachel Cade*) Collins
SIROCCO COL 1951	Kessel, J. Random House, N.Y.
SISTER KENNY RKO 1946	Kenny, E. *and* Ostenso, M. (*And they shall walk*) Dodd, N.Y.
SISTERS, THE WAR 1938	Brinig, M. Cobden-Sanderson
SITTING PRETTY FOX 1948	Davenport, *Mrs.* G. (*Belvedere*) Bobbs Merrill, Boston
SITUATION HOPELESS BUT NOT SERIOUS PAR 1964	Shaw, R. (*Hiding place, The*) Chatto & Windus
SIX BRIDGES TO CROSS GFD 1954	Dinneen, J. F. (*Anatomy of a crime*) Scribner, N.Y.
633 SQUADRON UA 1964	Smith, F. E. Hutchinson
SKIN GAME BI 1931	Galsworthy, J. (P) Duckworth

SKINNER STEPS OUT
UA 1929

Dodge, H. I. *and others* (*Skinner's dress suit*) (P)
French, N.Y.

SKYLARK
PAR 1941

Raphaelson, S. (P)
Various

SKYSCRAPER SOULS
MGM 1932

Baldwin, F. (*Skyscraper*)
Sampson Low

SLAUGHTER ON 10TH AVENUE
UI 1957

Keating, W. J. *and* Carter, H. (*Man who rocked the boat, The*)
Harper, N.Y.

SLEEPERS EAST
FOX 1934

Nebel, F.
Collins

SLEEPING TIGER, THE
INSIGNIA 1954

Moiseiwitsch, M.
Heinemann

SLIGHTLY HONOURABLE
UA 1939

Presnell, F. G. (*Send another coffin*)
Heinemann

SMALL BACK ROOM, THE
LF 1949

Balchin, N.
Collins

SMILEY
FOX 1955

Raymond, M.
Sylvan Press

SMOKY
FOX 1933
FOX 1946

James, W.
Various

SNAKE PIT, THE
FOX 1948

Ward, M. J.
Cassell

SNOWBOUND
RKO 1948

Innes, M. H. (*Lonely skier, The*)
Collins

SNOW DOG
ABP 1951

Curwood, J. O. (*Tentacles of the North*)
Various

SNOWS OF KILMANJARO, THE
FOX 1952

Hemingway, E.
Cape

SO BIG
WAR 1932
WAR 1953

Ferber, E.
Heinemann

SO BRIGHT THE FLAME
MGM 1952

Barringer, E. D. (*Bowery to Bellevue*)
Norton, N.Y.

SO DEAR TO MY HEART
RKO 1948

North, S.
Odhams

TITLE OF FILM	AUTHOR AND PUBLISHER
SO ENDS OUR NIGHT UA 1941	Remarque, E. M. (*Flotsam*) Hutchinson
SO EVIL MY LOVE PAR 1948	Shearing, J. (*For her to see*) Hutchinson
SO GOES MY LOVE UN 1946	Maxim, H. P. World, N.Y.
SOHO INCIDENT COL 1956	Westerby, R. (*Wide boys never work*) Methuen
SOLDIER AND THE LADY, THE RKO 1937	Verne, J. (*Michael Strogoff*) Sampson Low
SOLDIER IN THE RAIN WAR 1965	Goldman, W. Eyre & Spottiswoode
SOLDIER OF FORTUNE FOX 1955	Gann, E. K. Hodder & Stoughton
SOLDIERS THREE MGM 1951	Kipling, R. Macmillan
SOLID GOLD CADILLAC, THE COL 1956	Teichman, H. *and* Kaufman, G. S. (P) Random House, N.Y.
SOLITARY CHILD, THE BL 1957	Bawden, N. Collins
SOLO FOR SPARROW AA 1962	Wallace, E. (*Gunner, The*) Long
SOLOMON AND SHEBA UA 1959	Williams, J. Macdonald
SO LONG AT THE FAIR GFD 1950	Thorne, A. Heinemann
SOMBRERO MGM 1953	Niggli, J. (*Mexican village, A*) Sampson Low
SOMEBODY UP THERE LIKES ME MGM 1956	Graziano, R. Hammond
SOME CAME RUNNING MGM 1958	Jones, J. Collins
SOME LIKE IT HOT UA 1959	Wilder, W. *and* Diamond, I. A. L. Panther Bks
SOMETHING OF VALUE MGM 1957	Ruark, R. Hamilton
SOMETHING WILD UA 1962	Karmel, A. (*Mary Ann*) Secker & Warburg

150

SONG OF BERNADETTE, THE FOX 1943	Werfel, F. V. Hamilton
SONG TO REMEMBER, A COL 1945	Leslie, D. (*Polonaise*) Hutchinson
SON OF INDIA MGM 1931	Crawford, F. M. (*Mr. Isaacs*) Macmillan
SONS AND LOVERS FOX 1960	Lawrence, D. H. Heinemann
SO RED THE ROSE PAR 1935	Young, S. Cassell
SORORITY HOUSE RKO 1939	Chase, M. C. (P) French, N.Y.
SORRELL AND SON UA 1934	Deeping, W. Cassell
SO THIS IS LOVE WAR 1953	Moore, G. (*You're only human once*) Invincible Press
SO THIS IS NEW YORK UA 1948	Lardner, R. W. (*Big town, The*) Garden City, N.Y.
SOUND AND THE FURY, THE FOX 1959	Faulkner, W. Chatto & Windus
SOUND OF MUSIC, THE FOX 1965	Trapp, M. A. (*Story of the Trapp family singers*) Bles
SOUND OF THE FURY, THE UA 1951	Pagano, J. (*Condemned, The*) Invincible Press
SOUTH BY JAVA HEAD RANK 1960	MacLean, A. Collins
SOUTHERNER, THE UA 1945	Perry, G. S. (*Hold Autumn in your hands*) Sun Dial, N.Y.
SOUTH PACIFIC TODD AO 1958	Michener, J. A. (*Tales from the South Pacific*) Collins
SOUTH RIDING UA 1938	Holtby, W. Collins
SO WELL REMEMBERED RKO 1947	Hilton, J. Macmillan
SPANIARD'S CURSE, THE BL 1957	Pargeter, E. (*Assize of the dying, The*) Heinemann

SPANISH CAPE MYSTERY, THE
REP 1935

Queen, E.
Gollancz

SPANISH GARDENER, THE
RANK 1956

Cronin, A. J.
Gollancz

SPARE THE ROD
BL 1961

Croft, M.
Pan Bks

SPARTACUS
RANK 1959

Fast, H.
Panther Bks

SPEAK EASILY
MGM 1932

Kelland, C. B.
Harper, N.Y.

SPELL BOUND
UA 1945

Beeding, F.
World, N.Y.

SPENCER'S MOUNTAIN
WAR 1963

Hamner, E.
Dial Press, N.Y.

SPIDER'S WEB, THE
UA 1960

Christie, A. (P)
French

SPINSTER, THE
MGM 1962

Ashton-Warner, S.
Secker & Warburg

SPIRAL ROAD, THE
UI 1962

Hartog, J. de.
Hamilton

SPIRAL STAIRCASE, THE
RKO 1946

White, E. L. (*Some must watch*)
Ward Lock

SPIRIT OF ST. LOUIS, THE
WAR 1956

Lindbergh, C. A. (*We*)
Putnam, N.Y.

SPOILERS, THE
UN 1942
UN 1955

Beach, R.
Cassell

SPOT OF BOTHER, A
AB 1938

Sylvaine, V. (P)
French

SPY IN BLACK, THE
COL 1938

Clouston, J. S.
Blackwood

SPY OF NAPOLEON
TWICKENHAM 1931

Orczy, *Baroness* E.
Hodder & Stoughton

SPY WHO CAME IN FROM THE COLD, THE
PAR 1964

Le Carré, J.
Gollancz

SQUARE RING, THE
GFD 1953

Peterson, R.
Barker

TITLE OF FILM	AUTHOR AND PUBLISHER
SQUEAKER, THE GB 1937	Wallace, E. (P) Hodder & Stoughton
SQUEAKER, THE GB 1937	Wallace, E. Hodder & Stoughton
STAGECOACH UA 1939 FOX 1965	Haycox, E. (*Stage to Lordsburgh*) Hodder & Stoughton
STAGE DOOR RKO 1937	Kaufman, G. S. *and* Ferber, E. (P) Heinemann
STAGE FRIGHT WAR 1949	Jepson, S. (*Man running*) Macdonald
STALAG 17 PAR 1953	Bevan, D. *and* Trzcinski, E. (P) Dramatists, N.Y.
STALLION ROAD WAR 1947	Longstreet, S. Jarrolds
STAMPEDE ABP 1950	Mann, E. B. Triangle Bks, N.Y.
STARS IN MY CROWN MGM 1950	Brown, J. D. Hodder & Stoughton
STARS LOOK DOWN, THE GN 1940	Cronin, A. J. Gollancz
STATE FAIR FOX 1945 FOX 1962	Stong, P. D. Grosset, N.Y.
STATION WEST RKO 1948	Short, L. Collins
STEEL CAGE, THE GN 1956	Duffy, C. T. (*San Quentin*) Davies
STELLA FOX 1950	Disney, D. M. (*Family skeleton*) Doubleday, N.Y.
STELLA DALLAS UA 1937	Prouty, *Mrs.* O. Hodder & Stoughton
STOLEN AIRLINER, THE BL 1955	Pudney, J. (*Thursday adventure*) Evans
STOPOVER TOKYO FOX 1957	Marquand, J. P. Collins
STOP, YOU'RE KILLING ME WAR 1952	Runyon, D. *and* Lindsay, H. (*Slight case of murder, A*) (P) Dramatists, N.Y.

STORM CENTRE COL 1956	Taradash, D. *and* Moll, E. Panther Bks
STORM FEAR UA 1955	Seeley, C. Holt, N.Y.
STORM IN A TEACUP LF 1937	Bridie, J. (P) French
STORM OVER THE NILE GFD 1955	Mason, A. E. W. (*Four feathers, The*) Hodder & Stoughton
STORY OF DR. WASSELL, THE PAR 1944	Hilton, J. Macmillan
STORY OF ESTHER COSTELLO, THE COL 1957	Monsarrat, N. Cassell
STORY OF G.I. JOE, THE UA 1945	Pyle, E. T. Various
STORY OF GILBERT AND SULLIVAN, THE BL 1953	Baily, L. (*Gilbert and Sullivan book, The*) Cassell
STORY OF MANKIND, THE WAR 1957	Van Loon, H. W. Harrap
STORY OF PRIVATE POOLEY, THE CONTEMPORARY 1962	Jolly, C. (*Vengeance of Private Pooley, The*) Heinemann
STRANGE AFFAIR OF UNCLE HARRY, THE UN 1945	Job, T. (*Uncle Harry*) (P) French
STRANGE AWAKENING, THE AA 1958	Quentin, P. (*Puzzle for fiends*) Gollancz
STRANGE BOARDERS GB 1938	Oppenheim, E. P. (*Strange boarders of Palace Crescent*) Hodder & Stoughton
STRANGE CARGO MGM 1940	Sale, R. (*Not too narrow, not too deep*) Cassell
STRANGE DOOR, THE UI 1951	Stevenson, R. L. (*Sire of Maletroit's door, The*) Various
STRANGE INCIDENT FOX 1943	Clark, W. van T. (*Ox-Bow incident, The*) Gollancz
STRANGE INTERLUDE MGM 1932	O'Neill, E. G. (P) Cape

STRANGE INTRUDER ABP 1957	Fowler, H. M. (*Shades will not vanish*) Angus & Robertson
STRANGER, THE GN 1963	Beaumont, C. (*Intruder, The*) Muller
STRANGER CAME HOME EXCLUSIVE 1954	Sanders, G. (*Stranger at home*) Pilot Press
STRANGER IN MY ARMS, A UI 1958	Wilder, R. (*And ride a tiger*) W. H. Allen
STRANGER IN THE HOUSE JARFID 1966	Simenon, G. (*Strangers in the house*) Routledge
STRANGER IN TOWN EROS 1957	Chitterden, F. (*Uninvited, The*) Boardman
STRANGERS IN LOVE PAR 1932	Locke, W. J. (*Shorn lamb, The*) Lane
STRANGERS MAY KISS MGM 1931	Parrott, U. Cape
STRANGERS ON A TRAIN WAR 1951	Highsmith, P. Cresset Press
STRANGERS ON HONEYMOON GB 1937	Wallace, E. (*Northing tramp, The*) Hodder & Stoughton
STRANGER'S RETURN MGM 1933	Stong, P. D. Harcourt, N.Y.
STRANGERS WHEN WE MEET COL 1959	Hunter, E. Constable
STRANGER WALKED IN, THE REN 1949	Vosper, F. (*Love from a stranger*) (P) Collins
STRANGE WOMAN, THE UA 1946	Williams, B. A. Houghton Mifflin, Boston
STRANGE WORLD OF PLANET X, THE EROS 1958	Ray, R. Jenkins
STRAWBERRY ROAN BN 1944	Street, A. G. Faber
STRAW MAN, THE UA 1953	Disney, D. M. Doubleday, N.Y.
STREETCAR NAMED DESIRE, A WAR 1951	Williams, T. (P) Lehmann

STREET OF CHANCE
PAR 1942

Woolrich, C. (*Black curtain, The*)
Grosset, N.Y.

STREET OF SHADOWS
AA 1953

Meynell, L. (*Creaking chair, The*)
Collins

STREET SCENE
UA 1931

Rice, E. (P)
French, N.Y.

STRICTLY DISHONOURABLE
UN 1931
MGM 1951

Sturges, P. (P)
Liveright, N.Y.

STRIKE ME PINK
UA 1936

Kelland, C. B. (*Dreamland*)
Miles

STRIP-TEASE MURDERS
UA 1943

Lee, G. R.
Lane

STRONGER THEN FEAR
RKO 1952

Brady, L. (*Edge of doom*)
Cresset Press

STUDS LONIGAN
UA 1964

Farrell, J. T.
W. H. Allen

STUDY IN SCARLET, THE
WW 1933

Doyle, *Sir* A. C.
Ward Lock

SUBTERRANEANS, THE
MGM 1960

Kerouac, J.
Deutsch

SUDDEN FEAR
RKO 1952

Sherry, E.
Hodder & Stoughton

SUDDENLY, LAST SUMMER
COL 1959

Williams, T. (P)
Secker & Warburg

SUGARFOOT
WAR 1951

Kelland, C. B.
Grosset, N.Y.

SUICIDE MISSION
EROS 1957

Howarth, D. (*Shetland bus, The*)
Nelson

SUMMER AND SMOKE
PAR 1959

Williams, T. (P)
Secker & Warburg

SUMMER HOLIDAY
MGM 1948

O'Neill, E. G. (*Ah wilderness*) (P)
Cape

SUMMER LIGHTNING
BD 1932

Wodehouse, P. G.
Jenkins

SUMMER MADNESS
UA 1955

Laurents, A. (*Time of the cuckoo, The*) (P)
Random House, N.Y.

SUMMER MAGIC DISNEY 1963	Wiggins, K. D. (*Mother Carey's chickens*) Hodder & Stoughton
SUMMER OF THE SEVENTEENTH DOLL, THE UA 1959	Lawler, R. (P) Fontana
SUMMER PLACE, A WAR 1959	Wilson, S. Cassell
SUN ALSO RISES, THE FOX 1957	Hemingway, E. (*Fiesta*) Cape
SUNDAY IN NEW YORK MGM 1964	Krasna, N. (P) Random House, N.Y.
SUNDOWN UA 1941	Lyndon, B. Lane
SUNDOWNERS, THE WAR 1960	Cleary, J. (*Back of Beyond*) Collins
SUNDOWN JIM FOX 1942	Haycox, E. Paul
SUNRISE AT CAMPOBELLO WAR 1960	Schary, D. (P) Random House, N.Y.
SUNSET PASS PAR 1933 RKO 1946	Grey, Z. Hodder & Stoughton
SUN SHINES BRIGHT, THE REP 1953	Cobb, I. S. (*Old Judge Priest*) Grosset, N.Y.
SURPRISE PACKAGE COL 1960	Buchwald, A. Gollancz
SURRENDER—HELL ABP 1959	Harkins, P. (*Blackburn's headhunters*) Cassell
SUSAN AND GOD MGM 1940	Crothers, R. (P) Random House, N.Y.
SUSAN SLADE WAR 1962	Hume, D. (*Sins of Susan Slade, The*) Dell, N.Y.
SUSPECT BL 1960	Balchin, N. (*Sort of traitors, A*) Collins
SUSPECT, THE UN 1944	Ronald, J. (*This way out*) Rich & Cowan
SUSPICION RKO 1941	Iles, F. (*Before the fact*) Gollancz

SUZY
  MGM 1936

Gorman, H.
Cassell

SVENGALI
  WAR 1931
  REN 1954

Du Maurier, G. (*Trilby*)
Various

SWAMP WATER
  FOX 1941

Bell, V.
Collins

SWAN, THE
  MGM 1956

Molnar, F. (P)
Boni, N.Y.

SWEET BIRD OF YOUTH
  MGM 1962

Williams, T. (P)
Secker & Warburg

SWISS FAMILY ROBINSON
  RKO 1940
  DISNEY 1960

Wyss, J. D.
Various

SWORD AND THE ROSE, THE
  RKO 1953

Kester, P. (*When knighthood was in flower*) (P)
French, N.Y.

SWORD AND THE ROSE, THE
  RKO 1953

Major, C. (*When knighthood was in flower*)
Grayson

SWORD IN THE STONE
  DISNEY 1963

White, T. H.
Collins

SYLVIA
  PAR 1963

Cunningham, E. V.
Deutsch

SYLVIA SCARLETT
  RKO 1935

Mackenzie, *Sir* C.
Various

SYMPHONY IN TWO FLATS
  GFD 1931

Novello, I. (P)
Methuen

T

TAGGART
  UI 1965

L'Amour, L.
Corgi Bks

TAKE CARE OF MY LITTLE GIRL
  FOX 1951

Goodin, P.
Dutton, N.Y.

TAKE HER, SHE'S MINE
  MGM 1963

Ephron, P. *and* Ephron, H. (P)
Random House, N.Y.

TAKE MY LIFE
  EL 1948

Graham, W.
Ward Lock

TALE OF TWO CITIES, A
  MGM 1935
  RANK 1957

Dickens, C.
Various

TALES OF TERROR WAR 1963	Poe, E. A. (*Morella; Black cat, The; Case of Dr. Valdemar*) Various
TALK OF A MILLION ABP 1951	D'Alton, L. L. (*Money doesn't matter*) (P) Duffy, Dublin
TALL HEADLINES, THE GN 1951	Lindop, A. E. Heinemann
TALL MAN RIDING WAR 1955	Fox, N. A. Collins
TALL MEN, THE FOX 1955	Fisher, C. Houghton Mifflin, Boston
TALL STORY WAR 1960	Nemerov, H. (*Homecoming game, The*) Gollancz
TALL STORY WAR 1960	Lindsay, H. *and* Crouse, R. (P) Random House, N.Y.
TAMAHINE WAR 1963	Niklaus, T. Lane
TAMANGO COL 1959	Merimee, P. Blackie
TAMING OF THE SHREW, THE INDIVIDUAL 1933 COL 1966	Shakespeare, W. (P) Various
TAMMY TELL ME TRUE RANK 1961	Sumner, G. Bobbs Merrill, Indianapolis
TAP ROOTS UI 1948	Street, J. Sun Dial, N.Y.
TARAS BULBA UA 1962	Gogol, N. Dent
TARNISHED ANGELS, THE UI 1957	Faulkner, W. (*Pylon*) Chatto & Windus
TASTE OF HONEY, A BRYANSTON 1961	Delaney, S. (P) Methuen
TAXI TO TOBRUK MIRACLE FILMS 1961	Havard, R. Collins
TEA AND SYMPATHY MGM 1956	Anderson, R. (P) Random House, N.Y.
TEAHOUSE OF THE AUGUST MOON, THE MGM 1957	Patrick, J. (P) Heinemann

TEAHOUSE OF THE AUGUST MOON,   Sneider, V. J.
THE   Macmillan
MGM 1957

TELL ENGLAND   Raymond, E.
CAPITOL 1931   Cassell

TELL TALE HEART, THE   Poe, E. A.
ABP 1960   Various

TEMPEST   Pushkin, A. (*Captain's daughter, The*)
PAR 1959   Various

TEMPTATION   Hichens, R. (*Bella Donna*)
COL 1930   Heinemann

TEMPTATION HARBOUR   Simenon, G. (*Newhaven-Dieppe*)
AB 1947   Routledge

TEN DAYS TO DIE   Musmanno, M. A.
INTERCONTINENTAL 1955   Davies

TENDER IS THE NIGHT   Fitzgerald, F. S. K.
FOX 1959   Grey Walls Press

TEN LITTLE INDIANS   Christie, A. (*Ten little niggers*) (P)
ABP 1965   French

TEN LITTLE INDIANS   Christie, A. (*Ten little niggers*)
ABP 1965   Collins

TEN LITTLE NIGGERS   Christie, A. (P)
FOX 1945   French

TEN LITTLE NIGGERS   Christie, A.
FOX 1945   Collins

TEN MINUTE ALIBI   Armstrong, A. *and* Shaw, H.
SOSKIN 1934   Methuen

TEN MINUTE ALIBI   Armstrong, A. (P)
SOSKIN 1934   Gollancz

TENNESSEE'S PARTNER   Harte, B.
RKO 1955   Various

TEN SECONDS TO HELL   Bachmann, L. (*Phoenix*)
UA 1958   Collins

10.30 p.m. SUMMER   Duras, M. (10.30 *p.m. on a summer night*)
UA 1965   Calder

TENSION AT TABLE ROCK   Gruber, G. (*Bitter Sage*)
RKO 1956   Wright & Brown

TERM OF TRIAL
WAR 1962

Barlow, J.
Hamilton

TERRIBLE BEAUTY, A
UA 1960

Roth, A.
Hutchinson

TERROR, THE
ALL 1941

Wallace, E.
Collins

TERROR, THE
ALL 1941

Wallace, E. (P)
French

TESS OF THE STORM COUNTRY
FOX 1960

White, G. M.
Various

THANK YOU, JEEVES
FOX 1936

Wodehouse, P. G.
Jenkins

THANK YOU MR. MOTO
FOX 1937

Marquand, J. P.
Jenkins

THARK
GB 1932

Travers, B. (P)
Bickers

THAT CERTAIN FEELING
PAR 1956

Kerr, J. *and* Brooke, E. (*King of hearts*) (P)
Doubleday, N.Y.

THAT DANGEROUS AGE
LF 1948

Kennedy, M. (*Autumn*) (P)
French

THAT DARN CAT
DISNEY 1964

Gordons, The. (*Undercover cat*)
Macdonald

THAT LADY
FOX 1954

O'Brien, K.
Heinemann

THAT WOMAN OPPOSITE
MON 1957

Carr, J. D. (*Emperor's snuffbox, The*)
Hamilton

THEIR SECRET AFFAIR
WAR 1956

Marquand, J. P. (*Melville Goodwin, USA*)
Hale

THÉRÈSE
GALA 1965

Mauriac, F.
Eyre & Spottiswoode

THESE CHARMING PEOPLE
PAR 1931

Arlen, M.
Collins

THESE THOUSAND HILLS
FOX 1958

Guthrie, A. B.
Hutchinson

THESE THREE
UA 1936

Hellman, L. F. (*Children's hour, The*) (P)
Knopf, N.Y.

THEY CAME BY NIGHT
FOX 1940

Lyndon, B. (P)
Hamilton

THEY CAME TO A CITY
EALING 1945

Priestley, J. B. (P)
Heinemann

THEY CAME TO CORDURA
COL 1959

Swarthout, G.
Heinemann

THEY DRIVE BY NIGHT
WAR 1940

Bezzerides, A. I. (*Long haul*)
Cape

THEY GAVE HIM A GUN
MGM 1937

Cowen, W. J.
Heinemann

THEY KNEW MR. KNIGHT
GFD 1946

Whipple, D.
Murray

THEY KNEW WHAT THEY WANTED
RKO 1940

Howard, S. C. (P)
Harcourt, N.Y.

THEY MADE ME A FUGITIVE
WAR 1947

Budd, J. (*Convict has escaped, A*)
Joseph

THEY'RE A WEIRD MOB
RANK 1965

Culotta, N.
Kaye

THEY SAVED LONDON
EROS 1957

Newman, B.
Hamilton

THEY WERE EXPENDABLE
MGM 1945

White, W. L.
Hamilton

THEY WERE SISTERS
GDF 1945

Whipple, D.
Murray

THEY WON'T FORGET
WAR 1937

Greene, W. (*Death in the deep South*)
Cassell

THIEVES' HIGHWAY
FOX 1949

Bezzarides, A. I. (*Thieves' market*)
Scribner, N.Y.

**THING FROM ANOTHER WORLD,
THE**
RKO 1951

Campbell, J. W. (*Who goes there?*)
Shasta Pubns, Chicago

THIN MAN, THE
MGM 1934

Hammett, D.
Barker

THINGS HAPPEN AT NIGHT
REN 1947

Harvey, F. (*Poltergeist, The*) (P)
Dent

THINGS TO COME
UA 1936

Wells, H. G. (*Shape of things to come, The*)
Hutchinson

THINGS TO COME
UA 1936

Wells, H. G. (P)
Cresset Press

THIRD DAY, THE
WAR 1965

Hayes, J.
W. H. Allen

THIRD, MAN, THE
GFD 1950

Greene, G.
Heinemann

THIRD MAN ON THE MOUNTAIN
DISNEY 1959

Ullman, J. R. (*Banner in the sky*)
Collins

THIRD PARTY RISK
EXCLUSIVE 1955

Bentley, N.
Joseph

THIRD TIME LUCKY
ANGOFILM 1948

Butler, G. (*They cracked her glass slipper*)
Jarrolds

13 WEST STREET
BL 1962

Brackett, L. (*Tiger amongst us, The*)
Boardman

THIRTY-NINE STEPS, THE
GB 1935
RANK 1959

Buchan, J.
Various

THIRTY SECONDS OVER TOKIO
MGM 1944

Lawson, T.
Hammond

THIS ABOVE ALL
FOX 1942

Knight, E. M.
Cassell

THIS EARTH IS MINE
UI 1959

Hobart, *Mrs.* A. T. (*Cup and the sword, The*)
Cassell

THIS GUN FOR HIRE
PAR 1942

Greene, G. (*Gun for sale, A*)
Various

THIS IS MY STREET
WAR 1963

Maynard, N.
Corgi Bks

THIS HAPPY BREED
TC 1944

Coward, N. (P)
Heinemann

THIS HAPPY FEELING
RANK 1958

Herbert, F. H. (*For love or money*) (P)
Dramatists, N.Y.

THIS ISLAND EARTH
UI 1955

Jones, R. F.
Shasta Pubns, Chicago

THIS IS MY AFFAIR
FOX 1951

Weidman, J. (*I can get it for you wholesale*)
Heinemann

THIS SPORTING LIFE
RANK 1962

Storey, D.
Longmans

THIS WAS A WOMAN
FOX 1948

Morgan, J. (P)
French

TITLE OF FILM	AUTHOR AND PUBLISHER
THIS WOMAN IS MINE UN 1941	Gabriel, G. W. (*I, James Lewis*) Doubleday, N.Y.
THOSE GALLOWAYS DISNEY 1965	Annixter, P. (*Swift water*) Houghton Mifflin, Boston
THOSE WERE THE DAYS PAR 1940	Pinero, *Sir* A. W. (*Magistrate, The*) (P) Heinemann
THOUSAND CLOWNS, A UA 1964	Gardner, H. (P) Random House, N.Y.
THREE CAME HOME FOX 1949	Keith, A. Joseph
THREE COINS IN THE FOUNTAIN FOX 1954	Secondari, J. (*Coins in the fountain*) Eyre & Spottiswoode
THREE COMRADES MGM 1938	Remarque, E. M. Hutchinson
THREE FACES OF EVE, THE FOX 1957	Thigpen, C. H. *and* Cleckley, H. M. Secker & Warburg
3 FOR BEDROOM C INT 1952	Lieberson, G. Doubleday, N.Y.
THREE GODFATHERS, THE MGM 1936	Kyne, P. B. Various
THREE LIVES OF THOMASINA, THE DISNEY 1963	Gallico, P. (*Thomasina*) Joseph
THREE MEN IN A BOAT BL 1956	Jerome, J. K. Various
THREE MUSKETEERS, THE RKO 1935 FOX 1939 MGM 1949	Dumas, A. Various
THREE ON A SPREE UA 1961	McCutcheon, G. B. (*Brewster's millions*) Various
THREE WEIRD SISTERS, THE BN 1948	Armstrong, C. (*Case of the weird sisters, The*) Gifford
THREE WORLDS OF GULLIVER, THE COL 1959	Swift, J. (*Gulliver's travels*) Various
THUNDERBALL UA 1964	Fleming, I. Cape
THUNDERHEAD, SON OF FLICKA FOX 1945	O'Hara, M. Eyre & Spottiswoode

TITLE OF FILM	AUTHOR AND PUBLISHER
THUNDER IN THE EAST PAR 1951	Moorehead, A. (*Rage of the vulture, The*) Hamilton
THUNDER MOUNTAIN FOX 1935	Grey, Z. Hodder & Stoughton
THUNDER ROCK MGM 1943	Ardrey, R. (P) Hamilton
THUNDERING HERD PAR 1933	Grey, Z. Hodder & Stoughton
TIARA TAHITI RANK 1962	Cotterell, G. Eyre & Spottiswoode
TIGER BY THE TAIL EROS 1955	Chase, J. H. Hale
TIGER IN THE SMOKE RANK 1956	Allingham, W. Chatto & Windus
TIGER WALKS, A DISNEY 1964	Niall, I. Heinemann
TILL THE END OF TIME RKO 1946	Busch, N. (*They dream of home*) Grosset, N.Y.
TIMBER FURY EL 1950	Curwood, J. O. (*Retribution*) Various
TIMBERJACK REP 1954	Cushman, D. (*Ripper from Rawhide*) Macmillan, N.Y.
TIME GENTLEMEN, PLEASE! ABP 1952	Minney, R. J. (*Nothing to lose*) Macdonald
TIME MACHINE, THE MGM 1960	Wells, H. G. Heinemann
TIME OF INDIFFERENCE CONT 1967	Moravia, A. Secker & Warburg
TIME OF YOUR LIFE UA 1948	Saroyan, W. (P) Faber
TIME OUT OF MIND UN 1947	Field, R. Macmillan
TIME TO LOVE AND A TIME TO DIE RANK 1957	Remarque, E. M. Hutchinson
TIME TO REMEMBER AA 1962	Wallace, E. (*Man who bought London*) Ward Lock

TIMOTHY'S QUEST
PAR 1936

Wiggin, K. D.
Partridge

TISH
MGM 1942

Rinehart, M. R. (*Tish marches on*)
Cassell

TOBACCO ROAD
FOX 1941

Caldwell, E.
Falcon Press

TOBACCO ROAD
FOX 1941

Caldwell, E. *and* Kirkland, J. (P)
Falcon Press

TOBY TYLER
DISNEY 1959

Kaler, J. O.
Various

TO CATCH A THIEF
PAR 1955

Dodge, D.
Penguin

TO DOROTHY, A SON
BL 1954

Macdougall, R. (P)
Evans

TO HAVE AND HAVE NOT
WAR 1944

Hemingway, E.
Cape

TO HELL AND BACK
UI 1955

Murphy, A.
Hammond

TO KILL A MOCKING BIRD
UI 1962

Lee, H.
Penguin

TOMAHAWK TRAIL, THE
UA 1950

Cooper, J. F. (*Leather stocking tales*)
Various

TO MARY—WITH LOVE
FOX 1936

Sherman, R.
Faber

TOM BROWN'S SCHOOLDAYS
RKO 1940
REN 1951

Hughes, T.
Various

TOM JONES
UA 1962

Fielding, H.
Various

TOMORROW IS FOREVER
RKO 1946

Bristow, G.
Heinemann

TOMORROW THE WORLD
UA 1944

D'Usseau, A. *and* Gow, J. (*Deep are the roots*) (P)
Dramatists, N.Y.

TOM THUMB
MGM 1958

Grimm, J. L. R. *and* Grimm, W. K.
Various

TONIGHT AT 8.30
GFD 1952

Coward, N. (P)
Heinemann

TONIGHT IS OURS PAR 1933	Coward, N. (*Queen was in the parlour, The*) (P) Heinemann
TONIGHT WE SING FQX 1953	Hurok, S. *and* Goode, R. (*Impressario*) Macdonald
TONKA DISNEY 1958	Appel, D. (*Comanche*) Various
TOO MUCH, TOO SOON WAR 1958	Barrymore, D. *and* Frank, G. Muller
TOO YOUNG TO MARRY WAR 1931	Flavin, M. (*Broken dishes*) (P) French, N.Y.
TOPKAPI UA 1964	Ambler, E. (*Light of day, The*) Heinemann
TOPPER MGM 1937	Smith, T. Sun Dial, N.Y.
TOPPER TAKES A TRIP UA 1939	Smith, T. Methuen
TORCH BEARERS, THE FOX 1935	Kelly, G. (P) French, N.Y.
TORTILLA FLAT MGM 1942	Steinbeck, J. Penguin
TO SIR, WITH LOVE COL 1966	Braithwaite, E. R. Bodley Head
TO THE LAST MAN PAR 1933	Grey, Z. Hodder & Stoughton
TO THE PUBLIC DANGER GFD 1948	Hamilton, P. (P) Constable
TOUCH OF LARCENY, A PAR 1959	Garve, A. (*Megstone plot, The*) Collins
TOWN LIKE ALICE, A RANK 1956	Shute, N. Heinemann
TOWN TAMER PAR 1965	Gruber, F. Barker
TOWN WITHOUT PITY UA 1961	Gregor, M. Heinemann
TOYS IN THE ATTIC UA 1963	Hellman, L. (P) Random House, N.Y.
TRACK OF THE CAT WAR 1954	Clark, W. van T. Gollancz

TRADER HORN
MGM 1931

Horn, A.
Cape

TRAIL DUST
PAR 1936

Mulford, C. E.
Hodder & Stoughton

TRAIL OF THE YUKON
MONOGRAM 1949

Curwood, J. O. (*Gold hunters, The*)
Various

TRANSCONTINENTAL EXPRESS
REP 1950

Nevins, F. J. (*Yankee dared, A*)
By the Author, Chicago

TRAPEZE
UA 1956

Catto, M. (*Killing frost, The*)
Heinemann

TRAVELLER'S JOY
GFD 1951

Macrae, A. (P)
French

TREAD SOFTLY
APEX 1952

Verner, G. (*Show must go on, The*)
Wright & Brown

TREASURE HUNT
BL 1952

Farrel, M. J. *and* Perry, J. (P)
Collins

TREASURE ISLAND
MGM 1934
RKO 1949

Stevenson, R. L.
Various

TREASURE OF LOST CANYON, THE
UI 1952

Stevenson, R. L. (*Treasure of Franchard*)
Various

TREASURE OF SIERRA MADRE
WAR 1948

Traven, B.
Cape

**TREASURE OF THE GOLDEN
CONDOR**
FOX 1953

Marshall, E. (*Jewel of Mahabar*)
Hodder & Stoughton

TREE GROWS IN BROOKLYN, A
FOX 1945

Smith, B.
Heinemann

TRENT'S LAST CASE
BL 1952

Bentley, E. C.
Various

TRIAL
MGM 1955

Mankiewicz, D. M.
Deutsch

TRIAL, THE
BL 1963

Kafka, F.
Secker & Warburg

TRIAL OF MARY DUGAN, THE
MGM 1929

Veiller, B. (P)
French

TRIALS OF OSCAR WILDE, THE
EROS 1960

Hyde, H. M.
Hodge

TRIO
GFD 1950

Maugham, W. S.
Heinemann

TRIPLE CROSS, THE
AA 1967

Owen, F. (*Eddie Chapman story, The*)
Hamilton

TROJAN BROTHERS, THE
BN 1946

Johnson, P. H.
Joseph

TROPIC ZONE
PAR 1953

Gill, T. (*No place for women*)
Putnam, N.Y.

TROTTIE TRUE
TC 1949

Brahms, C. *and* Simon, S. J.
Joseph

TROUBLE FOR TWO
MGM 1936

Stevenson, R. L. (*Suicide club, The*)
Various

TROUBLE IN THE GLEN
REP 1954

Walsh, M.
Chambers

TROUBLE WITH ANGELS, THE
COL 1965

Trahey, J. (*Life with Mother Superior*)
Joseph

TROUBLE WITH HARRY, THE
PAR 1955

Story, J. T.
Boardman

TRUE AS A TURTLE
RANK 1957

Coates, J.
Gollancz

TRUSTED OUTLAW, THE
REP 1937

McCulley, J.
Hutchinson

TUNES OF GLORY
UA 1960

Kennaway, J.
Putnam

TUNNEL OF LOVE, THE
MGM 1959

De Vries, P.
Gollancz

TUNNEL OF LOVE, THE
MGM 1959

Fields, J. *and* De Vries, P. (P)
French

TURNABOUT
UA 1940

Smith, T.
Methuen

TURN THE KEY SOFTLY
GFD 1953

Brophy, J.
Collins

TUTTLES OF TAHITI, THE
RKO 1942

Nordhoff, C. B. *and* Hall, J. N. (*No more gas*)
Chapman & Hall

TWELVE O'CLOCK HIGH
FOX 1949

Lay, B. *and* Bartlett, S.
Harper, N.Y.

27TH DAY
COL 1957

Mantley, J.
Joseph

20,000 LEAGUES UNDER THE SEA
DISNEY 1954

Verne, J.
Various

20,000 YEARS IN SING SING
IN 1933

Lawes, L. E.
Garden City, N.Y.

TWENTY-ONE DAYS
LF 1940

Galsworthy, J. (*First and the last, The*)
Heinemann

29, ACACIA AVENUE
COL 1945

Constanduros, M. *and* Constanduros, D.
(*Acacia Avenue*) (*P*)
French

TWICE ROUND THE DAFFODILS
AA 1962

Cargill, P. and Beale, J. (*Ring for Catty*) (P)
French

TWILIGHT FOR THE GODS
RANK 1957

Gann, E. K.
Hodder & Stoughton

TWO FACES OF DR. JEKYLL, THE
COL 1958

Stevenson, R. L. (*Dr. Jekyll and Mr. Hyde*)
Various

TWO FOR THE ROAD
FOX 1967

Raphael, F.
Cape

TWO FOR THE SEESAW
UA 1962

Gibson, W. (P)
French

TWO IN THE DARK
RKO 1936

Burgess, G. (*Two o'clock courage*)
Triangle Bks, N.Y.

TWO KINDS OF WOMAN
PAR 1932

Sherwood, R. E. (*This is New York*) (P)
Scribner, N.Y.

TWO LEFT FEET
BL 1965

Leslie, D. S. (*In my solitude*)
Hutchinson

TWO-LETTER ALIBI
BL 1962

Garve, A. (*Death and the sky above us*)
Pan Bks

TWO LOVES
MGM 1960

Ashton-Warner, S.
Secker & Warburg

TWO MRS CARROLLS, THE
WAR 1947

Vale, M. (P)
Allen & Unwin

TWO RODE TOGETHER
COL 1961

Cooke, W. E.
Mills & Boon

TWO WEEKS IN ANOTHER TOWN
MGM 1962

Shaw, I.
Cape

TWO YEARS BEFORE THE MAST
PAR 1946

Dana, R. H.
Various

U

UGLY AMERICAN, THE
UI 1962

Lederer, W. J. *and* Burdick, E. L.
Gollancz

UGLY DACHSHUND, THE
DISNEY 1966

Stern, G. B.
Cassell

ULYSSES
ARCHWAY 1954

Homer (*Iliad*)
Various

ULYSSES
BL 1966

Joyce, J.
Lane

UNCHAINED
WAR 1954

Scudder, K. J. (*Prisoners are people*)
Doubleday, N.Y.

UNCLE SILAS
TC 1947

Le Fanu, S.
Oxford U.P.

UNCONQUERED
PAR 1947

Swanson, N. H.
Doubleday, N.Y.

UNDER CAPRICORN
WAR 1949

Simpson, H.
Heinemann

UNDER MY SKIN
FOX 1950

Hemingway, E. (*My old man*)
Cape

UNDER NEW MANAGEMENT
BUTCHER 1946

Jacobs, N.
Hutchinson

UNDER THE CARIBBEAN
BL 1954

Hass, H. (*Diving for adventure*)
Jarrolds

UNDER THE RED ROBE
FOX 1937

Weyman, S.
Various

UNDER THE TONTO RIM
PAR 1933

Grey, Z.
Hodder & Stoughton

UNDER TWO FLAGS
FOX 1936

Ouida
Chatto & Windus

UNEASY TERMS
BN 1948

Cheyney, P.
Collins

UNEXPECTED UNCLE
RKO 1941

Hatch, E.
Farrar, N.Y.

UNFORGIVEN, THE
UA 1960

LeMay, A. (*Siege at Dancing Bird, The*)
Collins

UNGUARDED HOUR, THE
MGM 1936

Merivale, B. (P)
French

UNHOLY LOVE HP 1932	Flaubert, G. (*Madame Bovary*) Cape
UNINVITED, THE PAR 1944	Macardle, D. (*Uneasy freehold*) Doubleday, N.Y.
UNION STATION PAR 1950	Walsh, T. (*Nighmare in Manhattan*) Little Brown, Boston
UNSEEN, THE PAR 1945	White, E. L. (*Her heart in her throat*) Grosset, N.Y.
UNSUSPECTED, THE WAR 1947	Armstrong, C. Harrap
UNTAMED PAR 1940	Lewis, S. (*Mantrap*) Cape
UNTAMED FOX 1955	Moray, H. Museum Press
UNTIL THEY SAIL MGM 1957	Michener, J. A. (*Return to paradise*) Secker & Warburg
UP FROM THE BEACH FOX 1964	Barr, G. (*Epitaph for an enemy*) Hutchinson
UP FRONT UI 1951	Mauldin, W. H. Various
UP PERISCOPE WAR 1959	White, R. Collins
UPSTAIRS AND DOWNSTAIRS RANK 1959	Thorn, R. S. Spearman
UP THE DOWN STAIRCASE WAR 1966	Kaufman, B. Barker

V

VAGABOND KING, THE PAR 1930 PAR 1956	McCarthy, J. H. (P) French
VALIANT IS THE WORD FOR CARRIE PAR 1938	Benefield, B. Heinemann
VALLEY OF DECISION MGM 1945	Davenport, M. Collins
VALLEY OF THE GIANTS WAR 1938	Kyne, P. B. Hodder & Stoughton

VALLEY OF THE SUN RKO 1942	Kelland, C. B. Various
VALUE FOR MONEY RANK 1955	Boothroyd, D. Laurie
VANESSA MGM 1935	Walpole, *Sir* H. Macmillan
VANISHING AMERICAN, THE REP 1955	Grey, Z. Hodder & Stoughton
VANISHING VIRGINIAN, THE MGM 1941	Williams, *Mrs.* R. (*Father was a handful*) Joseph
VANITY FAIR HOL 1932	Thackeray, W. M. Various
VEILED WOMAN FOX 1929	Reed, M. (*Spinner in the sun*) Putnam
VENDETTA RKO 1951	Merimee, P. (*Columbia*) Hamilton
VENETIAN AFFAIR, THE MGM 1966	McInnes, H. Collins
VENETIAN BIRD GFD 1952	Canning, V. Hodder & Stoughton
VENGEANCE BL 1963	Siodmak, C. (*Donovan's brain*) Corgi Bks
VENGEANCE VALLEY MGM 1950	Short, L. Collins
VERTIGO PAR 1958	Boileau, P. *and* Narcejac, T. (*Living and the dead, The*) Arrow Bks
VESSEL OF WRATH, THE PAR 1938	Maugham, W. S. (*Beachcomber*) Heinemann
VICE VERSA TC 1948	Anstey, F. Murray
VICKI FOX 1953	Fisher, S. (*I wake up screaming*) Hale
VICTORIA REGINA RKO 1937	Housman, L. (P) Cape
VICTORS, THE BL 1963	Barons, A. (*Human kind, The*) Cape

173

TITLE OF FILM	AUTHOR AND PUBLISHER
VICTORY PAR 1940	Conrad, J. Various
VIKINGS, THE UA 1958	Marshall, E. (*Viking, The*) Muller
VILLAGE OF THE DAMNED, THE MGM 1960	Wyndham, J. (*Midwich cuckoos, The*) Penguin
VINTAGE, THE MGM 1957	Keir, U. Collins
VIOLATORS, THE RKO 1957	Beckhardt, I. *and* Brown, W. Arco
VIOLENT SATURDAY FOX 1955	Heath, W. L. Hamilton
V.I.P.'S, THE MGM 1963	Albert, M. Mayflower
VIRGINIAN, THE PAR 1929	Wister, O. Various
VIRGIN ISLAND BL 1958	White, R. (*Our virgin island*) Gollancz
VIRTUOUS HUSBAND UN 1931	Davis, D. (*Apron strings*) (P) French, N.Y.
VISIT, THE FOX 1964	Durrenmatt, F. (P) French, N.Y.
VISIT TO A SMALL PLANET PAR 1959	Vidal, G. (P) Little, Toronto
VIVA ZAPATA! FOX 1952	Pinchon, E. (*Zapata the unconquerable*) Doubleday, N.Y.
VOICE OF BUGLE ANN MGM 1936	Kantor, M. Selwyn & Blount
VOICE OF THE TURTLE WAR 1947	Druten, J. van. (P) Joseph
VOLPONE SIRITZKY 1947	Jonson, B. (P) Allen & Unwin
VON RYAN'S EXPRESS FOX 1964	Westheimer, D. Joseph

W

WACO PAR 1967	Sanford, H. *and* Lamb, M. (*Emporia*) Hale

WAGES OF FEAR FILMS DE FRANCE 1953	Arnaud, G. British Publishers Guild
WAGON WHEELS PAR 1934	Grey, Z. (*Fighting caravans*) Hodder & Stoughton
WAKE ME WHEN IT'S OVER FOX 1960	Singer, H. Putnam, N.Y.
WAKE OF THE RED WITCH REP 1948	Roark, G. Aldor
WALK IN THE SUN, A FOX 1945	Brown, H. P. M. Secker & Warburg
WALK ON THE WILD SIDE, A COL 1962	Algren, N. Ace
WALLS OF GOLD FOX 1933	Norris, K. Murray
WALLS OF JERICHO, THE FOX 1949	Wellman, P. I. Laurie
WALTZ OF THE TOREADORS RANK 1962	Anouilh, J. (P) French
WANDERER OF THE WASTELAND PAR 1935 RKO 1945	Grey, Z. Hodder & Stoughton
WANDERING JEW, THE OLY 1935	Thurston, E. T. (P) Putnam
WAR AND PEACE PAR 1956	Tolstoy, L. Macmillan
WAR CORRESPONDENT INT 1951	Pyle, E. T. (*Here's your war*) Various
WARE CASE, THE FOX 1939	Bancroft, G. P. (P) Methuen
WARLOCK FOX 1959	Hall, O. Bodley Head
WAR LOVER, THE COL 1963	Hersey, J. Hamilton
WARN THAT MAN AB 1942	Sylvaine, V. (P) French
WARNING TO WANTONS, A AQUILA 1949	Mitchell, M. Heinemann

175

WAR OF THE WORLDS PAR 1953	Wells, H. G. Heinemann
WAR WAGON UI 1966	Huffaker, C. (*Badman*) Muller
WATCH IT SAILOR COL 1961	Cary, F. L. *and* King, P. (P) Elek
WATCH ON THE RHINE WAR 1943	Hellman, L. F. (P) Random House, N.Y.
WATERFRONT GFD 1950	Brophy, J. Various
WATER GYPSIES, THE SDC 1932	Herbert, *Sir* A. P. Methuen
WATERLOO BRIDGE UN 1932 MGM 1940	Sherwood, R. E. (P) Scribner, N.Y.
WATUSI MGM 1958	Haggard, *Sir* H. R. (*King Solomon's mines*) Various
WAY OF A GAUCHO FOX 1952	Childs, H. (*Gaucho*) Prentice-Hall, N.Y.
WAYS AND MEANS GFD 1952	Coward, N. (P) Heinemann
WAY TO THE GOLD, THE FOX 1957	Steele, W. D. Doubleday, N.Y.
WAYWARD BUS, THE FOX 1957	Steinbeck, J. Heinemann
WAY WEST, THE UA 1966	Guthrie, A. B. Corgi
WEAK AND THE WICKED, THE ABP 1953	Henry, J. (*Who lie in gaol*) Gollancz
WEAKER SEX, THE TC 1948	McCracken, E. (*No medals*) (P) French
WE ARE NOT ALONE WAR 1939	Hilton, J. Macmillan
WE DIE ALONE REN 1959	Howarth, D. (*Escape alone*) Collins
WEE WILLIE WINKIE FOX 1937	Kipling, R. Macmillan

WEEKEND AT DUNKIRK FOX 1965	Merle, R. (*Weekend at Zuydcoote*) Lehmann
WEEK-END AT THE WALDORF MGM 1945	Bolton, G. Grosset, N.Y.
WEEK-END MARRIAGE IN 1932	Baldwin, F. (*Part-time wives*) Sampson Low
WEEK-ENDS ONLY FOX 1932	Fabian, W. (*Week-end girl*) Paul
WE JOINED THE NAVY WAR 1962	Winton, J. Joseph
WE LIVE AGAIN UA 1934	Tolstoy, L. N. (*Resurrection*) Various
WE'RE IN THE MINK RANK 1959	Coke, P. (*Breath of Spring*) (P) French
WE'RE NO ANGELS PAR 1955	Husson, A. (*My three angels*) (P) Random House, N.Y.
WEST II WAR 1963	Del Rivo, L. (*Furnished room, The*) Hutchinson
WEST LAND CASE, THE UN 1937	Latimer, J. (*Headed for a hearse*) Methuen
WEST OF THE PECOS RKO 1934 RKO 1945	Grey, Z. Hodder & Stoughton
WET PARADE MGM 1932	Sinclair, U. Laurie
WE WERE STRANGERS COL 1949	Sylvester, R. (*Rough sketch*) Dial Press, N.Y.
WHATEVER HAPPENED TO BABY JANE? WAR 1962	Farrell, H. (*Baby Jane*) Eyre & Spottiswoode
WHAT EVERY WOMAN KNOWS MGM 1934	Barrie, *Sir* J. M. (P) Hodder & Stoughton
WHAT EVERY WOMAN WANTS ADELPHI 1954	Lewis, E. (*Relations are best apart*) (P) Playscripts
WHAT LOLA WANTS WAR 1958	Addler, R. *and* Ross, J. (*Damn Yankees*) (P) Random House, N.Y.
WHAT PRICE GLORY FOX 1952	Anderson, M. *and* Stallings, L. (P) Dodd, N.Y.

WHEN WE ARE MARRIED BN 1943	Priestley, J. B. (P) Heinemann
WHEN WORLDS COLLIDE PAR 1951	Balmer, E. *and* Wylie, P. Paul
WHERE LOVE HAS GONE PAR 1964	Robbins, H. Blond
WHERE SINNERS MEET RKO 1934	Milne, A. A. (*Dover Road*) (P) Houghton Mifflin, Boston
WHERE THE BOYS ARE MGM 1960	Swarthout, G. Heinemann
WHERE THERE'S A WILL EROS 1955	Delderfield, R. F. (P) French
WHERE THE SIDEWALK ENDS FOX 1950	Stuart, W. L. (*Night cry*) Dial Press, N.Y.
WHERE THE SPIES ARE MGM 1965	Leasor, J. (*Passport to oblivion*) Heinemann
WHEREVER SHE GOES ABP 1950	Abrahall, C. H. (*Prelude*) Oxford U.P.
WHILE PARENTS SLEEP SOSKIN 1936	Kimmins, A. (P) French
WHILE THE PATIENT SLEPT IN 1935	Eberhart, M. G. Heinemann
WHILE THE SUN SHINES ABP 1947	Rattigan, T. (P) Hamilton
WHIRLPOOL FOX 1951	Endore, G. (*Methinks the lady*) Cresset Press
WHISKY GALORE EALING 1949	Mackenzie, *Sir* C. Chatto & Windus
WHISPERING SMITH SPEAKS FOX 1935	Spearman, F. H. (*Whispering Smith*) Grosset, N.Y.
WHISPERERS, THE UA 1966	Nicolson, R. (*Mrs. Ross*) Constable
WHISTLE-STOP UA 1946	Wolff, M. M. Constable
WHITE BANNERS WAR 1938	Douglas, L. C. Davies

WHITE CARGO
BI 1930
MGM 1942

Gordon, L. (P)
Various

WHITE COCKATOO
WAR 1935

Eberhart, M. G.
Lane

WHITE CORRIDORS
GFD 1951

Ashton, H. (*Yeoman's hospital*)
Collins

WHITE FANG
FOX 1936

London, J.
Methuen

WHITE TOWER, THE
RKO 1950

Ullman, J. R.
Collins

WHITE UNICORN, THE
CORNFIELD 1947

Sandstrom, F. (*Milk white unicorn, The*)
Cassell

WHITE WITCH DOCTOR
FOX 1953

Stinetorf, L. A.
Westminster Press, Philadelphia

WHO GOES THERE?
BL 1952

Dighton, J. (P)
Elek

WHO IS HOPE SCHUYLER?
FOX 1942

Ransome, S. (*Hearses don't hurry*)
Doubleday, N.Y.

WHO KILLED AUNT MAGGIE?
REP 1940

Field, M.
Jarrolds

**WHO'S AFRAID OF VIRGINIA
WOOLF?**
WAR 1965

Albee, E. (P)
Cape

WHO'S GOT THE ACTION?
PAR 1963

Rose, A. (*Four punters are missing*)
Hamilton

WHO WAS THAT LADY?
COL 1960

Krasna, N. (*Who was that lady I saw you
with?*) (P)
Random House, N.Y.

WICKED LADY, THE
GFD 1946

King-Hall, M. (*Life and death of the
wicked Lady Skelton, The*)
Davies

WILD AFFAIR, THE
BL 1965

Sansom, W. (*Last hours of Sandra Lee, The*)
Hogarth Press

WILD AND THE WILLING, THE
RANK 1962

Dobie, L. *and* Sloman, R. (*Tinker, The*) (P)
French

WILD HARVEST
GN 1961

Longstreet, S.
Muller

WILD HORSE MESA
PAR 1932

Grey, Z.
Hodder & Stoughton

WILD IN THE COUNTRY
FOX 1961

Salamanca, J. R. (*Lost country, The*)
Four Square Bks

WILD RIVER
FOX 1960

Deal, B. (*Dunbar's Cove*)
Hutchinson

WILL ANY GENTLEMAN . . . ?
ABP 1953

Sylvaine, V. (P)
French

WIND CANNOT READ, THE
RANK 1958

Mason, R.
Hodder & Stoughton

WINDOM'S WAY
RANK 1957

Ullman, J. R.
Collins

WINGED VICTORY
FOX 1944

Hart, M. (P)
Various

**WINNIE THE POOH AND THE
HONEY TREE**
DISNEY 1965

Milne, A. A.
Methuen

WINSLOW BOY, THE
IS 1949

Rattigan, T. (P)
Hamilton

WINTERSET
RKO 1936

Anderson, M. (P)
Lane

WIRETAPPER, THE
EXCLUSIVE 1955

Vaus, J. (*Why I quit syndicated crime*)
Van Kempen, Wheaton, Ill.

WITCHES, THE
HAMMER 1966

Curtis, P. (*Devil's own, The*)
Pan

WITCHES OF SALEM, THE
FILMS DE FRANCE 1957

Miller, A. (*Crucible, The*) (P)
Secker & Warburg

WITH REGRET
PAR 1935

Pertwee, R. *and* Dearden, H. (*Interference*)
(P)
French, N.Y.

WITHOUT LOVE
MGM 1945

Barry, P. (P)
Coward-McCann, N.Y.

WITHOUT RESERVATIONS
RKO 1946

Allen, J. *and* Livingston, M. (*Thanks God,
I'll take it from here*)
Faber

WITNESS FOR THE PROSECUTION
UA 1957

Christie, A. (P)
French

WITNESS VANISHES, THE
UN 1939

Ronald, J. (*They can't hang me*)
Rich & Cowan

TITLE OF FILM	AUTHOR AND PUBLISHER
WIZARD OF OZ, THE MGM 1939	Baum, L. F. Hutchinson
WOLF HUNTERS, THE MONOGRAM 1949	Curwood, J. O. Various
WOLF LARSEN ABP 1959	London, J. (*Sea wolf, The*) Heinemann
WOMAN IN THE DARK REP 1952	Cosentino, N. (*Moon over Mulberry Street*) (P) Dramatic Pubns, Chicago
WOMAN IN THE HALL, THE GFD 1947	Stern, G. B. Cassell
WOMAN IN THE NIGHT WW 1929	Barcynska, *Countess* (*Tesha*) Hurst & Blackett
WOMAN IN THE WINDOW, THE RKO 1944	Wallis, J. H. (*Once off guard*) Jarrolds
WOMAN IN WHITE, THE WAR 1948	Collins, W. Various
WOMAN I STOLE, THE COL 1933	Hergesheimer, J. (*Tampico*) Various
WOMAN OBSERVED, THE FOX 1959	Mantley, J. (*Snow birch, The*) Joseph
WOMAN OF AFFAIRS, A MGM 1929	Arlen, M. (*Green hat, The*) Collins
WOMAN OF STRAW UA 1964	Arley, C. Collins
WOMAN OF SUMMER FOX 1963	Inge, W. (*Loss of roses, A*) (P) Random House, N.Y.
WOMAN REBELS, A RKO 1936	Syrett, N. (*Portrait of a rebel*) Bles
WOMAN OF ROME, A EXCLUSIVE 1956	Moravia, A. Secker & Warburg
WOMAN OF THE DUNES, THE CONTEMPORARY 1965	Abe, K. Secker & Warburg
WOMAN'S ANGLE, A ABP 1951	Feiner, R. (*Three cups of coffee*) Dakers
WOMAN'S SECRET, A RKO 1949	Baum, V. (*Mortgage on life*) Doubleday, N.Y.
WOMAN'S VENGEANCE, A UN 1947	Huxley, A. L. (*Gioconda smile, The*) Harper

WOMAN WITH NO NAME, THE
ABP 1950

Charles, T. (*Happy now I go*)
Longmans

WOMEN, THE
MGM 1939

Boothe, C. (P)
Gollancz

WOMEN AREN'T ANGELS
AB 1943

Sylvaine, V. (P)
French

WOMEN OF TWILIGHT
ROMULUS 1952

Rayman, S. (P)
Evans

WOMEN WHO PLAY
GB 1932

Lonsdale, F. (*Spring cleaning*) (P)
Collins

WONDERFUL COUNTRY, THE
UA 1959

Lea, T.
Heinemann

**WONDERFUL WORLD OF THE
BROTHERS GRIMM, THE**
MGM 1962

Grimm, J. L. K. *and* Grimm, W. K.
(*Grimms' fairy tales*)
Dent

WOODEN HORSE, THE
BL 1950

Williams, E.
Collins

WORLD AND HIS WIFE, THE
MGM 1948

Lindsay, H. *and* Crouse, R. (*State of the
Union*) (P)
Dramatists, N.Y.

WORLD IN HIS ARMS, THE
GFD 1952

Beach, R.
Hutchinson

WORLD OF HENRY ORIENT, THE
UA 1964

Johnson, N.
Gollancz

WORLD OF SUZIE WONG, THE
PAR 1959

Mason, R.
Collins

WORLD OF SUZIE WONG, THE
PAR 1959

Osborn, P. (P)
Random House, N.Y.

WORM'S EYE VIEW
ABP 1951

Delderfield, R. F. (P)
Sampson Low

W PLAN
RKO 1931

Seton, G.
Butterworth

**WRECK OF THE MARY DEARE,
THE**
MGM 1959

Innes, H. (*Mary Deare, The*)
Collins

WRONG BOX, THE
COL 1965

Stevenson, R. L. *and* Osbourne, L.
Longmans

WUTHERING HEIGHTS
UA 1939

Bronte, E. J.
Various

Y

YANGTSE INCIDENT
BL 1957

Earl, L. (*Escape of the Amethyst, The*)
Harrap

YANK AT OXFORD, A
MGM 1938

Garland, A. P.
Collins

YANKEE PASHA
GFD 1954

Marshall, E.
Redman

YANK IN ERMINE, A
MON 1955

Carstairs, J. P. (*Solid! said the Earl*)
Hurst & Blackett

YEARLING, THE
MGM 1946

Rawlings, *Mrs.* M.
Heinemann

YEARS BETWEEN, THE
BOX 1946

Du Maurier, D. (P)
Gollancz

YELLOW CANARY, THE
FOX 1963

Masterson, W. (*Evil come, evil go*)
W. H. Allen

YELLOW SANDS, THE
AB 1938

Phillpotts, E. (P)
Duckworth

YELLOWSTONE KELLY
WAR 1959

Fisher, C.
Houghton Mifflin, Boston

YES, MY DARLING DAUGHTER
WAR 1939

Reed, M. W. (P)
French, N.Y.

YIELD TO THE NIGHT
ABP 1956

Henry, J.
Gollancz

YOU CAN'T ESCAPE
ABP 1955

Kennington, A. (*She died young*)
Jarrolds

YOU CAN'T TAKE IT WITH YOU
COL 1938

Kaufman, G. S. *and* Hart, M. (P)
Barker

YOU KNOW WHAT SAILORS ARE
GFD 1953

Hyams, E. (*Sylvester*)
Longmans

YOUNG AND WILLING
UA 1943

Swan, F. (*Out of the frying pan*) (P)
French, N.Y.

YOUNG BESS
MGM 1953

Irwin, M.
Chatto & Windus

YOUNGBLOOD HAWKE
WAR 1963

Wouk, H.
Cape

YOUNG CASSIDY
MGM 1962

O'Casey, S. (*Mirror in my house*)
Macmillan

YOUNG DOCTORS, THE
UA 1961

Hailey, A. (*Final diagnosis, The*)
Joseph

YOUNG DON'T CRY, THE
COL 1957

Jessup, R. (*Man in charge*)
Secker & Warburg

YOUNG DR. KILDARE, THE
MGM 1938

Brand, M.
Hodder & Stoughton

YOUNG HAVE NO TIME, THE
CROSS CHANNEL 1959

Allen, J. (*Young love*)
Pan Bks

YOUNG IN HEART, THE
UA 1938

Wylie, I. A. R.
Cassell

YOUNG LIONS, THE
FOX 1957

Shaw, I.
Cape

YOUNG LOVERS, THE
MGM 1964

Halevy, J.
Mayflower

YOUNG MAN OF MANHATTAN
PAR 1930

Brush, K.
Cassell

YOUNG SAVAGES, THE
UA 1960

Hunter, E. (*Matter of conviction, A*)
Constable

YOUNG WIDOW
UA 1946

Cushman, C.
Triangle Bks, N.Y.

YOUNG WIVE'S TALE
ABP 1951

Jeans, R. (P)
French

YOUNG WOODLEY
BI 1930

Druten, J. van. (P)
Putnam

YOUNG WOODLEY
BI 1930

Druten, J. van.
Gollancz

YOUNGEST PROFESSION, THE
MGM 1943

Day, L.
Laurie

YOU ONLY LIVE TWICE
UA 1966

Fleming, I.
Cape

YOU PAY YOUR MONEY
BUTCHER 1956

Cronin, M.
Museum Press

YOU'RE A BIG BOY NOW
WAR 1966

Benedictus, D.
Blond

YOU'RE ONLY YOUNG TWICE
ABP 1952

Bridie, J. (*What say they*) (P)
Constable

YUKON FLIGHT
MON 1940

Erskine, L. Y. (*Renfrew rides North*)
Grosset, N.Y.

184

Z

ZARAK COL 1956	Bevan, A. J. (*Story of Zarak Khan, The*) Jarrolds
ZAZIE CONNOISSEUR 1962	Queneau, R. Lane
ZORBA THE GREEK FOX 1964	Kazantzakis, N. Faber

AUTHOR INDEX

Author's works which have been filmed are listed under the original title. Film titles which differ from the original are shown in italics.

A

ABBEY, Edward
   BRAVE COWBOY, THE   UI 1962
   (Hodder & Stoughton)   (*Lonely are the brave*)

ABBOTT, Anthony
   MURDER OF THE CIRCUS   COL 1933
   QUEEN, THE   (*Circus queen murder*)
   (Collins)

ABBOTT, George *and* **BISSELL,**
   Richard Pike
   PAJAMA GAME (P)   WAR 1957
   (Random House, N.Y.)

ABE, Kobo
   WOMAN OF THE DUNES, THE   CONTEMPORARY 1965
   (Secker & Warburg)

ABRAHALL, Clare Hoskyns
   PRELUDE   ABP 1950
   (Oxford U.P.)   (*Wherever she goes*)

ABRAHAMS, Doris Caroline *see*
   BRAHMS, C. *pseud.*

ACKLAND, Rodney
   BIRTHDAY (P)   FOX 1943
   (French, N.Y.)   (*Heaven can wait*)

ADAMS, Samuel Hopkins
   NIGHT BUS   COL 1934
   (Longmans)   (*It happened one night*)

ADAMSON, Hans Christian *see*
   LOCKWOOD, C. A. *jt. author*

ADAMSON, Joy
   BORN FREE   BL 1964
   (Collins)

ADDYMAN, Elizabeth
   SECRET TENT (P)   BL 1956
   (English Theatre Guild)

ADLER, Polly
   HOUSE IS NOT A HOME, A   PAR 1964
   (Heinemann)

ADLER, Richard *and* **ROSS, Jerry**

WHAT LOLA WANTS (P)   WAR 1958
(Random House, N.Y.)

AGEE, James

DEATH IN THE FAMILY, A   PAR 1963
(Gollancz)   (*All the way home*)

ALBEE, Edward

WHO'S AFRAID OF VIRGINIA   WAR 1965
WOOLF? (P)
(Cape)

ALBERT, Marvin H.

APACHE RISING   UA 1966
(Muller)   (*Duel at Diablo*)
V.I.P.'s, THE   MGM 1963
(Mayflower)

ALBRAND, Martha

DESPERATE MOMENT   GFD 1953
(Chatto & Windus)

ALCOTT, Louise May

LITTLE MEN   RKO 1940
(Various)
LITTLE WOMEN   RKO 1933
(Various)   MGM 1948
OLD FASHIONED GIRL, AN   EL 1948
(Sampson Low)

ALDINGTON, Richard

ALL MEN ARE ENEMIES   FOX 1934
(Heinemann)

ALDRICH, *Mrs.* **Bess**

MISS BISHOP   UA 1941
(Hodder & Stoughton)   (*Cheers for Miss Bishop*)

ALEXANDER, Ronald

TIME OUT FOR GINGER (P)   UA 1965
(Dramatists, N.Y.)   (*Billie*)

ALGREN, Nelson

MAN WITH THE GOLDEN ARM, UA 1955
THE
(Doubleday, N.Y.)
WALK ON THE WILD SIDE, A COL 1962
(Ace)

ALLAN, Edward *see*
   MACDOUGALL, R. *jt. author*

ALLARDICE, James
   AT WAR WITH THE ARMY (P)   PAR 1951
   (French, N.Y.)

ALLEN, Henry *see*
   FISHER, Clay. *pseud.*

ALLEN, Hervey
   ANTHONY ADVERSE   WAR 1936
   (Gollancz)

ALLEN, Jane *pseud. and*
   LIVINGSTONE, May
   THANKS GOD, I'LL TAKE IT   RKO 1946
   FROM HERE   (*Without reservation*)
   (Faber)

ALLEN, Johannes
   YOUNG LOVE   CC 1959
   (Pan Bks.)   (*Young have no time, The*)

ALLINGHAM, Margery
   TIGER IN THE SMOKE   RANK 1956
   (Chatto & Windus)

ALLISTER, Ray
   FRIESE-GREENE   BL 1951
   (Marsland)   (*Magic box, The*)

AMBLER, Eric
   EPITAPH FOR A SPY   RKO 1944
   (Hodder & Stoughton)   (*Hotel reserve*)
   JOURNEY INTO FEAR   RKO 1942
   (Hodder & Stoughton)
   LIGHT OF DAY, THE   UA 1964
   (Heinemann)   (*Topkapi*)
   MASK OF DIMITRIOS, THE   WAR 1944
   (Hodder & Stoughton)
   NIGHTCOMERS   RANK 1959
   (Hodder & Stoughton)
   UNCOMMON DANGER   WAR 1943
   (Hodder & Stoughton)   (*Background to danger*)

AMES, Delano L.
   SHE SHALL HAVE MURDER   BL 1950
   (Hodder & Stoughton)

AMIS, Kingsley

  LUCKY JIM   BL 1957
  (Gollancz)

  THAT UNCERTAIN FEELING   BL 1961
  (Gollancz)   *(Only two can play)*

ANDERS, Curt

  HELL IS FOR HEROES   PAR 1962
  (Corgi Bks.)

ANDERSON, Maxwell

  BAD SEED (P)   WAR 1956
  (Dodd, N.Y.)

  ELIZABETH THE QUEEN (P)   WAR 1939
  (Longmans, N.Y.)   *(Private lives of Elizabeth and Essex, The)*

  EVE OF ST. MARK, THE (P)   FOX 1944
  (Lane)

  JOAN OF LORRAINE (P)   RKO 1948
  (Anderson House, N.Y.)   *(Joan of Arc)*

  KEY LARGO (P)   WAR 1948
  (Anderson House, N.Y.)

  LOST IN THE STARS (P)   BL 1951
  (Sloane, N.Y.)   *(Cry, the beloved country)*

  SATURDAY'S CHILDREN (P)   WAR 1934
  (Longmans, N.Y.)   *(Maybe it's love)*
                         WAR 1940

  WINTERSET (P)   RKO 1936
  (Lane)

ANDERSON, Maxwell *and*
    STALLINGS, Laurence

  WHAT PRICE GLORY (P)   FOX 1952
  (*In* Best Plays of 1924–25: Dodd, N.Y.)

ANDERSON, Robert

  TEA AND SYMPATHY (P)   MGM 1956
  (Random House, N.Y.)

ANDERSON, Verily

  BEWARE OF CHILDREN   AA 1960
  (Hart-Davis)   *(No kidding)*

ANDREWS, Robert Hardy

  GREAT DAY IN THE MORNING RKO 1955
  (Lane)

  IF I HAD A MILLION   PAR 1932
  (Hurst & Blackett)

ANNIXTER, Paul

  SWIFT WATER   DISNEY 1965
  (Houghton Mifflin, Boston)   *(Those Calloways)*

ANOUILH, Jean
  BECKET (P)   PAR 1963
  (Methuen)
  WALTZ OF THE TOREADORS (P)   RANK 1962
  (French)

ANSTEY, F. *pseud.*
  BRASS BOTTLE, THE   RANK 1964
  (Murray)
  VICE VERSA   TC 1948
  (Murray)

ANTHONY, C. L. *pseud.*
  AUTUMN CROCUS (P)   AUT 1934
  (Gollancz)
  SERVICE (P)   MGM 1933
  (French)   (*Looking forward*)

APPEL, Benjamin
  FORTRESS IN THE RICE   WAR 1964
  (Bobbs-Merrill, Indianapolis)   (*Cry of battle*)

APPEL, David
  COMANCHE   DISNEY 1958
  (Various)   (*Tonka*)

APPLEBY, John
  CAPTIVE CITY, THE   WAR 1965
  (Hodder & Stoughton)

ARCHER, William
  GREEN GODDESS, THE (P)   WAR 1930
  (Heinemann)

ARDREY, Robert
  THUNDER ROCK (P)   MGM 1943
  (Hamilton)

ARENT, Arthur *ed.*
  ONE THIRD OF A NATION (P)   PAR 1939
  (*In* Federal theatre plays: Random
  House, N.Y.)

ARKELL, Reginald
  CHARLEY MOON   BL 1956
  (Joseph)

ARLEN, Michael
  GREEN HAT, THE   MGM 1929
  (Collins)   (*Woman of affairs, A*)
  LILY CHRISTINE   PAR 1932
  (Collins)
  THESE CHARMING PEOPLE   PAR 1931
  (Collins)

G   193

ARLEY, Catherine

WOMAN OF STRAW   UA 1964
(Collins)

ARMSTRONG, Anthony

HE WAS FOUND IN THE ROAD   GN 1956
(Methuen)   (*Man in the road, The*)
TEN MINUTE ALIBI (P)   SOSKIN 1934
(Gollancz)

ARMSTRONG, Anthony *see also*
   HAY, Ian *jt. author*

ARMSTRONG, Anthony *and*
   SHAW, Herbert
TEN MINUTE ALIBI   SOSKIN 1934
(Methuen)

ARMSTRONG, Charlotte

MISCHIEF   FOX 1952
(Davies)   (*Don't bother to knock*)
THREE WEIRD SISTERS   BN 1948
(Gifford)   (*Case of the weird sisters, The*)
UNSUSPECTED, THE   WAR 1947
(Harrap)

ARMSTRONG, Richard

PASSAGE HOME   GFD 1955
(Dent)

ARMSTRONG, Thomas

CROWTHERS OF BANKDAM, THE   ALL 1947
(Collins)   (*Master of Bankdam, The*)

ARNAUD, Georges

WAGES OF FEAR   FILMS DE FRANCE 1953
(British Publishers Guild)

ARNOLD, Elliott

BLOOD BROTHER   FOX 1950
(Collins)   (*Broken arrow*)
COMMANDOS, THE   COL 1943
(Rich & Cowan)   (*First comes courage*)
DEEP IN MY HEART   MGM 1954
(Duell, N.Y.)
FLIGHT FROM ASHIYA   UA 1963
(Muller)

ARUNDEL, Edith

PERSISTENT WARRIORS, THE   BN 1947
(Jenkins)   (*Green fingers*)

ASCH, Scholem
EAST RIVER   MGM 1949
(Macdonald)

ASHBROOK, Harriet
MURDER OF STEPHEN KESTER   CHESTERFIELD 1934
(Eyre & Spottiswoode)   (*Green-eyes*)

ASHTON, Helen
YEOMAN'S HOSPITAL   GFD 1951
(Collins)   (*White corridors*)

ASHTON, Winifred *see*
    DANE, Clemence *pseud.*

ASHTON-WARNER, Sylvia
SPINSTER, THE   MGM 1960
(Secker & Warburg)   (*Two loves*)

ATKINSON, Eleanor
GREYFRIAR'S BOBBY   MGM 1949
(Hamilton)   (*Challenge to Lassie*)

ATLAS, Leopold
WEDNESDAY'S CHILD (P)   RKO 1946
(French, N.Y.)   (*Child of divorce*)

ATHANAS, Verne
PROUD ONES   FOX 1956
(Rich & Cowan)

AUSTEN, Jane
PRIDE AND PREJUDICE   MGM 1940
(Various)

AXELROD, George
GOODBYE CHARLIE (P)   FOX 1965
(French, N.Y.)
SEVEN YEAR ITCH, THE (P)   FOX 1955
(Heinemann)

WILL SUCCESS SPOIL ROCK   FOX 1957
HUNTER? (P)   (*Oh! for a man!*)
(Random House, N.Y.)

AXELSON, *Mrs.* **Mary Dougal**
CHILD IS BORN, A   WAR 1940
(Caldwell, Idaho)

AYRES, Ruby Mildred
  SECOND HONEYMOON   CONTINENTAL 1931
  (Hodder & Stoughton)

B

BABER, Douglas
  MY DEATH IS A MOCKERY   ADELPHI 1952
  (Heinemann)

BACHMANN, Lawrence
  KISS OF DEATH   MGM 1952
  (Knopf, N.Y.)   (*Devil makes three, The*)
  PHOENIX   UA 1958
  (Collins)   (*Ten seconds to hell*)

BACCHELLI, Riccardo
  MILL ON THE PO   LUX FILMS 1950
  (Hutchinson)

BAGNOLD, Enid
  CHALK GARDEN, THE (P)   RANK 1963
  (French)
  NATIONAL VELVET (P)   MGM 1944
  (Heinemann)

BAILEY, C. W. *see*
  KNEBEL, F. *jt. author*

BAILY, Leslie
  GILBERT AND SULLIVAN   BL 1953
  BOOK, THE   (*Story of Gilbert and Sullivan, The*)
  (Cassell)

BAKER, Elliott
  FINE MADNESS, A   WAR 1965
  (Joseph)

BAKER, Frank
  LEASE OF LIFE   EALING 1954
  (Angus & Robertson)

BAKER, Louise
  HER TWELVE MEN   MGM 1954
  (McGraw-Hill, N.Y.)

BALCHIN, Nigel
 MINE OWN EXECUTIONER BL 1948
 (Collins)
 SMALL BACK ROOM, THE LF 1949
 (Collins)
 SORT OF TRAITORS, A BL 1960
 (Collins)   (*Suspect*)

BALDERSTON, John Lloyd
 BERKELEY SQUARE (P) FOX 1933
 (French)   FOX 1951
          (*House in the Square, The*)

BALDWIN, Faith
 BEAUTY   MGM 1933
 (Sampson Low)   (*Beauty for sale*)
 MEN ARE SUCH FOOLS WAR 1938
 (Sampson Low)
 MOON'S OUR HOME, THE PAR 1936
 (Sampson Low)
 OFFICE WIFE   WAR 1930
 (Sampson Low)
 PART-TIME WIVES   IN 1932
 (Sampson Low)   (*Week-end marriage*)
 SKYSCRAPER   MGM 1932
 (Sampson Low)   (*Skyscraper souls*)

BALL, John
 IN THE HEAT OF THE NIGHT UA 1967
 (Joseph)

BALMER, Edwin *and* WYLIE, Philip
 WHEN WORLDS COLLIDE PAR 1951
 (Paul)

BANCROFT, George Pleydell
 WARE CASE, THE (P) FOX 1939
 (Methuen)

BANKS, Lynne Reid
 L-SHAPED ROOM, THE BL 1962
 (Chatto & Windus)

BANNERMAN, K. *see*
 BROOKE, H. *jt. author*

BARBER, Elsie Oaks
 JENNY ANGEL   CONT 1961
 (Putnam)   (*Angel baby*)

BARCYNSKA, *Countess*
 TESHA   WW 1929
 (Hurst & Blackett)   (*Woman in the night, The*)

BARD, Mary
  DOCTOR WEARS THREE   FOX 1950
  FACES, THE   (*Mother didn't tell me*)
  (Hammond)

BARLING, Maurice *see*
  BARRINGTON, Pamela *pseud.*

BARLOW, James
  TERM OF TRIAL   WAR 1962
  (Hamilton)

BARON, Alexander
  HUMAN KIND, THE   BL 1963
  (Cape)   (*Victors, The*)

BARR, George
  EPITAPH FOR AN ENEMY   FOX 1964
  (Hutchinson)   (*Up from the beach*)

BARRETT, Michael
  APPOINTMENT IN ZAHREIN   PAR 1962
  (Pan Bks.)   (*Escape from Zahrein*)

BARRETT, William Edward
  LEFT HAND OF GOD, THE   FOX 1955
  (Corgi Bks.)
  LILIES OF THE FIELD, THE   UA 1963
  (Heinemann)

BARRETT, Wilson
  SIGN OF THE CROSS, THE   PAR 1932
  (Various)   PAR 1944

BARRIE, *Sir* **James Matthew**
  ADMIRABLE CRICHTON, THE (P)   COL 1957
  (Hodder & Stoughton)
  ALICE SIT BY THE FIRE   PAR 1950
  (Hodder & Stoughton)   (*Rendezvous*) (U.S.A. title *Darling how could you?*)
  LITTLE MINISTER, THE   RKO 1934
  (Cassell)
  OLD LADY SHOWS HER   PAR 1930
  MEDALS, THE (P)   (*Seven days leave*)
  (Hodder & Stoughton)
  PETER PAN (P)   RKO 1953
  (Hodder & Stoughton)
  QUALITY STREET (P)   RKO 1937
  (Hodder & Stoughton)
  ROSALIND (P)   PAR 1953
  (Hodder & Stoughton)   (*Forever female*)
  WHAT EVERY WOMAN KNOWS (P)   MGM 1934
  (Hodder & Stoughton)

BARRINGER, Emily Dunning
  BOWERY TO BELLEVUE   MGM 1952
  (Norton, N.Y.)   *(Girl in white, The)*
                              MGM 1952
                              (So bright the flame)

BARRINGTON, Pamela *pseud.*
  ACCOUNT RENDERED   RANK 1957
  (Barker)

BARSTOW, Stanley
  KIND OF LOVING, A   AA 1962
  (Joseph)

BARTLETT, Lanier *and*
  BARTLETT, Virginia Stievers
  ADIOS   IN 1931
  (Murray)   *(Lash, The)*

BARTLETT, Sy *see*
  LAY, B. *jt. author*

BARTLETT, V. *see*
  SHERRIFF, R. C. *jt. author*

BARTLETT, V. S. *see*
  BARTLETT, L. *jt. author*

BARTOLINI, Luigi
  BICYCLE THIEVES   MGM 1949
  (Joseph)

BARTON, Reyner
  ENVY MY SIMPLICITY   GN 1932
  (Chapman & Hall)   *(Killer Walks, A)*

BARRY, Philip
  ANIMAL KINGDOM, THE (P)   RKO 1932
  (French, N.Y.)   WAR 1946
                              (One more tomorrow)

  PHILADELPHIA STORY (P)   MGM 1940
  (French, N.Y.)   MGM 1956
                              (High society)

  WITHOUT LOVE (P)   MGM 1945
  (Coward-McCann, N.Y.)

BARRYMORE, Diana *and*
  FRANK, Gerold
  TOO MUCH, TOO SOON   WAR 1958
  (Muller)

BASSETT, James

HARM'S WAY   COL 1965
(Heinemann)   (*In harm's way*)

BASSING, Eileen

HOME BEFORE DARK   WAR 1958
(Longmans)

BASSO, Hamilton

VIEW FROM POMPEY'S HEAD   FOX 1955
(Collins)   (*Secret interlude*)

BATES, Herbert Ernest

DARLING BUDS OF MAY, THE   MGM 1959
(Joseph)   (*Mating game, The*)
PURPLE PLAIN, THE   GFD 1954
(Joseph)

BAUM, Lyman Frank

WIZARD OF OZ, THE   MGM 1939
(Hutchinson)

BAUM, Vicki

BERLIN HOTEL   WAR 1945
(Joseph)   (*Hotel Berlin*)
GRAND HOTEL   MGM 1932
(Bles)
MORTGAGE ON LIFE   RKO 1949
(Doubleday, N.Y.)   (*Woman's secret, A*)

BAWDEN, Nina

SOLITARY CHILD, THE   BL 1957
(Collins)

BAX, Roger *pseud.*

CAME THE DAWN   MGM 1953
(Hutchinson)   (*Never let me go*)

BEACH, Rex Ellingwood

ALASKA   UN 1942
(Harper, N.Y.)   (*Spoilers, The*)
DON CARELESS   REP 1950
(Hutchinson)   (*Avengers, The*)
SILVER HORDE, THE   RKO 1930
(Hodder & Stoughton)
SON OF THE GODS   IN 1930
(Hutchinson)   PAR 1930
                                    UN 1942
SPOILERS, THE   UI 1955
(Harper, N.Y.)
WORLD IN HIS ARMS, THE   GFD 1952
(Hutchinson)

BEALE, J. *see* **CARGILL, P.** *jt. author*

BEATTY, David
  CONE OF SILENCE   BL 1959
  (Secker & Warburg)

BEAUMONT, Charles
  INTRUDER, THE   GN 1963
  (Muller)   (*Stranger, The*)

BECKER, Stephen
  COVENANT WITH DEATH, A   WAR 1966
  (Hamilton)

BECKHARDT, Israel *and* **BROWN, Wezel**
  VIOLATORS, THE   RKO 1957
  (Arco)

BECKWITH, Reginald
  BOYS IN BROWN (P)   GFD 1949
  (Marshall)

BEEDING, Francis *pseud.*
  NORWICH VICTIMS, THE   ALL 1939
  (Hodder & Stoughton)   (*Dead men tell no tales*)
  SPELL BOUND   UA 1945
  (World, N.Y.)
  Formerly published as
  The House of Dr. Edwardes

BEHAN, Brendan
  QUARE FELLOW, THE (P)   BL 1962
  (Methuen)

BEHREND, Arthur
  HOUSE OF THE SPANIARD, THE GB 1936
  (Heinemann)

BEHRMAN, Samuel Nathaniel
  BIOGRAPHY (P)   MGM 1934
  (French)   (*Biography of a bachelor girl*)
  NO TIME FOR COMEDY (P)   WAR 1940
  (Hamilton)
  PIRATE, THE (P)   MGM 1948
  (Random House, N.Y.)
  SECOND MAN (P)   RKO 1930
  (Various)   (*He knew women*)

BEHRMAN, Samuel Nathaniel *and*
    LOGAN, Joshua
  FANNY (P)   WAR 1960
  (Random House, N.Y.)

BEITH, *Sir* **John Hay** *see* **HAY, Ian** *pseud.*

BELL, John Keble *see*
    HOWARD, Keble *pseud.*

BELL, Thomas
    ALL BRIDES ARE BEAUTIFUL   RKO 1946
    (Grosset, N.Y.)   (*From this day forward*)

BELL, Vereen
    SWAMP WATER   FOX 1941
    (Collins)   FOX 1952
        (*Lure of the wilderness*)

BELLAMANN, Henry
    KING'S ROW   WAR 1941
    (Cape)

BENCHLEY, Nathaniel
    OFF-ISLANDERS, THE   UA 1966
    (Penguin)   (*Russians are coming—the Russians are
        coming, The*)

    SAIL A CROOKED SHIP   COL 1961
    (Hutchinson)

BENEDICTUS, David
    YOU'RE A BIG BOY NOW   WAR 1966
    (Blond)

BENEFIELD, Barry
    CHICKEN-WAGON FAMILY   FOX 1939
    (Triangle Bks., N.Y.)
    VALIANT IS THE WORD FOR
    CARRIE   PAR 1936
    (Heinemann)

BENET, Stephen Vincent
    DEVIL AND DANIEL WEBSTER,
    THE   RKO 1941
    (Oxford U.P.)   (*All that money can buy*)
    FAMOUS   PAR 1952
    (*In* Last circle: (*Just for you*)
    Farrar, N.Y.)
    SOBBIN' WOMEN, THE   MGM 1954
    (*In* Thirteen o'clock: Heinemann)   (*Seven brides for seven brothers*)

BENGTSSON, Franz
    LONG SHIPS, THE   BL 1963
    (Collins)

BENNETT, Arnold

CARD, THE
(Methuen)
GFD 1951

GREAT ADVENTURE
(Methuen)
PAR 1933
(*His double life*)

MR. PROHACK
(Various)
GFD 1949
(*Dear Mr. Prohack*)

BENTLEY, Edmund Clerihew

TRENT'S LAST CASE
(Various)
BL 1952

BENTLEY, Nicolas

FLOATING DUTCHMAN, THE
(Joseph)
AA 1953

THIRD PARTY RISK
(Joseph)
EXCLUSIVE 1955

BENSON, *Mrs.* Sally

JUNIOR MISS
(Sun Dial, N.Y.)
FOX 1945

MEET ME IN ST. LOUIS
(Random House, N.Y.)
MGM 1944

**BENTHAM, Josephine *and*
WILLIAMS, Herschel V.**

JANIE (P)
(French, N.Y.)
WAR 1944

BERKELEY, Reginald

FRENCH LEAVE (P)
(French)
AB 1937

LADY WITH A LAMP, THE (P)
(Gollancz)
BL 1951

BERKMAN, Ted

CAST A GIANT SHADOW
(Doubleday, N.Y.)
UA 1965

BERNA, Paul

HUNDRED MILLION FRAMES, A
(Penguin)
DISNEY 1963
(*Horse without a head*)

BERNANOS, Georges

DIARY OF A COUNTRY PRIEST
(Lane)
GCT 1950

BERNSTEIN, Morey

SEARCH FOR BRIDEY
MURPHY, THE
(Hutchinson)
PAR 1956

BESIER, Rudolf

BARRETTS OF WIMPOLE
STREET, THE   MGM 1934
(Gollancz)   MGM 1956

BARRETTS OF WIMPOLE
STREET, THE (P)   MGM 1934
(Gollancz)   MGM 1956

BEVAN, Anthony J.

STORY OF ZARAK KHAN, THE   COL 1956
(Jarrolds)   (*Zarak*)

BEVAN, Donald *and* TRZCINSKI, Edmund

STALAG 17 (P)   PAR 1953
(Dramatists, N.Y.)

BEZZERIDES, Albert Isaac

LONG HAUL   WAR 1940
(Cape)   (*They drive by night*)
THIEVES' MARKET   FOX 1949
(Scribner, N.Y.)   (*Thieves' highway*)

BICKERTON, Derek

PAYROLL   AA 1961
(Eyre & Spottiswoode)

BIDDLE, Francis

MR. JUSTICE HOLMES   MGM 1950
(Scribner, N.Y.)   (*Magnificient Yankee, The*)

BIGGERS, Earl Derr

AGONY COLUMN   WAR 1941
(Bobbs-Merrill, Indianapolis)   (*Passage from Hong Kong*)
BEHIND THAT CURTAIN   FOX 1930
(Harrap)
BLACK CAMEL   FOX 1931
(Cassell)
CHARLIE CHAN CARRIES ON   FOX 1931
(Cassell)
INSIDE THE LINES (P)   RKO 1930
(French, N.Y.)
SEVEN KEYS TO BALDPATE   RKO 1930
(Grosset, N.Y.)   RKO 1935
                                     RKO 1947

BIRDWELL, Russell

I RING DOORBELLS   PRC 1946
(Messner, N.Y.)

BIRTLES, D.

OVERLANDERS, THE   EALING 1946
(World Film Pubns.)

BISHOP, Curtis
  SHADOW RANGE   ABP 1953
  (Macmillan, N.Y.)   (*Cow country*)

BISHOP, Curtis *see also*
  BRANDON, Curt *pseud.*

BISSELL, Richard Pike
  7½ CENTS   WAR 1957
  (Little Brown, Boston)   (*Pajama game*)

BLACK, Ian Stewart
  HIGH BRIGHT SUN, THE   RANK 1964
  (Hutchinson)
  IN THE WAKE OF A STRANGER BUTCHER 1959
  (Dakers)

BLACKBURN, Thomas Wakefield
  SHORT GRASS   ABP 1951
  (Sampson Low)
  SIERRA BARON   FOX 1958
  (Random House, N.Y.)

BLACKMORE, Richard Doddridge
  LORNA DOONE   ATP 1935
  (Various)   COL 1951

BLAIR, C. F. *jt. author see* **WALLIS, A. J.**

BLAIR, Eric *see*
  ORWELL, George *pseud.*

BLAISDELL, Anne *pseud.*
  NIGHTMARE   COL 1965
  (Gollancz)   (*Fanatic*)

BLAKE, George
  SHIPBUILDERS, THE   BN 1944
  (Faber)

BLANKFORT, Michael
  JUGGLER, THE   COL 1953
  (Dobson)

BLASCO IBANEZ, Vicente
  BLOOD AND SAND   FOX 1941
  (Benn)
  FOUR HORSEMEN OF THE
  APOCALYPSE, THE   MGM 1961
  (Various)

BLOCH, B. *see*
  BREWER, G. E. *jt. author*

BLOCH, Robert
  PSYCHO   PAR 1960
  (Hale)

BLOCHMAN, Lawrence Goldtree
  BOMBAY MAIL   UN 1934
  (Collins)

BLOCK, Libbie
  WILD CALENDAR   MGM 1948
  (World, N.Y.)   (*Caught*)

BLYTON, Enid
  FIVE ON TREASURE ISLAND   BL 1957
  (Hodder & Stoughton)

BOCCACCIO, Giovanni
  DECAMERON, THE   EROS 1953
  (Various)   (*Decameron nights*)

BOILEAU, Pierre *and* **NARCEJAC,**
  Thomas
  LIVING AND THE DEAD, THE PAR 1958
  (Arrow Bks.)   (*Vertigo*)

BOLAND, Bridget
  COCKPIT (P)   GFD 1949
  (*In* Plays of the year, 1948–49: Elek) (*Lost people, The*)
  PRISONER, THE (P)   COL 1955
  (Elek)

BOLAND, John
  LEAGUE OF GENTLEMEN, THE RANK 1960
  (Boardman)

BOLDREWOOD, Rolf
  ROBBERY UNDER ARMS   RANK 1957
  (Macmillan)

BOLT, Robert
  MAN FOR ALL SEASONS, A (P) COL 1966
  (French)

BOLTON, Guy
  WEEK-END AT THE WALDORF MGM 1945
  (Grosset, N.Y.)

BOLTON, Guy *adaptor*
ANASTASIA (P)   FOX 1956
(French)

BONESTELL, Chesley *and* **LEY, Willy**
CONQUEST OF SPACE   PAR 1954
(Sidgwick)

BONETT, Emery *pseud.*
GIRL MUST LIVE, A   UA 1941
(Miles)
HIGH PAVEMENT   GFD 1948
(Heinemann)   (*My sister and I*)

BONHAM, Frank
LOST STAGE VALLEY   COL 1951
(Simon & Schuster, N.Y.)

BONNER, Charles
NOR PERFUME NOR WINE   COL 1941
(Cassell)   (*Adam had four sons*)
Formerly published as Legacy

BONNET, Theodore
MUDLARK, THE   FOX 1950
(W. H. Allen)

BOOTH, Charles Gordon
GENERAL DIED AT DAWN, THE   PAR 1936
(Bell)
MR. ANGEL COMES ABOARD   RKO 1945
(Doubleday, N.Y.)   (*Johnny Angel*)

BOOTHE, Clare
KISS THE BOYS GOODBYE (P)   PAR 1941
(Various)
MARGIN FOR ERROR (P)   FOX 1943
(*In* Five plays of 1940: Hamilton)
WOMEN, THE (P)   MGM 1939
(*In* Famous plays of 1937: Gollancz)   MGM 1956
        (*Opposite sex, The*)

BOOTHROYD, Derrick
VALUE FOR MONEY   RANK 1955
(Laurie)

BOWEN, Catherine Drinker
YANKEE FROM OLYMPUS   MGM 1952
(Benn)   (*Man with thirty sons, The*)

BORDEN, Mary
ACTION FOR SLANDER   UA 1938
(Heinemann)

BOTTOME, Phyllis
HEART OF A CHILD   RANK 1958
(Faber)
MORTAL STORM, THE   MGM 1940
(Faber)
MURDER IN THE BUD   WAR 1945
(Faber)   (*Danger signal*)
PRIVATE WORLDS   PAR 1935
(Lane)
RAT, THE   RKO 1938
(Allan)

BOULLE, Pierre
BRIDGE ON THE RIVER
KWAI, THE   COL 1957
(Collins)

BOWER, B. M.
CHIP OF THE FLYING U   UN 1940
(Grosset, N.Y.)

BOYLE, Kay
AVALANCHE   PRC 1946
(Faber)

BRACKETT, Leigh
TIGER AMONGST US, THE   BL 1962
(Boardman)   (13 *West Street*)

BRADBURY, Ray
FAHRENHEIT 451   UI 1966
(Hart-Davis)

BRADY, Leo
EDGE OF DOOM   RKO 1950
(Cresset Press)   RKO 1952
        (*Stronger than fear*)

BRADLEY, Mary Hastings
I PASSED FOR WHITE   WAR 1960
(Davies)

BRAHMS, Caryl *and* **SIMON, S. J.** *pseud.*
ELEPHANT IN WHITE, THE   GFD 1944
(Joseph)   (*Give us the moon*)
NO NIGHTINGALES   BN 1947
(Joseph)   (*Ghosts of Berkeley Square, The*)
TROTTIE TRUE   TC 1949
(Joseph)

BRAINE, John
   LIFE AT THE TOP   BL 1965
   (Eyre & Spottiswoode)
   ROOM AT THE TOP   BL 1958
   (Eyre & Spottiswoode)

BRAITHWAITE, E. R.
   TO SIR, WITH LOVE   COL 1966
   (Bodley Head)

BRANCH, Houston *and* WATERS, Frank
   RIVER LAY   UN 1948
   (Cassell)

BRAND, Christanna
   GREEN FOR DANGER   INDIVIDUAL 1947
   (Lane)

BRAND, Max *pseud.*
   CALLING DR. KILDARE MGM 1939
   (Hodder & Stoughton)
   DESTRY RIDES AGAIN   UN 1932
   (Hodder & Stoughton)   UN 1939
                 UI 1954
                 (*Destry*)
   DR. KILDARE'S CRISIS MGM 1940
   (Hodder & Stoughton)
   DR. KILDARE'S TRIAL   MGM 1941
   (Dodd, N.Y.)   (*People versus Dr. Kildare, The*)
   SECRET OF DR. KILDARE, THE MGM 1939
   (Hodder & Stoughton)
   UNTAMED, THE   FOX 1931
   (Wright & Brown)   (*Fair warning*)
   YOUNG DR. KILDARE, THE MGM 1938
   (Hodder & Stoughton)

BRANDON, Curt *pseud.*
   BUGLE'S WAKE   EROS 1955
   (Dutton, N.Y.)   (*Seminole uprising*)

BREUER, Bessie
   MEMORY OF LOVE   RKO 1939
   (Rich & Cowan)   (*In name only*)

**BREWER, George Emerson *and*
   BLOCH, Bertram**
   DARK VICTORY (P)   WAR 1939
   (Dramatists, N.Y.)

BRICKHILL, Paul

DAM BUSTERS, THE   ABP 1954
(Evans)

GREAT ESCAPE, THE   UA 1963
(Faber)

REACH FOR THE SKY   RANK 1956
(Collins)

BRIDIE, James *pseud.*

IT DEPENDS WHAT YOU MEAN (P) BL 1952
(Constable)   *(Folly to be wise)*
SLEEPING CLERGYMAN, A (P) BL 1951
(French)   *(Flesh and blood)*
WHAT SAY THEY? (P)   ABP 1952
(Constable)   *(You're only young twice)*

BRIGHOUSE, Harold

HOBSON'S CHOICE (P)   BI 1931
(French)   BL 1953

BRINKLEY, William

DON'T GO NEAR THE WATER   MGM 1957
(Cape)

BRINIG, Myron

SISTERS, THE   WAR 1938
(Cobden Sanderson)

BRISTOW, Gwen

JUBILEE TRAIL   REP 1954
(Eyre & Spottiswoode)
TOMORROW IS FOREVER   RKO 1946
(Heinemann)

BROMFIELD, Louis

BETTER THAN LIFE   WAR 1940
(*In* A collection of nine novels: Cassell) *(It all came true)*
McLEOD'S FOLLY   UA 1943
(*In* It takes all kinds: Cassell) *(Johnny Vagabond)*
MRS. PARKINGTON   MGM 1944
(Cassell)
RAINS CAME, THE   FOX 1939
(Cassell)   FOX 1955
     (Rains of Ranchipur, The)

BRONTE, Charlotte

JANE EYRE   MON 1934
(Various)   FOX 1944

BRONTE, Emily Jane

WUTHERING HEIGHTS   UA 1939
(Various)

BROOKE, E. *see* **KERR, J.** *jt. author*

BROOKE, Harold *and*
    BANNERMAN, Kay
    HOW SAY YOU? (P)   RANK 1961
    (Evans)   (*Pair of briefs*)

BROOKE, Hugh
    SATURDAY ISLAND   RKO 1951
    (Heinemann)

BROOKS, Richard
    BRICK FOXHOLE, THE   RKO 1947
    (Harper, N.Y.)   (*Crossfire*)

BROPHY, John
    DAY THEY ROBBED THE
    BANK OF ENGLAND, THE   MGM 1959
    (Collins)
    IMMORTAL SERGEANT, THE   FOX 1943
    (Collins)
    TURN THE KEY SOFTLY   GFD 1953
    (Collins)
    WATERFRONT   GFD 1950
    (Various)

BROWN, Francis Yeats *see*
    YEATS-BROWN, F.

BROWN, Frederic
    SCREAMING MIMI   COL 1957
    (Boardman)

BROWN, Harry
    SOUND OF HUNTING, A (P)   COL 1952
    (Knopf, N.Y.)   (*Eight iron men*)

BROWN, Harry Peter McNab
    STARS IN THEIR COURSES, THE PAR 1967
    (Cape)   (*El Dorado*)
    WALK IN THE SUN, A   FOX 1945
    (Secker & Warburg)

BROWN, Helen Gurney
    SEX AND THE SINGLE GIRL   WAR 1964
    (Muller)

BROWN, Joe David
   KINGS GO FORTH   UA 1958
   (Cassell)
   STARS IN MY CROWN   MGM 1950
   (Hodder & Stoughton)

BROWN, R. G. *see*
   HARWOOD, H. M. *jt. author*

BROWN, Wenzell
   MONKEY ON MY BACK   UA 1957
   (Elek)

BROWNE, Wynyard
   HOLLY AND THE IVY, THE (P)   BL 1952
   (French)

BRUSH, Katherine
   YOUNG MAN OF MANHATTAN   PAR 1930
   (Cassell)

BRYAN, Michael
   INTENT TO KILL   FOX 1958
   (Eyre & Spottiswoode)

BUCHAN, John *Ist Baron Tweedsmuir*
   HUNTINGTOWER   PAR 1928
   (Hodder & Stoughton)
   THIRTY-NINE STEPS, THE   GB 1935
   (Hodder & Stoughton)   RANK 1959

BUCHWALD, Art
   GIFT FROM THE BOYS, A   COL 1959
   (Harper, N.Y.)
   SURPRISE PACKAGE   COL 1960
   (Gollancz)

BUCK, Pearl
   CHINA SKY   RKO 1945
   (Blue Ribbon Bks., N.Y.)
   DEVIL NEVER SLEEPS, THE   FOX 1962
   (Pan Bks.)
   DRAGON SEED   MGM 1944
   (Methuen)
   GOOD EARTH, THE   MGM 1937
   (Methuen)
   HOUSE DIVIDED, A   UN 1932
   (Methuen)

BUDD, Jackson
   CONVICT HAS ESCAPED, A   WAR 1947
   (Joseph)   (*They made me a fugitive*)

BULLETT, Gerald
JURY, THE   COL 1956
(Dent)   (*Last man to hang*)

BURDICK, Eugene *and*
     WHEELER, Harvey
FAIL SAFE   BL 1963
(Hutchinson)

BURDICK, E. *see also*
     LEDERER, W. J. *jt. author*

BURGESS, Alan
SMALL WOMAN, THE   FOX 1958
(Evans)   (*Inn of the Sixth Happiness, The*)

BURGESS, Gelett
TWO O'CLOCK COURAGE   RKO 1936
(Triangle Bks., N.Y.)   (*Two in the dark*)

BURKE, Jonathan
ECHO OF BARBARA   RANK 1960
(Long)

BURNETT, William Riley
ADOBE WALLS   PAR 1953
(Knopf, N.Y.)   (*Arrowhead*)
ASPHALT JUNGLE, THE   MGM 1950
(Corgi Bks.)   MGM 1963
                         (*Cairo*)
CAPTAIN LIGHTFOOT   UI 1954
(Macdonald)
DARK COMMAND   REP 1940
(Heinemann)
HIGH SIERRA   WAR 1941
(Heinemann)   WAR 1955
                         (*I died a thousand times*)
IRON MAN   UI 1951
(Heinemann)
LITTLE CAESAR   IN 1930
(Cape)
NOBODY LIVES FOREVER   WAR 1946
(World, N.Y.)
SAINT JOHNSON   UN 1932
(Heinemann)   (*Law and order*)
VANITY ROW   REP 1956
(Corgi Bks.)   (*Accused of murder*)

BURNFORD, Sheila
INCREDIBLE JOURNEY, THE   DISNEY 1962
(Hodder & Stoughton)

BURNHAM, B. *see*
     HILTON, J. *jt. author*

BURNS, Robert Elliott
I AM A FUGITIVE FROM THE
CHAIN GANG   WAR 1932
(Paul)   (*I am a fugitive*)

BURNS, Walter Noble
SAGA OF BILLY THE KID   MGM 1941
(Grosset, N.Y.)   (*Billy the Kid*)

BURRESS, John
MISSOURI TRAVELLER, THE DISNEY 1958
(Vanguard, N.Y.)

BURT, Kendal *and* LEASOR, James
ONE THAT GOT AWAY, THE RANK 1957
(Collins *and* Joseph)

BURTIS, Thomson
NEW GUINEA GOLD   PAR 1951
(Doubleday, N.Y.)   (*Crosswinds*)

BUSCH, Niven
DUEL IN THE SUN   MGM 1946
(W. H. Allen)
FURIES, THE   PAR 1950
(W. H. Allen)
THEY DREAM OF HOME RKO 1946
(Grosset, N.Y.)   (*Till the end of time*)

BUTLER, Gerald
KISS THE BLOOD OFF MY
  HANDS   UI 1949
(Jarrolds)   (*Blood on my hands*)
THEY CRACKED HER GLASS
SLIPPER   ANGOFILM 1948
(Jarrolds)   (*Third time lucky*)

BUTTERFIELD, Roger Place
AL SCHMID, MARINE   WAR 1945
(Norton, N.Y.)   (*Pride of the Marines*)

BYRNE, M. St. C. *see*
SAYERS, D. L. *jt. author*

C

CAILLOU, Allan
KHARTOUM   CINERAMA 1966
(W. H. Allen)
RAMPAGE   WAR 1963
(Davies)

CAIN, James Mallahan

DOUBLE INDEMNITY   PAR 1944
(*In* Three of a kind: Hale)

MILDRED PIERCE   WAR 1945
(Hale)

POSTMAN ALWAYS RINGS
TWICE, THE   MGM 1946
(Cape)

SERENADE   WAR 1956
(Penguin)

CAIRN, James

GUY NAMED JOE, A   MGM 1943
(Hollywood Pubns.)

CALDWELL, Erskine

CLAUDELLE   WAR 1961
(Pan Bks.)   (*Young and eager*)

GOD'S LITTLE ACRE   UA 1958
(Heinemann)

TOBACCO ROAD   FOX 1941
(Falcon Press)

**CALDWELL, Erskine *and*
   KIRKLAND, Jack**

TOBACCO ROAD (P)   FOX 1941
(Falcon Press)

CALDWELL, Taylor

DEAR AND GLORIOUS PHYSICIAN   PAR 1963
(Collins)

CAMP, William

IDLE ON PARADE   COL 1959
(MacGibbon)

CAMPBELL, George

CRY FOR HAPPY   COL 1960
(Harcourt, N.Y.)

CAMPBELL, John W.

WHO GOES THERE?   RKO 1951
(Shasta Pubns., Chicago)   (*Thing from another world, The*)

CAMPBELL, *Sir* Malcolm

SALUTE TO THE GODS   MGM 1939
(Cassell)   (*Burn 'em up O'Connor*)

CAMPBELL, Reginald

DEATH IN TIGER VALLEY   REP 1936
(Hodder & Stoughton)   (*Girl from Mandalay*)

CAMPION, N. R. *see*
  MAHER, M. *jt. author*

CANAWAY, W. H.
  SAMMY GOING SOUTH
  (Hutchinson) — BL 1962

CANNING, Victor
  CASTLE MINERVA
  (Hodder & Stoughton) — UA 1965
  GOLDEN SALAMANDER
  (Hodder & Stoughton) — GFD 1949
  HOUSE OF THE SEVEN
  FLIES, THE
  (Hodder & Stoughton) — MGM 1959
  (*House of the seven hawks, The*)
  PANTHER'S MOON
  (Hodder & Stoughton) — GFD 1950
  VENETIAN BIRD
  (Hodder & Stoughton) — GFD 1952

CAPON, Paul
  DEATH AT SHINGLE STRAND
  (Ward Lock) — RANK 1958
  (*Hidden homicide*)

CAPOTE, Truman
  BREAKFAST AT TIFFANYS
  (Hamilton) — PAR 1961

CARGILL, Patrick *and* **BEALE, Jack**
  RING FOR CATTY (P)
  (French) — AA 1962
  (*Twice round the daffodils*)

CARLETON, *Mrs.* **Marjorie Chalmers**
  CRY WOLF
  (Sun Dial, N.Y.) — WAR 1947

CARPENTER, Margaret
  EXPERIMENT PERILOUS
  (Harrap) — RKO 1944

CARR, James Dickson
  EMPEROR'S SNUFFBOX, THE
  (Hamilton) — MON 1957
  (*That woman opposite*)

CARROLL, Curt
  GOLDEN HERD
  (Morrow, N.Y.) — REP 1952
  (*San Antone*)

CARROLL, Gladys

   AS THE EARTH TURNS   WAR 1934
   (Macmillan)

CARROLL, Lewis *pseud.*

   ALICE IN WONDERLAND   PAR 1933
   (Various)   RKO 1951

CARS, Guy des

   BRUTE, THE   BL 1954
   (Wingate)   (*Green scarf, The*)

CARSON, Rachel L.

   SEA AROUND US, THE   RKO 1953
   (Staples)

CARSTAIRS, John Paddy

   SOLID! SAID THE EARL   MON 1955
   (Hurst & Blackett)   (*Yank in ermine, A*)

CARTER, Arthur

   OPERATION MADBALL (P)   COL 1962
   (French, N.Y.)

CARTER, Felicity Winifred *see*
   BONETT, Emery *pseud.*

CARTER, R. *see*
   KEATING, W. J. *jt. author*

CASE, Robert Ormond

   GOLDEN PORTAGE, THE   REP 1942
   (Jarrolds)   (*Girl from Alaska, The*)

CARY, E. *see*
   GILBRETH, F. B. *jt. author*

CARY, F. L. *see also* **KING, P.** *jt. author*

CARY, Falkland L. *and* **KING, Philip**

   WATCH IT SAILOR (P)   COL 1961
   (*In* Plays of the year 1961: Elek)

CARY, Falkland L. *and*
   WEATHERS, Philip

   MADAM TIC-TAC (P)   RKO 1956
   (French)   (*No road back*)

CARY, Joyce

   HORSE'S MOUTH, THE   UA 1958
   (Joseph)

CASPARY, Vera

BACHELOR IN PARADISE   MGM 1961
(Pan)

BEDELIA   GFD 1946
(Eyre & Spottiswoode)

EASY LIVING   PAR 1937
(Longmans)

LAURA   FOX 1944
(Eyre & Spottiswoode)

CASPARY, Vera *and* **SKLAR, George**

LAURA (P)   FOX 1944
(Dramatists, N.Y.)

CASTLE, John

PASSWORD IS COURAGE, THE   MGM 1962
(Souvenir Press)

CATTO, Max

DEVIL AT 4 O'CLOCK, THE   COL 1961
(Pan Bks.)

HILL IN KOREA, A   BL 1956
(Hutchinson)

KILLING FROST, A   UA 1956
(Heinemann)   (*Trapeze*)

LIONS AT THE KILL   FOX 1960
(Hutchinson)   (*Seven thieves*)

MISTER MOSES   UA 1965
(Heinemann)   (*Mr. Moses*)

PRIZE OF GOLD, A   COL 1954
(Heinemann)

THEY WALK ALONE (P)   PAR 1948
(Secker & Warburg)   (*Daughter of darkness*)

CATTO, Max *see also*
   KENT, Simon *pseud.*

CECIL, Henry

BROTHERS IN LAW   BL 1956
(Joseph)

CHABER, M. E. *pseud.*

MAN INSIDE, THE   COL 1958
(Eyre & Spottiswoode)

CHAMALES, Thomas T.

GO NAKED IN THE WORLD   MGM 1960
(Deutsch)

NEVER SO FEW   MGM 1959
(Pan Bks.)

CHAMBERLAIN, George Agnew

SCUDDA HOO! SCUDDA HAY!   FOX 1948
(Grosset, N.Y.)

CHAMBERLAIN, William

TRUMPETS OF COMPANY K   MGM 1958
(Ballentine, N.Y.)   (*Imitation General*)

CHAMBERS, Whitman

MURDER FOR A WANTON   MGM 1936
(Melrose)   (*Sinner take all*)

CHANDLER, Raymond

BIG SLEEP, THE   WAR 1946
(Hamilton)
FAREWELL, MY LOVELY   RKO 1942
(Hamilton)   (*Falcon takes over, The*)
    RKO 1944
HIGH WINDOW, THE   FOX 1947
(Hamilton)   (*Brasher doubloon*)

LADY IN THE LAKE   MGM 1946
(Hamilton)

CHANSLOR, Roy

BALLAD OF CAT BALLOU   COL 1965
(Little Brown, Boston)   (*Cat Ballou*)
HAZARD   PAR 1948
(Various)
JOHNNY GUITAR   REP 1954
(Hale)

CHAPMAN, Edward

JOEY BOY   BL 1965
(Cassell)

CHAPMAN, John

DRY ROT (P)   BL 1956
(English Theatre Guild)

CHAPMAN, Robert

BEHIND THE HEADLINES   RANK 1956
(Laurie)
MURDER FOR THE MILLIONS   COL 1957
(Laurie)   (*Murder reported*)
ONE JUMP AHEAD   GFD 1955
(Laurie)
WINTER WEARS A SHROUD   MON 1954
(Laurie)   (*Delavine affair, The*)

CHAPMAN, R. H. *see*
    COXE, L. O. *jt. author*

CHARTERIS, Leslie

GETAWAY
(Hodder & Stoughton)

RKO 1941
(*Saint's vacation, The*)

MEET THE TIGER
(Ward Lock)

REP 1943
(*Saint meets the Tiger, The*)

SAINT IN NEW YORK, THE
(Hodder & Stoughton)

RKO 1938

CHASE, James Hadley *pseud.*

EVE
(Panther)

GALA 1963

I'LL GET YOU FOR THIS
(Jarrolds)

BL 1951

LAST PAGE, THE (P)
(French)

EXCLUSIVE 1952

NO ORCHIDS FOR MISS
BLANDISH
(Jarrolds)

ALL 1948

TIGER BY THE TAIL
(Hale)

EROS 1955

WORLD IN MY POCKET, THE
(Pan Bks.)

BL 1961
(*On Friday at II*)

CHASE, Mary Coyle

BERNARDINE (P)
(Oxford U.P.)

FOX 1957

HARVEY (P)
(Dramatists, N.Y.)

GFD 1950

SORORITY HOUSE (P)
(French, N.Y.)

RKO 1939

CHATTERTON, Edward Keble

'Q' SHIPS AND THEIR STORY
(Sidgwick & Jackson)

RKO 1928
(*Blockade*)

CHAYEFSKY, Paddy

MIDDLE OF THE NIGHT (P)
(Random House, N.Y.)

COL 1959

CHESSMAN, Caryl

CELL 2455, DEATH ROW
(Longmans)

COL 1955

CHESTERTON, Gilbert Keith

FATHER BROWN STORIES
(Cassell)

COL 1954
(*Father Brown*)

WISDOM OF FATHER
BROWN, THE
(Cassell)

PAR 1935
(*Father Brown, detective*)

CHETHAM-STRODE, Warren

BACKGROUND (P)   ABP 1953
(French)

GUINEA PIG, THE (P)   PILGRIM-PATHE 1949
(Sampson Low)

CHEVALIER, Gabriel
CLOCHEMERLE   BLUE RIBBON 1951
(Secker & Warburg)

CHEYNEY, Peter

DAMES DON'T CARE   FANCEY 1954
(Collins)

SINISTER ERRAND   FOX 1952
(Collins)   (*Diplomatic courier*)

UNEASY TERMS   BN 1948
(Collins)

URGENT HANGMAN, THE   EROS 1954
(Collins)   (*Meet Mr. Callaghan*)

CHILDS, Herbert

GAUCHO   FOX 1952
(Prentice-Hall, N.Y.)   (*Way of a Gaucho*)

CHITTERDEN, Frank

UNINVITED, THE   EROS 1957
(Boardman)   (*Stranger in town*)

CHODOROV, Edward

OH MEN! OH, WOMEN! (P) FOX 1957
(French)

KIND LADY (P)   MGM 1935
(French)   MGM 1951

CHODOROV, Jerome *see also*
   FIELDS, J. *jt. author*

CHODOROV, Jerome *and*
   FIELDS, Joseph
JUNIOR MISS (P)   FOX 1945
(Dramatists, N.Y.)

CHRISTIE, Agatha

ABC MURDERS, THE   MGM 1966
(Collins)   (*Alphabet murders, The*)

AFTER THE FUNERAL   MGM 1963
(Collins)   (*Murder at the gallop*)

4.50 FROM PADDINGTON MGM 1961
(Collins)   (*Murder she said*)

MRS. McGINTY'S DEAD MGM 1963
(Collins)   (*Murder most foul*)

CHRISTIE, Agatha (*continued*)

SPIDER'S WEB, THE (P) (French)	UA 1960
TEN LITTLE NIGGERS (Collins)	FOX 1945 ABP 1965 (*Ten little Indians*)
TEN LITTLE NIGGERS (P) (French)	FOX 1945 ABP 1965 (*Ten little Indians*)
WITNESS FOR THE PROSECUTION (P) (French)	UA 1957

CHRISTIE, Dorothy *and*
    CHRISTIE, Campbell

CARRINGTON, V.C. (P) (Heinemann)	INDEPENDENT 1954
GRAND NATIONAL NIGHT (P) (French)	REN 1953
HIS EXCELLENCY (P) (*In* Plays of the year, 1950: Elek)	GFD 1951

CLARK, Walter Van Tilburg

OX-BOW INCIDENT, THE (Gollancz)	FOX 1943 (*Strange incident*) FOX 1956
TRACK OF THE CAT (Gollancz)	WAR 1954

CLARKE, Donald Henderson

HOUSEKEEPER'S DAUGHTER, THE (Laurie)	UA 1939
IMPATIENT VIRGIN (Long)	UN 1932 (*Impatient maiden*)
LOUIS BERETTI (Long)	FOX 1930 (*Born reckless*)
MILLIE (Long)	RKO 1931
MILLIE'S DAUGHTER (Laurie)	COL 1947

CLAVELL, J.

KING RAT (Joseph)	BL 1964

CLEARY, Jon

BACK OF SUNSET (Collins)	WAR 1960 (*Sundowners, The*)
GREEN HELMET, THE (Collins)	MGM 1960
JUSTIN BAYARD (Collins)	WAR 1958 (*Dust in the sun*)

222

CLECKLEY, H. M. *see*
 THIGPEN, C. H. *jt. author*

CLELAND, John
 FANNY HILL   GALA 1965
 (Luxor Press)

CLEMENS, Samuel Langhorne *see*
 TWAIN, Mark *pseud.*

CLEWES, Howard
 GREEN GROW THE RUSHES BL 1951
 (Lane)
 LONG MEMORY, THE GFD 1953
 (Macmillan)

CLIFFORD, Charles L.
 REAL GLORY, THE UA 1939
 (Heinemann)

CLIFFORD, Francis
 ACT OF MERCY   WAR 1964
 (Hamilton)   (*Guns of darkness*)
 NAKED RUNNER, THE WAR 1966
 (Hodder & Stoughton)

CLIFT, Denison
 MAN ABOUT TOWN FOX 1932
 (Long)

CLOETE, Stuart
 FIERCEST HEART, THE FOX 1960
 (Collins)

CLOU, John
 CARAVAN TO CARNAL, A RKO 1955
 (Redman)   (*Conqueror, The*)

CLOUSTON, J. Storer
 SPY IN BLACK, THE COL 1938
 (Blackwood)

COATES, John
 TRUE AS A TURTLE RANK 1957
 (Gollancz)

COATES, Robert M.
 WISTERIA COTTAGE UA 1958
 (Gollancz)   (*Edge of fury*)

COBB, Humphrey
  PATHS OF GLORY   UA 1957
  (Heinemann)

COBB, Irving Shrewsbury
  OLD JUDGE PRIEST   REP 1953
  (Grosset, N.Y.)   (*Sun shines bright, The*)

COCHRAN, Rice E.
  BE PREPARED   FOX 1953
  (Sloane, N.Y.)   (*Mister Scoutmaster*)

COCKRELL, Francis Marion *and*
  COCKRELL, Marion
  DARK WATERS   UA 1944
  (World, N.Y.)

COEN, Franklin
  NIGHT OF THE QUARTER MOON   MGM 1959
  (Corgi Bks.)

COFFEE, Lenore
  WEEP NO MORE   PAR 1958
  (Cassell)   (*Another time, another place*)

COHN, Arthur
  JOKER IS WILD   PAR 1957
  (Random House, N.Y.)

COKE, Peter
  BREATH OF SPRING (P)   RANK 1960
  (French)   (*Make mine mink*

COLE, Burt
  OLIMPIA   WAR 1967
  (W. H. Allen)   (*Bobo, The*)

COLETTE
  GIGI   MGM 1958
  (Penguin)

COLLINS, Dale
  ORDEAL, THE   MGM 1930
  (Allan)   (*Ship from Shanghai*)

  SENTIMENTALISTS   PATHE 1929
  (Little Brown, Boston)   (*Sal of Singapore*)
          PAR 1931
          (*His woman*)

COLLINS, L. *and* **LAPIERRE, D.**
IS PARIS BURNING?   PAR 1965
(Gollancz)

COLLINS, Norman
LONDON BELONGS TO ME   UN 1948
(Collins)
American title is Dulcimer Street

COLLINS, Wilkie
MOONSTONE, THE   MON 1934
(Various)
WOMAN IN WHITE, THE   WAR 1948
(Various)

COLLISON, Wilson *pseud.*
CONGO LANDING   MGM 1940
(McBride, N.Y.)   (*Congo Maisie*)
FAREWELL TO WOMEN (P)   MGM 1953
(McBride, N.Y.)   (*Mogambo*)

COMBER, *Mrs.* **Elizabeth** *see*
HAN SUYIN *pseud.*

COMDEN, Betty *and* **GREEN, Adolph**
BELLS ARE RINGING (P)   MGM 1960
(Random House, N.Y.)

CONDON, Richard
MANCHURIAN CANDIDATE   UA 1962
(Pan Bks.)
OLDEST CONFESSION, THE   UA 1961
(Longmans)   (*Happy thieves, The*

CONNELL, Richard Edward
BROTHER ORCHID (P)   WAR 1940
(French, N.Y.)

CONNELL, Vivian
CHINESE ROOM, THE   FOX 1959
(Secker & Warburg)   (*In the Chinese room*)

CONNELLY, Marc
GREEN PASTURES (P)   WAR 1936
(Gollancz)

CONNELLY, M. *see also*
KAUFMAN, G. S. *jt. author*

CONNER, Rearden
SHAKE HANDS WITH THE DEVIL   UA 1959
(Dent)

CONNERS, Harry
  APPLESAUCE (P)   IN 1936
  (French, N.Y.)   *(Brides are like that)*

CONRAD, Joseph *pseud.*
  LORD JIM   COL 1964
  (Dent)
  OUTCAST OF THE ISLANDS, AN   LF 1951
  (Various)
  SECRET AGENT, THE   GB 1936
  (Various)   *(Sabotage)*
  VICTORY   PAR 1930
  (Various)   *(Dangerous paradise)*
                       PAR 1940
  WITHIN THE TIDES   REP 1953
  (Dent)   *(Laughing Anne)*

CONSTANDUROS, Mabel *and*
  CONSTANDUROS, Denis
  ACACIA AVENUE (P)   COL 1945
  (French)   (29 *Acacia Avenue*)
  HERE COME THE HUGGETTS   GFD 1948
  (Sampson Low)
  HUGGETTS ABROAD, THE   GFD 1949
  (Sampson Low)

COOK, William Everett
  TWO RODE TOGETHER   COL 1961
  (Mills & Boon)

COOKSON, Catherine
  ROONEY   RANK 1958
  (Macdonald)

COOPER, James Fenimore
  DEERSLAYER, THE   REP 1943
  (Various)   FOX 1957
  LAST OF THE MOHICANS, THE UA 1936
  (Various)   COL 1949
                       (Last of the Redskins)
  LEATHER STOCKING TALES   UA 1950
  (Various)   *(Tomahawk trail, The)*
  PATHFINDER, THE   COL 1953
  (Various)

COPPEL, Alec
  I KILLED THE COUNT (P)   GN 1939
  (Heinemann)
  I KILLED THE COUNT   GN 1939
  (Blackie)
  MAN ABOUT A DOG, A   GFD 1949
  (Harrap)   *(Obsession)*
  MR. DENNING DRIVES NORTH BL 1951
  (Harrap)

CORMACK, Bartlett

   RACKET, THE (P)   RKO 1952
   (French, N.Y.)

COSTAIN, Thomas Bertram

   BLACK ROSE, THE   FOX 1949
   (Staples)
   SILVER CHALICE, THE   WAR 1954
   (Hodder & Stoughton)

COSENTINO, Nicholas

   MOON OVER MULBERRY
   STREET (P)   REP 1952
   (Dramatic Pubns., Chicago)   (*Woman in the dark*)

COTLER, Gordon

   BOTTLETOP AFFAIR, THE   MGM 1962
   (Panther Bks.)   (*Horizontal lieutenant, The*)

COTTERELL, Geoffrey

   Tiara Tahiti   RANK 1962
   (Eyre & Spottiswoode)

COTTRELL, Dorothy

   SILENT REEFS   FOX 1960
   (Hodder & Stoughton)   (*Secret of the purple reef, The*)

COUSINS, E. G.

   SAPPHIRE   RANK 1959
   (Panther Bks.)

COUSTEAU, Jacques

   SILENT WORLD, THE   RANK 1955
   (Hamilton)

COWAN, Samuel Kinkade
SERGEANT YORK AND HIS
PEOPLE   WAR 1941
(Various)   (*Sergeant York*)

COWARD, Noel

   ASTONISHED HEART, THE (P)   GFD 1949
   (*In* Tonight at 8.30: Heinemann)
   BITTER SWEET (P)   MGM 1940
   (Heinemann)
   BLITHE SPIRIT (P)   CIN 1945
   (Heinemann)
   CAVALCADE (P)   FOX 1933
   (Heinemann)   FOX 1955
   DESIGN FOR LIVING (P)   PAR 1933
   (Heinemann)

227

COWARD, Noel (*continued*)

FUMED OAK (P)   GFD 1952
(French)

MEET ME TONIGHT (P)   GFD 1952
(Heinemann)

PRIVATE LIVES (P)   MGM 1931
(Heinemann)

QUEEN WAS IN THE PARLOUR, PAR 1933
THE (P)   (*Tonight is ours*)
(Heinemann)

RED PEPPERS (P)   GFD 1952
(Heinemann)

STILL LIFE (P)   CIN 1946
(French)   (*Brief encounter*)

THIS HAPPY BREED (P)   CIN 1944
(Heinemann)

TONIGHT AT 8.30 (P)   GFD 1952
(Heinemann)

WAYS AND MEANS (P)   GFD 1952
(Heinemann)

COWEN, William Joyce

THEY GAVE HIM A GUN   MGM 1937
(Heinemann)

COX, A. B. *see* **ILES, Francis** *pseud.*

COXE, George Harmon

MURDER WITH PICTURES   PAR 1936
(Heinemann)

COXE, Louis Osborne *and*
    CHAPMAN, Robert H.

BILLY BUDD (P)   AA 1962
(Hill & Wang, N.Y.)

COXHEAD, Elizabeth

FRIEND IN NEED, A   EROS 1958
(Collins)   (*Cry from the streets, A*)

COZZENS, James Gould

BY LOVE POSSESSED   UA 1961
(Longmans)

CURE OF THE FLESH   FOX 1933
(Longmans)   (*Doctor Bull*)

CRANE, Stephen

BRIDE COMES TO YELLOW
SKY, THE   RKO 1952
(*In* 20 stories: Knopf, N.Y.) (*Face to face*)
RED BADGE OF COURAGE, THE MGM 1951
(Heritage, N.Y.)

CRAWFORD, Francis Marion

  MR. ISAACS   MGM 1931
  (Macmillan)   *(Son of India)*

CREASEY, John

  HAMMER THE TOFF   BUTCHER 1952
  (Long)
  SALUTE THE TOFF   BUTCHER 1951
  (Long)

CREASEY, John *see also*

  HALLIDAY, Michael *pseud.*
  MARRIC, J. J. *pseud.*

CRICHTON, Robert

  GREAT IMPOSTER, THE   UI 1960
  (Gollancz)

CROCKETT, Lucy Heron

  MAGNIFICENT DEVILS   PAR 1956
  (Dymock)   *(Proud and profane)*

CROFT, Michael

  SPARE THE ROD   BL 1960
  (Pan)

CROFT-COOKE, Rupert

  SEVEN THUNDERS   RANK 1957
  (Macmillan)

CROMPTON, Richmal

  JUST WILLIAM   AB 1940
  (Newnes)

CRONIN, Archibald Joseph

  BEYOND THIS PLACE   REN 1959
  (Gollancz)
  CITADEL, THE   MGM 1938
  (Gollancz)
  GREEN YEARS, THE   MGM 1946
  (Gollancz)
  HATTER'S CASTLE   PAR 1941
  (Gollancz)
  JUPITER LAUGHS (P)   WAR 1941
  (Gollancz)   *(Shining victory)*
  KEYS OF THE KINGDOM, THE FOX 1944
  (Gollancz)
  SPANISH GARDENER, THE   RANK 1956
  (Gollancz)
  STARS LOOK DOWN, THE   GN 1940
  (Gollancz)

CRONIN, Michael

PAID IN FULL   FANCEY 1954
(Museum Press)   *(Johnny on the spot)*

YOU PAY YOUR MONEY   BUTCHER 1956
(Museum Press)

CROSS, *Mrs* Mary Ann *see*
   ELIOT, George *pseud.*

CROTHERS, Rachel

AS HUSBANDS GO (P)   FOX 1934
(French)

'OLD LADY 31' (P)   MGM 1940
(Various)   *(Captain is a lady, The)*

SUSAN AND GOD (P)   MGM 1940
(Random House, N.Y.)

CROUSE, R. *see*
   LINDSAY, H. *jt. author*

CROY, Homer

FAMILY HONEYMOON   UN 1949
(Hurst & Blackett)

SIXTEEN HANDS   PAR 1939
(Hamilton)   *(I'm from Missouri)*

CULOTTA, Nina

THEY'RE A WEIRD MOB   RANK 1965
(Kaye)

CUNNINGHAM, E. V. *pseud.*

PENELOPE   MGM 1966
(Deutsch)

SYLVIA   PAR 1963
(Deutsch)

CURIE, Eve

MADAME CURIE   MGM 1943
(Heinemann)

CURRY, Ellsworth

HAPPENING, THE   PAR 1967
(Corgi)

CURTIS, Peter

DEVIL'S OWN, THE   HAMMER 1966
(Pan)   *(Witches, The)*

YOU'RE BEST ALONE   ABP 1950
(Macdonald)   *(Guilt is my shadow)*

CURWOOD, James Oliver

BACK TO GOD'S COUNTRY   GFD 1953
(Triangle Bks., N.Y.)

GOLD HUNTERS, THE   MON 1949
(Various)   (*Trail of the Yukon*)

KAZAN THE WOLF DOG   COL 1949
(Grosset, N.Y.)

NOMADS OF THE NORTH   ABP 1954
(Nelson)   (*Northern patrol*)
     DISNEY 1961
     (*Nikki, wild dog of the North*)

RETRIBUTION   EL 1950
(Various)   (*Timber fury*)

RIVER'S END   WAR 1940
(Grosset, N.Y.)

TENTACLES OF THE NORTH   ABP 1951
(Various)   (*Snow dog*)

WOLF HUNTERS, THE   MON 1949
(Various)

CUSHMAN, Clarissa

YOUNG WIDOW   UA 1946
(Triangle Bks., N.Y.)

CUSHMAN, Dan

RIPPER FROM RAWHIDE   REP 1954
(Macmillan, N.Y.)   (*Timberjack*)

D

D'ALTON, Louis Lynch

MONEY DOESN'T MATTER (P)   ABP 1951
(Duffy, Dublin)   (*Talk of a million*)

DANA, Richard Henry

TWO YEARS BEFORE THE MAST   PAR 1946
(Various)

DANE, Clemence *pseud.*

BILL OF DIVORCEMENT, A (P)   RKO 1932
(Heinemann)   RKO 1940

DANE, Clemence *and* **SIMPSON, H. de G.**

ENTER SIR JOHN   BI 1930
(Hodder & Stoughton)   (*Murder*)

DANINOS, Pierre

MAJOR THOMPSON LIVES   GALA 1957
IN FRANCE   (*Diary of Major Thompson, The*)
(Cape)   (U.S.A. title *French are a funny race, The*)

DANNAY, Frederic *see*
QUEEN, Ellery *pseud.*

DAVENPORT, Mrs. Gwen
  BELVEDERE   FOX 1948
  (Bobbs Merrill, Boston)   *(Sitting pretty)*

DAVENPORT, Marcia
  EAST SIDE, WEST SIDE   MGM 1949
  (Collins)
  VALLEY OF DECISION, THE   MGM 1945
  (Collins)

DAVIDSON, Lionel
  NIGHT OF WENCELAS   RANK 1963
  (Gollancz)   *(Hot enough for June*

DAVIES, Hunter
  HERE WE GO ROUND THE
  MULBERRY BUSH   UA 1967
  (Panther)

DAVIES, Joseph Edward
  MISSION TO MOSCOW   WAR 1943
  (Gollancz)

DAVIES, Valentine
  IT HAPPENS EVERY SPRING   FOX 1950
  (Farrar, N.Y.)
  MIRACLE ON 34th STREET   FOX 1947
  (Harcourt, N.Y.)   FOX 1956

DAVIS, Clyde Brion
  ANOINTED, THE   MGM 1945
  (Barker)   *(Adventure)*

DAVIS, Dorrence
  APRON STRINGS (P)   UN 1931
  (French, N.Y.)   *(Virtuous husband)*

DAVIS, Frederick Clyde *see*
RANSOME, Stephen *pseud.*

DAVIS, Mrs. Lavinia
  COME BE MY LOVE   UN 1949
  (Doubleday, N.Y.)   *(Once more my darling)*

DAVIS, Owen
  MR. AND MRS. NORTH (P)   MGM 1941
  (French, N.Y.)

DAVIS, Richard Harding
  BAR SINISTER, THE   MGM 1955
  (Scribner, N.Y.)   (*It's a dog's life*)

DAWSON, Peter
  RENEGADE CANYON   COL 1953
  (Collins)

DAY, Clarence
  LIFE WITH FATHER (P)   WAR 1947
  (Chatto & Windus)

DAY, Lillian
  YOUNGEST PROFESSION, THE   MGM 1943
  (Laurie)

DEAL, Borden
  DUNBAR'S COVE   FOX 1960
  (Hutchinson)   (*Wild river*)

DEARDON, H. *see*
  PERTWEE, R. *jt. author*

DEARSLEY, A. P.
  FLY AWAY PETER (P)   GFD 1948
  (French)

DEBRETT, Hal
  BEFORE I WAKE   GN 1955
  (Dodd, N.Y.)

DEEPING, Warwick
  SORRELL AND SON   UA 1934
  (Cassell)

DEFOE, Daniel
  ADVENTURES OF ROBINSON
    CRUSOE, THE   UA 1954
  (Various)
  MOLL FLANDERS   FOX 1954
  (Various)   PAR 1964
         (*Amorous adventures of Moll Flanders, The*)

DE FRECE, *Lady*
  RECOLLECTIONS OF VESTA
  TILLEY   BL 1957
  (Hutchinson)   (*After the ball*)

DEIGHTON, Leonard
  FUNERAL IN BERLIN   PAR 1966
  (Cape)
  IPCRESS FILE, THE   RANK 1964
  (Hodder & Stoughton)

DEKOBRA, Maurice

    HELL IS SOLD OUT   EROS 1951
    (Laurie)

    SPHINX HAS SPOKEN, THE   RKO 1931
    (Laurie)   (*Friends and lovers*)

DELANEY, Shelagh

    TASTE OF HONEY, A (P)   BL 1961
    (Methuen)

DELDERFIELD, R. F.

    ALL OVER THE TOWN (P)   WESSEX 1948
    (French)

    GLAD TIDINGS (P)   EROS 1953
    (Rylee)

    ORCHARD WALLS, THE (P)   ABP 1955
    (French)   (*Now and forever*)

    STOP AT A WINNER   AA 1961
    (Hodder & Stoughton)   (*On the fiddle*)

    WHERE THERE'S A WILL (P)   EROS 1955
    (French)

    WORM'S EYE VIEW (P)   ABP 1951
    (*In* Embassy successes, Vol. I:
       Sampson Low)

DELL, Jeffery

    NOBODY ORDERED WOLVES   GFD 1951
    (Heinemann)   (*Dark man, The*)

DELMAR, Vina

    ABOUT MRS. LESLIE   PAR 1954
    (Hale)

DEL RIVO, Laura

    FURNISHED ROOM, THE   WAR 1963
    (Hutchinson)   (*West II*)

DEMING, Richard

    CAREFUL MAN, THE   PAR 1967
    (W. H. Allen)   (*Arrivederci, baby!*)

DENHAM, R. *see* **PERCY, E.** *jt. author*

DENNIS, Patrick

    AUNTIE MAME   WAR 1956
    (Vanguard, N.Y.)

DE VOTO, Bernard

    ACROSS THE WIDE MISSOURI MGM 1951
    (Eyre & Spottiswoode)

DE VRIES, Peter
  TUNNEL OF LOVE, THE   MGM 1959
  (Gollancz)

DE VRIES, P. *see also*
  FIELDS, J. *jt. author*

DEWLEN, Al
  NIGHT OF THE TIGER, THE   COL 1966
  (Longmans)   (*Ride beyond vengeance*)
  TWILIGHT OF HONOUR   MGM 1963
  (Longmans)   (*Charge is murder, The*)

DIAMOND, I. A. L. *see*
  WILDER, W. *jt. author*

DIBNER, Martin
  DEEP SIX, THE   WAR 1957
  (Cassell)

DICK, R. A. *pseud.*
  GHOST AND MRS. MUIR, THE   FOX 1947
  (Harrap)

DICKENS, Charles
  CHRISTMAS CAROL, A   PAR 1935
  (Various)   MGM 1938
                        REN 1951
                        (*Scrooge*)
  DAVID COPPERFIELD   MGM 1935
  (Various)
  GREAT EXPECTATIONS   UN 1934
  (Various)   CINE 1946
  MYSTERY OF EDWIN
  DROOD, THE   UN 1935
  (Various)
  NICHOLAS NICKLEBY   EALING 1948
  (Various)
  OLIVER TWIST   MONOGRAM 1933
  (Various)   CINE 1948
  PICKWICK PAPERS   REN 1952
  (Various)
  TALE OF TWO CITIES, A   MGM 1935
  (Various)   RANK 1957

DICKENS, Monica
  ONE PAIR OF FEET   TC 1943
  (Joseph)   (*Lamp still burns, The*)

DI DONATO, Pietro
  CHRIST IN CONCRETE   GFD 1949
  (World, N.Y.)   (*Give us this day*)

DIGHTON, John
  HAPPIEST DAYS OF YOUR
  LIFE, THE (P)   BL 1949
  (*In* Plays of the year, 1948–49: Elek)
  WHO GOES THERE? (P)   BL 1952
  (*In* Plays of the year, 1951: Elek)

DINE, S. S. van
  BENSON MURDER CASE, THE   PAR 1930
  (Benn)
  BISHOP MURDER CASE, THE   MGM 1930
  (Cassell)
  CANARY MURDER CASE, THE   PAR 1929
  (Benn)
  CASINO MURDER CASE, THE   MGM 1935
  (Cassell)
  GARDEN MURDER CASE, THE   MGM 1936
  (Cassell)
  GRACIE ALLEN MURDER
  CASE, THE   PAR 1939
  (Cassell)
  KENNEL MURDER CASE, THE   WAR 1933
  (Cassell)   WAR 1940
                           (*Calling Philo Vance*)

DINELLI, Mel
  MAN, THE (P)   RKO 1952
  (Dramatists, N.Y.)   (*Beware my lovely*)

DINNEEN, Joseph F.
  ANATOMY OF A CRIME   GFD 1954
  (Scribner, N.Y.)   (*Six bridges to cross*)

DINNER, William *and* MORUM, William
  LATE EDWINA BLACK, THE (P)   GFD 1951
  (French)

DISNEY, Doris Miles
  FAMILY SKELETON   FOX 1950
  (Doubleday, N.Y.)   (*Stella*)
  STRAW MAN, THE   UA 1953
  (Doubleday, N.Y.)

DIVINE, David *pseud.*
  BOY ON A DOLPHIN, THE   FOX 1957
  (Murray)

DOBIE, Laurence *and* SLOMAN, Robert
  TINKER, THE (P)   RANK 1962
  (French)   (*Wild and willing, The*)

DODGE, David
  PLUNDER OF THE SUN   WAR 1953
  (Random House, N.Y.)
  TO CATCH A THIEF   PAR 1955
  (Penguin)

AUTHOR AND ORIGINAL TITLE	FILM TITLE

DODGE, Henry Irving *and others*
SKINNER'S DRESS SUIT (P)   UN 1929
(French, N.Y.)   (*Skinner steps out*)

DODGSON, Charles Lutwidge *see*
    CARROLL, Lewis *pseud.*

DODSON, Kenneth
AWAY ALL BOATS   UI 1955
(Angus & Robertson)

DONOVAN, Robert J.
WARTIME ADVENTURES OF
PRESIDENT JOHN F. KENNEDY,
THE   WAR 1963
(Panther Bks.)   (*PT.* 109)

DOSTOEVSKI, Fedor Mikhailovich
BROTHERS KARAMAZOV, THE   MGM 1957
(Various)
CRIME AND PUNISHMENT   COL 1935
(Various)   WAR 1958
    (*Crime and punishment U.S.A.*)
GAMBLER AND OTHER
STORIES, THE   MGM 1949
(Various)   (*Great sinner, The*)

DOUGLAS, Felicity
IT'S NEVER TOO LATE (P)   ABP 1956
(Evans)

DOUGLAS, Lloyd Cassel
DISPUTED PASSAGE   PAR 1939
(Davies)
GREEN LIGHT, THE   WAR 1937
(Davies)
MAGNIFICENT OBSESSION   UN 1935
(Allen & Unwin)   UI 1954
ROBE, THE   FOX 1953
(Davies)
WHITE BANNERS   WAR 1938
(Davies)

DOWNES, Donald
EASTER DINNER, THE   PAR 1962
(Rinehart, N.Y.)   (*Pigeon that took Rome, The*)

DOYLE, *Sir* **Arthur Conan**
ADVENTURE OF THE FIVE PIPS   UN 1945
(Murray)

237

DOYLE, *Sir* **Arthur Conan** (*continued*)

HIS LAST BOW (Murray)	UN 1942 (*Sherlock Holmes and the voice of terror*)
HOUND OF THE BASKERVILLES, THE (Murray)	ID 1932 FOX 1939 UA 1959
LOST WORLD, THE (Murray)	FOX 1960
MAN WITH THE TWISTED LIP, THE (*In* Adventures of Sherlock Holmes: Murray)	GN 1951
RETURN OF SHERLOCK HOLMES (Murray)	PAR 1929
SIGN OF FOUR (Murray)	WW 1932
SIX NAPOLEONS (Murray)	UN 1944 (*Pearl of death*)
STUDY IN SCARLET, A (Murray)	WW 1933

DOYLE, Monte

SIGNPOST TO MURDER (P) (French)	MGM 1965

DRATLER, Jay

PITFALL (Oxford U.P.)	UA 1948

DREISER, Theodore

AMERICAN TRAGEDY, AN (Constable)	PAR 1931 PAR 1951 (*Place in the sun, A*)
JENNIE GERHARDT (Constable)	PAR 1933
SISTER CARRIE (Constable)	PAR 1952 (*Carrie*)

DRESSER, Davis *see*
  HALLIDAY, Brett *pseud.*

DRUMMOND, John D.

BUT FOR THESE MEN (W. H. Allen)	RANK 1965 (*Heroes of the Telemark*)

DRUMMOND, William

LIFE FOR RUTH (Corgi Bks.)	RANK 1962

DRUON, Maurice

    CURTAIN FALLS, THE   BL 1964
    (Hart-Davis)

DRURY, Allen

    ADVISE AND CONSENT   BL 1962
    (Collins)

DRUTEN, John van

    AFTER ALL (P)   MGM 1932
    (*In* Famous plays of 1931: Gollancz)   (*New morals for old*)
    BEHOLD WE LIVE (P)   RKO 1933
    (Gollancz)   (*If I were free*)
    BELL, BOOK AND CANDLE (P)   COL 1958
    (French)
    I AM A CAMERA (P)   BL 1955
    (Random House, N.Y.)
    I REMEMBER MAMA (P)   RKO 1948
    (Dramatists, N.Y.)
    LONDON WALL (P)   BI 1931
    (Gollancz)   (*After office hours*)
    OLD ACQUAINTANCE (P)   WAR 1943
    (French)
    THERE'S ALWAYS JULIET (P)   PAR 1941
    (French, N.Y.)   (*One night in Lisbon*)
    VOICE OF THE TURTLE (P)   WAR 1947
    (Joseph)
    YOUNG WOODLEY (P)   BI 1930
    (Putnam)
    YOUNG WOODLEY   BI 1930
    (Gollancz)

DRYER, Bernard Victor

    PORT AFRIQUE   COL 1956
    (Cassell)

DUFFY, Clinton *and* JENNINGS, Dean

    SAN QUENTIN   ABP 1954
    (Davies)   (*Men behind bars*)
                         GN 1956
                         (*Steel cage, The*)

DUGUID, Julian

    GREEN HELL   UN 1940
    (Various)

DUMAS, Alexandre (*père*)

    BLACK TULIP   CINERAMA 1965
    (Various)
    COMPANIONS OF JEHU, THE   COL 1945
    (Dent)   (*Fighting guardsmen*)

DUMAS, Alexandre (*continued*)

COUNT OF MONTE CRISTO, THE (Various)	UA 1934
MAN IN THE IRON MASK, THE (Collins)	UA 1939
MEMOIRS OF A PHYSICIAN (Routledge)	UA 1949 (*Black magic*)
THREE MUSKETEERS, THE (Various)	RKO 1935 FOX 1939 MGM 1949

DUMAS, Alexandre (*fils*)

LADY OF THE CAMELIAS, THE (Various)	MGM 1936 (*Camille*)

DU MAURIER, Daphne

BIRDS, THE (*In* Short stories: Gollancz)	RANK 1963
FRENCHMAN'S CREEK (Gollancz)	PAR 1944
HUNGRY HILL (Gollancz)	TC 1947
JAMAICA INN (Gollancz)	PAR 1939
MY COUSIN RACHEI (Gollancz)	FOX 1952
REBECCA (Gollancz)	UA 1940
REBECCA (P) (Gollancz)	UA 1940
SCAPEGOAT, THE (Gollancz)	MGM 1958
YEARS BETWEEN, THE (P) (Gollancz)	BOX 1946

DU MAURIER, George

PETER IBBOTSON (Various)	PAR 1935
TRILBY (Various)	WAR 1931 (*Svengali*) REN 1954 (*Svengali*)

DUNCAN, Alex

IT'S A VET'S LIFE (Joseph)	RANK 1961 (*In the doghouse*)

DUPREZ, Fred

MY WIFE'S FAMILY (P) (French)	ABP 1956

DURAS, Marguerite

SAILOR FROM GIBRALTAR, THE   UA 1967
(Calder)

SEA OF TROUBLES, A   RANK 1958
(Methuen)   *(Sea wall)*

10.30 p.m. ON A SUMMER NIGHT   UA 1965
(Calder)   *(10.30 p.m. summer)*

DURRANT, Theo

MARBLE FOREST   ABP 1957
(Wingate)   *(Macabre)*

DURRELL, Lawrence

JUSTINE   FOX 1969
(Faber)   *(Alexandria Quartet)*

DURRENMATT, Friedrich

VISIT, THE (P)   FOX 1964
(French, N.Y.)

D'USSEAU, Arnaud *and* GOW, James

DEEP ARE THE ROOTS (P)   UA 1944
(Dramatists, N.Y.)   *(Tomorrow the world)*

DYER, Charles

RATTLE OF A SIMPLE MAN (P)   WAR 1964
(French)

E

EARL, Lawrence

ESCAPE OF 'THE AMETHYST' THE   BL 1957
(Harrap)   *(Yangtse incident)*

EASTWOOD, James

MURDER INC.   WAR 1952
(Dakers)

ECHARD, Margaret

DARK FANTASTIC   WAR 1951
(Invincible Press)   *(Lightning strikes twice)*

EDMONDS, Walter Dumaux

ROME HAUL   FOX 1953
(Triangle Bks., N.Y.)   *(Farmer takes a wife, The)*

EDWARDS, Samuel

55 DAYS AT PEKING   RANK 1962
(Bantam Bks., N.Y.)

241

EHRLICH, Max

FIRST TRAIN TO BABYLON   UA 1961
(Gollancz)   (*Naked edge, The*)

ELIOT, Thomas Stearns

MURDER IN THE CATHEDRAL (P) FILM TRADERS 1951
(Faber)

ELLIN, Stanley

DREADFUL SUMMIT   UA 1954
(Simon & Schuster, N.Y.)   (*Big night, The*)

ELLIS, Ruth

WHITE COLLARS (P)   MGM 1929
(French, N.Y.)   (*Idle rich*)

ELY, David

SECONDS   PAR 1965
(Deutsch)

EMMONS, Della Gould

SACAJAWEA OF THE SHOSHONES PAR 1955
(Binfords, Portland, Ore)   (*Far horizons, The*)

ENDORE, Guy

METHINKS THE LADY   FOX 1951
(Cresset Press)   (*Whirlpool*)
WEREWOLF OF PARIS, THE   RANK 1960
(Long)   (*Curse of the werewolf, The*)

ENGSTRAND, Stuart David

BEYOND THE FOREST   WAR 1951
(Cape)

EPHRON, Phoebe *and* **EPHRON, Henry**

TAKE HER, SHE'S MINE (P)   FOX 1963
(Random House, N.Y.)

ERSKINE, John

EXPERIMENT IN SINCERITY   UN 1930
(Putnam)   (*Lady surrenders, A*)

ERSKINE, Laurie York

RENFREW'S LONG TRAIL   MON 1940
(Grosset, N.Y.)   (*Danger ahead*)
RENFREW RIDES AGAIN   MON 1939
(Appleton, N.Y.)   (*Fighting mad*)
RENFREW RIDES NORTH   MON 1940
(Grosset, N.Y.)   (*Yukon flight*)
RENFREW RIDES THE RANGE   MON 1939
(Appleton, N.Y.)   (*Crashing thru'*)

ERTZ, Susan

  IN THE COOL OF THE DAY   MGM 1963
  (Collins)

ERVINE, St John Green

  BOYD'S SHOP (P)   RANK 1960
  (Allen & Unwin)

  FIRST MRS FRASER, THE (P)   STERLING 1932
  (Chatto & Windus)

EUNSON, D. *see* **WILDE, H.** *jt. author*

EURIPIDES

  ELECTRA (P)   UA 1963
  (Various)

EUSTACE, C. J.

  DAMAGED LIVES   PAR 1935
  (Putnam, N.Y.)

EVANS, E. Eynon

  BLESS THIS HOUSE (P)   MON 1955
  (French)   (Room in the house)

  WISHING WELL (P)   ADELPHI 1954
  (French)   (*Happiness of three women, The*)

EVANS, Evan

  BRANDED   PAR 1950
  (Various)

EVANS, Max

  ROUNDERS, THE   MGM 1965
  (Macmillan, N.Y.)

F

FABIAN, Robert

  FABIAN OF THE YARD   EROS 1954
  (Naldrett Press)

FABIAN, Warner

  WEEK-END GIRL   FOX 1932
  (Paul)   (*Week-ends only*

FAIRLIE, Gerard

  CALLING BULLDOG DRUMMOND MGM 1951
  (Hodder & Stoughton)

FALLADA, Hans

  LITTLE MAN, WHAT NOW?   UN 1934
  (Putnam)

FANTE, John
    FULL OF LIFE   COL 1957
    (Little Brown, Boston)

FARNOL, Jeffrey
    AMATEUR GENTLEMAN, THE   UA 1936
    (Sampson Low)

FARRELL, Henry
    BABY JANE   WAR 1962
    (Eyre & Spottiswoode)   (*Whatever happened to Baby Jane*)

FARRELL, James Thomas
    STUDS LONIGAN   UA 1959
    (W. H. Allen)   UA 1964

FARRELL, M. J. *and* PERRY, John
    TREASURE HUNT (P)   BL 1952
    (Collins)

FAST, Howard
    MY GLORIOUS BROTHERS   UA 1959
    (Panther Bks.)
    SPARTACUS   RANK 1959
    (Panther Bks.)
    WINSTON AFFAIR, THE   FOX 1963
    (Methuen)   (*Man in the middle*)

FAST, Howard *see also*
    CUNNINGHAM, E. V. *pseud.*

FAUCHIOS, Rene
    LATE CHRISTOPHER
    BEAN, THE (P)   MGM 1933
    (Gollancz)   (*Christopher Bean*)

FAULKNER, John Meade
    MOONFLEET   MGM 1955
    (Little Brown, Boston)

FAULKNER, William
    HAMLET, THE   FOX 1957
    (Chatto & Windus)   (*Long hot summer, The*)
    INTRUDER IN THE DUST   MGM 1949
    (Random House, N.Y.)
    PYLON   UA 1957
    (Chatto & Windus)   (*Tarnished angels, The*)
    REQUIEM FOR A NUN   FOX 1960
    (Chatto & Windus)   (*Sanctuary*)

    SANCTUARY   FOX 1960
    (Chatto & Windus)
    SOUND AND THE FURY, THE   FOX 1959
    (Chatto & Windus)

FAUST, Frederick *see*
    BRAND, Max *pseud.*

FEARING, Kenneth
  BIG CLOCK, THE   PAR 1948
  (Lane)

FEDER, S. *see* **TURKUS, B.** *jt. author*

FEINER, Ruth
  THREE CUPS OF COFFEE   ABP 1951
  (Dakers)   (*Woman's angle, A*)

FENTON, Edward
  MYSTERY IN FLORENCE   DISNEY 1963
  (Constable)   (*Escapade in Florence*)

FERBER, Edna
  CIMARRON   RKO 1931
  (Gollancz)   MGM 1960
  COME AND GET IT   UA 1936
  (Heinemann)
  GIANT   WAR 1956
  (Gollancz)
  ICE PALACE   WAR 1960
  (Gollancz)
  OLD MAN MINICK   WAR 1932
  (Doubleday, N.Y.)   (*Expert, The*)
  SARATOGA TRUNK   WAR 1945
  (Heinemann)
  SHOW BOAT   UN 1929
  (Heinemann)   UN 1936
                       MGM 1951
  SO BIG   WAR 1932
  (Heinemann)   WAR 1953

FERBER, Edna *see also*
    KAUFMAN, G. S. *jt. author*

FERGUSON, Margaret
  SIGN OF THE RAM, THE   COL 1948
  (Hale)

FETHERSTONHAUGH, Robert Collier
  ROYAL CANADIAN MOUNTED
  POLICE   PAR 1940
  (Various)   (*North West mounted police*)

FEUCHTWANGER, Leon
  JEW SÜSS (P)   GB 1935
  (Hutchinson)
  JEW SÜSS   GB 1935
  (Hutchinson)

FIELD, Medora

  BLOOD ON HER SHOE   REP 1944
  (Jarrolds)   *(Girl who dared. The)*

  WHO KILLED AUNT MAGGIE   REP 1940
  (Jarrolds)

FIELD, Rachel

  ALL THIS AND HEAVEN TOO   WAR 1940
  (Collins)

  AND NOW TOMORROW   PAR 1944
  (Collins)

  TIME OUT OF MIND   UA 1947
  (Macmillan)

FIELDING, Henry

  TOM JONES   UA 1962
  (Dent)

FIELDS, Joseph

  DOUGHGIRLS, THE (P)   WAR 1944
  (Random House, N.Y.)

FIELDS, Joseph *see also*
  CHODOROV, J. *jt. author*

FIELDS, Joseph *and* **CHODOROV, Jerome**

  ANNIVERSARY WALTZ (P)   UA 1959
  (Random House, N.Y.)   *(Happy anniversary)*
  MY SISTER EILEEN (P)   COL 1942
  (Macmillan)   COL 1955

FIELDS, Joseph *and* **DE VRIES, Peter**

  TUNNEL OF LOVE, THE (P)   MGM 1959
  (French)

FIENBURGH, Wilfred

  NO LOVE FOR JOHNNIE   RANK 1960
  (Hutchinson)

FINCH, M.

  DENTIST IN THE CHAIR   REN 1960
  (Ace Bks.)

FINDLEY, Ferguson *pseud.*

  REMEMBER THAT FACE!   COL 1951
  (Reinhardt & Evans)

FINEMAN, Irving

  THESE OUR LOVERS   WAR 1962
  (Long)   *(Lovers must learn)*

FINKLEHOFFE, F. R. *see*
MONKS, J. *jt. author*

FINNEY, Jack
   ASSAULT ON A QUEEN   PAR 1966
   (Eyre & Spottiswoode)
   BODY SNATCHERS, THE   COL 1956
   (Eyre & Spottiswoode)   (*Invasion of the body snatchers, The*)
   GOOD NEIGHBOUR SAM   COL 1965
   (Eyre & Spottiswoode)
   HOUSE OF NUMBERS   MGM 1957
   (Eyre & Spottiswoode)

FISHER, Clay
   TALL MEN, THE   FOX 1955
   (Houghton Mifflin, Boston)
   YELLOWSTONE KELLY   WAR 1959
   (Houghton Mifflin, Boston)

FISHER, Michael
   BETHNAL GREEN   BL 1964
   (Cassell)   (*Place to go, A*)

FISHER, Stephen Gould
   DESTINATION TOKYO   WAR 1943
   (Appleton, N.Y.)

FISHER, Steve
   I WAKE UP SCREAMING   FOX 1953
   (Hale)   (*Vicki*)

FITCH, Clyde
   BEAU BRUMMELL (P)   MGM 1954
   (Lane, N.Y.)

FITZGERALD, Francis Scott Key
   BABYLON REVISITED   MGM 1954
   (Scribner, N.Y.)   (*Last time I saw Paris, The*)
   GREAT GATSBY, THE   PAR 1949
   (Grey Walls Press)
   TENDER IS THE NIGHT   FOX 1962
   (Grey Walls Press)

FITZ-SIMONS, Foster
   BRIGHT LEAF   WAR 1950
   (Rinehart, N.Y.)

FLAUBERT, Gustave
   MADAME BOVARY   HOLLYWOOD 1932
   (Cape)   (*Unholy love*)
                     MGM 1949
   SALAAMBO   FOX 1959
   (Dent)

FLAVIN, Martin
  BROKEN DISHES (P)   IN 1936
  (French, N.Y.)   (*Love begins at twenty*)
                          WAR 1961
                          (*Too young to marry*)

  ONE WAY OUT (P)   COL 1950
  (French, N.Y.)   (*Convicted*)

FLEISCHMAN, Albert Sidney
  BLOOD ALLEY   WAR 1955
  (Corgi Bks.)
  YELLOWLEG   WAR 1961
  (Muller)   (*Deadly companions, The*)

FLEMING, Berry
  COLONEL EFFINGHAM'S RAID   FOX 1945
  (Various)

FLEMING, Ian
  CASINO ROYALE   COL 1966
  (Cape)
  DR. NO   UA 1962
  (Cape)
  FROM RUSSIA WITH LOVE   UA 1963
  (Cape)
  GOLDFINGER   UA 1963
  (Cape)
  THUNDERBALL   UA 1964
  (Cape)
  YOU ONLY LIVE TWICE   UA 1966
  (Cape)

FLEMING, Joan
  DEEDS OF DR. DEADCERT, THE   FOX 1957
  (Hutchinson)   (*Family doctor*)

FLENDER, Harold
  PARIS BLUES   UA 1961
  (Panther Bks.)

FLETCHER, Lucille
  BLINDFOLD   UI 1965
  (Eyre & Spottiswoode)

FLEXNER, James Thomas
  DOCTORS ON HORSEBACK   MGM 1949
  (Heinemann)   (*Big Jack*)

FOLDES, Yolande
  GOLDEN EARRINGS   PAR 1947
  (Hale)
  MAKE YOU A GOOD WIFE   PAR 1948
  (Hutchinson)   (*My own true love*)

248

FONTAINE, Robert L.

 HAPPY TIME, THE   COL 1952
 (Hamilton)

FOOTE, Horton

 CHASE, THE (P)   COL 1965
 (Dramatists, N.Y.)

 TRAVELLING LADY, THE (P) COL 1965
 (Dramatists, N.Y.)   *(Baby, the rain must fall)*

FOOTE, John Taintor

 LOOK OF EAGLES   FOX 1938
 (Appleton, N.Y.)   *(Kentucky)*

FORBES, Esther

 JOHNNY TREMAIN   DISNEY 1957
 (Constable)

 RUNNING OF THE TIDE, THE MGM 1949
 (Houghton Mifflin, Boston)

FORBES, Murray

 HOLLOW TRIUMPH   EL 1948
 (Martin)

FOREMAN, Leonard London

 DON DESPERADO   PAR 1952
 (Cassell)   *(Savage, The)*

 ROAD TO SAN JACINTO ABP 1954
 (Dutton, N.Y.)   *(Arrow in the dust)*

FORESTER, Cecil Scott

 AFRICAN QUEEN, THE ROMULUS 1951
 (Joseph)

 BROWN ON 'RESOLUTION' GB 1933
 (Lane)   FOX 1952
    (Single handed)

 CAPTAIN HORNBLOWER, R.N. WAR 1951
 (Joseph)   *(Captain Horatio Hornblower, R.N.)*

 GUN, THE   UA 1957
 (Joseph)   *(Pride and the passion, The)*

 HUNT THE BISMARK   FOX 1960
 (Joseph)   *(Sink the Bismark)*

 PAYMENT DEFERRED   MGM 1932
 (Lane)

 PAYMENT DEFERRED (P) MGM 1932
 (Lane)

FORREST, A. J.

 INTERPOL   COL 1957
 (Wingate)

FORSTER, Margaret
   GEORGY GIRL   COL 1966
   (Secker & Warburg)

FOWLER, Gene
   BEAU JAMES   PAR 1957
   (Viking, N.Y.)

FOWLER, Helen Marjorie
   SHADES WILL NOT VANISH   ABP 1957
   (Angus & Robertson)   (*Strange intruder*)

FOWLES, John
   COLLECTOR, THE   BL 1964
   (Cape)

FOX, John
   LITTLE SHEPHERD OF
   KINGDOM COME, THE   FOX 1961
   (Scribner, N.Y.)

FOX, Norman A.
   RAWHIDE YEARS, THE   UI 1955
   (Collins)
   ROUGHSHOD   GFD 1952
   (Dodd, N.Y.)   (*Gunsmoke*)
   TALL MAN RIDING   WAR 1955
   (Collins)

FRAILEY, O. *see* **NESS, E.** *jt. author*

FRANCE, Anatole
   CRIME OF SYLVESTRE
   BONNARD, THE   RKO 1935
   (Collins)   (*Chasing yesterday*)

FRANK, Anne
   DIARY OF ANNE FRANK, THE   FOX 1959
   (Gollancz)

FRANK, Gerold *see*
   BARRYMORE, D. *jt. author*

FRANK, Leonhard
   CARL AND ANNA   MGM 1932
   (Various)   (*As you desire me*)

FRANK, Patrick
   HOLD BACK THE NIGHT   ABP 1956
   (Hamilton)

FRANKAU, Pamela
  JEZEBEL   WAR 1938
  (Rich & Cowan)

FRANKEN, Rose
  CLAUDIA   FOX 1943
  (W. H. Allen)
  CLAUDIA (P)   FOX 1943
  (French, N.Y.)
  CLAUDIA AND DAVID   FOX 1946
  (W. H. Allen)

FRAZEE, Steve
  DESERT GUNS   WAR 1961
  (World, N.Y.)   (*Gold of the seven saints*)
  HIGH CAGE   PAR 1958
  (Macmillan, N.Y.)   (*High hell*)

FREDE, Richard
  INTERNS, THE   COL 1962
  (Corgi Bks.)

FREEDMAN, Benedict *and*
  FREEDMAN, Nancy Mars
  MRS. MIKE   UA 1950
  (Hamilton)

FREEMAN, Gillian *see*
  GEORGE, Eliot *pseud.*

FREY, Charles F. *see*
  FINDLEY, Ferguson *pseud.*

FRINGS, *Mrs.* **Ketti**
  HOLD BACK THE DAWN   PAR 1941
  (Duell, N.Y.)

FULLER, Samuel
  DARK PAGE, THE   COL 1952
  (Duell, N.Y.)

G

GABRIEL, Gilbert Wolf
  I, JAMES LEWIS   UN 1941
  (Doubleday, N.Y.)   (*This woman is mine*)

GADDIS, Thomas E.
  BIRD MAN OF ALCATRAZ   UA 1962
  (Four Square Bks.)

GAINES, Robert

FINAL NIGHT   BL 1953
(Heinemann)   (*Front page story*)

GALLICO, Paul

SMALL MIRACLE, THE   IND 1951
(Joseph)   (*Never take no for an answer*)

THOMASINA   DISNEY 1963
(Joseph)   (*Three lives of Thomasina, The*)

TRIAL BY TERROR   COL 1952
(Joseph)   (*Assignment-Paris*)

GALSWORTHY, John

ESCAPE (P)   RKO 1930
(Duckworth)   FOX 1948

FIRST AND THE LAST, THE   LF 1940
(Heinemann)   (*Twenty-one days*)

LOYALTIES (P)   AUTEN 1934
(Duckworth)

MAN OF PROPERTY, THE   MGM 1949
(Heinemann)   (*Forsyte saga, The*)

OLD ENGLISH (P)   WAR 1930
(Duckworth)

SKIN GAME (P)   BI 1931
(Duckworth)

GANN, Ernest Kellogg

BLAZE AT NOON   PAR 1937
(Aldor)

FATE IS THE HUNTER   FOX 1964
(Hodder & Stoughton)

FIDDLER'S GREEN   UI 1951
(Sloane, N.Y.)   (*Raging tide, The*)

HIGH AND THE MIGHTY, THE   WAR 1954
(Hodder & Stoughton)

ISLAND IN THE SKY   WAR 1953
(Joseph)

SOLDIER OF FORTUNE   FOX 1955
(Hodder & Stoughton)

TWILIGHT FOR THE GODS   RANK 1957
(Hodder & Stoughton)

GARDEN, John

ALL ON A SUMMER'S DAY   ABP 1950
(Joseph)   (*Double confession*)

GARDNER, Erle Stanley

CASE OF THE CARETAKER'S
CAT, THE   IN 1936
(Cassell)   (*Case of the black cat, The*)

GARDENER, Erle Stanley (*continued*)

CASE OF THE CURIOUS
BRIDE, THE   IN 1935
(Cassell)

CASE OF THE HOWLING
DOG, THE   WAR 1934
(Grosset, N.Y.)

CASE OF THE LUCKY LEGS, THE   WAR 1935
(Harrap)

CASE OF THE STUTTERING
BISHOP, THE   WAR 1937
(Cassell)

CASE OF THE VELVET
CLAWS, THE   IN 1936
(Harrap)

GARDNER, Herbert

THOUSAND CLOWNS, A (P)   UA 1964
(Random House, N.Y.)

GARDNER, John

LIQUIDATOR, THE   MGM 1965
(Muller)

GARLAND, A. P.

YANK AT OXFORD, A   MGM 1938
(Collins)

GARSTIN, Crosbie

CHINA SEAS   MGM 1935
(Chatto & Windus)

GARVE, Andrew

DEATH AND THE SKY ABOVE US   BL 1962
(Pan Bks.)   (*Two-letter alibi*)

MEGSTONE PLOT, THE   PAR 1959
(Collins)   (*Touch of larceny, A*)

GARY, Romain

COLOURS OF THE DAY, THE   FOX 1959
(Joseph)   (*Man who understood women*)

LADY L.   MGM 1965
(Joseph)

ROOTS OF HEAVEN, THE   FOX 1958
(Joseph)

GAY, John

BEGGAR'S OPERA, THE (P)   BL 1953
(French)

GAZZO, Michael Vincente
    HATFUL OF RAIN, A (P)   FOX 1957
    (Random House, N.Y.)

GEBLER, Ernest
    PLYMOUTH ADVENTURE, THE   MGM 1952
    (Cassell)

GEER, Andrew Clare
    SEA CHASE, THE   WAR 1954
    (Collins)

GENET, Jean
    BALCONY, THE (P)   BL 1963
    (Faber)

GEORGE, Eliot *pseud.*
    LEATHER BOYS, THE   BL 1962
    (Blond)

GEORGE, Peter
    TWO HOURS TO DOOM   COL 1963
    (Corgi Bks.)   (*Dr Strangelove: or How I learned to stop worrying and love the bomb*)

GIBBS, Anthony Hamilton
    YOUNG APOLLO, THE   MUNDUS 1935
    (Hutchinson)   (*Men of tomorrow*)

GIBSON, William
    MIRACLE WORKER, THE (P)   UA 1962
    (Knopf, N.Y.)
    TWO FOR THE SEESAW (P)   UA 1962
    (French)

GIELGUD, Val Henry
    DEATH AT BROADCASTING
    HOUSE   PHOENIX 1935
    (Rich & Cowan)

GILBERT, Anthony *pseud.*
    WOMAN IN RED, THE   COL 1945
    (Collins)   (*My name is Julia Ross*)

GILBERT, Michael
    DEATH HAS DEEP ROOTS   GN 1956
    (Pan Bks.)   (*Guilty ?*)
    DEATH IN CAPTIVITY   BL 1958
    (Pan Bks.)   (*Danger within*)

GILBERT, *Sir* William Schwenck
    MIKADO, THE (P)   UN 1939
    (Macmillan)

GILBRETH, Frank Bunker *and*
    CAREY, Ernestine

BELLS ON THEIR TOES   FOX 1952
(Heinemann)

CHEAPER BY THE DOZEN   FOX 1950
(Heinemann)

GILDEN, K. B.

HURRY SUNDOWN   PAR 1966
(Heinemann)

GILL, Tom

GAY BANDIT OF THE BORDER   FOX 1932
(Collins)   (*Gay Caballero*)

NO PLACE FOR WOMEN   PAR 1953
(Putnam, N.Y.)   (*Tropic zone*)

GILLIAT, S. *see* **LAUNDER, F.** *jt. author*

GILLIGAN, Edmund

GAUNT WOMAN, THE   RKO 1950
(Scribner, N.Y.)

GILMAN, Peter

DIAMOND HEAD   COL 1962
(Joseph)

GILPATRIC, Guy

ACTION IN THE NORTH
ATLANTIC   WAR 1943
(Dutton, N.Y.)

GINSBURY, Norman

FIRST GENTLEMAN, THE (P)   COL 1948
(Hammond)

GIPSON, Frederick Benjamin

CIRCLES ROUND THE WAGON FOX 1959
(Joseph)   (*Hound dog man*)

OLD YELLER   DISNEY 1958
(Harper, N.Y.)

SAVAGE SAM   DISNEY 1963
(Hodder & Stoughton)

GLASGOW, Ellen

IN THIS OUR LIFE   WAR 1942
(Cape)

GLEMSER, Bernard

GIRL ON A WING   MGM 1963
(Macdonald)   (*Come fly with me*)

GLICKMAN, William *and* **STEIN, Joseph**

MRS. GIBBONS' BOYS (P)   BL 1962
(French, N.Y.)

GLOAG, Julian

OUR MOTHER'S HOUSE   MGM 1967
(Pan)

GODDEN, Rumer

BATTLE OF THE VILLA
FIORITA, THE   WAR 1964
(Macmillan)   (*Affair at the Villa Fiorita, The*)

BLACK NARCISSUS   ARCHERS 1947
(Davies)

EPISODE OF SPARROWS, AN   RANK 1957
(Macmillan)   (*Innocent sinners*)

FUGUE IN TIME   RKO 1949
(Joseph)   (*Enchantment*)

GREENGAGE SUMMER, THE   RANK 1960
(Macmillan)

RIVER, THE   UA 1951
(Joseph)

GOETZ, Ruth *and* **GOETZ, Augustus**

HEIRESS, THE (P)   PAR 1949
(Reinhardt & Evans)

GOGOL, Nikolai Vasilevich

INSPECTOR GENERAL, THE (P)   WAR 1949
(French, N.Y.)

TARAS BULBA   UA 1962
(Dent)

GOLDING, Louis

MR. EMMANUEL   TC 1944
(Rich & Cowan)

GOLDING, William

LORD OF THE FLIES   BL 1963
(Faber)

GOLDMAN, William

SOLDIER IN THE RAIN   WAR 1965
(Eyre & Spottiswoode)

GOLDSMITH, Martin M.

DETOUR   PRC 1946
(Hurst & Blackett)

256

GOODCHILD, George

SPLENDID CRIME, THE   RKO 1931
(Hodder & Stoughton)   (*Public defender*)

GOODE, R. *see* **HUROK, S.** *jt. author*

GOODIN, Peggy

CLEMENTINE   EL 1948
(Dutton, N.Y.)   (*Mickey*)

TAKE CARE OF MY LITTLE GIRL   FOX 1951
(Dutton, N.Y.)

GOODIS, David

DARK PASSAGE   WAR 1947
(World, N.Y.)

GOODMAN, George J. W.

WHEELER-DEALERS, THE   MGM 1964
(Doubleday, N.Y.)   (*Separate beds*)

GOODRICH, Frances *and*
   HACKETT, Albert

DIARY OF ANNE FRANK, THE (P)   FOX 1959
(French)

GORDON, Arthur

REPRISAL   COL 1956
(Hamilton)

GORDON, Leon

WHITE CARGO (P)   BI 1930
(Various)   MGM 1942

GORDON, *Mrs.* **Mildred and GORDON, G.**

CASE FILE: F.B.I.   UA 1954
(Doubleday, N.Y.)   (*Down 3 dark streets*)

MAKE HASTE TO LIVE   REP 1954
(Doubleday, N.Y.)

OPERATION TERROR   COL 1962
(Macdonald)   (*Grip of fear*)

UNDERCOVER CAT   DISNEY 1964
(Macdonald)   (*That darn cat*)

GORDON, Richard

CAPTAIN'S TABLE, THE   RANK 1958
(Joseph)

DOCTOR AT LARGE   RANK 1957
(Joseph)

DOCTOR AT SEA   BFD 1955
(Joseph)

GORDON, Richard (*continued*)

DOCTOR IN CLOVER   RANK 1965
(Joseph)

DOCTOR IN LOVE   RANK 1959
(Joseph)

DOCTOR IN THE HOUSE   GFD 1954
(Joseph)

GORDON, Ruth

LEADING LADY (P)   MGM 1953
(Dramatists, N.Y.)   (*Actress, The*)
OVER 21 (P)   COL 1945
(Dramatists, N.Y.)

GORMAN, Herbert

SUZY   MGM 1936
(Cassell)

GOUDGE, Elizabeth

GREEN DOLPHIN STREET   MGM 1947
(Hodder & Stoughton)

GOUZENKO, Igor

THIS WAS MY CHOICE   FOX 1948
(Dent)   (*Iron curtain*)

GOW, J. *see* **D'USSEAU, A.** *jt. author*

GRAEME, Bruce *pseud.*

FOG FOR A KILLER   GN 1962
(Hutchinson)   (*Out of the fog*)
HATE SHIP   BI 1930
(Hutchinson)
SUSPENSE   GN 1956
(Hutchinson)   (*Face in the night*)
WAY OUT, THE   AA 1955
(Hutchinson)   (*Dial 999*)

GRAHAM, Sheilah *and* **FRANK, Gerold**

BELOVED INFIDEL   FOX 1959
(Cassell)

GRAHAM, Winston

FORTUNE IS A WOMAN   COL 1957
(Hodder & Stoughton)
MARNIE   UI 1964
(Hodder & Stoughton)
NIGHT WITHOUT STARS   GFD 1951
(Hodder & Stoughton)
TAKE MY LIFE   EL 1948
(Ward Lock)

GRANGER, Kathleen R. G.

   TEN AGAINST CAESAR   COL 1954
   (Houghton Mifflin, Boston)   *(Gun fury)*

GRANT, Neil

   DUSTY ERMINE (P)   TWICKENHAM 1936
   (French)

GRAZIANO, Rocky

   SOMEBODY UP THERE LIKES ME   MGM 1956
   (Hammond)

GREEN, A. *see* **COMDEN, B.** *jt. author*

GREEN, Frederick Lawrence

   ODD MAN OUT   TC 1947
   (Joseph)

   ON THE NIGHT OF THE FIRE   SOMLO 1939
   (Joseph)

GREEN, Gerald

   LAST ANGRY MAN, THE   COL 1959
   (Pan Bks.)

GREEN, G. *see*
   KLINGMAN, L. *jt. author*

GREEN, Janet

   MURDER MISTAKEN (P)   EROS 1955
   (Evans)   *(Cast a dark shadow)*

GREEN, Paul Eliot *and* **WRIGHT, Richard**

   NATIVE SON (P)   CLASSIC 1951
   (Harper, N.Y.)

GREENE, Graham

   ACROSS THE BRIDGE   RANK 1957
   (*In* 21 short stories: Heinemann)

   BASEMENT ROOM, THE   FOX 1948
   (Cresset Press)   *(Fallen idol, The)*

   BRIGHTON ROCK   ABP 1948
   (Heinemann)

   COMEDIANS, THE   MGM 1967
   (Heinemann)

   CONFIDENTIAL AGENT   WAR 1945
   (Heinemann)

   END OF THE AFFAIR, THE   COL 1954
   (Heinemann)

AUTHOR AND ORIGINAL TITLE	FILM TITLE

GREENE, Graham (*continued*)

GUN FOR SALE
(Various)
PAR 1942
(*This gun for sale*)
PAR 1957
(*Short cut to hell*)

HEART OF THE MATTER, THE
(Heinemann) — BL 1953

LOSER TAKES ALL
(Heinemann) — BL 1956

MAN WITHIN, THE
(Heinemann) — BOX 1947

MINISTRY OF FEAR
(Heinemann) — PAR 1944

OUR MAN IN HAVANA
(Heinemann) — COL 1959

POWER AND THE GLORY, THE
(Heinemann)
RKO 1947
(*Fugitive, The*)
PAR 1962

QUIET AMERICAN, THE
(Heinemann) — UA 1957

THIRD MAN, THE
(Heinemann) — GFD 1950

GREENE, Ward

DEATH IN THE DEEP SOUTH
(Cassell)
WAR 1937
(*They won't forget*)

LADY AND THE TRAMP
(Simon & Schuster, N.Y.) — DISNEY 1955

GREENWALD, Harold

CALL GIRL, THE
(Elek)
WAR 1960
(*Girl of the night*)

GREENWOOD, Robert

MR. BUNTING AT WAR
(Dent)
BN 1942
(*Salute John Citizen*)

GREENWOOD, Walter

CURE FOR LOVE, THE (P)
(French) — BL 1949

LOVE ON THE DOLE
(Cape) — UA 1941

GREENWOOD, W. *see also*
GOW, R. *jt. author*

GREGOR, Manfred

TOWN WITHOUT PITY
(Heinemann) — UA 1961

GRESHAM, W.

NIGHTMARE ALLEY   FOX 1947
(Heinemann)

GREY, Zane

BORDER LEGION   PAR 1930
(Hodder & Stoughton)   PAR 1934
                              (*Last round up, The*)

CODE OF THE WEST   PAR 1935
(Hodder & Stoughton)   (*Home on the Range*)
                              RKO 1947

DESERT GOLD   PAR 1936
(Nelson)

DRIFT FENCE   PAR 1935
(Hodder & Stoughton)

FIGHTING CARAVANS   PAR 1931
(Hodder & Stoughton)   PAR 1934
                              (*Wagon wheels*)

FORLORN RIVER   PAR 1937
(Hodder & Stoughton)

HERITAGE OF THE DESERT   PAR 1933
(Nelson)   PAR 1939

KNIGHTS OF THE RANGE   PAR 1940
(Hodder & Stoughton)

LAST TRAIL, THE   FOX 1933
(Hodder & Stoughton)

LIGHT OF WESTERN STARS, THE   PAR 1930
(Nelson)   PAR 1940

LONE STAR RANGER   FOX 1930
(Harper)   FOX 1942

MAN OF THE FOREST   PAR 1933
(Hodder & Stoughton)

MAVERICK QUEEN, THE   REP 1956
(Hodder & Stoughton)

MYSTERIOUS RIDER, THE   PAR 1933
(Hodder & Stoughton)   PAR 1938

NEVADA   PAR 1935
(Hodder & Stoughton)

RAINBOW TRAIL   FOX 1932
(Harper)

RIDERS OF THE PURPLE SAGE   FOX 1931
(Harper)   FOX 1941

ROBBERS' ROOST   FOX 1933
(Hodder & Stoughton)   UA 1955

SUNSET PASS   PAR 1933
(Hodder & Stoughton)

THUNDERING HERD   PAR 1933
(Hodder & Stoughton)

GREY, Zane (*continued*)

THUNDER MOUNTAIN   FOX 1935
(Hodder & Stoughton)

TO THE LAST MAN   PAR 1933
(Hodder & Stoughton)

TWIN SOMBREROS   COL 1947
(Hodder & Stoughton)   (*Gunfighters*)

UNDER THE TONTO RIM   PAR 1933
(Hodder & Stoughton)

VANISHING AMERICAN, THE   REP 1955
(Hodder & Stoughton)

WANDERER OF THE WASTELAND   PAR 1935
(Hodder & Stoughton)   RKO 1945

WEST OF THE PECOS   RKO 1934
(Hodder & Stoughton)   RKO 1945

WILD FIRE   UN 1949
(Harper)   (*Red Canyon*)

WILD HORSE MESA   PAR 1932
(Hodder & Stoughton)

GRIMBLE, *Sir* **Arthur**

PATTERN OF ISLANDS   BL 1956
(Murray)   (*South Pacific*)

GRIMM, Jakob Ludwig Karl *and*
   GRIMM, Wilhelm Karl

GRIMMS' FAIRY TALES   MGM 1962
(Dent)   (*Wonderful world of the brothers Grimm,*
      The)

HANSEL AND GRETEL   RKO 1954
(Various)

TOM THUMB   MGM 1958
(Various)

GROVER, C. *see*
   GULLICK, Bill *pseud.*

GRUBB, Davis

NIGHT OF THE HUNTER, THE   UA 1955
(Hamilton)

GRUBER, Frank

BITTER SAGE   RKO 1956
(Wright & Brown)   (*Tension at Table Rock*)

LOCK AND THE KEY, THE   RKO 1957
(World Work)   (*Man in the vault*)

TOWN TAMER   PAR 1965
(Barker)

TWENTY PLUS TWO   WAR 1961
(Boardman)   (*It started in Tokyo*)

GUARESCHI, Giovanni
DON CAMILLO AND THE
PRODIGAL SON   MIRACLE FILMS 1954
(Gollancz)   *(Return of Don Camillo, The)*
LITTLE WORLD OF DON
CAMILLO, THE   LF 1952
(Gollancz)

GULLICK, Bill *pseud.*
BEND OF THE SNAKE   UI 1952
(Museum Press)   *(Where the river bends)*
HALLELUJAH TRAIL, THE   UA 1965
(Doubleday, N.Y.)
Originally called Hallelujah train, The

GUNN, James Edward
DEADLIER THAN THE MALE   RKO 1947
(World, N.Y.)   *(Born to kill)*

GUNN, Neil Miller
SILVER DARLINGS, THE   AA 1947
(Faber)

GUTHRIE, Alfred B.
BIG SKY, THE   RKO 1952
(Boardman)
THESE THOUSAND HILLS   FOX 1958
(Hutchinson)
WAY WEST, THE   UA 1966
(Corgi)

GUTHRIE, Thomas Anstey *see*
    ANSTEY, F. *pseud.*

GWALTNEY, Francis Irby
DAY THE CENTURY ENDED, THE   FOX 1956
(Secker & Warburg)   *(Between heaven and hell)*

H

HAASE, John
ERASMUS WITH FRECKLES   FOX 1965
(Simon & Schuster, N.Y.)   *(Dear Brigitte)*

HABE, Hans
THOUSAND SHALL FALL, A   UA 1943
(Harrap)   *(Hangmen also die)*

HACKETT, A. *see*
    GOODRICH, F. *jt. author*

HACKNEY, Alan
PRIVATE LIFE   BL 1959
(Gollancz)   *(I'm alright Jack)*
PRIVATE'S PROGRESS, A   BL 1956
(Gollancz)

HAEDRICH, Marcel
  CRACK IN THE MIRROR   FOX 1960
  (W. H. Allen)

HAGAN, James
  ONE SUNDAY AFTERNOON (P)   PAR 1933
  (French, N.Y.)   WAR 1941
                               (*Strawberry blonde, The*)
                               WAR 1948

HAGGARD, *Sir* Henry Rider
  KING SOLOMON'S MINES   GB 1937
  (Cassell)   MGM 1950
                               MGM 1958
                               (*Watusi*)

  SHE   RKO 1935
  (Macdonald)   WAR 1964

HAIGHT, G. *see* **SCOTT, A.** *jt. author*

HAILEY, Arthur
  FINAL DIAGNOSIS, THE   UA 1961
  (Joseph)   (*Young doctors, The*)
  HOTEL   WAR 1966
  (Pan)

HAINES, William Wister
  COMMAND DECISION   MGM 1948
  (Cassell)
  COMMAND DECISION (P)   MGM 1948
  (Random House, N.Y.)

HALEVY, Julian
  YOUNG LOVERS, THE   MGM 1964
  (Mayflower)

HALL, Adam
  BERLIN MEMORANDUM, THE RANK 1965
  (Collins)   (*Quiller memorandum, The*)

HALL, J. N. *see* **NORDHOFF, C.** *jt. author*

HALL, Magdalen King *see* **KING-HALL, M.**

HALL, Oakley
  WARLOCK   FOX 1959
  (Bodley Head)

HALL, Willis
  LONG AND THE SHORT AND
  THE TALL (P)   WAR 1960
  (Heinemann)

HALL, Willis *see also*
WATERHOUSE, K. *jt. author*

HALLIDAY, Brett *pseud.*
MURDER IS MY BUSINESS   PRC 1946
(Dodd, N.Y.)

HALLIDAY, Michael *pseud.*
CAT AND MOUSE   EROS 1958
(Hodder & Stoughton)

HAMBLEDON, Phyllis
NO DIFFERENCE TO ME   ABP 1950
(Sampson Low)   (*No place for Jennifer*)

HAMILTON, Donald
BIG COUNTRY, THE   UA 1958
(Wingate)
MURDERER'S ROW   BL 1966
(Muller)
ROUGH COMPANY   COL 1954
(Wingate)
SILENCERS, THE   COL 1965
(Hodder & Stoughton)

HAMILTON, Patrick
GASLIGHT (P)   BN 1940
(French)   MGM 1944
                               (*Murder in Thornton Square*)
ROPE (P)   WAR 1948
(French)
TO THE PUBLIC DANGER (P)   GFD 1948
(*In* Two radio plays: Constable)
TWENTY THOUSAND STREETS
UNDER THE SKY   RANK 1962
(Constable)   (*Bitter harvest*)

HAMMETT, Dashiell
GLASS KEY, THE   PAR 1935
(Cassell)   PAR 1942
MALTESE FALCON, THE   WAR 1931
(Cassell)   WAR 1941
THIN MAN, THE   MGM 1934
(Barker)

HAMNER, Earl *jun.*
SPENCER'S MOUNTAIN   WAR 1963
(Dial Press, N.Y.)

HANLEY, Clifford
LOVE FROM EVERYBODY   WAR 1961
(Hutchinson)   (*Don't bother to knock*)

HANNUM, *Mrs.* **Alberta**
   ROSEANNA McCOY   RKO 1951
   (Holt, N.Y.)

HANSBERRY, Loraine
   RAISIN IN THE SUN, A (P)   COL 1960
   (Methuen)

HAN SUYIN *pseud.*
   MANY SPLENDOURED THING, A   FOX 1955
   (Cape)   (*Love is a many splendoured thing*)
   MOUNTAIN IS YOUNG, THE   PAR 1959
   (Cape)

HARDING, Bertita
   MAGIC FIRE   REP 1956
   (Harrap)
   PHANTOM CROWN   WAR 1939
   (Harrap)   (Juarez)

HARDY, Jocelyn Lee
   EVERYTHING IS THUNDER   GB 1936
   (Lane)

HARDY, Lindsay
   GRAND DUKE AND
   MR. PIMM, THE   UA 1963
   (Cape)   (*All this and money too*)

HARDY, Stuart *pseud.*
   MOUNTAINS ARE MY KINGDOM UN 1938
   (Macaulay, N.Y.)   (*Forbidden valley*)

HARDY, Thomas
   FAR FROM THE MADDING
   CROWD   WAR 1966
   (Macmillan)

HARGROVE, Marion
   GIRL HE LEFT BEHIND, THE   WAR 1957
   (Viking, N.Y.)
   SEE HERE, PRIVATE HARGROVE MGM 1944
   (Hodder & Stoughton)

HARKINS, Philip
   BLACKBURN'S HEADHUNTERS ABP 1959
   (Cassell)   (*Surrender – hell*)

HARRER, Heinrich
   SEVEN YEARS IN TIBET   CURZON 1956
   (Hart-Davis)

HARRIS, Frank

  ON THE TRAIL   COL 1957
  (Lane)   (*Cowboy*)

HARRIS, John

  SEA SHALL NOT HAVE
  THEM, THE   EROS 1954
  (Hurst & Blackett)

HART, Moss

  CHRISTOPHER BLAKE (P)   WAR 1948
  (Random House, N.Y.)   (*Decision of Christopher Blake*)
  WINGED VICTORY (P)   FOX 1944
  (Various)

HART, Moss *see also*
  KAUFMAN, G. S. *jt. author*

HARTE, Bret

  OUTCASTS OF POKER FLAT   RKO 1937
  (Various)   FOX 1952
  TENNESSEE'S PARTNER   RKO 1955
  (Various)

HARTOG, Jan de

  FOUR POSTER, THE (P)   COL 1952
  (Sampson Low)
  INSPECTOR, THE   FOX 1962
  (Hamilton)
  SPIRAL ROAD, THE   UI 1962
  (Hamilton)
  STELLA   COL 1958
  (Hamilton)   (*Key, The*)

HARVEY, Frank

  POLTERGEIST, THE (P)   REN 1947
  (Deane)   (*Things happen at night*)

HARVEY, Frank *jun.*

  SALOON BAR (P)   EALING 1942
  (French)

HARVEY, William Fryer

  BEAST WITH FIVE FINGERS   WAR 1946
  (Dent)

HARWOOD, Harold Marsh

  MAN IN POSSESSION (P)   MGM 1931
  (Benn)   MGM 1937
                   (*Personal property*)

HARWOOD, Harold Marsh *and*
  BROWN, Robert Gore
  CYNARA   UA 1932
  (Benn)

HASS, Hans
  DIVING TO ADVENTURE   BL 1954
  (Jarrolds)   (*Under the Caribbean*)

HASTINGS, Charlotte
  BONADVENTURE (P)   GFD 1951
  (French)

HASTINGS, Hugh
  SEAGULLS OVER SORRENTO (P)   MGM 1954
  (*In* Plays of the year 1950: Elek)

HASTINGS, *Sir* Patrick
  BLIND GODDESS, THE (P)   FOX 1948
  (French)

HASTINGS, Phyllis
  RAPTURE IN MY RAGS   FOX 1964
  (Dent)   (*Rapture*)

HATCH, Eric
  MY MAN GODFREY   UN 1936
  (Barker)   UI 1957
  UNEXPECTED UNCLE   RKO 1941
  (Farrar, N.Y.)

HAVARD, René
  TAXI TO TOBRUK   MIRACLE FILMS 1961
  (Collins)

HAWKINS, John *and* **HAWKINS, Ward**
  FLOODS OF FEAR   RANK 1958
  (Eyre & Spottiswoode)

HAWLEY, Cameron
  CASH McCALL   WAR 1959
  (Hammond)
  EXECUTIVE SUITE   MGM 1954
  (Hammond)

HAWTHORNE, Nathaniel
  HOUSE OF THE SEVEN
  GABLES, THE   UN 1940
  (Various)
  SCARLET LETTER, THE   MAJESTIC 1934
  (Various)

HAY, Ian *pseud.*

HOUSEMASTER (P)   ALL 1939
(French)
HOUSEMASTER   ALL 1939
(Hodder & Stoughton)

HAY, Ian *and* **ARMSTRONG, Anthony**

ORDERS ARE ORDERS (P)   BL 1954
(French)

HAY, Ian *and* **KING-HALL, Stephen**

MIDDLE WATCH (P)   BI 1930
(French)   AB 1940
MIDSHIPMAID, THE (P)   GB 1932
(French)
OFF THE RECORD (P)   REN 1957
(French)   (*Carry on Admiral*)

HAYCOX, Ernest

BUGLES IN THE AFTERNOON   WAR 1952
(Hodder & Stoughton)
CANYON PASSAGE   UN 1946
(Hodder & Stoughton)
STAGE TO LORDSBURGH   UA 1939
(*In* By rope and lead: (*Stagecoach*)
Hodder & Stoughton)   FOX 1965
                                   (*Stagecoach*)
SUNDOWN JIM   FOX 1942
(Paul)

HAYES, Alfred

GIRL ON THE VIA
FLAMINIA, THE   UA 1954
(Gollancz)   (*Act of love*)

HAYES, Douglas

COMEDY MAN, THE   BL 1964
(Abelard-Schuman)

HAYES, Joseph

DESPERATE HOURS, THE   PAR 1955
(Deutsch)
DESPERATE HOURS, THE (P)   PAR 1955
(Random House, N.Y.)
THIRD DAY, THE   WAR 1965
(W. H. Allen)

HAYES, Marrijane *and*
    HAYES, Joseph Arnold
BONVOYAGE   DISNEY 1962
(Deutsch)

HAYES, Nelson

    DILDO CAY   PAR 1941
    (Davies)   (*Bahama passage*)

HEATH, W. L.

    VIOLENT SATURDAY   FOX 1955
    (Hamilton)

HECHT, Ben

    FLORENTINE DAGGER, THE   WAR 1935
    (Harrap)
    MIRACLE IN THE RAIN   WAR 1956
    (Knopf, N.Y.)

HECHT, Ben *and* **MacARTHUR, Charles**

    FRONT PAGE, THE (P)   UA 1931
    (Covici, N.Y.)   COL 1940
                                 (*His girl Friday*)

HEGGEN, Thomas

    MISTER ROBERTS   WAR 1955
    (Nicholson)

HEGGEN, Thomas *and* **LOGAN, Joshua**

    MISTER ROBERTS (P)   WAR 1955
    (Random House, N.Y.)

HELLMAN, Lillian Florence

    ANOTHER PART OF THE
    FOREST (P)   UN 1948
    (Viking, N.Y.)
    CHILDREN'S HOUR, THE (P)   UA 1936
    (Knopf, N.Y.)   (*These three*)
                                 UA 1962
                                 (*Loudest whisper, The*
    LITTLE FOXES, THE (P)   RKO 1941
    (Hamilton)
    NORTH STAR   RKO 1943
    (Macmillan)
    SEARCHING WIND, THE (P)   PAR 1946
    (Viking, N.Y.)
    TOYS IN THE ATTIC (P)   UA 1963
    (Random House, N.Y.)
    WATCH ON THE RHINE (P)   WAR 1943
    (French, N.Y.)

HELSETH, Henry Edward

    CHAIR FOR MARTIN ROME, THE   FOX 1948
    (Dodd, N.Y.)   (*Cry of the city*)

HEMINGWAY, Ernest

FAREWELL TO ARMS, A   PAR 1932
(Cape)   FOX 1957

FIESTA   FOX 1957
(Cape)   (*Sun also rises, The*)

FOR WHOM THE BELL TOLLS   PAR 1943
(Cape)

KILLERS, THE   UN 1946
(*In* First 49 stories: Cape)   RANK 1964

MACOMBER AFFAIR, THE   UN 1947
(*In* First 49 stories: Cape)

MY OLD MAN   FOX 1950
(*In* First 49 stories: Cape)   (*Under my skin*)

OLD MAN AND THE SEA, THE   WAR 1957
(Cape)

SNOWS OF KILMANJARO, THE   FOX 1952
(Cape)

TO HAVE AND HAVE NOT   WAR 1944
(Cape)   WAR 1950
         (*Breaking point, The*)

HEMON, Louis

MARIA CHAPDELAINE   BL 1950
(Macmillan)   (*Naked heart, The*)

M. RIPOIS AND HIS NEMESIS   ABP 1954
(Allen & Unwin)   (*Knave of hearts*)

HENRY, Harriet

JACKDAWS STRUT   WAR 1931
(Paul)   (*Bought*)

HENRY, Joan *pseud.*

WHO LIE IN GAOL   ABP 1953
(Gollancz)   (*Weak and the wicked, The*)

YIELD TO THE NIGHT   ABP 1953
(Gollancz)

HENRY, Marguerite

MISTY OF CHINCOTEAGUE   FOX 1961
(Collins)   (*Misty*)

HENRY, O.

CLARION CALL, THE

COP AND THE ANTHEM, THE

GIFT OF MAGI, THE   FOX 1952

LAST LEAF, THE   (*Full house*)

RANSOM OF RED CHIEF, THE
(*In* Best of O. Henry: Hodder & Stoughton)

PASSING OF THE BLACK EAGLE   COL 1948
(Various)   (*Black Eagle*)

HERBERT, *Sir* **Alan Patrick**

HOUSE BY THE RIVER, THE   REP 1950
(Methuen)

WATER GIPSIES, THE   SDC 1932
(Methuen)

HERBERT, Frederick Hugh

FOR LOVE OR MONEY (P)   RANK 1958
(Dramatists, N.Y.)   (*This happy feeling*)

KISS AND TELL (P)   COL 1945
(Longmans)

MOON IS BLUE, THE (P)   UA 1953
(Random House, N.Y.)

HERGESHEIMER, Joseph

JAVA HEAD   ID 1935
(Heinemann)

TAMPICO   COL 1933
(Various)   (*Woman I stole, The*)

HERLIHY, James Leo

ALL FALL DOWN   MGM 1961
(Dutton, N.Y.)

HERLIHY, James Leo *and*
    NOBLE, William

BLUE DENIM (P)   FOX 1959
(Random House, N.Y.)   (*Blue jeans*)

HERSEY, John Richard

BELL FOR ADANO, A   FOX 1945
(Gollancz)

WAR LOVER, THE   COL 1963
(Hamilton)

HESSE, Dean E.

BATTLE HYMN   UI 1956
(Davies)

HEYER, Georgette *pseud.*

RELUCTANT WIDOW, THE   GFD 1950
(Heinemann)

HEYERDAHL, Thor

KON-TIKI EXPEDITION   RKO 1951
(Allen & Unwin)   (*Kon-Tiki*)

HEYM, Stefan

HOSTAGES   PAR 1943
(Putnam)

HICHENS, Robert
   BELLA DONNA   COL 1930
   (Heinemann)   OLY 1935
                           (Temptation)
                           UN 1945

   GARDEN OF ALLAH, THE   UA 1936
   (Methuen)
   PARADINE CASE, THE   BL 1949
   (Convoy)

HIGHSMITH, Patricia
   STRANGERS ON A TRAIN   WAR 1951
   (Cresset Press)
   TALENTED MR. RIPLEY, THE   HILLCREST 1961
   (Pan Bks.)   *(Purple noon)*

HILL, Weldon
   ONIONHEAD   WAR 1958
   (Deutsch)

HILTON, James
   DAWN OF RECKONING   MGM 1941
   (Butterworth)   *(Rage in heaven)*
   GOODBYE MR. CHIPS   MGM 1939
   (Hodder & Stoughton)
   KNIGHT WITHOUT ARMOUR   UA 1937
   (Macmillan)
   Originally called Without armour
   LOST HORIZON   COL 1937
   (Macmillan)
   RANDOM HARVEST   MGM 1942
   (Macmillan)
   SO WELL REMEMBERED   RKO 1947
   (Macmillan)
   STORY OF DR. WASSELL, THE   PAR 1944
   (Macmillan)
   WE ARE NOT ALONE   WAR 1939
   (Macmillan)

HILTON, James *and* BURNHAM, Barbara
   GOODBYE MR. CHIPS (P)   MGM 1939
   (French, N.Y.)

HINE, Al
   LORD LOVE A DUCK   UA 1965
   (Atheneum Press, N.Y.)

HOBART, *Mrs.* Alice Tisdale
   CUP AND THE SWORD, THE   UI 1959
   (Cassell)   *(This earth is mine)*
   OIL FOR THE LAMPS OF CHINA   WAR 1935
   (Cassell)   WAR 1941
                           (Law of the tropics

HOBSON, *Mrs.* **Laura**
 GENTLEMEN'S AGREEMENT   FOX 1947
 (Cassell)

HODGINS, Eric
 MR BLANDINGS BUILDS HIS
 DREAM HOUSE   RKO 1948
 (Joseph)

HODSON, James Lansdale
 RETURN TO WOODS   WAR 1965
 (Gollancz)   (*King and country*)

HOLDING, Charles H.
 SCAR, THE   ABP 1949
 (Eerdmans, Grand Rapids)

HOLDING, *Mrs.* **Elizabeth**
 BLANK WALL   COL 1949
 (Simon & Schuster, N.Y.)   (*Reckless moment, The*)

HOLDRIDGE, Desmond
 DEATH OF A COMMON MAN ARCHERS 1947
 (Hale)   (*End of the river, The*)

HOLLAND, Marty
 FALLEN ANGEL   FOX 1945
 (Dutton, N.Y.)

HOLLES, Robert
 SIEGE OF BATTERSEA, THE FOX 1964
 (Joseph)   (*Guns at Batasi*)

HOLT, Felix
 GABRIEL HORN   UA 1955
 (Various)   (*Kentuckian, The*)

HOLTBY, Winifred
 SOUTH RIDING   UA 1938
 (Collins)

HOME, William Douglas
 CHILTERN HUNDREDS, THE (P) TC 1949
 (French)
 NOW BARABBAS (P)   WAR 1949
 (Longmans)   (*Now Barabbas was a robber*)
 RELUCTANT DEBUTANTE, THE (P) MGM 1958
 (French)

HOMER
 ILIAD   ARCHWAY 1954
 (Various)   (*Ulysses*)

HOMES, Geoffrey *pseud*

BUILD MY GALLOWS HIGH   RKO 1947
(Grosset, N.Y.)

FORTY WHACKS   WAR 1946
(Grosset, N.Y.)   (*Crime by night*)

NO HANDS ON THE CLOCK   PAR 1941
(Various)

HOOKE, Nona Warner

DARKNESS I LEAVE YOU   RANK 1957
(Hale)   (*Gypsy and the gentleman, The*)

DEADLY RECORD   AA 1959
(Hale)

HOOVER, John Edgar

PERSONS IN HIDING   PAR 1939
(Dent)   PAR 1940
      (*Queen of the mob*)
      PAR 1940
      (*Parole fixer*)

HOPE, Anthony

PRISONER OF ZENDA   UA 1937
(Dent)   MGM 1952

HOPLEY, George *pseud.*

NIGHT HAS A THOUSAND EYES   PAR 1948
(Oxford U.P.)

HORGAN, Paul

DISTANT TRUMPET, A   WAR 1964
(Macmillan)

HORN, Aloysius

TRADER HORN   MGM 1931
(Cape)

HORNE, Kenneth

FOOLS RUSH IN (P)   PINEWOOD 1949
(French)

LADY MISLAID, A (P)   ABP 1958
(English Theatre Guild)

HORNUNG, Ernest William

RAFFLES   UA 1930
(Grayson)   UA 1940

HOUGH, Emerson

NORTH OF 36   PAR 1931
(Appleton, N.Y.)   (*Conquering horde*)

HOUGHTON, Stanley

HINDLE WAKES (P
(Sidgwick)

GB 1932
MON 1952

HOUGRON, Jean

BLAZE OF THE SUN
(Hurst & Blackett)

PAR 1959

HOUSEHOLD, Geoffrey

BRANDY FOR THE PARSON
(*In* Tales of adventure: Joseph)

MGM 1952

ROGUE MALE
(Chatto & Windus)

FOX 1941
(*Manhunt*)

ROUGH SHOOT
(Joseph)

UA 1953

HOUSMAN, Laurence

Victoria Regina (P)
(Cape)

RKO 1937

HOWARD, Keble *pseud.*

LORD BABS
(Benn)

GFD 1932

HOWARD, Leigh

BLIND DATE
(Longmans)

RANK 1959

HOWARD, Sidney Coe

DODSWORTH (P)
(Harcourt, N.Y.)

UA 1936

THEY KNEW WHAT THEY
WANTED (P)
(*In* Modern plays, edited by
J. F. MacDermott. Harcourt, N.Y.

MGM 1930
(*Lady to love, A*)
RKO 1940

HOWARTH, David

ESCAPE ALONE
(Collins)

REN 1959
(*We die alone*)

SHETLAND BUS, THE
(Nelson)

FORLONG 1954
EROS 1957
(*Suicide mission*)

HOWE, George Locke

CALL IT TREASON
(Hart-Davis)

FOX 1951
(*Decision before dawn*)

HOYT, Vance Joseph
SEQUOIA   MGM 1934
(Grosset, N.Y.)

HUBBARD, Elbert
MESSAGE TO GARCIA, A (Poem)   FOX 1936
(Lothian, N.Y.)

HUBLER, Richard Gibson
I'VE GOT MINE   UA 1953
(Putnam, N.Y.)   (*Beachhead*)

HUDSON, William Henry
GREEN MANSIONS   MGM 1959
(Various)

HUFFAKER, Clair
BADMAN   UI 1966
(Muller)   (*War wagon*)
FLAMING LANCE   FOX 1960
(Simon & Schuster, N.Y.) (*Flaming star*)
GUNS OF THE RIO CONCHOS FOX 1964
(Muller)   (*Rio Conchos*)
SEVEN WAYS FROM SUNDOWN UI 1960
(Muller)

HUGGINS, Roy
DOUBLE TAKE   COL 1948
(Grosset, N.Y.)   (*I love trouble*)

HUGHES, Dorothy Belle
FALLEN SPARROW, THE   RKO 1943
(Nicholson & Watson)
IN A LONELY PLACE   COL 1950
(Duell, N.Y.)
RIDE THE PINK HORSE   UI 1947
(Duell, N.Y.)

HUGHES, Ken
HIGH WRAY   ABP 1954
(Gifford)   (*House across the lake, The*)

HUGHES, Richard
HIGH WIND IN JAMAICA, A FOX 1964
(Chatto & Windus)

HUGHES, Rupert
NO ONE MAN   PAR 1932
(Jarrolds)

HUGHES, Thomas

  TOM BROWN'S SCHOOLDAYS   RKO 1940
    (Various)   REN 1951

HUGO, Victor

  HUNCHBACK OF NOTRE
  DAME, THE   RKO 1939
    (Various)   RANK 1957
  LES MISERABLES   UA 1935
    (Various)   FOX 1952

HUIE, William Bradford

  AMERICANIZATION OF
  EMILY, THE   MGM 1963
    (W. H. Allen)
  REVOLT OF MAMIE
  STOVER, THE   FOX 1956
    (W. H. Allen)

HULL, Alexander

  SHEP OF THE PAINTED HILLS   MGM 1951
    (Chapman & Hall)   (*Painted hills*)

HULL, Helen Rose

  HEAT LIGHTNING   WAR 1934
    (Cobden Sanderson)

HULME, Kathryn

  NUN'S STORY, THE   WAR 1958
    (Muller)

HUME, Doris

  SIN OF SUSAN SLADE, THE   WAR 1962
    (Duell, N.Y.)   (*Susan Slade*)

HUMPHREY, William

  HOME FROM THE HILL   MGM 1959
    (Pan Bks.)

HUNTER, Evan

  BLACKBOARD JUNGLE   MGM 1954
    (Constable)
  BUDDWING   MGM 1967
    (Constable)   (*Mister Buddwing*)
  MATTER OF CONVICTION, A   UA 1960
    (Constable)   (*Young savages, The*)
  STRANGERS WHEN WE MEET   COL 1959
    (Constable)

HUNTER, Jack D.

  BLUE MAX, THE   FOX 1965
    (Muller)

HUNTER, John Alexander

AFRICAN BUSH ADVENTURES   COL 1959
(Various)   (*Killers of Kilimanjaro*)

HUROK, Sol *and* **GOODE, Ruth**

IMPRESSARIO   FOX 1953
(Macdonald)   (*Tonight we sing*)

HURST, Fannie

ANATOMY OF ME   UN 1934 (*Imitation of life*)
(Cape)   RANK 1959 (*Imitation of life*)
BACK STREET   UN 1931
(Cape)   UN 1941
     UI 1961

FIVE AND TEN   MGM 1931
(Cape)
HUMORESQUE   WAR 1946
(Smith, N.Y.)
LUMMOX   UA 1930
(Cape)

HUSSON, Albert

MY THREE ANGELS (P)   PAR 1955
(Random House, N.Y.)   (*We're no angels*)

HUTCHINSON, Arthur Stuart-Menteth

IF WINTER COMES   MGM 1947
(Hodder & Stoughton)

HUTCHISON, Graham Seton *see*
     SETON, G. *pseud.*

HUTTON, Michael Clayton

HAPPY FAMILY, THE (P)   APEX 1952
(Deane)

HUXLEY, Aldous Leonard

GIOCONDA SMILE, THE   UN 1947
(Harper, N.Y.)   (*Woman's vengeance, A*)
YOUNG ARCHIMEDES   GFD 1950
(Chatto & Windus)   (*Prelude to fame*)

HYAMS, Edward

SYLVESTER   GFD 1953
(Longmans)   (*You know what sailors are*)

HYDE, Harford Montgomery

TRIALS OF OSCAR WILDE, THE   EROS 1960
(Hodge)

279

HYMAN, Max

  NO TIME FOR SERGEANTS   WAR 1958
  (Dent)

HYMAN, Max *see also*
  LEVIN, I. *jt. author*

HYND, Alan

  BETRAYAL FROM THE EAST   RKO 1945
  (McBride, N.Y.)

I

IBANEZ, Vicente Blasco *see* **BLASCO, I. V.**

IDELL, Albert Edward

  CENTENNIAL SUMMER   FOX 1946
  (Sampson Low)

ILES, Francis *pseud*

  BEFORE THE FACT   RKO 1941
  (Gollancz)   (*Suspicion*)

INGE, William

  DARK AT THE TOP OF THE
  STAIRS, THE (P)   WAR 1960
  (Random House, N.Y.)
  COME BACK LITTLE SHEBA (P)   PAR 1952
  (Random House, N.Y.)
  LOSS OF ROSES, A (P)   FOX 1963
  (Random House, N.Y.)   (*Stripper, The*)
            FOX 1963
            (*Woman of summer*)

  PICNIC (P)   COL 1955
  (Random House, N.Y.)

INNES, Hammond

  CAMPBELL'S KINGDOM   RANK 1957
  (Collins)
  LONELY SKIER, THE   RKO 1948
  (Collins)   (*Snowbound*)
  MARY DEARE, THE   MGM 1959
  (Collins)   (*Wreck of the Mary Deare*)
  WHITE SOUTH, THE   COL 1953
  (Collins)

IRISH, William *pseud.*

  DEADLINE AT DAWN   RKO 1946
  (Lippincott, Philadelphia)

IRISH, William *pseud.* (*continued*)

I MARRIED A DEAD MAN	PAR 1950
(Lippincott, Philadelphia)	(*No man of her own*)
I WOULDN'T BE IN YOUR SHOES	MON 1948
(Lippincott, Philadelphia)	
PHANTOM LADY	UN 1944
(Lippincott, Philadelphia)	

IRWIN, Margaret

YOUNG BESS	MGM 1953
(Chatto & Windus)	

J

JACKSON, Charles Reginald

LOST WEEK-END, THE	PAR 1945
(Lane)	

JACKSON, *Mrs.* Helen Maria

RAMONA	FOX 1936
(Sampson Low)	

JACKSON, Shirley

BIRD'S NEST, THE	MGM 1957
(Farrar, N.Y.)	(*Lizzie*)
HAUNTING OF HILL HOUSE, THE	MGM 1963
(Joseph)	(*Haunting, The*)

JACOBS, Naomi

UNDER NEW MANAGEMENT	BUTCHER 1946
(Hutchinson)	

JACOBS, William Wymark

INTERRUPTION, THE	COL 1955
(*In* Sea whispers: Methuen)	(*Footsteps in the fog*)

JACOBS, William Wymark *and*
    PARKER, Louis Napoleon

MONKEY'S PAW, THE (P)	RKO 1932
(*In* One-act plays of to-day,	BUTCHER 1948
series 2: Harrap)	

JAFFÉ, Rona

BEST OF EVERYTHING, THE	FOX 1959
(Cape)	

JAMES, Henry

ASPERN PAPERS, THE   UN 1947
(Macmillan)   (*Lost moment, The*)

TURN OF THE SCREW, THE   FOX 1961
(Dent)   (*Innocents, The*)

WASHINGTON SQUARE   PAR 1949
(Macmillan)   (*Heiress, The*)

JAMES, Meyrich Edward Clifton

I WAS MONTY'S DOUBLE   ABP 1958
(Rider)

JAMES, Montague Rhodes

CASTING THE RUNES   COL 1957
(Arnold)   (*Night of the demon*)

JAMES, Will

SAND   FOX 1949
(Cassell)

SMOKY   FOX 1933
(Various)   FOX 1946

JANEWAY, *Mrs*. Elizabeth

DAISY KENYON   FOX 1947
(Doubleday, N.Y.)

JANNEY, Russell

MIRACLE OF THE BELLS, THE   RKO 1948
(W. H. Allen)

JAYNES, Clare

MY REPUTATION   WAR 1946
(World, N.Y.)
(*Originally called* Instruct my sorrows)

JEANS, Ronald

YOUNG WIVES' TALE (P)   ABP 1951
(*In* Plays of the year, 1949–50: Elek)

JEFFRIES, Graham Montague *see*
    GRAEME, Bruce *pseud.*

JELLICOE, Ann

KNACK, THE (P)   UA 1965
(Dell, N.Y.)

JENNINGS, D. *see* **DUFFY, C.** *jt. author*

JEPSON, Selwyn

MAN RUNNING   WAR 1949
(Macdonald)   (*Stage fright*)

JEROME, Jerome Klapka
PASSING OF THE THIRD FLOOR
BACK, THE   GB 1936
(Hurst & Blackett)
THREE MEN IN A BOAT   BL 1956
(Various)

JERUSALEM, Else
RED HOUSE, THE   UN 1947
(Laurie)

JESSUP, Richard
CHUKA   PAR 1966
(Jenkins)
CINCINNATI KID, THE   MGM 1965
(Gollancz)
DEADLY DUO, THE   UA 1962
(Boardman)
MAN IN CHARGE   COL 1957
(Secker & Warburg)   (*Young don't cry, The*)

JOB, Thomas
UNCLE HARRY (P)   UN 1945
(French)   (*Strange affair of Uncle Harry, The*)

JOHNSON, Dorothy M.
HANGING TREE, THE   WAR 1958
(Deutsch)

JOHNSON, Nora
WORLD OF HENRY ORIENT, THE UA 1964
(Gollancz)

JOHNSON, Osa Helen
I MARRIED ADVENTURE   COL 1940
(Hutchinson)

JOHNSON, Owen
LAWRENCEVILLE SCHOOL TALES MGM 1950
(Grosset, N.Y.)   (*Happy years, The*)

JOHNSON, Pamela Hansford
TROJAN BROTHERS, THE   BN 1946
(Joseph)

JOHNSTON, Annie Fellows
LITTLE COLONEL   FOX 1935
(Various)

AUTHOR AND ORIGINAL TITLE	FILM TITLE

JOLLY, Cyril

VENGEANCE OF PRIVATE
POOLEY, THE   CONT 1962
(Heinemann)   (*Story of Private Pooley, The*)

JONES, Guy Pearce *and*
  JONES, Constance Bridges

PEABODY'S MERMAID   UN 1948
(Joseph)   (*Mr Peabody and the mermaid*)
THERE WAS A LITTLE MAN   FOX 1948
(Random House, N.Y.)   (*Luck of the Irish*)

JONES, James

FROM HERE TO ETERNITY   COL 1953
(Collins)
SOME CAME RUNNING   MGM 1958
(Collins)

JONES, Joanna

NURSE IS A NEIGHBOUR   WAR 1963
(Joseph)   (*Nurse on wheels*)

JONES, Raymond F.

THIS ISLAND EARTH   UI 1955
(Sharta Pubns., Chicago)

JONSON, Ben

Volpone (P)   SIRITZKY 1947
(Allen & Unwin)

JOPE-SLADE, Christine *and*
  STOKES, Sewell

BRITANNIA OF BILLINGSGATE (P) GB 1933
(French)

JORDAN, Elizabeth Garver

DADDY AND I   RKO 1936
(Grosset, N.Y.)   (*Make way for a lady*)

JOYCE, James

ULYSSES   BL 1966
(Lane)

K

KAFKA, Franz

TRIAL, THE   BL 1963
(Secker & Warburg)

284

AUTHOR AND ORIGINAL TITLE	FILM TITLE

KALER, James Otis
TOBY TYLER   DISNEY 1959
(Various)

KANDEL, Aben
CITY FOR CONQUEST   WAR 1940
(Joseph)

KANIN, Fay
GOODBYE, MY FANCY (P)   WAR 1951
(French, N.Y.)

KANIN, Garson
BORN YESTERDAY (P)   COL 1951
(Viking, N.Y.)
RAT RACE, THE (P)   PAR 1960
(Dramatists, N.Y.)

KANTOR, Mackinlay
ANDERSONVILLE   COL 1959
(W. H. Allen)
AROUSE AND BEWARE   MGM 1940
(Gollancz)   (*Man from Dakota, The*)
GENTLE ANNIE   MGM 1944
(Various)
GLORY FOR ME   RKO 1946
(Coward-McCann, N.Y.)   (*Best years of our lives, The*)
GOD AND MY COUNTRY   DISNEY 1967
(World, N.Y.)   (*Follow me, boys!*)
GUN CRAZY   UA 1949
(*In* Author's choice   (*Deadly is the female*)
Coward-McCann, N.Y.)
HAPPY LAND   FOX 1943
(Longmans)
VOICE OF BUGLE ANN   MGM 1936
(Selwyn & Blount)

KARMEL, Alex
MARY ANN   UA 1962
(Secker & Warburg)   (*Something wild*)

KASTNER, Erich
EMIL AND THE DETECTIVES   UFA 1931
(Cape)   DISNEY 1964
LOTTIE AND LISA   DISNEY 1961
(Cape)
THREE MEN IN THE SNOW   MGM 1938
(Cape)   (*Paradise for three*)

KATA, Elizabeth
BE READY WITH BELLS
AND DRUMS   MGM 1966
(Penguin)   (*Patch of blue, A*)

KATCHER, Leon

BIG BANKROLL   WAR 1961
(Gollancz)

HARD MAN, THE   COL 1957
(Macmillan, N.Y.)

KAUFMAN, Bel

UP THE DOWN STAIRCASE   WAR 1966
(Barker)

KAUFMAN, George Simon *and*
   CONNELLY, Marc

DULCY (P)   MGM 1940
(Various)

KAUFMAN, George Simon *and*
   FERBER, Edna

DINNER AT EIGHT (P)   MGM 1933
(Heinemann)

ROYAL FAMILY, THE (P)   PAR 1930
(French, N.Y.)   (*Royal family of Broadway*)

STAGE DOOR (P)   RKO 1937
(Heinemann)

KAUFMAN, George Simon *and*
   HART, Moss

GEORGE WASHINGTON SLEPT
HERE (P)   WAR 1942
(*In* Six plays. Random House, N.Y.)

MAN WHO CAME TO
DINNER, THE (P)   WAR 1941
(Random House, N.Y.)

YOU CAN'T TAKE IT
WITH YOU (P)   COL 1938
(Barker)

KAUFMAN, G. S. *see also*
   TEICHMAN, H. *jt. author*

KAUS, Gina

DARK ANGEL   PRC 1946
(Cassell)   (*Her sister's secret*)

LUXURY LINER   PAR 1933
(Cassell)

KAYE-SMITH, Sheila

JOANNA GODDEN   GFD 1947
(Cassell)   (*Loves of Joanna Godden, The*)

KAZAN, Elia

AMERICA, AMERICA   WAR 1964
(Collins)   (*Anatolian smile, The*)

KAZANTZAKIS, Nikes
  ZORBA THE GREEK   FOX 1964
  (Faber)

KEATING, William J. *and*
    CARTER, Richard
  MAN WHO ROCKED THE
  BOAT, THE   UI 1957
  (Harper, N.Y.)   (*Slaughter on* 10*th Avenue*)

KEELER, Harry Stephen
  SING SING NIGHTS   MON 1934
  (Ward Lock)

KEENE, Day
  JOY HOUSE   MGM 1965
  (Consul Bks.)   (*Love cage, The*)

KEIR, Ursula
  VINTAGE, THE   MGM 1937
  (Collins)

KEITH, Agnes
  THREE CAME HOME   FOX 1949
  (Joseph)

KELLAND, Clarence Buddington
  ARIZONA   COL 1940
  (Harper)
  DREAMLAND   UA 1936
  (Miles)   (*Strike me pink*)
  GREAT CROONER, THE   WAR 1937
  (Barker)   (*Mr. Dodd takes the air*)
  MR. DEEDS GOES TO TOWN   COL 1936
  (Barker)
  SCATTERGOOD BAINES   RKO 1941
  (Hodder & Stoughton)
  SKIN DEEP   FOX 1941
  (Various)   (*For beauty's sake*)
  SPEAK EASILY   MGM 1932
  (Harper)
  SUGARFOOT   WAR 1951
  (Grosset, N.Y.)
  VALLEY OF THE SUN   RKO 1942
  (Various)

KELLINO, Pamela
  DEL PALMA   REP 1951
  (Hale)   (*Lady possessed, A*)

KELLOCK, Harold
  HOUDINI   PAR 1953
  (Heinemann)

KELLY, George
  CRAIG'S WIFE (P)   COL 1936
  (French)   COL 1950
                         (*Harriet Craig*)

  TORCH BEARERS (P)   FOX 1935
  (French, N.Y.)

KELLY, Judith
  MARRIAGE IS A PRIVATE AFFAIR MGM 1944
  (Cassell)

KENDRICK, Baynard Hardwick
  LIGHTS OUT   UI 1951
  (W. H. Allen)   (*Bright victory*)
  ODOUR OF VIOLETS   MGM 1942
  (Methuen)   (*Eyes in the night*)

KENNAWAY, James
  MIND BENDERS, THE   AA 1963
  (Pan Bks.)
  TUNES OF GLORY   UA 1960
  (Putnam)

KENNEDY, Margaret
  AUTUMN (P)   LF 1949
  (French)   (*That dangerous age*)
  CONSTANT NYMPH, THE (P) FOX 1934
  (Heinemann)   WAR 1943
  CONSTANT NYMPH, THE   FOX 1934
  (Heinemann)   WAR 1943
  ESCAPE ME NEVER   UA 1935
  (Heinemann)

KENNETT, John
  PERIL FOR THE GUY   BL 1953
  (Brockhampton)

KENNINGTON, Alan
  NIGHT HAS EYES, THE   ANGLO-AMERICAN 1952
  (Jarrolds)
  SHE DIED YOUNG   ABP 1955
  (Jarrolds)   (*You can't escape*)

KENNY, Elizabeth *and* OSTENSO, Martha
  AND THEY SHALL WALK   RKO 1946
  (Dodd, N.Y.)   (*Sister Kenny*)

KENT, Simon *pseud.*

  FERRY TO HONG KONG   RANK 1959
  (Hutchinson)

  FIRE DOWN BELOW   COL 1957
  (Hutchinson)

KENT, Willis *see*
  COLLISON, Wilson *pseud*

KENWARD, Alan Richard

  CRY HAVOC (P)   MGM 1943
  (French, N.Y.)

KEON, Michael

  DURIAN TREE, THE   UA 1964
  (Hamilton)   (*7th dawn*)

KERR, Geoffrey

  COTTAGE TO LET (P   GFD 1941
  (French)

KERR, Jean

  MARY, MARY (P)   WAR 1963
  (Doubleday, N.Y.)

  PLEASE DON'T EAT THE DAISIES   MGM 1960
  (Heinemann)

KERR, Jean *and* **BROOKE, Eleanor**

  KING OF HEARTS (P)   PAR 1956
  (Doubleday, N.Y.)   (*That certain feeling*)

KERSH, Gerald

  NIGHT AND THE CITY   FOX 1950
  (Heinemann)

KESSEL, Joseph

  LION, THE   FOX 1962
  (Hart-Davis)

  SIROCCO   COL 1951
  (Random House, N.Y.)

KESSELRING, Joseph Otto

  ARSENIC AND OLD LACE (P)   WAR 1944
  (French)

KESTER, Paul

  WHEN KNIGHTHOOD WAS IN
  FLOWER (P)   RKO 1953
  (French, N.Y.)   (*Sword and the rose, The*)

KEYHOE, Donald E.

  FLYING SAUCERS FROM OUTER
  SPACE   COL 1956
  (Hutchinson)   (*Earth versus the flying saucers*)

KIMBROUGH, E. *see*
    SKINNER, C. O. *jt. author*

KIMMINS, Anthony
    AMOROUS PRAWN, THE (P)   BL 1962
    (French)
    WHILE PARENTS SLEEP (P)   SOSKIN 1936
    (French)

KING, Philip
    ON MONDAY NEXT (P)   GFD 1952
    (French)   (*Curtain up*)
    SEE HOW THEY RUN (P)   BL 1955
    (French)
    SERIOUS CHARGE (P)   EROS 1959
    (French)

KING, Philip *see also*
    CARY, F. L. *jt. author*

KING, Philip *and* **CARY, Falkland L.**
    SAILOR BEWARE (P)   BL 1956
    (*In* Plays of the year Vol. 12: Elek)

KING, Rufus
    CASE OF THE CONSTANT GOD   UN 1936
    (Methuen)   (*Love letters of a star*)
    SECRET BEYOND THE
    DOOR, THE   UI 1948
    (Various)

KING-HALL, Magdalen
    LIFE AND DEATH OF THE
    WICKED LADY SKELTON, THE   GFD 1946
    (Davies)   (*Wicked lady, The*)

KING-HALL, S. *see* **HAY, I.** *jt. author*

KINGSLEY, Sidney
    DEAD END (P)   UA 1937
    (Dramatists, N.Y.)
    DETECTIVE STORY (P)   PAR 1951
    (Random House, N.Y.)
    MEN IN WHITE   MGM 1934
    (Gollancz)

KIPLING, Rudyard
    CAPTAINS COURAGEOUS   MGM 1937
    (Macmillan)
    JUNGLE BOOK, THE   DISNEY 1966
    (Macmillan)

KIPLING, Rudyard (*continued*)

KIM   MGM 1949
(Macmillan)

LIGHT THAT FAILED, THE   PAR 1939
(Macmillan)

SOLDIERS THREE   MGM 1951
(Macmillan)

TOOMAI OF THE ELEPHANTS   UA 1937
(Macmillan)   (*Elephant boy*)

WEE WILLIE WINKIE   FOX 1937
(Macmillan)

KIRK, Jeremy

BUILD-UP BOYS, THE   FOX 1960
(Hart-Davis)   (*Madison Avenue*)

KIRKBRIDE, Ronald

GIRL NAMED TAMIKO, A   PAR 1963
(Pan Bks.)

KIRKLAND, J. *see*
  CALDWELL, E. *jt. author*

KIRST, Hans Helmuth

NIGHT OF THE GENERALS, THE   BL 1966
(Collins)

KJELGAARD, James Arthur

BIG RED   DISNEY 1962
(Grosset, N.Y.)

KLEIN, Alexander

DOUBLE DEALERS   PAR 1962
(Faber)   (*Counterfeit traitor, The*)

KLEMPNER, John

LETTER TO FIVE WIVES, A   FOX 1948
(Scribner, N.Y.)   (*Letter to three wives, A*)

KLINGMAN, Lawrence *and*
  GREEN, Gerald

HIS MAJESTY O'KEEFE   WAR 1954
(Hale)

KNEBEL, Fletcher *and*
  BAILEY, Charles W.

SEVEN DAYS IN MAY   PAR 1963
(Corgi Bks.)

KNIGHT, Eric Mowbray

LASSIE COME HOME   MGM 1943
(Cassell)

THIS ABOVE ALL   FOX 1942
(Cassell)

KNOBLOCK, Edward

KISMET (P)   IN 1931
(Methuen)   MGM 1955

LULLABY, THE (P)   MGM 1931
(Putnam)   (*Sin of Madelon Claudet, The*)

KNOTT, Frederick

DIAL 'M' FOR MURDER (P)   WAR 1954
(Random House, N.Y.)

KOBER, Arthur

HAVING WONDERFUL TIME (P)   RKO 1938
(Dramatist, N.Y.)

KOHNER, Frederick

GIDGET   COL 1959
(Joseph)

KOMROFF, Manuel

MAGIC BOW   GFD 1946
(Heinemann)

KOPIT, Arthur

OH DAD, POOR DAD (P)   PAR 1966
(Methuen)

KRAMM, Joseph

SHRIKE, THE (P)   UI 1955
(Random House, N.Y.)

KRASNA, Norman

DEAR RUTH (P)   PAR 1947
(*In* Best plays of 1944–45: Gollancz)

JOHN LOVES MARY (P)   WAR 1949
(Dramatists, N.Y.)

'KIND SIR' (P)   WAR 1958
(Dramatists, N.Y.)   (*Indiscreet*)

SMALL MIRACLE (P)   PAR 1935
(French, N.Y.)   (*Four hours to kill*)

SUNDAY IN NEW YORK (P)   MGM 1964
(Random House, N.Y.)

WHO WAS THAT LADY I SAW
YOU WITH? (P)   COL 1960
(Random House, N.Y.)   (*Who was that lady?*)

AUTHOR AND ORIGINAL TITLE   FILM TITLE

KURNITZ, Harry
  ONCE MORE WITH FEELING (P)   COL 1959
  (Random House, N.Y.)

KURNITZ, Harry *see also*
  PAGE, M. *pseud.*

KYNE, Peter Bernard
  CAPPY RICKS   REP 1937
  (Hodder & Stoughton)   (*Affairs of Cappy Ricks, The*)
  NEVER THE TWAIN SHALL MEET   MGM 1931
  (Various)
  PARSON OF PANAMINT, THE   PAR 1941
  (Grosset, N.Y.)
  THREE GODFATHERS   UN 1930
  (Various)   (*Hell's heroes*)
                                MGM 1936
  VALLEY OF THE GIANTS   WAR 1938
  (Hodder & Stoughton)

L

LA BERN, Arthur Jack
  IT ALWAYS RAINS ON SUNDAYS   EALING 1948
  (Nicholson & Watson)
  NIGHT DARKENS THE STREETS   GFD 1948
  (Nicholson & Watson)   (*Good-time girl*)
  PAPER ORCHID   COL 1949
  (Marlowe)

LAGERKVIST, Par
  BARABBAS   COL 1962
  (Four Square Bks.)

LAKE, Stuart N.
  WYATT EARP: FRONTIER
  MARSHAL   FOX 1939
  (Various)   (*Frontier marshal*)

LAMBERT, Gavin
  INSIDE DAISY CLOVER   WAR 1965
  (Hamilton)

L'AMOUR, Louis
  BURNING HILLS   COL 1958
  (Jason Press, N.Y.)   (*Apache territory*)
  GUNS OF THE TIMBERLANDS   WAR 1959
  (Jason Press, N.Y.)
  HELLER WITH A GUN   PAR 1960
  (Muller)   (*Heller in pink tights*)
  TAGGART   UI 1965
  (Corgi Bks.)

LAMPEDUSA, Guiseppe di
LEOPARD, THE   FOX 1962
(Collins)

LAMPELL, Millard
HERO, THE   COL 1951
(Messner, N.Y.)   (*Saturday's hero*)

LAMPLUGH, Lois
ROCKETS IN THE DUNES   RANK 1960
(Cape)

LA MURE, Pierre
MOULIN ROUGE   UA 1952
(Collins)

LANDERY, Charles
MR. SMITH GOES TO
WASHINGTON   COL 1939
(Dent)

LANDON, Christopher
ICE COLD IN ALEX   ABP 1957
(Heinemann)

LANDON, Margaret
ANNA AND THE KING OF SIAM   FOX 1946
(Harrap)   FOX 1956
                                 (*King and I, The*)

LANE, Kendall
GAMBIT   UI 1966
(Hodder & Stoughton)

LANGHAM, James R.
SING A SONG OF MURDER   PAR 1942
(Hale)   (*Night in New Orleans, A*)

LANGLEY, Adria Locke
LION IS IN THE STREETS, A   WAR 1953
(McGraw-Hill, N.Y.)

LANGLEY, Noel
LITTLE LAMBS EAT IVY (P)   ABP 1952
(French)   (*Father's doing fine*)

LANGLEY, Noel *See also*
  MORLEY, E. *jt. author*

LAPIERRE, D. *See*
  COLLINS, L. *jt. author*

AUTHOR AND ORIGINAL TITLE	FILM TITLE

LARDNER, Ring Wilmer
ALIBI IKE
(*In* Best stories. Garden City Press, N.Y.)   WAR 1935

BIG TOWN, THE   UA 1948
(*In* Best stories. Garden City Press, N.Y.)   (*So this is New York*)

LARTEGUY, Jean
CENTURIANS, THE   COL 1966
(Hutchinson)   (*Lost Command*)
YELLOW FEVER   COL 1965
(Hutchinson)   (*Not for honour and glory*)

LASKI, Marghanita
LITTLE BOY LOST   PAR 1953
(Cresset Press)

LATIMER, Jonathan
DEAD DON'T CARE, THE   UN 1939
(Methuen)   (*Last warning, The*)
HEADED FOR A HEARSE   UN 1937
(Methuen)   (*Westland case, The*)
LADY IN THE MORGUE   UN 1938
(Methuen)

LAUNDER, Frank *and* **GILLIAT, Sidney**
MEET A BODY (P)   BL 1956 (*Green man, The*)
(French)

LAURENTS, Arthur
TIME OF THE CUCKOO, THE (P)   UA 1955
(Random House, N.Y.)   (*Summer madness*)

LAURITZEN, Jonreed
ROSE AND THE FLAME, THE   GFD 1955
(Hurst & Blackett)   (*Kiss of fire*)

LAVERY, Emmet Godfrey
FIRST LEGION, THE (P)   UA 1951
(French, N.Y.)

LAVIN, Nora *and* **THORP, Molly**
HOP DOG, THE   ABP 1954
(Oxford U.P.)   (*Adventure in the hopfields*)

LAWES, Lewis Edward
20,000 YEARS IN SING SING   IN 1933
(Garden City Press, N.Y.)

LAWLER, Ray
SUMMER OF THE SEVENTEENTH   UA 1959
DOLL, THE (P)
(Collins)

LAWRENCE, David Herbert

LADY CHATTERLEY'S LOVER   COL 1956
(Heinemann)

ROCKING HORSE WINNER, THE   TC 1949
(*In* Complete tales. Heinemann)

SONS AND LOVERS   FOX 1960
(Heinemann)

LAWRENCE, H. L.

CHILDREN OF LIGHT   BL 1963
(Macdonald)   (*Damned, The*)

LAWRENCE, Jerome *and* LEE, Robert E.

AUNTIE MAME (P)   WAR 1958
(Vanguard, N.Y.)

INHERIT THE WIND (P)   UA 1960
(Random House, N.Y.)

LAWRENCE, Margery

MADONNA OF THE SEVEN   GFD 1945
   MOONS
(Hurst & Blackett)

LAWRENCE, Thomas Edward

SEVEN PILLARS OF WISDOM   BL 1962
(Cape)   (*Lawrence of Arabia*)

LAWSON, Ted

THIRTY SECONDS OVER TOKIO   MGM 1944
(Hammond)

LAY, Beirne *and* BARTLETT, Sy

TWELVE O'CLOCK HIGH   FOX 1949
(Harper, N.Y.)

LEA, Fanny Heaslip

FOUR MARYS   MGM 1938
(Nicholson & Watson)   (*Man-proof*)

LEA, Thomas

BRAVE BULLS, THE   COL 1950
(Heinemann)

WONDERFUL COUNTRY, THE   UA 1959
(Heinemann)

LEASOR, James

PASSPORT TO OBLIVION   MGM 1965
(Heinemann)   (*Where the spies are*)

LEBLANC, Maurice

ARSENE LUPIN   MGM 1932
(Newnes)

LE CARRÉ, John

CALL FOR THE DEAD   BL 1966
(Gollancz)   (*Deadly affair, The*)

SPY WHO CAME IN FROM THE   PAR 1963
  COLD, THE
(Gollancz)

LEDERER, William Julius *and* BURDICK, Eugene L.

UGLY AMERICAN, THE   UI 1962
(Gollancz)

LEE, Chin Yang

FLOWER DRUM SONG   UI 1961
(Gollancz)

LEE, Edna

QUEEN BEE   COL 1955
(Hurst & Blackett)

LEE, Gypsy Rose

GYPSY   WAR 1962
(Pan Bks)

STRIP-TEASE MURDERS   UA 1943
(Lane)

LEE, Harper

TO KILL A MOCKING BIRD   UI 1962
(Penguin)

LEE, James

CAREER (P)   PAR 1959
(Random House, N.Y.)

LEE, Manfred *see*
QUEEN, Ellery, *pseud*

LEE, R. E. *see*
LAWRENCE, J. *jt. author*

LE FANU, Sheridan

UNCLE SILAS   TC 1947
(Oxford U.P.)

LeMAY, Alan
  SEARCHERS, THE   WAR 1956
  (Collins)

  SIEGE AT DANCING BIRD, THE   UA 1960
  (Collins)   (*Unforgiven, The*)
  USELESS COWBOY, THE   RKO 1945
  (Collins)   (*Along came Jones*)

LEONARD, Elmore
  HOMBRE   FOX 1966
  (Hale)

LERNER, Alan Jay
  BRIGADOON (P)   MGM 1954
  (Theatre Arts)

LEROUX, Gaston
  PHANTOM OF THE OPERA, THE   UN 1943
  (Various)   UI 1962

LESLIE, David Stuart
  IN MY SOLITUDE   BL 1965
  (Hutchinson)   (*Two left feet*)

LESLIE, Doris
  POLONAISE   COL 1945
  (Hutchinson)   (*Song to remember, A*)

LEVIN, Ira
  CRITIC'S CHOICE (P)   WAR 1962
  (Random House, N.Y.)
  KISS BEFORE DYING, A   UA 1956
  (Joseph)

LEVIN, Ira *and* HYMAN, Mac
  NO TIME FOR SERGEANTS (P)   FOX 1959
  (Random House, N.Y.)

LEVIN, Meyer
  COMPULSION   WAR 1958
  (Muller)

LeWIS, Edin
  RELATIVES ARE BEST APART (P) ADELPHI 1954
  (Playscripts)   (*What every woman wants*)

LEWIS, Hilda
  DAY IS OURS, THE   GFD 1952
  (Macdonald)   (*Mandy*)

LEWIS, Sinclair

ANN VICKERS   RKO 1933
(Cape)

BABBITT   IN 1934
(Cape)

DODSWORTH   UA 1936
(Cape)

ELMER GANTRY   UA 1959
(Cape)

MAIN STREET   IN 1936
(Cape)   (*I married a doctor*)

MANTRAP   PAR 1940
(Cape)   (*Untamed*)

MARTIN ARROWSMITH   UA 1931
(Cape)   (*Arrowsmith*)

LEY, Willy *see*
BONESTELL, C. *jt. author*

LIEBERSON, Goddard

3 FOR BEDROOM C   UI 1952
(Doubleday, N.Y.)

LIGGETT, Thomas

PIGEON FLY HOME   DISNEY 1958
(Holiday, N.Y.)   (*Pigeon that worked a miracle*)

LIGNERIS, Françoise de

PSYCHE 63   BL 1964
(Spearman)   (*Psyche 59*)

LINDBERGH, Charles Augustus

WE   WAR 1956
(Putnam, N.Y.)   (*Spirit of St Louis, The*)

LINDNER, Robert

FIFTYMINUTE HOUR, THE   UA 1963
(Corgi Bks)   (*Pressure point*)

LINDFORD, Dee

MAN WITHOUT A STAR   UI 1955
(Morrow, N.Y.)

LINDOP, Audrey Erskine

I THANK A FOOL   MGM 1962
(Collins)

SINGER NOT THE SONG, THE   RANK 1960
(Heinemann)

TALL HEADLINES, THE   GN 1951
(Heinemann)

LINDSAY, Howard *and* **CROUSE, Russell**

LIFE WITH FATHER (P)   PAR 1946
(French)

REMAINS TO BE SEEN (P)   MGM 1953
(Dramatists, N.Y.)

STATE OF THE UNION (P)   MGM 1948
(Dramatists, N.Y.)   (*World and his wife, The*)

TALL STORY (P)   WAR 1960
(Random House, N.Y.)

LINDSAY, Howard *see also*
RUNYON, D. *jt. author*

LINDSAY, Philip

IRON DUKE, THE   GB 1935
(Queensway Press)

LININGTON, Elizabeth *see*
BLAISDELL, Anne *pseud*

LINKLATER, Eric

POET'S PUB   AQUILA 1949
(Cape)

LAXDALE HALL   ABP 1953
(Cape)

PRIVATE ANGELO   ABP 1949
(Cape)

LIPSCOMB, William Percy *and* **MINNEY,
R. J.**

CLIVE OF INDIA (P)   UA 1935
(Gollancz)

LIPSKY, Eleazar

PEOPLE AGAINST O'HARA, THE MGM 1951
(Wingate)

LLEWELLYN, Richard

HOW GREEN WAS MY VALLEY FOX 1941
(Joseph)

NONE BUT THE LONELY HEART RKO 1944
(Joseph)

POISON PEN (P)   AB 1940
(French)

LOCKE, William John

BELOVED VAGABOND, THE   COL 1937
(Lane)

LOCKE, William John (*continued*)

MORALS OF MARCUS ORDEYNE
(Lane)

GB 1935
(*Morals of Marcus, The*)

MOUNTEBANK
(Lane)

WAR 1931
(*Sideshow of life*)

SHORN LAMB, THE
(Lane)

PAR 1932
(*Strangers in love*)

LOCKHART, *Sir* **Robert Hamilton Bruce**

MEMOIRS OF A BRITISH AGENT
(Putnam)

IN 1934
(*British Agent*)

LOCKRIDGE, Ross

RAINTREE COUNTY
(Macdonald)

MGM 1957

LOCKWOOD, Charles Andrew *and*
   ADAMSON, Hans Christian

HELLCATS OF THE SEA
(Greenberg, N.Y.)

COL 1957
(*Hellcats of the Navy*)

LOFTING, Hugh

DR. DOLITTLE
(Cape)

FOX 1966

LOFTS, Norah

JASSY
(Joseph)

GFD 1947

LOGAN, J. *see*

BEHRMAN, S. N. *jt. author*
HEGGEN, T. *jt. author*

LOMAX, Bliss

LEATHER BURNERS, THE
(Muller)

UA 1943

LONDON, Jack

CALL OF THE WILD
(Heinemann)

UA 1935

MARTIN EDEN
(Heinemann)

COL 1942
(*Adventures of Martin Eden*)

MEXICAN, THE
(*In* Nightborn and other stories:
  Appleton, N.Y.)

UA 1952
(*Fighter, The*)

SEA WOLF, THE
(Heinemann)

FOX 1930
WAR 1941
ABP 1959
(*Wolf Larsen*)

WHITE FANG
(Methuen)

FOX 1936

LONG, Gabrielle Margaret Vere *see*
 PREEDY, George *pseud*
 SHEARING, Joseph *pseud*

LONG, Sumner Arthur

  NEVER TOO LATE (P)   WAR 1965
  (French, N.Y.)

LONGFELLOW, Henry Wadsworth

  HIAWATHA (Poem)   ABP 1952
  (Various)

LONGSTREET, Stephen

  STALLION ROAD   WAR 1947
  (Jarrolds)

  WILD HARVEST   GN 1961
  (Muller)

LONSDALE, Frederick

  AREN'T WE ALL (P)   PAR 1932
  (Heinemann)

  LAST OF MRS. CHEYNEY, THE (P)   MGM 1937
  (Collins)   MGM 1951
                            (*Law and the lady, The*)

  HIGH ROAD, THE (P)   MGM 1930
  (Collins)   (*Lady of scandal, The*)

  ON APPROVAL (P)   BOX 1944
  (Collins)

  SPRING CLEANING (P)   GB 1932
  (Collins)   (*Women who play*)

LOOS, Anita

  BUT GENTLEMEN MARRY   UA 1955
    BRUNETTES   (*Gentlemen marry brunettes*)
  (Brentano, N.Y.)

  GENTLEMEN PREFER BLONDES   FOX 1953
  (Cape)

LORAINE, Philip

  BREAK IN THE CIRCLE   EXCLUSIVE 1954
  (Hodder & Stoughton)

  DUBLIN NIGHTMARE   RANK 1957
  (Hodder & Stoughton)   (*Nightmare in Dublin*)

LORD, Walter

  NIGHT TO REMEMBER, A   RANK 1957
  (Longmans)

AUTHOR AND ORIGINAL TITLE	FILM TITLE

LOTHAR, Ernst

ANGEL WITH THE TRUMPET (Harrap)	BL 1950
CLAIRVOYANT, THE (Secker)	GB 1935
MILLS OF GOD, THE (Secker)	UN 1948 (*Act of murder, An*)

LOTT, Milton

| LAST HUNT, THE (Houghton Mifflin, Boston) | MGM 1955 |

LOWNDES, Mrs. Marie Belloc

LETTY LYNTON (Benn)	MGM 1932
LODGER, THE (Benn)	FOX 1944 FOX 1953 (*Man in the attic, The*)
STORY OF IVY, THE (Eyre & Spottiswoode)	UI 1947 (*Ivy*)

LUSTGARTEN, Edgar

| GAME FOR THREE LOSERS (Museum Press) | WAR 1965 |

LYNDON, Barre

AMAZING DR. CLITTERHOUSE, THE (Hamilton)	WAR 1938
AMAZING DR. CLITTERHOUSE, THE (P) (*In* Four plays of 1936: Hamilton)	WAR 1938
MAN IN HALF-MOON STREET, THE (P) (Hamilton)	PAR 1944 PAR 1959 (*Man who could cheat death, The*)
SUNDOWN (Lane)	UA 1941
THEY CAME BY NIGHT (P) (Hamilton)	FOX 1940

LYON, Dana

| TENTACLES (Harper, N.Y.) | FOX 1951 (*House on Telegraph Hill, The*) |

LYTTON, Edward George Earle Lytton Bulwer Lytton, 1st baron

| HAUNTED AND THE HAUNTERS, THE (P) (Various) | BUTCHER 1947 (*Night comes too soon*) |

M

MacARTHUR, C. *see*
HECHT, B. *jt. author*

McCALL, Mary
  GOLD FISH BOWL, THE   IN 1932
  (Paul)   (*It's tough to be famous*)

MACARDLE, Donald
  UNEASY FREEHOLD   PAR 1944
  (Doubleday, N.Y.)   (*Uninvited, The*)

McCARTHY, Justin Huntly
  VAGABOND KING, THE (P)   PAR 1930
  (French)   PAR 1956

McCARTHY, Mary
  GROUP, THE   UA 1965
  (Weidenfeld & Nicolson)

McCOY, Horace
  KISS TOMORROW GOODBYE   WAR 1950
  (Barker)

McCRACKEN, Esther
  NO MEDALS (P)   TC 1948
  (French)   (*Weaker sex, The*)
  QUIET WEDDING (P)   PAR 1941
  (French)
  QUIET WEEK-END (P)   AB 1946
  (French)

McCULLERS, Mrs. Carson
  MEMBER OF THE WEDDING, THE COL 1952
  (Cresset Press)
  REFLECTIONS IN A GOLDEN EYE WAR 1966
  (Cresset Press)

McCULLEY, Johnston
  MARK OF ZORRO, THE   FOX 1940
  (Grosset, N.Y.)   UI 1951
       (*Mark of the renegade*)
  TRUSTED OUTLAW, THE   REP 1937
  (Hutchinson)

McCUTCHEON, George Barr
  BREWSTER'S MILLIONS   UA 1945
  (Various)   UA 1961
       (*Three on a spree*)

McCUTCHEON, Hugh

TO DUSTY DEATH   BUTCHER 1961
(Long)   (*Pit of darkness*)

MACDONALD, Betty

EGG AND I, THE   UN 1947
(Hammond)

MACDONALD, John D.

EXECUTIONERS, THE   UI 1962
(Hale)   (*Cape Fear*)
RESTLESS   PAR 1961
(Pan Bks)   (*Man trap*)

MACDONALD, Philip

LIST OF ADRIAN MESSENGER   UI 1963
(Penguin)
PATROL   RKO 1934
(Collins)   (*Lost patrol*)

MACDONALD, Ross

MOVING TARGET, THE   WAR 1967
(Pan)   (*Harper*)

MACDONALD, William Colt

POWDERSMOKE RANGE   RKO 1935
(Collins)
ROARIN' LEAD   REP 1937
(Collins)

MACDOUGALL, Roger

ESCAPADE (P)   EROS 1955
(Heinemann)
GENTLE GUNMAN, THE (P)   GFD 1952
(*In* Plays of the year 1950–51: Elek)
TO DOROTHY, A SON (P)   BL 1954
(Evans)

MACDOUGALL, Roger *and* **ALLAN,
   Edward**

DOUBLE IMAGE (P)   FOX 1959
(French)

McENROE, Robert G.

SILVER WHISTLE, THE (P)   FOX 1951
(Theatre Arts)   (*Mr. Belvedere rings the bell*)

McEVOY, Charles

LIKES OF 'ER, THE (P)   ABP 1932
(*In* Great modern British plays: Harrap)   (*Sally in our alley*)

McGILL, Angus

YEA, YEA, YEA
(Secker & Warburg)

JARFID 1966
(*Press for time*)

McGIVERN, William P.

BIG HEAT, THE
(Hamilton)

COL 1953

DARKEST HOUR
(Collins)

WAR 1955
(*Hell on Frisco Bay*)

ODDS AGAINST TOMORROW
(Collins)

UA 1959

ROGUE COP
(Collins)

MGM 1954

SHIELD FOR MURDER
(Dodd, N.Y.)

UA 1954

McGOVERN, James

FRAULEIN
(Calder)

FOX 1957

McILVAINE, Jane

IT HAPPENS EVERY THURSDAY
(McRae-Smith)

GFD 1953

MacINNES, Helen

ABOVE SUSPICION
(Harrap)

MGM 1943

ASSIGNMENT IN BRITTANY
(Harrap)

MGM 1943

VENETIAN AFFAIR, THE
(Collins)

MGM 1966

MACKEN, Walter

HOME IS THE HERO (P)
(Macmillan)

BL 1959

McKENNA, Marthe

I WAS A SPY
(Jarrolds)

FOX 1934

McKENNA, Richard

SAND PEBBLES, THE
(Gollancz)

FOX 1966

McKENNEY, Ruth

MY SISTER EILEEN
(Chatto & Windus)

COL 1942
COL 1955

MACKENZIE, *Sir* **Compton**
   CARNIVAL   BI 1931
   (Various)   (*Dance pretty lady*)
                           COL 1935
                           TC 1946

   ROCKETS GALORE   RANK 1958
   (Chatto & Windus)
   SYLVIA SCARLETT   RKO 1935
   (Various)
   WHISKY GALORE   EALING 1949
   (Chatto & Windus)

MACKENZIE, Donald
   MOMENT OF DANGER   ABP 1959
   (Pan Bks)
   NOWHERE TO GO   MGM 1958
   (Elek)

MACKINTOSH, Elizabeth *see*
   TEY, Josephine *pseud*

MACLEAN, Alistair
   GUNS OF NAVARONE, THE   COL 1959
   (Collins)
   LAST FRONTIER   RANK 1960
   (Collins)   (*Secret, ways The*)
   SOUTH BY JAVA HEAD   FOX 1959
   (Collins)

McLELLAN, C. M. S.
   BELLE OF NEW YORK, THE (P)   MGM 1952
   (French)

McMURTY, Larry
   HORSEMAN, PASS BY   PAR 1963
   (Hamilton)   (*Hud*)

McNEILE, Herman Cyril *see*
   'SAPPER' *pseud*

McNEILL, Janet
   CHILD IN THE HOUSE   EROS 1956
   (Hodder & Stoughton)

McNULTY, John Lawrence
   3RD AVENUE, NEW YORK   PAR 1947
   (Little Brown, Boston)   (*Easy come, easy go*)

McPARTLAND, John
   KINGDOM OF JOHNNY COOL,   UA 1964
      THE   (*Johnny Cool*)
   (Muller)
   NO DOWN PAYMENT   FOX 1957
   (Macdonald)

MACREA, Arthur
    TRAVELLER'S JOY (P)   GFD 1951
    (French)

McSHANE, Mark
    SEANCE ON A WET AFTERNOON   RANK 1964
    (Cassell)

McVEIGH, Sue
    GRAND CENTRAL MURDER   MGM 1942
    (Houghton Mifflin, Boston)

MAETERLINCK, Maurice
    BLUE BIRD, THE (P)   FOX 1940
    (Various)

MAHER, Marty *and* **CAMPION, Nardi**
     Reeder
    BRINGING UP THE BRASS   COL 1954
    (McKay, N.Y.)   (*Long gray line*)

MAIER, William
    PLEASURE ISLAND   PAR 1953
    (Wingate)   (*Girls of Pleasure island*)

MAILER, Norman
    AMERICAN DREAM, AN   WAR 1966
    (Deutsch)   (*See you in hell, darling*)
    NAKED AND THE DEAD, THE   WAR 1958
    (Wingate)

MAINWARING, Daniel *see*
HOMES, Geoffrey *pseud*

MAJOR, Charles
    WHEN KNIGHTHOOD WAS IN   RKO 1953
     FLOWER   (*Sword and the rose, The*)
    (Grayson)

MALLESON, Lucy Beatrice *see*
GILBERT, A. *pseud*

MALLORY, Jay
    SWEET ALOES   WAR 1936
    (Cassell)   (*Give me your heart*)

MALORY, *Sir* **Thomas**
LE MORTE D'ARTHUR   MGM 1954
(Various)   (*Knights of the Round Table, The*)

MANKIEWICZ, Donald
TRIAL   MGM 1955
(Deutsch)

MANKOWITZ, Wolf
KID FOR TWO FARTHINGS, A   INDEPENDENT 1954
(Deutsch)
MAKE ME AN OFFER   BL 1954
(Deutsch)

MANN, Edward Beverly
STAMPEDE   ABP 1950
(Triangle Bks, N.Y.)

MANN, Heinrich
BLUE ANGEL   PAR 1930
(Jarrolds)   FOX 1959

MANTLEY, John
SNOW BIRCH, THE   FOX 1959
(Joseph)   (*Woman obsessed, The*)
27TH DAY   COL 1957
(Joseph)

MARCH, William
BAD SEED, THE   WAR 1956
(Hamilton)

MARKS, Leo
GIRL WHO COULDN'T QUITE,   MONARCH 1949
  THE (P)
(French)

MARLOWE, Christopher
DR. FAUSTUS (P)   BL 1966
(Various)

MARQUAND, John Phillips
H. M. PULHAM, ESQ   MGM 1941
(Hale)
LATE GEORGE APLEY, THE   FOX 1947
(Hale)
MELVILLE GOODWIN, USA   WAR 1956
(Hale)   (*Their secret affair*)
POLLY FULTON   MGM 1949
(Hale) *Title in U.S.A.*
B. F.'S DAUGHTER
STOPOVER TOKYO   FOX 1957
(Collins)
THANK YOU, MR. MOTO   FOX 1937
(Jenkins)

MARRIC, J. J. *pseud*
  GIDEON'S DAY   COL 1958
  (Hodder & Stoughton)

MARRYAT, Frederick
  MR. MIDSHIPMAN EASY   ATP 1935
  (Various)   (*Midshipman Easy*)

MARSH, Ronald
  IRENE   ARGYLE 1950
  (Chatto & Windus)

MARSHALL, Bruce
  RED DANUBE   MGM 1949
  (Constable)

MARSHALL, Catherine
  STORY OF PETER MARSHALL, FOX 1954
  THE   (*Man called Peter, A*)
  (Davies)

MARSHALL, Edison
  JEWEL OF MAHABAR   FOX 1953
  (Hodder & Stoughton)   (*Treasure of the Golden Condor*)
  VIKING, THE   UA 1958
  (Muller)   (*Vikings, The*)
  YANKEE PASHA   GFD 1954
  (Redman)

MARSHALL, James Leslie
  SANTA FE   COL 1951
  (Random House, N.Y.)

MARSHALL, *Mrs*. Rosamund
  BRIXBY GIRLS, THE   MGM 1960
  (Redman)   (*All the fine young cannibals*)
  KITTY   ABP 1953
  (Collins)

MARSHALL, Samuel Lyman A
  PORK CHOP HILL   UA 1959
  (Panther Bks)

MARTIN, Archibald Edward
  CURIOUS CRIME   EXCLUSIVE 1955
  (Muller)   (*Glass cage, The*)

MARTIN, George Victor
  FOR OUR VINES HAVE TENDER MGM 1945
    GRAPES   (*Our vines have tender grapes*)
  (Joseph)

MASON, Alfred Edward Woodley

AT THE VILLA ROSE   AB 1940
(Hodder & Stoughton)

DRUM, THE   UA 1938
(Hodder & Stoughton)   (*Drums*)

FIRE OVER ENGLAND   UA 1937
(Hodder & Stoughton)

FOUR FEATHERS, THE   PAR 1930
(Hodder & Stoughton)   UA 1939
       IFD 1955
       (*Storm over the Nile*)

HOUSE OF THE ARROW   AB 1940
(Hodder & Stoughton)   ABP 1953

MASON, Howard *pseud*

PHOTOFINISH   WAR 1959
(Joseph)   (*Follow that horse*)

MASON, Richard

SHADOW AND THE PEAK, THE   RANK 1958
(Collins)   (*Passionate summer*)

WIND CANNOT READ, THE   RANK 1958
(Hodder & Stoughton)

WORLD OF SUZIE WONG, THE   PAR 1959
(Collins)

MASSIE, Christopher

CORRIDOR OF MIRRORS   GFD 1948
(Faber)

PITY MY SIMPLICITY   PAR 1945
(Faber)   (*Love letters*)

MASTERS, John

BHOWANI JUNCTION   MGM 1955
(Joseph)

MASTERSON, Whit

ALL THROUGH THE NIGHT   WAR 1956
(W. H. Allen)   (*Cry in the night, A*)

EVIL COME, EVIL GO   FOX 1963
(W. H. Allen)   (*Yellow canary, The*)

MATHESON, Richard

INCREDIBLE SHRINKING MAN,   RANK 1957
THE
(*In* Born of man, and woman:
Chamberlain Press, Philadelphia)

MAUGHAM, Robert

LINE ON GINGER   BL 1953
(Chapman & Hall)   (*Intruder, The*)

311

MAUGHAM, Robin

ROUGH AND THE SMOOTH, THE MGM 1959
(Chapman & Hall)

SERVANT, THE WAR 1963
(Heinemann)

MAUGHAM, William Somerset

ASHENDEN GB 1936
(Heinemann) (*Secret agent*)

BEACHCOMBER PAR 1938
(Heinemann) (*Vessel of wrath, The*)

CHRISTMAS HOLIDAY UN 1944
(Heinemann)

ENCORE GFD 1951
(Heinemann)

HOUR BEFORE THE DAWN PAR 1944
(Doubleday, N.Y.)

LETTER, THE (P) PAR 1929
(Heinemann) WAR 1940

MOON AND SIXPENCE, THE UA 1942
(Heinemann)

NARROW CORNER WAR 1933
(Heinemann)

OF HUMAN BONDAGE RKO 1934
(Heinemann) WAR 1946
 MGM 1963

OUR BETTERS (P) RKO 1933
(Heinemann)

PAINTED VEIL, THE (P) MGM 1934
(Heinemann) MGM 1957
 (*Seventh sin, The*)

PAINTED VEIL, THE MGM 1934
(Heinemann) MGM 1957
 (*Seventh sin, The*)

QUARTETTE GFD 1949
(Heinemann)

RAIN (P) UA 1932
(French) COL 1954
 (*Miss Sadie Thompson*)

RAZOR'S EDGE, THE FOX 1946
(Heinemann)

SACRED FLAME, THE (P) WAR 1929
(Heinemann) WAR 1935
 (*Right to live, The*)

TRIO GFD 1950
(Heinemann)

VESSEL OF WRATH GFD 1954
(Heinemann) (*Beachcomber*)

MAULDIN, William Henry
  UP FRONT   UI 1951
  (Various)

MAUPASSANT, Guy de
  BEL AMI   UA 1947
  (Various)   (*Private affairs of Bel Ami*)

MAURIAC, François
• THÉRÈSE   GALA 1965
  (Eyre & Spottiswoode)

MAVOR, Osborne Henry *see*
  BRIDIE, James *pseud*

MAXFIELD, Henry S.
  LEGACY FOR A SPY   WAR 1966
  (Heinemann)   (*Double man, The*)

MAXIM, Hiram Percy
  SO GOES MY LOVE   UN 1946
  (World, N.Y.) *Originally called:*
  GENIUS IN THE FAMILY

MAXWELL, William Babington
  RAGGED MESSENGER, THE   COL 1930
  (Butterworth)   (*Madonna of the streets*)

MAYER, Edwin Justus
  FIREBRAND, THE (P)   UA 1934
  (French)   (*Affairs of Cellini*)

MAYNARD, Nan
  THIS IS MY STREET   WAR 1963
  (Corgi Bks)

MAYSE, Arthur
  DESPERATE SEARCH   MGM 1952
  (Harrap)

MEAD, Shepherd
  HOW TO SUCCEED IN BUSINESS   UA 1966
    WITHOUT REALLY TRYING
  (Macdonald)

MEERSCH, Maxence van der
  BODIES AND SOULS   MGM 1949
  (Pilot Press)   (*Doctor and the girl, The*)

MELVILLE, Alan
  CASTLE IN THE AIR (P)   ABP 1952
  (French)
  SIMON AND LAURA (P)   RANK 1955
  (French)

313

MELVILLE, Herman

BILLY BUDD   ANGLO-ALLIED 1962
(Various)

MOBY DICK   WAR 1930
(Various)   (*Sea beasts, The*)
                                    WAR 1954

TYPEE   RANK 1964
(Various)   (*Enchanted island*)

MERCER, Charles

RACHEL CADE   WAR 1960
(Collins)   (*Sins of Rachel Cade, The*)

MERCER, David

MORGAN – A SUITABLE CASE   BL 1966
FOR TREATMENT (P)
(Calder)

MERGENDAHL, Charles

BRAMBLE BUSH, THE   WAR 1959
(Muller)

MÉRIMÉE, Prosper

COLOMBA   RKO 1951
(Hamilton)   (*Vendetta*)

TAMANGO   COL 1959
(Blackie)

MERIVALE, Bernard

UNGUARDED HOUR, THE (P)   MGM 1936
(French)

MERLE, Robert

WEEKEND AT ZUYDCOOTE   FOX 1965
(Lehmann)   (*Weekend at Dunkirk*)

MERRIAM, Robert E.

BATTLE OF THE BULGE   CINERAMA 1965
(Panther Books)

MERRITT, Abraham

BURN, WITCH, BURN   MGM 1936
(Methuen)   (*Devil-doll, The*)

METALIOUS, Grace

PEYTON PLACE   FOX 1957
(Muller)

RETURN TO PEYTON PLACE   FOX 1960
(Muller)

MEYNELL, Laurence W.

BREAKING POINT, THE   BUTCHER 1960
(Collins)

CREAKING CHAIR, THE   AA 1953
(Collins)   *(Street of shadows)*

HOUSE IN MARSH ROAD, THE   GN 1960
(Collins)

ONE STEP FROM MURDER   GN 1959
(Collins)   *Price of silence, The)*

MICHAEL, George

AFRICAN FURY   ABP 1955
(Joseph)

MICHAELS IN AFRICA, THE   NEW REALM 1962
(Muller)   *(Drums of destiny)*

MICHENER, James Albert

BRIDGES AT TOKO-RI, THE   PAR 1954
(Secker & Warburg)

HAWAII   UA 1965
(Secker & Warburg)

RETURN TO PARADISE   UA 1953
(Random House, N.Y.)

SAYONARA   WAR 1957
(Secker & Warburg)

TALES FROM THE SOUTH PACIFIC   TODD AO 1958
(Collins)   *(South Pacific)*

UNTIL THEY SAIL   MGM 1957
(*In* Return To Paradise:
Secker & Warburg)

MIDDLETON, Edgar

POTIPHAR'S WIFE   POWERS 1932
(Laurie)   *(Her strange desire)*

MILLAR, Ronald

FRIEDA (P)   EALING 1947
(English Theatre Guild)

MILLER, Alice Duer

AND ONE WAS BEAUTIFUL   MGM 1940
(Methuen)

GOWNS BY ROBERTA   RKO 1935
(Various)   *(Roberta)*
      MGM 1952
      (Lovely to look at)

MANSLAUGHTER   PAR 1930
(*In* Summer holiday. Dodd, N.Y.)

MILLER, Arthur
  CRUCIBLE, THE (P)   FILMS DE FRANCE 1957
  (Secker & Warburg)   *(Witches of Salem, The)*
  DEATH OF A SALESMAN (P)   COL 1951
  (Cresset Press)

MILLIN, Sarah Gertrude
  RHODES   GB 1936
  (Chatto & Windus)

MILLS, Mervyn
  LONG HAUL, THE   COL 1957
  (Pan Bks)

MILNE, Alan Alexander
  DOVER ROAD (P)   RKO 1934
  (*In* Chief contemporary dramatists. *(Where sinners meet)*
    Houghton Mifflin, Boston)
  FOUR DAYS' WONDER   UN 1937
  (Methuen)
  MICHAEL AND MARY (P)   UN 1932
  (Chatto & Windus)
  PERFECT ALIBI, THE (P)   RKO 1931
  (*In* Four plays: Putnam, N.Y.)
  WINNIE THE POOH AND THE DISNEY 1965
    HONEY TREE
  (Methuen)

MINNEY, Raleigh James
  CARVE HER NAME WITH PRIDE RANK 1957
  (Newnes)
  NOTHING TO LOSE   ABP 1952
  (Macdonald)   *(Time gentlemen, please!)*

MINNEY, R. J. *see*
LIPSCOMB, W. P. *jt. author*

MITCHELL, Margaret
  GONE WITH THE WIND   MGM 1939
  (Macmillan)

MITCHELL, Mary
  WARNING TO WANTONS, A AQUILA 1949
  (Heinemann)

MITFORD, Nancy
  BLESSING, THE   MGM 1959
  (Hamilton)   *(Count your blessings)*

MOISEIWITSCH, Maurice
  SLEEPING TIGER, THE INSIGNIA FILMS 1954
  (Heinemann)

MOLL, Elick *see*
TARADASH, D. *jt author*

MOLNAR, Ferenc

GUARDSMAN, THE (P)   MGM 1941
(Macy-Masius, N.Y.)   (*Chocolate soldier, The*)

OLYMPIA (P)   PAR 1960
(Brentano, N.Y.)   (*Breath of scandal, A*)

SWAN, THE (P)   UA 1930
(Longmans, N.Y.)   (*One romantic night*)
     MGM 1956

MONAGHAN, James [Jay]

LAST OF THE BADMEN   ABP 1949
(Bobbs-Merrill, Indianapolis)   (*Bad men of Tombstone*)

MONKS, John *and* **FINKLEHOFFE, Fred R.**

BROTHER RAT (P)   WAR 1938
(Random House, N.Y.)   WAR 1952
     (*About face*)

MONRO, Robert

FRENCH MISTRESS, A (P)   BL 1960
(French)

MONSARRAT, Nicholas

CRUEL SEA, THE   GFD 1952
(Cassell)

STORY OF ESTHER COSTELLO   COL 1957
THE
(Cassell)

MONTAGUE, Ewen Edward Samuel

MAN WHO NEVER WAS, THE   FOX 1955
(Evans)

MONTEILHET, Hubert

RETURN FROM THE ASHES   UA 1965
(Panther Bks.)

MONTGOMERY, Lucy Maud

ANNE OF GREEN GABLES   RKO 1934
(Harrap)

ANNE OF WINDY POPLARS   RKO 1940
(Harrap) *Also published as*
ANNE OF WINDY WILLOWS

MOODY, William Vaughan

GREAT DIVIDE, THE   IN 1930
(Macmillan)

MOORE, Brian
   LUCK OF GINGER COFFEY, THE   BL 1965
   (Deutsch)

MOORE, George
   ESTHER WATERS   WESSEX 1948
   (Various)
   ESTHER WATERS (P)   WESSEX 1948
   (Heinemann)

MOORE, Grace
   YOU'RE ONLY HUMAN ONCE   WAR 1953
   (Invincible Press)   (*So this is love*)

MOORE, Ruth
   SPOONHANDLE   FOX 1948
   (Grosset, N.Y.)   (*Deep waters*)

MOOREHEAD, Alan
   RAGE OF THE VULTURE, THE   PAR 1951
   (Hamilton)   (*Thunder in the East*)

MORANTE, Elsa
   ARTURO'S ISLAND   GALA 1963
   (Collins)

MORAVIA, Alberto
   APPOINTMENT AT THE BEACH   COMPTON 1965
   (*In* Fetish, The: Secker & Warburg)   (*Naked hours, The*)
   TIME OF INDIFFERENCE   CONT 1967
   (Secker & Warburg)
   WOMAN OF ROME, A   EXCLUSIVE 1956
   (Secker & Warburg)

MORAY, Helga
   UNTAMED   FOX 1955
   (Museum Press)

MORELL, Parker
   DIAMOND JIM   UN 1935
   (Hurst & Blackett)

MORGAN, Albert
   GREAT MAN, THE   UI 1956
   (Dutton, N.Y.)

MORGAN, Charles
   FOUNTAIN, THE   RKO 1934
   (Macmillan)

MORGAN, Joan

  THIS WAS A WOMAN (P)   FOX 1948
(French)

MORIER, James Justian

  ADVENTURES OF HAJJI BABA   FOX 1954
    OF ISPAHAN   (*Adventures of Hajji Baba, The*)
(Modern Library, N.Y.)

MORLEY, Christopher Darlington

  KITTY FOYLE   RKO 1940
(Lippincott, Philadelphia)

MORLEY, Edward *and* **LANGLEY, Noel**

  EDWARD, MY SON (P)   MGM 1948
(French)

MORRIS, Colin

  RELUCTANT HEROES (P)   ABP 1951
(English Theatre Guild)

MORROS, Boris

  MY TEN YEARS AS A   RANK 1960
    COUNTERSPY   (*Confessions of a counterspy*)
(Laurie)

MORTIMER, John

  DOCK BRIEF, THE (P)   MGM 1962
(Elek)

MORTIMER, Penelope

  PUMPKIN EATER, THE   BL 1963
(Penguin)

MOSEL, Ted

  DEAR HEART (P)   WAR 1964
(Obolensky, N.Y.)

MOSLEY, Leonard

  CAT AND THE MICE, THE   BL 1960
(Barker)   (*Foxhole in Cairo*)

MOSS, Arthur *and* **MARVEL, Evelyn**

  LEGEND OF THE LATIN   COL 1950
    QUARTER   (*Her wonderful lie*)
(W. H. Allen)

MOSS, W. Stanley

  ILL MET BY MOONLIGHT   RANK 1956
(Corgi Bks)

MOTLEY, Willard

KNOCK ON ANY DOOR   COL 1949
(Collins)

LET NO MAN WRITE MY   COL 1960
  EPITAPH   (*Reach for tomorrow*)
(Collins)

MOTTRAM, Ralph Hale

SPANISH FARM, THE   EXCELLENT 1930
(Chatto & Windus)   (*Roses of Picardy*)

MOYZISCH, L. C.

OPERATION CICERO   FOX 1952
(Wingate)   (*Five fingers*)

MULFORD, Clarence Edward

BAR 20   UA 1943
(Hodder & Stoughton)

BAR 20 RIDES AGAIN   PAR 1935
(Hodder & Stoughton)

COTTONWOOD GULCH   PAR 1937
(Hodder & Stoughton)   (*North of Rio Grande*)

HOP-ALONG CASSIDY   PAR 1935
(Hodder & Stoughton)

HOP-ALONG CASSIDY RETURNS   PAR 1936
(Hodder & Stoughton)

ROUND-UP, THE   PAR 1937
(Hodder & Stoughton)   (*Hills of old Wyoming*)

TRAIL DUST   PAR 1936
(Hodder & Stoughton)

MULLEN, Pat

MAN OF ARAN   GB 1934
(Faber)

MULVIHILL, William

SANDS OF THE KALIHARI   PAR 1965
(Longmans)

MUNDY, Talbot

KING OF THE KHYBER RIFLES   FOX 1954
(Hutchinson)

MURPHY, Audie

TO HELL AND BACK   UI 1955
(Hammond)

MUSMANNO, Michael A.

TEN DAYS TO DIE   INTERCONTINENTAL 1955
(Davies)

MYERS, Elizabeth
 MRS CHRISTOPHER   GFD 1951
 (Chapman & Hall)   (*Blackmailer*)

MYRER, Anton
 BIG WAR, THE   FOX 1958
 (Hamilton)   (*In love and war*)

N

NABOKOV, Vladimir
 LOLITA   MGM 1962
 (Corgi Bks)

NARCEJAC, T. *see*
BOILEAU, P. *jt. author*

NASH, N. Richard
 RAINMAKER, THE (P)   PAR 1956
 (Random House, N.Y.)

NASH, N. Robert
 GIRLS OF SUMMER (P)   PAR 1959
 (French, N.Y.)

NASH, O. *see*
PERELMAN, S. J. *jt. author*

NATHAN, Robert
 BISHOP'S WIFE, THE   RKO 1947
 (*In* Barley fields: Constable)
 ONE MORE SPRING   FOX 1950
 (Cassell)
 PORTRAIT OF JENNIE   SELZNICK 1948
 (Heinemann)

NATHANSON, E. M.
 DIRTY DOZEN, THE   MGM 1966
 (Barker)

NAUGHTON, Bill
 ALFIE (P)   PAR 1965
 (French)
 ALFIE   PAR 1965
 (MacGibbon & Kee)

NEBEL, Frederick
 SLEEPERS EAST   FOX 1934
 (Collins)

L

NEIDER, Charles

  AUTHENTIC DEATH OF HENDRY   PAR 1960
    JONES, THE   (*One eyed Jacks*)
  (Harper, N.Y.)

NEMEROV, Howard

  HOMECOMING GAME, THE   WAR 1960
  (Gollancz)   (*Tall story*)

NEMIROWSKY, I.

  DAVID GOLDEN   BL 1950
  (Constable)   (*My daughter Joy*)

NESS, Eliot *and* **FRALEY, Oscar**

  UNTOUCHABLES, THE   WAR 1959
  (Messner, N.Y.)   (*Scarface mob, The*)

NEUMANN, Robert

  QUEEN'S DOCTOR, THE   BL 1959
  (Gollancz)   (*King in shadow*)

NEVINS, Frank J.

  YANKEE DARED, A   REP 1950
  (Chicago. Published by the author)   (*Transcontinental express*)

NEWMAN, Bernard

  THEY SAVED LONDON   EROS 1957
  (Hamilton)

NIALL, Ian *pseud*

  NO RESTING PLACE   ABP 1951
  (Heinemann)
  TIGER WALKS, A   DISNEY 1964
  (Heinemann)

NIALL, Michael

  BAD DAY AT BLACK ROCK   MGM 1955
  (Muller)

NICHOLSON, Meredith

  HOUSE OF THE THOUSAND   REP 1936
    CANDLES, THE
  (Black)

NICHOLSON, Robert

  MRS. ROSS   UA 1966
  (Constable)   (*Whisperers, The*)

NIELAND, D'Arcy

  SHIRALEE, THE   MGM 1957
  (Angus & Robertson)

NIELSON, Helen
   MURDER BY PROXY   EXCLUSIVE 1954
   (Gollancz)

NIGGLI, Josephine
   MEXICAN VILLAGE, A   MGM 1953
   (Sampson Low)   *(Sombrero)*

NIKLAUS, Thelma
   TAMAHINE   WAR 1963
   (Lane)

NILES, Blair
   CONDEMNED TO DEVIL'S ISLAND   UA 1939
   (Cape)   *(Condemned)*

NOBLE, Hollister
   WOMAN WITH A SWORD   RKO 1952
   (Doubleday, N.Y.)   *(Drums in the deep South)*

NOBLE, W. *see*
HERLIHY, J. L. *jt. author*

NOEL, Sterling
   HOUSE OF SECRETS, THE   RANK 1956
   (Deutsch)

NOLAN, Jeanette
   GATHER YE ROSEBUDS   PAR 1948
   (Appleton, N.Y.)   *(Isn't it romantic)*

NORDHOFF, Charles Bernard *and* **HALL,**
   James Norman
   BOTANY BAY   PAR 1952
   (Chapman & Hall)
   HIGH BARBAREE, THE   MGM 1947
   (Faber)
   HURRICANE   UA 1937
   (Chapman & Hall)
   MUTINY ON THE BOUNTY   MGM 1935
   (Chapman & Hall)   MGM 1962
   NO MORE GAS   RKO 1942
   (Chapman & Hall)   *(Tuttles of Tahiti, The)*

NORRIS, Charles Gilman
   SEED   UN 1931
   (Heinemann)

NORRIS, Kathleen
   BEAUTY'S DAUGHTER   FOX 1935
   (Murray)

NORRIS, Kathleen (*continued*)

PASSION FLOWER   MGM 1930
(Murray)

SECOND HAND WIFE   FOX 1933
(Murray)

WALLS OF GOLD   FOX 1933
(Murray)

NORTH, Sperling

SO DEAR TO MY HEART   RKO 1948
(Odhams)

NORWAY, Nevil Shute *see*
SHUTE, Nevil *pseud*

NOVELLO, Ivor

I LIVED WITH YOU (P)   GB 1935
(Methuen)

SYMPHONY IN TWO FLATS (P)   GFD 1931
(*In* Three plays: Methuen)

TRUTH GAME, THE (P)   MGM 1932
(French, N.Y.)   (*But the flesh is weak*)

NUGENT, E. *see*
THURBER, J. *jt. author*

O

O'BRIEN, Edna
LONELY GIRL, THE   UA 1964
(Cape)   (*Girl with green eyes*)

O'BRIEN, Kate
THAT LADY   FOX 1954
(Heinemann)

O'BRINE, Mannering
PASSPORT TO TREASON   EROS 1956
(Hammond)

O'CASEY, Sean
JUNO AND THE PAYCOCK (P)   BI 1930
(Macmillan)

JUNO AND THE PAYCOCK   BI 1930
(Macmillan)

MIRROR IN MY HOUSE   MGM 1964
(Macmillan)   (*Young Cassidy*)

PLOUGH AND THE STARS (P)   RKO 1936
(Macmillan)

AUTHOR AND ORIGINAL TITLE	FILM TITLE

O'CONNOR, Edwin

LAST HURRAH, THE   COL 1958
(Pan Bks)

O'DELL, Scott

ISLAND OF THE BLUE DOLPHINS   RANK 1964
(Constable)

ODETS, Clifford

BIG KNIFE, THE (P)   UA 1955
(Random House, N.Y.)
CLASH BY NIGHT (P)   RKO 1952
(Random House, N.Y.)
GOLDEN BOY (P)   COL 1938
(Gollancz)
WINTER JOURNEY (P)   PAR 1954
(Viking, N.Y.)   (*Country girl, The*)

ODLUM, Jerome

EACH DAWN I DIE   WAR 1939
(Various)

O'DONNELL, Peter

MODESTY BLAISE   FOX 1965
(Souvenir Press)

O'FLAHERTY, Liam

INFORMER, THE   RKO 1935
(Cape)

OGBURN, Charlton

MERRILL'S MARAUDERS   WAR 1962
(Hodder & Stoughton)   (*Marauders, The*)

O'GRADY, Rohan

LET'S KILL UNCLE   UI 1967
(Longmans)

O'HARA, John

BUTTERFIELD 8   MGM 1960
(Cresset Press)
FROM THE TERRACE   FOX 1960
(Cresset Press)
PAL JOEY (P)   COL 1957
(Cresset Press)
RAGE TO LIVE, A   UA 1964
(Cresset Press)

O'HARA, Mary *pseud*

  GREEN GRASS OF WYOMING   FOX 1949
  (Eyre & Spottiswoode)

  MY FRIEND FLICKA   FOX 1943
  (Eyre & Spottiswoode)

  THUNDERHEAD—SON OF FLICKA FOX 1945
  (Eyre & Spottiswoode)

'OLIVIA' *pseud*

  OLIVIA   FILMS DE FRANCE 1950
  (Hogarth Press)

OLLIVANT, Alfred

  OWD BOB   GB 1937
  (Various)

O'NEILL, Eugene Gladstone

  AH WILDERNESS (P)   MGM 1935
  (Cape)   MGM 1948
    (*Summer holiday*)

  ANNA CHRISTIE (P)   MGM 1930
  (Random House, N.Y.)

  DESIRE UNDER THE ELMS (P)   PAR 1958
  (Cape)

  EMPEROR JONES (P)   UA 1933
  (Cape)

  HAIRY APE, THE (P)   UA 1944
  (Cape)

  LONG DAY'S JOURNEY INTO FOX 1962
    NIGHT (P)
  (Cape)

  LONG VOYAGE HOME, THE (P) UA 1940
  (Various)

  MOURNING BECOMES ELECTRA RKO 1948
    (P)
  (Cape)

  STRANGE INTERLUDE (P)   MGM 1932
  (Cape)

OPPENHEIM, Edward Phillips

  AMAZING QUEST OF MR ERNEST KLEMENT 1936
    BLISS, THE   (*Amazing quest, The*)
  (Hodder & Stoughton)

  GREAT IMPERSONATION, THE UN 1935
  (Hodder & Stoughton)   UN 1942

  LION AND THE LAMB, THE   COL 1931
  (Hodder & Stoughton)

  STRANGE BOARDERS OF PALACE GB 1938
    CRESCENT   (*Strange boarders*)
  (Hodder & Stoughton)

ORCZY, *Baroness* **Emmuska**

ELUSIVE PIMPERNEL, THE   BL 1950
(Hutchinson)

EMPEROR'S CANDLESTICKS, THE   MGM 1937
(Hodder & Stoughton)

SCARLET PIMPERNEL, THE   UA 1935
(Hodder & Stoughton)

O'ROURKE, Frank

BRAVADOS, THE   FOX 1958
(Heinemann)

MULE FOR THE MARQUESA, A   COL 1966
(Fontana)   *(Professionals, The)*

ORWELL, George *pseud*

ANIMAL FARM   ABP 1954
(Secker & Warburg)
1984   ABP 1956
(Gollancz)

OSBORN, Paul

ON BORROWED TIME (P)   MGM 1939
(Dramatists, N.Y.)

WORLD OF SUZIE WONG, THE   PAR 1959
   (P)
(Random House, N.Y.)

OSBORNE, Hubert

SHORE LEAVE (P)   MGM 1954
(French, N.Y.)   *(Hit the deck)*

OSBORNE, John

ENTERTAINER, THE (P)   BL 1960
(Evans)

LOOK BACK IN ANGER (P)   ABP 1959
(Faber)

OSBOURNE, L. *see*
STEVENSON, R. L. *jt. author*

OSTENSO, M. *see*
KENNY, E. *jt. author*

OUIDA

DOG OF FLANDERS, A   RKO 1935
(Chatto & Windus)   FOX 1959
UNDER TWO FLAGS   FOX 1936
(Chatto & Windus)

OURSLER, Fulton

GREATEST STORY EVER TOLD,
THE
(Worlds Work)

UA 1965

OVERHOLSTER, Wayne D.

CAST A LONG SHADOW
(Ward Lock)

UA 1959

OWEN, Frank

EDDIE CHAPMAN STORY, THE
(Hamilton)

AA 1967
(*Triple cross, The*)

OWEN, Guy

BALLAD OF THE FLIM-FLAM
MAN
(Macmillan, N.Y.)

FOX 1966
(*Flim-flam man, The*)

P

PACKER, Joy

NOR THE MOON BY NIGHT
(Eyre & Spottiswoode)

RANK 1958

PAGANO, Jo

CONDEMNED, THE
(Invincible Press)

UA 1951
(*Sound of the fury, The*)

PAGE, Elizabeth

TREE OF LIBERTY
(Collins)

COL 1940
(*Howards of Virginia, The*)

PAGE, Gertrude

PADDY THE NEXT BEST THING
(Hurst & Blackett)

FOX 1933

PAGE, Marco

FAST COMPANY
(Heinemann)

MGM 1939
(*Fast and loose*)

PALEY, Frank

RUMBLE ON THE DOCKS
(Crown, N.Y.)

COL 1957

PALMER, John Leslie *see*
BEEDING, Francis *pseud*

PALMER, Stuart

PUZZLE OF THE BRIAR PIPE
(Collins)

RKO 1936
(*Murder on a bridle path*)

PUZZLE OF THE PEPPER TREE
(Jarrolds)

RKO 1935
(*Murder on a honeymoon*)

PAPASHVILY, George *and*
PAPASHVILY, Helen
 ANYTHING CAN HAPPEN   PAR 1952
 (Heinemann)

PARGETER, Edith
 SPANIARD'S CURSE, THE   BL 1957
 (Heinemann)   *(Assize of the dying, The)*

PARKER, Gilbert
 TRANSLATIONS OF A SAVAGE PAR 1935
 (Methuen)   *(Behold my wife)*

PARKER, Louis N.
 JOSEPH AND HIS BRETHREN (P) COL 1954
 (Bodley Head)

PARRISH, Ann
 ALL KNEELING   RKO 1950
 (Benn)   *(Born to be bad)*

PARROTT, Ursula
 STRANGERS MAY KISS   MGM 1931
 (Cape)

PASCAL, Ernest
 MARRIAGE BED, THE   PAR 1931
 (Allen & Unwin)   *(Husband's holiday)*

PASTERNAK, Boris
 DOCTOR ZHIVAGO   MGM 1965
 (Collins)

PATON, Alan
 CRY, THE BELOVED COUNTRY BL 1951
 (Cape)

PATRICK, John
 TEAHOUSE OF THE AUGUST MGM 1957
  MOON, THE (P)
 (Heinemann)

PATTON, Frances Gray
 GOOD MORNING, MISS DOVE FOX 1955
 (Gollancz)

PAYNE, Laurence
 NOSE ON MY FACE, THE   BL 1963
 (Hodder & Stoughton)   *(Girl in the headlines)*

PAYNE, Stephen
 BLACK ACES   UN 1937
 (Wright & Brown)

PEARSON, William
    FEVER IN THE BLOOD   WAR 1960
    (Macmillan)

PERCY, Edward
    SHOP AT SLY, CORNER THE (P)   BL 1946
    (French)

PERCY, Edward *and* **DENHAM,**
    Reginald
    LADIES IN RETIREMENT (P)   COL 1941
    (Random House, N.Y.)

PERDUE, Virginia
    HE FELL DOWN DEAD   WAR 1946
    (Doubleday, N.Y.)   *(Shadow of a woman)*

PERELMAN, Sidney Joseph *and* **NASH,**
    Ogden
    ONE TOUCH OF VENUS (P)   UN 1948
    (Little Brown, Boston)

PERKINS, Grace
    NO MORE ORCHIDS   COL 1932
    (Wright & Brown)

PERKINS, Kenneth
    DESERT VOICES   ABP 1952
    (Wright & Brown)   *(Desert pursuit)*

PERRY, George Sessions
    HOLD AUTUMN IN YOUR HANDS UA 1945
    (Sun Dial, N.Y.)   *(Southerner, The)*

PERRY, J. *see*
    FARRELL, M. J. *jt. author*

PERTWEE, Michael
    NIGHT WAS OUR FRIEND (P)   MONARCH 1951
    (English Theatre Guild)

PERTWEE, Roland
    HEAT WAVE (P)   WAR 1931
    (*In* Five three-act plays: French N.Y.) *(Road to Singapore)*
    PARAGON, THE (P)   ABP 1948
    (*In* Plays of the year 1948–49: Elek) *(Silent dust)*
    PINK STRING AND SEALING   EALING 1946
      WAX (P)
    (English Theatre Guild)

PERTWEE, Roland *and* **DEARDEN, Harold**

INTERFERENCE (P)   PAR 1935
(French, N.Y.)   (*With regret*)

PETERSON, Ralph

SQUARE RING, THE   GFD 1953
(Barker)

PHILLPOTTS, Eden

FARMER'S WIFE, THE (P)   ABP 1940
(French)

YELLOW SANDS, THE (P)   AB 1938
(Duckworth)

PIERSON, *Mrs.* **Louise**

ROUGHLY SPEAKING   WAR 1945
(Simon & Schuster, N.Y.)

PILKINGTON, Roger

NEPOMUK OF THE RIVER   CINERAMA 1965
(Macmillan)   (*Golden head, The*)

PINCHON, Edgcomb

ZAPATA, THE UNCONQUERABLE   FOX 1952
(Doubleday, N.Y.)   (*Viva Zapata*)

PINERO, *Sir* **Arthur Wing**

ENCHANTED COTTAGE, THE (P)   RKO 1945
(Heinemann)

MAGISTRATE, THE (P)   PAR 1940
(Heinemann)   (*Those were the days*)

SECOND MRS. TANQUERAY, THE   VANDYKE 1952
   (P)
(Heinemann)

PINTER, Harold

CARETAKER, THE (P)   BL 1963
(Grove Press, N.Y.)

PIPER, Evelyn

BUNNY LAKE IS MISSING   COL 1965
(Secker & Warburg)

NANNY, THE   WAR 1965
(Secker & Warburg)

PODHAJSKY, Alois

WHITE STALLIONS OF VIENNA,   DISNEY 1963
   THE   (*Flight of the white stallions, The*)
(Harrap)

POE, Edgar Allan

   BLACK CAT, THE   WAR 1963
   (*In* Tales of mystery and imagination: (*Tales of terror*)
   Various)

   CALYPSO   BL 1956
   (*In* Best tales: Various)   (*Gold bug, The*)

   CASE OF DR. VALDEMAR   WAR 1963
   (*In* Tales of mystery and imagination: (*Tales of terror*)
   Various)

   FALL OF THE HOUSE OF USHER,   AA 1960
      THE
   (Various)

   MASQUE OF THE RED DEATH   AA 1964
      THE
   (Various)

   MORELLA   WAR 1963
   (*In* Tales of mystery and imagination: (*Tales of terror*)
   Various)

   MURDERS IN THE RUE MORGUE   UN 1932
   (Various)   WAR 1954
                        (*Phantom of the Rue Morgue*)

   MYSTERY OF MARIE ROGET   UN 1942
   (Various)

   PIT AND THE PENDULUM, THE   AA 1961
   (*In* Tales of mystery and imagination:
   Various)

   PREMATURE BURIAL, THE   AA 1962
   (*In* Tales of mystery and imagination:
   Various)

   TELL-TALE HEART, THE   ABP 1960
   (*In* Tales of mystery and imagination:
   Various)

PORTER, Eleanor H.

   POLLYANNA   DISNEY 1960
   (Harrap)

PORTER, Gene Stratton *see*
STRATTON-PORTER, GENE

PORTER, Katherine Anne

   SHIP OF FOOLS   COL 1964
   (Secker & Warburg)

PORTER, William Sidney *see*
HENRY, O. *pseud*

POTTER, Stephen

   GAMESMANSHIP   WAR 1960
   (Hart-Davis)   (*School for scoundrels*)

POTTER, Stephen (*continued*)

LIFEMANSHIP
(Hart-Davis)

WAR 1960
(*School for scoundrels*)

ONEUPMANSHIP
(Hart-Davis)

WAR 1960
(*School for scoundrels*)

POWELL, Michael

GRAF SPEE
(Hodder & Stoughton)

RANK 1956
(*Battle of the River Plate, The*)

POWELL, Richard

PHILADELPHIAN, THE
(Hodder & Stoughton)

WAR 1959
(*City jungle, The*)

PIONEER GO HOME
(Hodder & Stoughton)

UA 1962
(*Follow that dream*)

PRAAG, Van Van

DAY WITHOUT END
(Sloane, N.Y.)

UA 1957
(*Men in war*)

PRATT, Theodore

BAREFOOT MAILMAN, THE
(Cassell)

COL 1951

MR. WINKLE GOES TO WAR
(Duell, N.Y.)

COL 1944

PREEDY, George *pseud*

GENERAL CRACK
(Lane)

WAR 1930

PRESNELL, Frank G.

SEND ANOTHER COFFIN
(Heinemann)

UA 1939
(*Slightly honourable*)

PRESSBURGER, Emeric

KILLING A MOUSE ON SUNDAY
(Harcourt, N.Y.)

COL 1964
(*Behold a pale horse*)

PRIESTLEY, John Boynton

BENIGHTED
(Heinemann)

BL 1963
(*Old dark house, The*)

DANGEROUS CORNER (P)
(French)

RKO 1943

GOOD COMPANIONS, THE
(Heinemann)

FOX 1933
ABP 1957

INSPECTOR CALLS, AN (P)
(French)

BL 1954

LABURNUM GROVE (P)
(Heinemann)

ATP 1935

LET THE PEOPLE SING
(Heinemann)

BN 1942

PRIESTLEY, John Boynton (*continued*)

OLD DARK HOUSE, THE   UN 1932
(Harper, N.Y.)   BL 1963

THEY CAME TO A CITY (P)   EALING 1945
(Heinemann)

WHEN WE ARE MARRIED (P)   BN 1943
(Heinemann)

PRIESTLEY, John Boynton *and*
KNOBLOCK, Edward

GOOD COMPANIONS, THE (P)   FOX 1933
(French, N.Y.)   ABP 1937

PROCTER, Maurice

HELL IS A CITY   WAR 1959
(Hutchinson)

PROKOSCH, Frederic

CONSPIRATORS, THE   WAR 1944
(Chatto & Windus)

PROUTY, Olive

NOW, VOYAGER   WAR 1942
(Hodder & Stoughton)

STELLA DALLAS   UA 1937
(Hodder & Stoughton)

PRYCE, Myfanwy

LADY IN THE DARK, THE   PAR 1944
(Lane)

PUDNEY, John

NET, THE   GFD 1952
(Joseph)

THURSDAY ADVENTURE   BL 1955
(Evans)   (*Stolen air-liner*)

PUGH, Marshall

COMMANDER CRABB   ROMULUS 1958
(Macmillan)   (*Silent enemy, The*)

PUSHKIN, Aleksandr Sergieevich

CAPTAIN'S DAUGHTER, THE   PAR 1959
(Various)   (*Tempest*)

QUEEN OF SPADES, THE   AB 1949
(Various)

PYLE, Ernest Taylor

HERE IS YOUR WAR   INT 1951
(Various)   (*War correspondent*)

STORY OF G.I. JOE, THE   UA 1945
(Various)

PYLE, Howard
   MEN OF IRON   UI 1954
   (Various)   (*Black shield of Falworth, The*)

Q

QUEEN, Ellery *pseud*
   ELLERY QUEEN, MASTER   COL 1940
     DETECTIVE
   (Grosset, N.Y.)
   PENTHOUSE MYSTERY   COL 1941
   (Grosset, N.Y.)   (*Ellery Queen and the penthouse mystery*)
   PERFECT CRIME   COL 1941
   (Grosset, N.Y.)   (*Ellery Queen and the perfect crime*)
   SPANISH CAPE MYSTERY, THE   REP 1935
   (Gollancz)

QUEFFELEC, Henri
   ISLE OF SINNERS   REGENT 1952
   (Verschoyle)

QUENEAU, Raymond
   ZAZIE   CONNOISSEUR 1962
   (Lane)

QUENTIN, Patrick *pseud*
   BLACK WIDOW   FOX 1954
   (Simon & Schuster, N.Y.)
   MAN IN THE NET THE   UA 1958
   (Gollancz)
   PUZZLE FOR FIENDS   AA 1958
   (Gollancz)   (*Strange awakening, The*)

R

RAE, John
   CUSTARD BOYS, THE   GALA 1962
   (Hart-Davis)   (*Reach for glory*)

RAINE, William McLeod
   RAWHIDE JUSTICE   GFD 1955
   (Hodder & Stoughton)   (*Man from Bitter Ridge*)

RAMAGE, Jennifer *see*
   MASON, Howard *pseud*

RAND, Ayn
    FOUNTAINHEAD, THE   WAR 1949
    (Cassell)

    NIGHT OF JANUARY 16TH (P)   PAR 1941
    (Longmans, N.Y.)

RANSOME, Stephen *pseud*
    HEARSES DON'T HURRY   FOX 1942
    (Doubleday, N.Y.)   *(Who is Hope Schuyler?)*

RAPHAEL, Frederic
    TWO FOR THE ROAD   FOX 1967
    (Cape)

RAPHAELSON, Samuel
    ACCENT ON YOUTH (P)   PAR 1935
    (French)   PAR 1959
    (But not for me)

    HILDA CRANE (P)   FOX 1956
    (Random House, N.Y.)

    PERFECT MARRIAGE, THE (P)   PAR 1946
    (Dramatists, N.Y.)

    SKYLARK (P)   PAR 1941
    (Various)

RASCOVICH, Mark
    BEDFORD INCIDENT, THE   BL 1964
    (Secker & Warburg)

RATTIGAN, Terence
    BROWNING VERSION, THE (P)   GFD 1951
    (French)

    DEEP BLUE SEA, THE (P)   FOX 1955
    (Hamilton)

    FRENCH WITHOUT TEARS (P)   PAR 1940
    (French)

    SEPARATE TABLES (P)   UA 1958
    (French)

    WHILE THE SUN SHINES (P)   ABP 1947
    (Hamilton)

    WHO IS SYLVIA (P)   BL 1954
    (Hamilton)   *(Man who loved redheads, The)*

    WINSLOW BOY, THE (P)   INTERNATIONAL 1949
    (Hamilton)

RAWLINGS, *Mrs*. Marjorie
    YEARLING, THE   MGM 1946
    (Heinemann)

RAWSON, Clayton
  NO COFFIN FOR THE CORPSE   FOX 1942
  (Little Brown, Boston)   *(Man who wouldn't die, The)*

RAWSON, Tabor
  I WANT TO LIVE   UA 1958
  (Muller)

RAY, Rene
  STRANGE WORLD OF PLANET X, EROS 1958
    THE
  (Jenkins)

RAYMAN, Sylvia
  WOMEN OF TWILIGHT (P)   ROMULUS 1952
  (Evans)

RAYMOND, Ernest
  BERG, THE (P)   BI 1930
  (Benn)   *(Atlantic)*
  FOR THEM THAT TRESPASS   ABP 1949
  (Cassell)
  TELL ENGLAND   CAPITOL 1931
  (Cassell)

RAYMOND, Moore
  SMILEY   FOX 1955
  (Sylvan Press)

RAYNER, Denys Arthur
  ESCORT   FOX 1957
  (Kimber)   *(Enemy below, The)*

REED, Mark White
  YES, MY DARLING DAUGHTER WAR 1939
    (P)
  (French, N.Y.)

REED, Myrtle
  SPINNER IN THE SUN   FOX 1929
  (Putnam)   *(Veiled woman)*

REID, P. R.
  COLDITZ STORY, THE   BL 1954
  (Hodder & Stoughton)

REMARQUE, Erich Maria
  ALL QUIET ON THE WESTERN UN 1930
    FRONT
  (Putnam)

REMARQUE, Erich Maria (*continued*)

ARCH OF TRIUMPH (Hutchinson)	UA 1948
FLOTSAM (Hutchinson)	UA 1941 (*So ends our night*
ROAD BACK (Putnam)	UN 1937
THREE COMRADES (Hutchinson)	MGM 1938
TIME TO LOVE AND A TIME TO DIE (Hutchinson)	RANK 1957

RESKO, John

Reprieve (MacGibbon)	WAR 1962

RESNIK, Muriel

SON OF ANY WEDNESDAY (P) (Stein & Day, N.Y.)	WAR 1966 (*Any Wednesday*)

RHODES, Eugene Manlove

PASO POR AQUI (Houghton Mifflin, Boston)	UA 1948 (*Four faces West*)

RICE, Alice Caldwell

MRS. WIGGS OF THE CABBAGE PATCH (Grosset, N.Y.)	PAR 1934

RICE, Craig

HAVING WONDERFUL CRIME (Nicholson & Watson)	RKO 1945
HOME SWEET HOMICIDE (World, N.Y.)	FOX 1946
LUCKY STIFF, THE (World, N.Y.)	UA 1948

RICE, Elmer L.

COUNSELLOR AT LAW (P) (Gollancz)	UN 1933
DREAM GIRL (P) (Coward-McCann, N.Y.)	PAR 1947
SEE NAPLES AND DIE (P) (French, N.Y.)	WAR 1931 (*Oh! sailor, behave!*)
STREET SCENE (P) (French, N.Y.)	UA 1931

RICHARDSON, Henry Handel

MAURICE GUEST (Heinemann)	MGM 1954 (*Rhapsody*)

RICHMAN, Arthur

NOT SO LONG AGO (P)   COL 1953
(French, N.Y.)   (*Let's do it again*)

RICHTER, Conrad Michael

LIGHT IN THE FOREST, THE   DISNEY 1958
(Gollancz)

SEA OF GRASS   MGM 1947
(Constable)

TRACEY CROMWELL   UI 1955
(Knopf, N.Y.)   (*One desire*)

RIDLEY, Arnold

BEGGAR MY NEIGHBOUR (P)   GFD 1953
(Evans)   (*Meet Mr. Lucifer*)

GHOST TRAIN, THE (P)   GFD 1931
(French, N.Y.)   GFD 1941

KEEPERS OF YOUTH   POWERS 1932
(Benn)

RINEHART, Mary Roberts

BAT, THE   UA 1931
(Cassell)   (*Bat whispers, The*)

BAT, THE (P)   WAR 1959
(French)

CASE OF ELINOR NORTON, THE   FOX 1935
(Cassell)

LOST ECSTASY   PAR 1931
(Doran, N.Y.)   (*I take this woman*)

MISS PINKERTON   WAR 1941
(Various)   (*Nurse's secret, The*)

TISH CARRIES ON   MGM 1942
(Cassell)   (*Tish*)

ROARK, Garland

FAIR WIND TO JAVA   REP 1953
(Falcon Press)

WAKE OF THE RED WITCH   REP 1948
(Aldor)

ROBB, John *pseud*

PUNITIVE ACTION   UA 1955
(Hamilton)   (*Desert sand*)

ROBBINS, Harold

CARPETBAGGERS, THE   PAR 1963
(Blond)   PAR 1963
     (*Nevada Smith*)

NEVER LOVE A STRANGER   ABP 1957
(Corgi Bks)

ROBBINS, Harold (*continued*)

  STONE FOR DANNY FISHER, A   PAR 1958
  (Hale)   (*King Creole*)

  WHERE LOVE HAS GONE   PAR 1964
  (Blond)

ROBERTS, Carl Eric Bechofer

  DON CHICAGO   BN 1945
  (Jarrolds)

ROBERTS, Denys

  SMUGGLERS CIRCUIT   BL 1958
  (Methuen)   (*Law and disorder*)

ROBERTS, Elizabeth Maddox

  GREAT MEADOW, THE   MGM 1931
  (Cape)

ROBERTS, Kenneth

  CAPTAIN CAUTION   UA 1940
  (Collins)

  LYDIA BAILEY   FOX 1952
  (Collins)

  NORTH-WEST PASSAGE   MGM 1940
  (Collins)   MGM 1959
                           (*Frontier Rangers*)
                           MGM 1959
                           (*Mission of danger*)

ROBERTS, Richard Emery

  GILDED ROOSTER, THE   COL 1955
  (Laurie)   (*Last frontier, The*)

  SECOND TIME ROUND   FOX 1961
  (Pocket Bks)
  Previously published as
  STAR IN THE WEST

ROBERTSON, Willard

  MOONTIDE   FOX 1942
  (Hamilton)

ROBINSON, Henry Morton

  CARDINAL, THE   COL 1963
  (Macdonald)

ROBINSON, Lennox

  BIG HOUSE, THE   MGM 1930
  (Macmillan)

ROBSON, Norman *see*
ROBB, John *pseud*

340

ROCHE, Arthur Somers

CASE AGAINST MRS. AMES, THE   PAR 1936
(Melrose)

ROCHE, Mazo de la

JALNA   RKO 1935
(Macmillan)

ROCK, Philip

EXTRAORDINARY SEAMAN   MGM 1967
(Souvenir Press)

ROE, Vingle

GOLDEN TIDE, THE   REP 1953
(Cassell)

ROHMER, Sax

DAUGHTER OF THE DRAGON   PAR 1931
(Cassell)

DRUMS OF FU MANCHU   REP 1943
(Cassell)

MYSTERY OF DR. FU MANCHU   PAR 1929
(Methuen)   (*Mysterious Dr. Fu Manchu*)

RETURN OF DR. FU MANCHU   PAR 1930
(*In* Book of Dr. Fu Manchu, The:
Hurst & Blackett)

RONALD, James

MEDAL FOR A GENERAL, A   BN 1944
(Hodder & Stoughton)

THEY CAN'T HANG ME   UN 1939
(Rich & Cowan)   (*Witness vanishes, The*)

THIS WAY OUT   UN 1944
(Rich & Cowan)   (*Suspect, The*)

ROONEY, Philip

CAPTAIN BOYCOTT   INDIVIDUAL 1947
(Talbot Press)

RORICK, Isabel Scott

MR. AND MRS. CUGAT   PAR 1942
(Jarrolds)   (*Are husbands necessary?*)

ROSE, Alexander

FOUR PUNTERS ARE MISSING   PAR 1963
(Hamilton)   (*Who's got the action?*)

ROSE, Anna Perrott

ROOM FOR ONE MORE   WAR 1952
(Houghton Mifflin, Boston)

ROSE, Edward Everett
  REAR CAR (P)   MGM 1934
  (French, N.Y.)   (*Murder in the private car*)

ROSS, J. *see*
ADLER, R. *jt. author*

ROSS, Sam
  HE RAN ALL THE WAY   UA 1951
  (Farrar, N.Y.)

ROSTEN, Leo
  CAPTAIN NEWMAN, M.D.   UI 1963
  (Gollancz)

ROTH, Arthur
  TERRIBLE BEAUTY, A   UA 1960
  (Hutchinson)

ROTH, Lillian
  I'LL CRY TOMORROW   MGM 1955
  (Gollancz)

ROUSSIN, Andre
  LITTLE HUT, THE (P)   MGM 1957
  (Random House, N.Y.)

RUARK, Robert
  SOMETHING OF VALUE   MGM 1957
  (Hamilton)

RUBIN, Theodore I.
  LISA AND DAVID   BL 1963
  (Macmillan)   (*David and Lisa*)

RUESCH, Hans
  RACER, THE   FOX 1954
  (Hurst & Blackett)   (*Racers, The*)
                 FOX 1958
                 (*Men against speed*)

RUGGLES, Eleanor
  PRINCE OF PLAYERS   FOX 1954
  (Davies)

RUNYON, Damon
  BLOODHOUNDS OF BROADWAY FOX 1952
  (Various)
  JOHNNY ONE-EYE   UA 1950
  (*In* Runyun à la carte: Constable)
  LEMON DROP KID, THE   PAR 1951
  (*In* Guys and dolls: Lippincott, N.Y.)
  MONEY FROM HOME   PAR 1953
  (Various)

RUNYON, Damon *and* **LINDSAY, Howard**

SLIGHT CASE OF MURDER, A (P)   WAR 1952
(Dramatists, N.Y.)   *(Stop, you're killing me)*

RUSSELL, John

WHERE THE PAVEMENT ENDS   PAR 1930
(Butterworth)   *(Sea god, The)*

RUSSELL, Mary Annette Beauchamp
Russell, *countess see*
'ELIZABETH' *pseud*

RUSSELL, Sheila MacKay

LAMP IS HEAVY, A   RANK 1956
(Angus & Robertson)   *(Feminine touch, The)*

RYAN, Cornelius

LONGEST DAY, THE   FOX 1962
(Gollancz)

RYAN, Patrick

HOW I WON THE WAR   UA 1967
(Muller)

S

SABATINI, Rafael

BLACK SWAN, THE   FOX 1942
(Hutchinson)
CAPTAIN BLOOD   IN 1935
(Hutchinson)
CAPTAIN BLOOD RETURNS   COL 1952
(Hutchinson)   *(Captain Blood fugitive)*
COLUMBUS   GFD 1949
(Hutchinson)   *(Christopher Columbus)*
FORTUNES OF CAPTAIN BLOOD,   COL 1950
   THE
(Hutchinson)
SCARAMOUCHE   MGM 1952
(Hutchinson)
SEA HAWK, THE   WAR 1940
(Various)

SADLEIR, Michael

FANNY BY GASLIGHT   GFD 1944
(Constable)

SAGAN, Françoise

AIMEZ-VOUS BRAHMS   UA 1961
(Murray)   *(Goodbye again)*

SAGAN, Françoise (*continued*)

  BONJOUR TRISTESSE   COL 1957
  (Murray)

  CERTAIN SMILE, A   FOX 1958
  (Murray)

SALAMANCA, J. R.

  LILITH   BL 1963
  (Heinemann)

  LOST COUNTRY, THE   FOX 1961
  (Four Square Bks)   (*Wild in the country*)

SALE, Richard

  NOT TOO NARROW, NOT TOO   MGM 1940
    DEEP   (*Strange cargo*)
  (Cassell)

  OSCAR, THE   PAR 1965
  (Cassell)

SALTEN, Felix

  BAMBI   RKO 1942
  (Various)

  FLORIAN   MGM 1940
  (Cape)

  PERRI   DISNEY 1957
  (Cape)

SALTER, James

  HUNTERS, THE   FOX 1958
  (Heinemann)

SANDERS, George

  STRANGER AT HOME   EXCLUSIVE 1954
  (Pilot Press)   (*Stranger came home*)

SANDOZ, Mari

  CHEYENNE AUTUMN   WAR 1964
  (McGraw-Hill, N.Y.)

SANDSTROM, Flora

  MADNESS OF THE HEART   TC 1949
  (Cassell)

  MIDWIFE OF PONT CLERY   UA 1961
  (Cassell)   (*Jessica*)

  MILK WHITE UNICORN, THE   BN 1947
  (Cassell)   (*White unicorn, The*)

SANFORD, Harry *and* **LAMB, H.**

  EMPORIA   PAR 1967
  (Hale)   (*Waco*)

SANSOM, William

LAST HOURS OF SANDRA LEE, THE
(Hogarth Press)

BL 1965
(*Wild affair, The*)

'SAPPER' *pseud*

BULLDOG DRUMMOND AT BAY
(Hodder & Stoughton)

REP 1937

CHALLENGE, THE
(Hodder & Stoughton)

PAR 1938
(*Bulldog Drummond in Africa*)

FEMALE OF THE SPECIES
(Hodder & Stoughton)

PAR 1937
(*Bulldog Drummond comes back*)

TEMPLE TOWER
(Hodder & Stoughton)

PAR 1939
(*Bulldog Drummond's secret police*)

THIRD ROUND, THE
(Hodder & Stoughton)

PAR 1938
(*Bulldog Drummond's peril*)

SAROYAN, William

HUMAN COMEDY, THE
(Faber)

MGM 1943

TIME OF YOUR LIFE (P)
(Faber)

UA 1948

SARTRE, Jean-Paul

CHIPS ARE DOWN, THE
(Rider)

LOPERT 1949

LOSER WINS (P)
(Hamilton)

FOX 1964

RESPECTABLE PROSTITUTE, THE
(P)
(*In* No exit and 3 other plays:
Vintage Bks, N.Y.)

GALA 1955

SAUNDERS, Hilary St. George *see also*
BEEDING, Francis *pseud*

SAUNDERS, Hilary St. George

RED BERET, THE
(Joseph)

COL 1953

SAUNDERS, John Monk

DAWN PATROL, THE
(Queensway Press)

IN 1930
WAR 1938

SAVAGE, Mildred

PARRISH
(Longmans)

WAR 1960

SAVORY, Gerald

GEORGE AND MARGARET (P)
(French)

WAR 1940

SAXON, Lyle
    LAFITTE THE PIRATE   PAR 1938
    (Appleton, N.Y.)   (*Buccaneer, The*)

SAYERS, Dorothy Leigh
    BUSMAN'S HONEYMOON   MGM 1940
    (Gollancz)   (*Busman's holiday*)

SAYERS, Dorothy Leigh *and* BYRNE, M.
  St. Clare
    BUSMAN'S HONEYMOON (P)   MGM 1940
    (Harcourt, N.Y.)   (*Busman's holiday*)

SCHAEFER, Jack Warner
    BIG RANGE   FOX 1953
    (Deutsch)   (*Silver whip, The*)
    SHANE   PAR 1953
    (Deutsch)

SCHARY, Dore
    SUNRISE AT CAMPOBELLO (P) WAR 1960
    (Random House, N.Y.)

SCHAUFFLER, Elsie
    PARNELL (P)   MGM 1937
    (Gollancz)

SCHIROKAUER, Alfred
    PAIVA: QUEEN OF LOVE   GFD 1948
    (Jarrolds)   (*Idol of Paris, The*)

SCHISGAL, Murray
    LUV (P)   BL 1966
    (Coward-McCann, N.Y.)

SCHISGALL, Oscar *see*
  HARDY, Stuart *pseud*

SCHNITZLER, Arthur
    LA RONDE
    (HCC Bks)   BL 1964
    MERRY GO ROUND   COMMERCIAL 1951
    (Weidenfeld & Nicolson)   (*La Ronde*)

SCHULBERG, Bud Wilson
    HARDER THEY FALL, THE   COL 1956
    (Lane)
    SOME FACES IN THE CROWD WAR 1957
    (Lane)   (*Face in the crowd, A*)

SCHULMAN, Arnold
  HOLE IN THE HEAD, A (P)   UA 1959
  (Random House, N.Y.)

SCHULMAN, Irving
  CHILDREN OF THE DARK   WAR 1955
  (World, N.Y.)   (*Rebel without a cause*)

SCHWEIZER, Richard
  LAST CHANCE, THE   MGM 1945
  (Drummond *and* Secker & Warburg)

SCOTT, Allan *and* HAIGHT, George
  GOODBYE AGAIN (P)   WAR 1941
  (French, N.Y.)   (*Honeymoon for three*)

SCOTT, J. D.
  SEA WYF AND BISCUIT   FOX 1957
  (Heinemann)   (*Sea-wife*)

SCOTT, Robert Lee
  GOD IS MY CO-PILOT   WAR 1945
  (Hodder & Stoughton)

SCOTT, Sir Walter
  IVANHOE   MGM 1951
  (Various)
  QUENTIN DURWARD   MGM 1955
  (Various)   (*Adventures of Quentin Durward*)
  TALISMAN, THE   WAR 1954
  (Various)   (*King Richard and the Crusaders*)

SCUDDER, Kenyon Judson
  PRISONERS ARE PEOPLE   WAR 1954
  (Doubleday, N.Y.)   (*Unchained*)

'SEAMARK' *pseud*
  MAN THEY COULDN'T ARREST,   GB 1933
    THE
  (Hodder & Stoughton)

SEARLS, Henry
  CROWDED SKY, THE   WAR 1960
  (Harper, N.Y.)

SECONDARI, John
  COINS IN THE FOUNTAIN   FOX 1954
  (Eyre & Spottiswoode)   (*Three coins in the fountain*)
                                  FOX 1965
                                  (*Pleasure seekers, The*)

SEELEY, Clinton
  STORM FEAR   UA 1955
  (Holt, N.Y.)

SEGALL, Harry

HALFWAY TO HEAVEN (P)   COL 1941
(French)   (*Here comes Mr. Jordan*)

SEGHERS, Anna

SEVENTH CROSS, THE   MGM 1944
(Hamilton)

SELINKO, Annemarie

DÉSIRÉE   FOX 1954
(Heinemann)

SEMPLE, Lorenzo

GOLDEN FLEECING, THE (P)   MGM 1961
(French, N.Y.)   (*Honeymoon machine, The*)

SETON, Anya

DRAGONWYCK   FOX 1946
(Hodder & Stoughton)

FOXFIRE   UI 1954
(Hodder & Stoughton)

SETON, Ernest Thompson

LOBO AND OTHER STORIES   DISNEY 1962
(Hodder & Stoughton)   (*Legend of Lobo, The*)

SETON, Graham *pseud*

W PLAN   RKO 1931
(Butterworth)

SEWARD, Florence A.

GOLD FOR THE CAESARS   MGM 1963
(Redman)

SEWELL, Anna

BLACK BEAUTY   FOX 1946
(Various)

SHAFFER, Peter

FIVE FINGER EXERCISE (P)   COL 1962
(French)

PRIVATE EAR, THE (P)   UI 1967
(French)   (*Pad, The (and how to use it)*)

SHAKESPEARE, William

AS YOU LIKE IT (P)   FOX 1936
(Various)

HAMLET (P)   TC 1948
(Various)

HENRY V (P)   TC 1945
(Various)

SHAKESPEARE, William (*continued*)

JULIUS CAESAR (P)   MGM 1953
(Various)

MACBETH (P)   REP 1951
(Various)   BL 1960

MIDSUMMER NIGHT'S DREAM, A WAR 1935
  (P)
(Various)

OTHELLO (P)   UA 1956
(Various)   EAGLE FILMS 1966

RICHARD III (P)   BL 1955
(Various)

ROMEO AND JULIET (P)   MGM 1936
(Various)   GFD 1954
      GALA 1956

TAMING OF THE SHREW, THE (P) INVICTA 1933

(Various)   MGM 1953
      (*Kiss me Kate*)
      COL 1966

SHAPIRO, Lionel

SEALED VERDICT   PAR 1948
(Doubleday, N.Y.)

SHARP, Don

CONFLICT OF WINGS   BL 1954
(Putnam, N.Y.)

SHARP, Margery

CLUNY BROWN   FOX 1946
(Collins)

NUTMEG TREE   MGM 1948
(Various)   (*Julia misbehaves*)

SHAW, Charles

HEAVEN KNOWS, MR. ALLISON FOX 1957
(Muller)

SHAW, George Bernard

ANDROCLES AND THE LION (P) RKO 1952
(Constable)

ARMS AND THE MAN (P)   GB 1932
(Various)

CAESAR AND CLEOPATRA (P) PASCAL 1945
(Various)

DEVIL'S DISCIPLE, THE (P)   UA 1959
(Constable)

DOCTOR'S DILEMMA, THE (P) MGM 1958
(Constable)

MAJOR BARBARA (P)   PASCAL 1941
(Various)

SHAW, George Bernard (*continued*)

MILLIONAIRESS, THE (P)   FOX 1960
(Constable)

PYGMALION (P)   MGM 1938
(Constable)   WAR 1964
        (*My Fair lady*)

SAINT JOAN (P)   UA 1957
(Constable)

SHAW, Irwin

GENTLE PEOPLE, THE (P)   WAR 1941
(Dramatists, N.Y.)   (*Out of the fog*)

IN THE FRENCH STYLE   COL 1963
(*In* Tip of a dead jockey: Cape)

TWO WEEKS IN ANOTHER TOWN MGM 1962
(Cape)

YOUNG LIONS, THE   FOX 1957
(Cape)

SHAW, Robert

HIDING PLACE, THE   PAR 1964
(Chatto & Windus)   (*Situation hopeless but not serious*)

SHEARING, Joseph *pseud*

AIRING IN A CLOSED CARRIAGE TC 1948
(Hutchinson)   (*Mark of Cain*)

BLANCHE FURY   CINEGUILD 1948
(Heinemann)

FOR HER TO SEE   PAR 1948
(Hutchinson)   (*So evil my love*)

MOSS ROSE   FOX 1947
(Heinemann)

SHELDON, Charles Monroe

IN HIS STEPS   GN 1936
(Warne)

SHELLABARGER, Samuel

CAPTAIN FROM CASTILE FOX 1948
(Macmillan)

PRINCE OF FOXES   FOX 1949
(Macmillan)

SHELLEY, Mary Wollstonecroft

FRANKENSTEIN   WAR 1931
(Dent)   WAR 1957
        (*Curse of Frankenstein, The*)

SHERMAN, Richard

TO MARY—WITH LOVE   FOX 1936
(Faber)

SHERRIFF, Robert Cedric

BADGERS GREEN (P)   HIGHBURY 1949
(Gollancz)

HOME AT SEVEN (P)   BL 1951
(Gollancz)

JOURNEY'S END (P)   TIFFANY 1930
(Gollancz)

SHERRIFF, Robert Cedric *and*
    BARTLETT, Vernon

JOURNEY'S END   TIFFANY 1930
(Gollancz)

SHERRY, Edna

SUDDEN FEAR   RKO 1952
(Hodder & Stoughton)

SHERRY, Gordon

BLACK LIMELIGHT (P)   ALL 1939
(French)

SHERWOOD, Robert Emmet

ABE LINCOLN OF ILLINOIS (P)   RKO 1940
(Scribner, N.Y.)   (*Abe Lincoln in Illinois*)

IDIOT'S DELIGHT (P)   MGM 1939
(Heinemann)

PETRIFIED FOREST, THE (P)   WAR 1936
(Scribner, N.Y.)   WAR 1945
      (*Escape in the desert*)

QUEEN'S HUSBAND, THE (P)   RKO 1931
(Scribner, N.Y.)   (*Royal bed*)

REUNION IN VIENNA (P)   MGM 1933
(Scribner, N.Y.)

ROAD TO ROME, THE (P)   MGM 1954
(French, N.Y.)   (*Jupiter's darling*)

THIS IS NEW YORK (P)   PAR 1932
(Scribner, N.Y.)   (*Two kinds of women*)

WATERLOO BRIDGE (P)   UN 1930
(Scribner, N.Y.)   MGM 1940
      MGM 1955
      (*Gaby*)

SHIBER, *Mrs.* **Ella**

PARIS-UNDERGROUND   UA 1945
(Harrap)

SHIELS, George

PROFESSOR TIM (P)   RKO 1957
(Macmillan)

SHIRREFS, Gordon Donald

 TRAILS END   ABP 1957
 (Avalon, N.Y.)   *(Oregon passage)*

SHORT, Luke *pseud*

 AMBUSH   MGM 1950
 (Collins)

 CORONER CREEK   COL 1948
 (Collins)

 HIGH VERMILION   PAR 1951
 (Collins)

 SILVER ROCK   REP 1954
 (Collins)   *(Hell's outpost)*

 STATION WEST   RKO 1948
 (Collins)

 VENGEANCE VALLEY, THE MGM 1950
 (Collins)

SHULMAN, Irving

 AMBOY DUKES, THE UI 1949
 (Doubleday, N.Y.)   *(City across the river)*

 CHILDREN OF THE DARK UA 1959
 (Holt, N.Y.)   *(Cry tough)*

 HARLOW   PAR 1964
 (Mayflower Bks)

 NOTORIOUS LANDLADY, THE COL 1962
 (Gold Medal Bks)

SHULMAN, Max

 'RALLY ROUND THE FLAG, FOX 1958
  BOYS!'
 (Heinemann)

SHUTE, Nevil *pseud*

 LANDFALL   AB 1948
 (Heinemann)

 NO HIGHWAY   FOX 1951
 (Heinemann)

 ON THE BEACH   UA 1959
 (Heinemann)

 PIED PIPER   FOX 1942
 (Heinemann)

 TOWN LIKE ALICE, A RANK 1956
 (Heinemann)

SIDNEY, Margaret *pseud*

 FIVE LITTLE PEPPERS AND HOW COL 1939
  THEY GREW
 (Various)

SIENKIEWICZ, Henryk

QUO VADIS   IN 1929
(Various)   MGM 1949

SILLIPHANT, Stirling

MARACAIBO   PAR 1958
(Farrar, N.Y.)

SILLITOE, Alan

LONELINESS OF THE LONG-   BL 1962
DISTANCE RUNNER, THE
(W. H. Allen)

SATURDAY NIGHT AND SUNDAY   BL 1960
   MORNING
(W. H. Allen)

SIMENON, Georges

ACT OF PASSION   CP 1952
(Routledge)   (*Forbidden fruit*)

BATTLE OF NERVES, A   BL 1950
(Routledge)   (*Man on the Eiffel Tower, The*)

BOTTOM OF THE BOTTLE   FOX 1955
(*In* Tidal wave: Doubleday, N.Y.) (*Beyond the river*)

BROTHER RICO   COL 1957
(*In* Tidal wave: Doubleday, N.Y.)

MAN WHO WATCHED THE   EROS 1952
   TRAINS GO BY
(Routledge)

MONSIEUR LA SOURIS   COL 1951
(Gallimard, Paris)   (*Midnight episode*)

NEWHAVEN-DIEPPE   AB 1947
(Routledge)   (*Temptation harbour*)

STRANGERS IN THE HOUSE   JARFID 1966
(Routledge)   (*Stranger in the house*)

SIMON, Neil

BAREFOOT IN THE PARK (P)   PAR 1966
(French, N.Y.)

COME BLOW YOUR HORN (P) PAR 1963
(Doubleday, N.Y.)

SIMON, S. J. *see*
BRAHMS, C. *jt. author*

SIMPSON, *Mrs.* **C. Fraser**

FOOTSTEPS IN THE NIGHT   AUTEN 1932
(Methuen)

M

SIMPSON, Helen

  SARABAND FOR DEAD LOVERS   EL 1949
  (Heinemann)

  UNDER CAPRICORN   WAR 1949
  (Heinemann)

SIMPSON, H. de G. *see*
  DANE, C. *jt. author*

SIMPSON, Norman Frederick

  ONE WAY PENDULUM   UA 1964
  (Grove Press, N.Y.)

SINCLAIR, Harold

  HORSE SOLDIERS, THE   UA 1959
  (Muller)

SINCLAIR, Upton

  GNOMOBILE   DISNEY 1966
  (Laurie)

  WET PARADE   MGM 1932
  (Laurie)

SINGER, Howard

  WAKE ME WHEN IT'S OVER   FOX 1960
  (Putnam, N.Y.)

SIODMAK, Carl

  DONOVAN'S BRAIN   BL 1963
  (Corgi Bks)   (*Vengeance*)

SITWELL, *Sir* **Osbert**

  PLACE OF ONE'S OWN, A   GFD 1945
  (Macmillan)

SKIDELSKY, Simon Jasha *see*
  SIMON, S. J. *pseud*

SKINNER, C. O. *see also*
  TAYLOR, S. A. *jt. author*

SKINNER, Cornelius Otis *and*
  KIMBROUGH, Emily

  OUR HEARTS WERE YOUNG AND PAR 1944
  GAY
  (Constable)

SKLAR, G. *see*
  CASPARY, V. *jt. author*

SLADE, C. Jope *see*
  JOPE-SLADE, C.

SLATER, Humphrey
CONSPIRATOR   MGM 1949
(Lehmann)

SLATER, Montague
ONCE A JOLLY SWAGMAN   WESSEX 1949
(Lane)

SLAUGHTER, Frank Gill
SANGAREE   PAR 1953
(Jarrolds)
WARRIOR, THE   RKO 1956
(Doubleday, N.Y.)   (*Naked in the sun*)

SLOMAN, R. *see*
   DOBIE, L. *jt. author*

SMALL, Austin J. *see*
   'SEAMARK' *pseud*

SMITH, Alson Jesse
BROTHER VAN   BL 1957
(Various)   (*Lawless Eighties, The*)

SMITH, Betty
JOY IN THE MORNING   MGM 1965
(Heinemann)
TREE GROWS IN BROOKLYN, A   FOX 1945
(Heinemann)
Originally published as:
A TREE GROWS IN THE YARD

SMITH, Dodie [Dorothy Gladys]
CALL IT A DAY (P)   WAR 1937
(Gollancz)
DEAR OCTOPUS (P)   GFD 1943
(Heinemann)
ONE HUNDRED AND ONE   DISNEY 1960
   DALMATIANS
(Heinemann)

SMITH, Dorothy Gladys *see*
   ANTHONY, C. L. *pseud*

SMITH, *Lady* **Eleanor**
BALLERINA   COL 1941
(Gollancz)   (*Men in her life*)
CARAVAN   FOX 1934
(Hutchinson)   EL 1947
MAN IN GREY, THE   GFD 1943
(Hutchinson)
RED WAGON   ALL 1938
(Gollancz)

SMITH, Frederick E.

633 SQUADRON   UA 1964
(Hutchinson)

SMITH, Harry Allen

RHUBARB   PAR 1951
(Barker)

SMITH, Shelley *pseud*

BALLAD OF THE RUNNING MAN   COL 1963
(Hamilton)   (*Running man, The*)

SMITH, Thorne

NIGHT LIFE OF THE GODS   UN 1935
(Methuen)

TOPPER   MGM 1937
(Methuen)

TOPPER TAKES A TRIP   UA 1939
(Methuen)

TURNABOUT   UA 1940
(Methuen)

SMITTER, Wessel

DETROIT, F.O.B.   PAR 1941
(Dent)   (*Reaching for the sun*)

SNEIDER, Vern J.

TEAHOUSE OF THE AUGUST   MGM 1957
  MOON, THE
(Macmillan)

BEGINNERS LUCK   AA 1959
(Collins)   (*Desperate man, The*)

SOPHOCLES

OEDIPUS REX (P)   OEDIPUS REX 1956
(Various)

SOUSA, John Philip

MARCHING ALONG   FOX 1952
(Hale)

SOUTAR, Andrew

DEVIL'S TRIANGLE   FOX 1932
(Hutchinson)   (*Almost married*)

SOUTHARD, Ruth

NO SAD SONGS FOR ME   COL 1950
(Doubleday, N.Y.)

SPEARMAN, Frank Hamilton

WHISPERING SMITH   FOX 1935
(Grosset, N.Y.)   (*Whispering Smith speaks*)

SPENCE, Hartzell

ONE FOOT IN HEAVEN   WAR 1941
(Harrap)

SPENCER, Elizabeth

LIGHT IN THE PIAZZA   MGM 1962
(Heinemann)

SPIGELGASS, Leonard

MAJORITY OF ONE, A (P)   WAR 1961
(French, N.Y.)

SPILLANE, Mickey

GIRL HUNTERS, THE   FOX 1964
(Barker)

I, THE JURY   UA 1953
(Barker)

KISS ME DEADLY   UA 1954
(Barker)

LONG WAIT, THE   UA 1954
(Barker)

MY GUN IS QUICK   UA 1957
(Barker)

SPRIGG, C. St. John

PERFECT ALIBI   RKO 1931
(Eldon)

SPRING, Howard

FAME IS THE SPUR   TC 1947
(Collins)

MY SON, MY SON   UA 1940
(Collins)
Originally published as:
O, ABSOLOM!

SPYRI, Johanna

HEIDI   FOX 1937
(Various)   UA 1954

STACPOOLE, Henry de Vere

BLUE LAGOON   INDIVIDUAL 1949
(Various)

STALLINGS, L. *see*
    ANDERSON, M. *jt. author*

STANDISH, Robert

  ELEPHANT WALK   PAR 1954
  (Davies)

STEELE, Wilbur Daniel

  WAY TO THE GOLD, THE   FOX 1957
  (Doubleday, N.Y.)

STEIN, J. *see*
  GLICKMAN, W. *jt. author*

STEINBECK, John

  EAST OF EDEN   WAR 1954
  (Heinemann)

  FORGOTTEN VILLAGE, THE   MGM 1941
  (Viking, N.Y.)

  GRAPES OF WRATH, THE   FOX 1940
  (Heinemann)

  MOON IS DOWN, THE   FOX 1943
  (Viking, N.Y.)

  OF MICE AND MEN   UA 1939
  (Heinemann)

  OF MICE AND MEN (P)   UA 1939
  (Covici, N.Y.)

  PEARL, THE   RKO 1948
  (Heinemann)   RKO 1954

  RED PONY, THE   BL 1949
  (Viking, N.Y.)

  TORTILLA FLAT   MGM 1942
  (Grosset, N.Y.)

  WAYWARD BUS, THE   FOX 1957
  (Heinemann)

STEPHENSON, Carl

  LEININGEN VERSUS THE ANTS PAR 1953
  (*In* Bedside Esquire: Barker)   (*Naked jungle, The*)

STERN, David

  FRANCIS   UI 1949
  (Farrar, N.Y.)

STERN, Gladys Bronwyn

  UGLY DACHSHUND. THE   DISNEY 1966
  (Cassell)

  WOMAN IN THE HALL, THE   GFD 1947
  (Cassell)

STEVENSON, Robert Louis

  BLACK ARROW   COL 1948
  (Various)

STEVENSON, Robert Louis (*continued*)

BODY SNATCHER   RKO 1945
(Various)

DR. JEKYLL AND MR. HYDE   PAR 1932
(Various)   MGM 1941
                              COL 1959
                              (*Two faces of Dr Jekyll, The*)

EBB TIDE   PAR 1947
(Various)   (*Adventure Island*)

KIDNAPPED   FOX 1938
(Various)   MON 1949
                              DISNEY 1959

MASTER OF BALLENTRAE, THE   WAR 1953
(Various)

ST. IVES   COL 1949
(Various)   (*Secret of St Ives, The*)

SIRE OF MALETROIT'S DOOR,   UI 1951
  THE   (*Strange door, The*)
(*In* New Arabian nights: Various)

SUICIDE CLUB, THE   MGM 1936
(Various)   (*Trouble for two*)

TREASURE ISLAND   MGM 1934
(Various)   RKO 1949

TREASURE OF FRANCHARD   UI 1952
(Various)   (*Treasure of Lost Canyon*)

STEVENSON, Robert Louis *and*
  OSBOURNE, Lloyd

WRONG BOX, THE   COL 1965
(Longmans)

STEWART, Donald Ogden

MR. AND MRS. HADDOCK   PAR 1931
  ABROAD   (*Finn and Hattie*)
(Doran, N.Y.)

STEWART, Mary

MOON-SPINNERS, THE   DISNEY 1964
(Hodder & Stoughton)

STEWART, Ramona

DESERT FURY   PAR 1947
(World, N.Y.)

STINETORF, Louise A.

WHITE WITCH DOCTOR   FOX 1953
(Westminster Press, Philadelphia)

STODDART, Dayton

PRELUDE TO NIGHT   EL 1948
(Coward-McCann, N.Y.)   (*Ruthless*)

STOKER, Bram
  DRACULA   UI 1931
  (Rider)   UI 1957

STOKES, S. *see*
  JOPE-SLADE, C. *jt. author*

STONE, *Mrs.* **Grace**
  BITTER TEA OF GENERAL YEN,   COL 1933
    THE
  (Bobbs-Merrill, Indianapolis)

STONE, Irving
  AGONY AND THE ECSTACY, THE FOX 1964
  (Collins)
  FALSE WITNESS   REP 1941
  (Doubleday, N.Y.)   (*Arkansas judge*)
  IMMORTAL WIFE   FOX 1953
  (Invincible Press)   (*President's lady, The*)
  LUST FOR LIFE   MGM 1956
  (Lane)

STONG, Philip
  CAREER   RKO 1939
  (Grosset, N.Y.)
  STATE FAIR   FOX 1945
  (Grosset, N.Y.)   FOX 1962
  STRANGER'S RETURN   MGM 1933
  (Harcourt, N.Y.)

STOREY, David
  THIS SPORTING LIFE   RANK 1962
  (Longmans)

STOREY, Robert
  TOUCH IT LIGHT (P)   BRYANSTON 1960
  (French)   (*Light up the sky*)

STORY, Jack Trevor
  LIVE NOW, PAY LATER   REGAL FILMS 1962
  (Secker & Warburg)
  MIX ME A PERSON   BL 1962
  (Corgi Bks)
  TROUBLE WITH HARRY, THE PAR 1955
  (Boardman)

STOUT, Rex
  FER DE LANCE   COL 1936
  (Cassell)   (*Meet Nero Wolfe*)
  LEAGUE OF FRIGHTENED MEN, COL 1937
    THE
  (Cassell)

STRABEL, Thelma

  REAP THE WILD WIND   PAR 1942
  (Collins)

STRATTON-PORTER, Gene

  FRECKLES   FOX 1960
  (Hodder & Stoughton)

  GIRL OF THE LIMBERLOST, A   MON 1934
  (Hodder & Stoughton)

  HARVESTER, THE   REP 1936
  (Hodder & Stoughton)

  HER FATHER'S DAUGHTER   MON 1940
  (Murray)   (*Her first romance*)

  KEEPER OF THE BEES   MON 1935
  (Hutchinson)

  LADDIE   RKO 1935
  (Murray)

  MICHAEL O'HALLORAN   REP 1937
  (Murray)   MON 1949

STREATFEILD, Noel

  AUNT CLARA   BL 1954
  (Collins)

STREET, Arthur George

  STRAWBERRY ROAN   BN 1944
  (Faber)

STREET, James Howell

  GOODBYE, MY LADY   WAR 1956
  (Invincible Press)

  TAP ROOTS   UI 1948
  (Sun Dial Press, N.Y.)

STREETER, Edward

  FATHER OF THE BRIDE   MGM 1950
  (Hamilton)

  MR. HOBB'S HOLIDAY   FOX 1962
  (Hamilton)   (*Mr. Hobbs takes a vacation*)

STRINDBERG, Johann August

  MISS JULIE (P)   LF 1951
  (Dent)

STRODE, William Chetham *see*
    CHETHAM-STRODE, William

STRONG, Austin

  SEVENTH HEAVEN, THE (P)   FOX 1937
  (French, N.Y.)

STRONG, Leonard Alfred George

  BROTHERS, THE   FOX 1947
  (Gollancz)

STRUTHER, Jan

  MRS MINIVER   MGM 1942
  (Chatto & Windus)

STUART, Aimee

  JEANNIE (P)   TANSA 1942
  (Hamilton)   ABP 1957
                    (Let's be happy)

STUART, Aimee *and* **STUART, Philip**

  NINE TILL SIX (P)   ATP 1932
  (French, N.Y.)

STUART, Donald

  SHADOW, THE   GLOBE 1936
  (Wright & Brown)

STUART, William

  NIGHT CRY   FOX 1950
  (Dial Press, N.Y.)   *(Where the sidewalk ends)*

STURE-VASA, Mary *see*
  O'HARA, Mary *pseud*

STURGES, Preston

  STRICTLY DISHONOURABLE (P)   UN 1931
  (Liveright, N.Y.)   MGM 1951

SUMMERS, Richard Aldrich

  VIGILANTE   WAR 1952
  (Duell, N.Y.)   *(San Francisco story, The)*

SUMNER, *Mrs.* Cid Ricketts

  QUALITY   FOX 1949
  (Dymock)   *(Pinky)*
  TAMMY TELL ME TRUE   RANK 1961
  (Bobbs-Merrill, Indianapolis)

SWANN, Francis

  OUT OF THE FRYING PAN (P)   UA 1943
  (French, N.Y.)

SWANSON, Neil Harmon

  FIRST REBEL, THE   RKO 1939
  (Grosset, N.Y.)   *(Allegheny uprising)*
  UNCONQUERED   PAR 1947
  (Doubleday, N.Y.)

SWARTHOUT, Glendon

THEY CAME TO CORDURA   COL 1959
(Heinemann)

WHERE THE BOYS ARE   MGM 1960
(Heinemann)

SWIFT, Jonathan

GULLIVER'S TRAVELS   PAR 1939
(Various)   COL 1959
(Three worlds of Gulliver, The)

SWIFT, Kay

WHO COULD ASK FOR   RKO 1950
  ANYTHING MORE   *(Never a dull moment)*
(Simon & Schuster, N.Y.)

SWIGGETT, Howard

POWER AND THE PRIZE, THE   MGM 1956
(Hodder & Stoughton)

SYLVAINE, Vernon

AREN'T MEN BEASTS   AB 1937
(Jenkins)

AREN'T MEN BEASTS (P)   AB 1937
(French)

AS LONG AS THEY'RE HAPPY (P)   GFD 1954
(French)

ONE WILD OAT (P)   EROS 1951
(French)

SPOT OF BOTHER, A (P)   AB 1938
(French)

WARN THAT MAN (P)   AB 1942
(French)

WILL ANY GENTLEMAN . . . ? (P)   ABP 1953
(French)

WOMEN AREN'T ANGELS (P)   AB 1943
(French)

SYLVESTER, Robert

BIG BOODLE, THE   UA 1957
(Random House, N.Y.)   *(Night in Havana)*

ROUGH SKETCH   COL 1949
(Dial Press, N.Y.)   *(We were strangers)*

SYMONS, Julian

NARROWING CIRCLE, THE   EROS 1955
(Gollancz)

SYRETT, Netta

PORTRAIT OF A REBEL   RKO 1936
(Bles)

T

TANNER, Edward Everett *see*
    DENNIS, Patrick *pseud*

TARADASH, Daniel *and* **MOLL, Elick**

STORM CENTRE	COL 1956
(Panther Bks)	

TARKINGTON, Booth

ALICE ADAMS	RKO 1935
(Odyssey Press, N.Y.)	
CLARENCE (P)	PAR 1937
(French, N.Y.)	
GENTLE JULIA	FOX 1936
(Grosset, N.Y.)	
LITTLE ORVIE	RKO 1940
(Heinemann)	
MAGNIFICENT AMBERSONS, THE	RKO 1942
(Grosset, N.Y.)	
MONSIEUR BEAUCAIRE	PAR 1946
(Grosset, N.Y.)	
PENROD	WAR 1937
(Hodder & Stoughton)	(*Penrod and Sam*)
	WAR 1953
	(*By the light of the silvery moon*)
PENROD AND SAM	IN 1931
(Hodder & Stoughton)	
SEVENTEEN	PAR 1940
(Grosset, N.Y.)	
SEVENTEEN (P)	PAR 1940
(French, N.Y.)	

TATE, Sylvia

FUZZY PINK NIGHTGOWN, THE	UA 1957
(Harper, N.Y.)	

TAYLOR, Kressman

ADDRESS UNKNOWN	COL 1944
(Hamilton)	

TAYLOR, Robert Louis

TRAVELS OF JAIMIE McPHEETERS,	MGM 1964
THE	(*Guns of Diablo*)
(Macdonald)	

TAYLOR, Rosemary

CHICKEN EVERY SUNDAY	FOX 1948
(Methuen)	FOX 1956
	(*Hefferan family, The*)

TAYLOR, Samuel A.

HAPPY TIME, THE (P)   COL 1952
(Dramatists, N.Y.)

SABRINA FAIR (P)   PAR 1954
(Random House, N.Y.)

TAYLOR, Samuel A. *and* SKINNER, C. O.

PLEASURE OF HIS COMPANY,   PAR 1959
   THE (P)
(Heinemann)

TAYLOR, Samuel Woolley

MAN WITH MY FACE, THE   UA 1951
(Hodder & Stoughton)

**TEICHMAN, Howard *and* KAUFMAN,
   George S.**

SOLID GOLD CADILLAC, THE (P)   COL 1956
(Random House, N.Y.)

TEILHET, Darwin L.

MY TRUE LOVE   UI 1952
(Gollancz)   (*No room for the groom*)

TELFER, Daniel

CARETAKERS, THE   UA 1962
(Macdonald)   (*Borderlines*)

TEMPLE, Joan

NO ROOM AT THE INN (P)   BN 1948
(*In* Embassy successes, Vol. 2:
   Sampson Low)

TEMPLE, William F.

FOUR-SIDED TRIANGLE   EXCLUSIVE 1952
(Long)

TERASAKI, Gwen

BRIDGE TO THE SUN   MGM 1961
(Joseph)

TERHUNE, Albert Payson

TREVE   UN 1937
(Grosset, N.Y.)   (*Mighty Treve, The*)

TERROT, Charles

ALLIGATOR NAMED DAISY, AN   RANK 1955
(Collins)

ANGEL WHO PAWNED HER   BL 1954
   HARP, THE
(Collins)

TEVIS, Walter

    HUSTLER, THE   FOX 1961
    (Joseph)

TEY, Josephine

    BRAT FARRAR   HAMMER 1958
    (Davies)

    FRANCHISE AFFAIR, THE   ABP 1951
    (Davies)

THACKERAY, William Makepeace

    VANITY FAIR   HOL 1932
    (Various)   RKO 1935
                            (*Becky Sharp*)

THAYER, Tiffany

    CALL HER SAVAGE   FOX 1932
    (Long)

THIGPEN, Corbett, H. *and* CLECKLEY, Harvey M.

    THREE FACES OF LOVE, THE   FOX 1957
    (Secker & Warburg)

THOMAS, Basil

    BOOK OF THE MONTH (P)   AA 1959
    (French)

    SHOOTING STAR (P)   ADELPHI 1953
    (Deane)   (*Great game, The*)

THOMAS, Brandon

    CHARLEY'S AUNT (P)   COL 1930
    (French, N.Y.)   FOX 1941

THOMPSON, J. Lee

    MURDER WITHOUT CRIME (P)   ABP 1950
    (French)

THOMPSON, Morton

    NOT AS A STRANGER   UA 1955
    (Joseph)

THORN, Ronald Scott

    FULL TREATMENT, THE   COL 1960
    (Heinemann)

    UPSTAIRS AND DOWNSTAIRS RANK 1959
    (Spearman)

366

THORNDIKE, Russell

  DR. SYN   GB 1937
  (Various)   DISNEY 1963

THORNE, Anthony

  BABY AND THE BATTLESHIP,   BL 1956
    THE
  (Heinemann)
  SO LONG AT THE FAIR   GFD 1950
  (Heinemann)

THORP, M. *see*
  LAVIN, N. *jt. author*

THURBER, James

  MY LIFE AND HARD TIMES   FOX 1941
  (Hamilton)   (*Rise and shine*)
  SECRET LIFE OF WALTER MITTY   RKO 1949
  (*In* Modern American short stories:
    World, N.Y.)

THURBER, James *and* **NUGENT, Elliot**

  MALE ANIMAL, THE (P)   WAR 1942
  (Random House, N.Y.)   WAR 1952
                     (*She's working her way through college*)

THURSTON, Ernest Temple

  WANDERING JEW, THE (P)   OLY 1935
  (Putnam)

TICKELL, Jerrard

  APPOINTMENT WITH VENUS   GFD 1951
  (Hodder & Stoughton)
  HAND AND THE FLOWER, THE   GFD 1953
  (Hodder & Stoughton)   *Day to remember, A*)
  ODETTE, G. C.   BL 1950
  (Chapman & Hall)

TIDMARSH, E. V.

  IS YOUR HONEYMOON REALLY   ADELPHI 1953
    NECESSARY? (P)
  (Deane)

TILSLEY, Frank

  MUTINY   COL 1962
  (Eyre & Spottiswoode)   (*H.M.S. Defiant*)

TOBY, Mark

  COURTSHIP OF EDDIE'S FATHER, MGM 1963
    THE
  (Gibbs & Phillips)

TOLLER, Ernst
  PASTOR HALL (P)   UA 1940
  (Lane)

TOLSTOY, Lev Nikolaevich
  ANNA KARENINA   MGM 1935
  (Various)   BL 1948
  RESURRECTION   UN 1931
  (Various)   UA 1934
                                 (*We live again*)
  WAR AND PEACE   PAR 1956
  (Macmillan)

TOOMBS, Alfred
  RAISING A RIOT   BL 1954
  (Hammond)

TOTHEROH, D.
  DEEP VALLEY   WAR 1947
  (Hutchinson)

TRACY, Don
  CRISS CROSS   UI 1949
  (Constable)

TRAHEY, Jane
  LIFE WITH MOTHER SUPERIOR   COL 1965
  (Joseph)   (*Trouble with angels, The*)

TRAIL, Armitage
  SCARFACE   UA 1932
  (Long)

TRANTER, Nigel
  BRIDAL PATH, THE   BL 1959
  (Hodder & Stoughton)

TRAPP, Maria Augusta
  STORY OF THE TRAPP FAMILY   FOX 1965
    SINGERS   (*Sound of music, The*)
  (Bles)

TRAVEN, Bruno
  TREASURE OF SIERRA MADRE   WAR 1948
  (Cape)

TRAVER, Robert *pseud*
  ANATOMY OF MURDER   COL 1959
  (Faber)

TRAVERS, Ben

  BANANA RIDGE (P)   ABP 1941
  (French)

  CUCKOO IN THE NEST   GB 1938
  (Lane)

  CUCKOO IN THE NEST (P)   GB 1938
  (Bickers)

  PLUNDER (P)   WILCOX 1937
  (Bickers)

  ROOKERY NOOK   MGM 1930
  (Lane)

  ROOKERY NOOK (P)   MGM 1930
  (Bickers)

  THARK (P)   GB 1932
  (Bickers)

TRAVERS, P. L.

  MARY POPPINS   DISNEY 1964
  (Penguin)

TREGASKIS, Richard William

  GUADALCANAL DIARY   FOX 1943
  (Wells & Gardner)

TREVOR, Elleston *pseud*

  BIG PICK-UP   MGM 1958
  (Heinemann)   (*Dunkirk*)

  FLIGHT OF THE PHOENIX, THE   FOX 1965
  (Heinemann)

  PILLARS OF MIDNIGHT   RANK 1963
  (Heinemann)

  QUEEN IN DANGER   EXCLUSIVE 1953
  (Boardman)   (*Mantrap*)

TRINIAN, John

  BIG GRAB, THE   GALA 1963
  (Pyramid Bks)   (*Big snatch, The*)

TROY, Una

  WE ARE SEVEN   ABP 1958
  (Heinemann)   (*She didn't say no*)

TROYAT, Henri

  MOUNTAIN, THE   PAR 1956
  (Allen & Unwin)

TRUESDELL, Jane

  BE STILL MY LOVE   PAR 1949
  (Boardman)   (*Accused, The*)

TRUSS, Seldon

  LONG NIGHT, THE   AA 1958
  (Hodder & Stoughton)   (*Long knife, The*)

TRZCINSKI, E. *see*
  BEVAN, D. *jt. author*

TUCHMAN, Barbara W.

  AUGUST 1914   RANK 1964
  (Constable)   (*Guns of August, The*)

TUCKER, Augusta

  MISS SUSIE SLAGLE'S   PAR 1945
  (Grosset, N.Y.)

TULLY, Jim

  BEGGARS OF LIFE   PAR 1928
  (Chatto & Windus)

TURKUS, Burton *and* **FEDER, Sid**

  MURDER, INCORPORATED   FOX 1960
  (Gollancz)

TURNEY, Catherine

  OTHER ONE, THE   FOX 1957
  (Holt, N.Y.)   (*Back from the dead*)

TWAIN, Mark *pseud*

  CELEBRATED JUMPING FROG OF   COL 1948
    CALAVERAS   (*Best man wins, The*)
  (Various)

  HUCKLBERRY FINN   MGM 1939
  (Various)   (*Adventures of Huckleberry Finn*)
                                                     MGM 1960
  MILLION POUND NOTE   GFD 1953
  (*In* Man that corrupted Hadleyburg:
    Harper, N.Y.)
  PRINCE AND THE PAUPER   WAR 1937
  (Chatto & Windus)   DISNEY 1961
  TOM SAWYER   UA 1938
  (Various)   (*Adventures of Tom Sawyer*)

TWISS, Clinton

  LONG, LONG TRAILER, THE   MGM 1954
  (Crowell, N.Y.)

U

ULLMAN, James Ramsey

  BANNER IN THE SKY   DISNEY 1959
  (Collins)   (*Third man on the mountain*)

AUTHOR AND ORIGINAL TITLE	FILM TITLE

ULLMAN, James Ramsey (*continued*)

WHITE TOWER, THE   RKO 1950
(Collins)

WINDOM'S WAY   RANK 1957
(Collins)

URIS, Leon

ANGRY HILLS, THE   MGM 1959
(Wingate)

BATTLE CRY   WAR 1954
(Wingate)

EXODUS   UA 1960
(Wingate)

USTINOV, Peter

ROMANOFF AND JULIET (P)   RANK 1961
(Random House, N.Y.)

V

VALE, Martin *pseud*

TWO MRS. CARROLLS, THE (P)   WAR 1947
(Allen & Unwin)

VAN ATTA, Winfred

SHOCK TREATMENT   FOX 1964
(Doubleday, N.Y.)

VANCE, Ethel *pseud*

ESCAPE   MGM 1940
(Collins)

VANCE, Louis Joseph

LONE WOLF RETURNS, THE   COL 1936
(Grosset, N.Y.)

VANE, Sutton

OUTWARD BOUND (P)   WAR 1930
(Boni, N.Y.)   WAR 1944
(*Between two worlds*)

VAN LOON, Hendrik Willem

STORY OF MANKIND, THE   WAR 1957
(Harrap)

VAUS, Jim *jun*

WHY I QUIT SYNDICATED CRIME   EXCLUSIVE 1955
(Van Kempen, Wheaton, Ill.)   (*Wiretapper, The*)

VEILLER, Bayard

TRIAL OF MARY DUGAN (P)   MGM 1929
(French, N.Y.)

VEILLER, *Mrs.* **Marguerite** *see*
    VALE, Martin *pseud*

VERNE, Jules

AROUND THE WORLD IN 80   UA 1957
    DAYS   (*Round the world in 80 days*)
(Various)

CAPTAIN GRANT'S CHILDREN   DISNEY 1962
(Various)   (*In search of the castaways*)

FIVE WEEKS IN A BALLOON   FOX 1962
(Various)

FROM THE EARTH TO THE   RANK 1958
    MOON
(Various)

JOURNEY TO THE CENTRE OF   FOX 1959
    THE EARTH
(Various)

MASTER OF THE WORLD   AA 1961
(Sampson Low)

MICHAEL STROGOFF   RKO 1937
(Sampson Low)   (*Soldier and the lady, The*)

MYSTERIOUS ISLAND   COL 1962
(Dent)

20,000 LEAGUES UNDER THE SEA   DISNEY 1954
(Various)

VERNER, Gerald

MEET MR. CALLAGHAN (P)   EROS 1954
(French)

WHISPERING WOMAN, THE   AA 1953
(Wright & Brown)   (*Noose for a lady*)

SHOW MUST GO ON, THE   APEX 1952
(Wright & Brown)   (*Tread softly*)

VICKERS, Roy

GIRL IN THE NEWS   FOX 1941
(Jenkins)

VIDAL, Gore

VISIT TO A SMALL PLANET (P)   PAR 1959
(Little, Toronto)

VOELKER, John D. *see*
    TRAVER, Robert *pseud*

VOSPER, Frank

  LOVE FROM A STRANGER (P)   UA 1937
  (French)   REN 1949
        (Stranger walked in, A)

  MURDER ON THE SECOND   WAR 1941
    FLOOR (P)
  (French)

VULLIAMY, C. E.

  DON AMONG THE DEAD MEN   BL 1964
  (Joseph)

W

WADE, Arthur Sarsfield *see*
  ROHMER, Sax *pseud*

WADELTON, Thomas Dorrington

  LITTLE MR. JIM   MGM 1946
  (Coward-McCann, N.Y.)   *(Army brat)*

WAKEMAN, Frederic

  HUCKSTERS, THE   MGM 1947
  (Falcon Press)

  SAXON CHARM, THE   UI 1948
  (Rinehart, N.Y.)

  SHORE LEAVE   FOX 1957
  (Farrar, N.Y.)   *(Kiss them for me)*

WALKER, David E.

  ADVENTURE IN DIAMONDS   RANK 1958
  (Evans)   *(Operation Amsterdam)*

  GEORDIE   BL 1955
  (Collins)

  HARRY BLACK   FOX 1958
  (Collins)

WALLACE, Edgar

  CALENDAR, THE (P)   GFD 1932
  (French)   GFD 1948

  CALENDAR, THE   WW 1932
  (Collins)   *(Bachelor's folly)*

  CASE OF THE FRIGHTENED   BL 1940
    LADY, THE (P)   *(Frightened lady, The)*
  (French, N.Y.)

  CLUE OF THE TWISTED CANDLE, AA 1960
    THE
  (Newnes)

  CRIMSON CIRCLE, THE   NEW ERA 1930
  (Hodder & Stoughton)

AUTHOR AND ORIGINAL TITLE	FILM TITLE
WALLACE, Edgar (*continued*)	
DAFFODIL MYSTERY (Ward Lock)	BL 1961 (*Devil's daffodil, The*)
DEBT DISCHARGED, A (Ward Lock)	AA 1961 (*Man detained*)
FACE IN THE NIGHT (Long)	AA 1960 (*Malpas mystery, The*)
FEATHERED SERPENT, THE (Hodder & Stoughton)	COL 1932 (*Menace, The*)
FLAT TWO (Long)	AA 1962
FOUR JUST MEN, THE (Various)	EALING 1939 (*Secret four, The*)
GREEN PACK, THE (Hodder & Stoughton)	BL 1936
GREEN PACK, THE (P) (French)	BL 1936
GREEN RIBBON, THE (Hutchinson)	AA 1962 (*Never back losers*)
GUNNER, THE (Long)	AA 1962 (*Solo for Sparrow*)
JACK O'JUDGEMENT (Ward Lock)	AA 1962 (*Share out, The*)
KATE PLUS TEN (Ward Lock)	WAINWRIGHT 1938
LONE HOUSE MYSTERY, THE (Collins)	AA 1961 (*Attempt to kill*)
MAN AT THE CARLTON (Hodder & Stoughton)	AA 1961 (*Man at the Carlton Tower*)
MAN WHO BOUGHT LONDON (Ward Lock)	AA 1962 (*Time to remember*)
MAN WHO KNEW, THE (Newnes)	AA 1960 (*Partners in Crime*)
MAN WHO WAS NOBODY, THE (Newnes)	AA 1960
MIND OF MR. REEDER, THE (Hodder & Stoughton)	RAYMOND 1939 (*Mind of Mr. J. G. Reeder, The*)
NORTHING TRAMP, THE (Hodder & Stoughton)	GB 1937 (*Strangers on a honeymoon*)
RINGER, THE (P) (Hodder & Stoughton)	ID 1932 MON 1939 (*Phantom strikes, The*) LF 1952
RINGER, THE (Hodder & Stoughton)	ID 1932 MON 1939 (*Phantom strikes, The*) LF 1952
ROOM 13 (Allied Press)	ALL 1941 (*Mystery of Room 13*)

WALLACE, Edgar (*continued*)

SANDERS OF THE RIVER UA 1935
(Ward Lock)

SINISTER MAN, THE AA 1961
(Hodder & Stoughton)

SQUEAKER, THE GB 1937
(Hodder & Stoughton) UA 1937
  (*Murder on Diamond Row*)
SQUEAKER, THE (P) GB 1937
(Hodder & Stoughton)

TERROR, THE ALL 1941
(Collins)

THREE OAK MYSTERY, THE AA 1960
(Ward Lock) (*Marriage of convenience*)

WALLACE, Francis

KID GALAHAD WAR 1937
(Hale) UA 1962

WALLACE, Irving

CHAPMAN REPORT, THE WAR 1962
(Cassell)

PRIZE, THE MGM 1963
(Cassell)

WALLACE, Lew

BEN HUR MGM 1931
(Various) MGM 1959

WALLACH, Ira

MUSCLE BEACH MGM 1966
(Gollancz) (*Don't make waves*)

WALLANT, Edward Lewis

PAWNBROKER, THE PAR 1964
(Gollancz)

WALLIS, Arthur James *and* **BLAIR, Charles F.**

THUNDER ABOVE RANK 1960
(Jarrolds) (*Beyond the Curtain*)

WALLIS, James Harold

ONCE OFF GUARD RKO 1944
(Jarrolds) (*Woman in the window, The*)

WALPOLE, *Sir* **Hugh**

MR. PERRIN AND MR. TRAILL TC 1948
(Various)
VANESSA MGM 1935
(Macmillan)

WALSH, Maurice

QUIET MAN, THE   REP 1952
(Angus & Robertson)

TROUBLE IN THE GLEN   REP 1954
(Chambers)

WALSH, Thomas

NIGHTMARE IN MANHATTAN   PAR 1950
(Little Brown, Boston)   *(Union Station)*

WALTARI, Mika

SINUHE, THE EGYPTIAN   FOX 1954
(Putnam)   *(Egyptian, The)*

WALTER, Eugene

EASIEST WAY, THE (P)   MGM 1931
(*In* Best plays of 1909–10: Dodd, N.Y.)

WARD, Mary Jane

SNAKE PIT, THE   FOX 1948
(Cassell)

WARNER, Douglas

DEATH OF A SNOUT   RANK 1963
(Cassell)   *(Informer, The)*

WARNER, Sylvia Ashton *see*
    ASHTON-WARNER, S.

WARREN, Charles Esme Thornton *and*
    BENSON, James

ABOVE US THE WAVES   GFD 1954
(Harrap)

WARREN, Charles Marquis

ONLY THE VALIANT   WAR 1950
(Macmillan, N.Y.)

WARREN, Robert Penn

ALL THE KING'S MEN   COL 1949
(Eyre & Spottiswoode)

BAND OF ANGELS   WAR 1956
(Eyre & Spottiswoode)

WATERHOUSE, Keith *and* **HALL, Willis**

BILLY LIAR (P)   WAR 1962
(Joseph)

WATERS, F. *see*
    BRANCH, H. *jt. author*

WATKIN, Lawrence Edward
  ON BORROWED TIME   MGM 1939
  (Davies)

WATKYN, Arthur
  FOR BETTER, FOR WORSE (P)   ABP 1954
  (*In* Plays of the year, 1952–53: Elek)

WAUGH, Alec
  GUY RENTON   FOX 1960
  (Consul Bks)   (*Circle of deception*)
  ISLAND IN THE SUN   FOX 1957
  (Cassell)

WAUGH, Evelyn
  LOVED ONE, THE   MGM 1965
  (Chatto & Windus)

WAUGH, Hillary
  SLEEP LONG, MY LOVELY   BL 1962
  (Gollancz)   (*Jigsaw*)

WEATHER, P. *see*
  CARY, F. L. *jt. author*

WEBB, Mary
  GONE TO EARTH   BL 1950
  (Cape)

WEBB, Richard *see*
  QUENTIN, Patrick *pseud*

WEBSTER, Jean
  DADDY LONG LEGS   FOX 1955
  (Hodder & Stoughton)

WEIDMAN, Jerome
  I CAN GET IT FOR YOU   FOX 1951
    WHOLESALE   (*This is my affair*)
  (Heinemann)

WELLES, Orson
  MR. ARKADIN   WAR 1955
  (W. H. Allen)   (*Confidential report*)

WELLMAN, Paul Iselin
  BRONCO APACHE   UA 1954
  (News of the World)   (*Apache*)
  CHAIN, THE   COL 1952
  (Laurie)
  COMANCHEROS, THE   FOX 1961
  (Doubleday, N.Y.)
  IRON MISTRESS   WAR 1952
  (Laurie)

WELLMAN, Paul Iselin (*continued*)

JUBAL TROOP (Grosset, N.Y.)	COL 1956 (*Jubal*)
WALLS OF JERICHO, THE (Laurie)	FOX 1949

WELLS, Herbert George

DOOR IN THE WALL, THE (*In* Short stories: Benn)	ABP 1956
FIRST MEN IN THE MOON, THE (Various)	COL 1963
HISTORY OF MR. POLLY (Various)	TC 1949
INVISIBLE MAN, THE (Various)	UA 1933
ISLAND OF DR. MOREAU, THE (Heinemann)	EROS 1959 (*Island of lost souls*)
KIPPS (Various)	FOX 1941
MAN WHO COULD WORK MIRACLES, THE (Cresset Press)	AU 1937
PASSIONATE FRIENDS, THE (Benn)	CINEGUILD 1949
SHAPE OF THINGS TO COME, THE (Hutchinson)	UA 1936 (*Things to come*)
THINGS TO COME (P) (Cresset Press)	UA 1936
TIME MACHINE, THE (Heinemann)	MGM 1960
WAR OF THE WORLDS (Heinemann)	PAR 1953

WELLS, Lee Edwin

DAY OF THE OUTLAW (Hale)	UA 1959

WERFEL, Franz V.

SONG OF BERNADETTE, THE (Hamilton)	FOX 1943

WESKER, Arnold

KITCHEN, THE (P) (Faber)	BL 1961

WEST, Jessamyn
  FRIENDLY PERSUASION   MGM 1956
  (Hodder & Stoughton)

WEST, Nathaniel
  MISS LONELYHEARTS   UA 1959
  (Grey Walls Press)   *(Lonelyhearts*

WESTERBY, Robert
  WIDE BOYS NEVER WORK   COL 1956
  (Methuen)   *(Soho incident)*

WESTHEIMER, David
  VON RYAN'S EXPRESS   FOX 1964
  (Joseph)

WEYMAN, Stanley John
  UNDER THE RED ROBE   FOX 1937
  (Various)

WHARTON, *Mrs.* **Edith Newbold**
  AGE OF INNOCENCE   RKO 1934
  (Appleton, N.Y.)
  OLD MAID, THE   WAR 1939
  (Grosset, N.Y.)

WHEATLEY, Dennis
  EUNUCH OF STAMBOUL, THE   HOB 1939
  (Hutchinson)   *(Secret of Stamboul, The)*
  FORBIDDEN TERRITORY   HOFFBERG 1938
  (Hutchinson)

WHEELER, H. *see*
  BURDICK, E. *jt. author*

WHIPPLE, Dorothy
  THEY KNEW MR. KNIGHT   GFD 1946
  (Murray)
  THEY WERE SISTERS   GFD 1945
  (Murray)

WHITE, Ethel Lina
  HER HEART IN HER THROAT PAR 1945
  (Grosset, N.Y.)   *(Unseen, The)*
  SOME MUST WATCH   RKO 1946
  (Ward Lock)   *(Spiral staircase, The)*
  WHEEL SPINS, THE   MGM 1938
  (Collins)   *(Lady vanishes, The)*

379

WHITE, Grace Miller

TESS OF THE STORM COUNTRY   FOX 1960
(Various)

WHITE, James Dillon

MAGGIE, THE   EALING 1954
(Heinemann)

WHITE, Jon Manchip Ewbank

MARK OF DUST   EXCLUSIVE 1954
(Hodder & Stoughton)   (*Mask of doubt*)

WHITE, Lionel

CLEAN BREAK   UA 1956
(Boardman)   (*Killing, The*)

MONEY TRAP   MGM 1965
(Boardman)

WHITE, Robb

OUR VIRGIN ISLAND   BL 1958
(Gollancz)   (*Virgin island*)

UP PERISCOPE   WAR 1958
(Collins)

WHITE, Theodore Harold

MOUNTAIN ROAD, THE   COL 1959
(Cassell)

ONCE AND FUTURE KING, THE   WAR 1966
(Collins)   (*Camelot*)

SWORD IN THE STONE, THE   DISNEY 1963
(Collins)

WHITE, William Lindsay

JOURNEY FOR MARGARET   MGM 1942
(Hurst & Blackett)

THEY WERE EXPENDABLE   MGM 1945
(Hamilton)

WHITEHEAD, Donald

FBI STORY, THE   WAR 1958
(Panther Bks)

WIBBERLEY, Leonard

MOUSE THAT ROARED, THE   UA 1962
(Bantam Bks)   (*Mouse on the moon*)

WRATH OF GRAPES   COL 1959
(Hale)   (*Mouse that roared, The*)

WIGGIN, *Mrs.* **Kate Douglas**

 MOTHER CAREY'S CHICKENS DISNEY 1963
 (Hodder & Stoughton)   (*Summer magic*)

 REBECCA OF SUNNYBROOK FOX 1932
  FARM   FOX 1938
 (Various)

 TIMOTHY'S QUEST   PAR 1936
 (Partridge)

WILDE, Hagar *and* **EUNSON, Dale**

 DEAR EVELYN (P)   UA 1944
 (French)   (*Guest in the house*)

WILDE, Oscar

 CANTERVILLE GHOST, THE MGM 1944
 (Collins)

 IDEAL HUSBAND, AN (P)   BL 1948
 (Methuen)

 IMPORTANCE OF BEING   GFD 1952
  EARNEST, THE (P)
 (Heinemann)

 LADY WINDERMERE'S FAN (P) FOX 1949
 (Methuen)

 LORD ARTHUR SAVILE'S CRIME UN 1943
 (Various)   (*Flesh and fantasy*)

 PICTURE OF DORIAN GRAY, THE MGM 1945
 (Unicorn Press)

WILDER, Margaret Applegate

 SINCE YOU WENT AWAY   UA 1944
 (McGraw-Hill, N.Y.)

WILDER, Robert

 AND RIDE A TIGER   UI 1958
 (W. H. Allen)   (*Stranger in my arms, A*)

 FLAMINGO ROAD   WAR 1949
 (Grosset, N.Y.)

WILDER, Thornton Niven

 BRIDGE OF SAN LUIS REY, THE MGM 1929
 (Longmans)   UA 1944

 MATCHMAKER, THE (P)   PAR 1958
 (French)

 OUR TOWN (P)   UA 1940
 (Coward-McCann, N.Y.)

WILDER, William *and* **DIAMOND,**
 I. A. L.

 SOME LIKE IT HOT   UA 1959
 (Panther Bks)

WILK, Max

DON'T RAISE THE BRIDGE   BL 1967
   LOWER THE RIVER
(Heinemann)

WILKINS, Vaughan

KING RELUCTANT, A   RANK 1957
(Cape)   (*Dangerous exile*)

WILLARD, John

CAT AND THE CANARY, THE   UN 1930
(Hudson)   (*Cat creeps, The*)
                    PAR 1939

WILLIAMS, Ben Ames

LEAVE HER TO HEAVEN   FOX 1945
(Hale)

STRANGE WOMAN, THE   UA 1946
(Houghton Mifflin, Boston)

WILLIAMS, Brock

EARL OF CHICAGO   MGM 1940
(Harrap)

UNCLE WILLIE AND THE   ABP 1953
   BICYCLE SHOP   (*Ain't life wonderful*)
(Harrap)

WILLIAMS, Emlyn

CORN IS GREEN, THE (P)   WAR 1945
(Heinemann)

LIGHT OF HEART, THE (P)   FOX 1942
(Heinemann)

NIGHT MUST FALL (P)   MGM 1937
(Gollancz)   MGM 1964

WILLIAMS, Eric

WOODEN HORSE, THE   BL 1950
(Collins)

**WILLIAMS, Hugh *and* WILLIAMS,
   Margaret**

GRASS IS GREENER, THE (P) UI 1960
(Gollancz)

WILLIAMS, H. V. *see*
BENTHAM, J. *jt. author*

WILLIAMS, Jay

SOLOMON AND SHEBA   UA 1959
(Macdonald)

WILLIAMS, *Mrs.* **Rebecca**

FATHER WAS A HANDFUL   MGM 1941
(Joseph)   (*Vanishing Virginian, The*)

WILLIAMS, Tennessee

BABY DOLL (P)   WAR 1956
(Secker & Warburg)

CAT ON A HOT TIN ROOF (P)   MGM 1958
(Secker & Warburg)

GLASS MENAGERIE, THE (P)   WAR 1950
(Lehmann)

NIGHT OF THE IGUANA, THE (P)   MGM 1963
(Secker & Warburg)

ORPHEUS DESCENDING (P)   UA 1960
(Secker & Warburg)   (*Fugitive kind, The*)

PERIOD OF ADJUSTMENT (P)   MGM 1962
(Secker & Warburg)

ROSE TATTOO, THE (P)   PAR 1954
(Secker & Warburg)

STREETCAR NAMED DESIRE, A   WAR 1951
   (P)
(Lehmann)

SUDDENLY LAST SUMMER (P)   COL 1959
(Secker & Warburg)

SUMMER AND SMOKE (P)   PAR 1962
(*In* Four plays: Secker & Warburg)

SWEET BIRD OF YOUTH (P)   MGM 1962
(Secker & Warburg)

WILLIAMS, Valentine

CROUCHING BEAST, THE   OLY 1936
(Hodder & Stoughton)

WILLIAMS, Wirt

ADA DALLAS   MGM 1960
(Muller)

WILLINGHAM, Calder

END AS A MAN   COL 1957
(Barker)

STRANGE ONE, THE (P)   COL 1957
(Grosset, N.Y.)   (*End as a man*)

WILLIS, Ted

HOT SUMMERNIGHT (P)   RANK 1961
(French)   (*Flame in the streets*)

AUTHOR AND ORIGINAL TITLE	FILM TITLE

WILSON, Cherry

EMPTY SADDLES   UN 1936
(Ward Lock)

WILSON, Donald Powell

MY SIX CONVICTS   COL 1952
(Hamilton)

WILSON, Harry Leon

BUNKER BEAN   RKO 1936
(Lane)
MERTON OF THE MOVIES   PAR 1932
(Cape)   (*Make me a star*)
RUGGLES OF RED GAP   PAR 1935
(Various)

WILSON, John

HAMP (P)   WAR 1965
(Evans)   (*King and Country*)

WILSON, John Raven

MASK, THE   BL 1958
(Heinemann)   (*Behind the mask*)

WILSON, Sloan

MAN IN THE GREY FLANNEL   FOX 1956
  SUIT, THE
(Cassell)

WILSTACH, Frank

WILD BILL HICKOK   PAR 1936
(Sun Dial, N.Y.)   (*Plainsman, The*)

WINSOR, KATHLEEN

FOREVER AMBER   FOX 1947
(Macdonald)

WINTER, Keith

SHINING HOUR, THE (P)   MGM 1938
(Heinemann)

WINTERTON, Paul *see*
  BAX, Roger *pseud*

WINTON, John

WE JOINED THE NAVY   WAR 1962
(Joseph)

WISEMAN, Nicholas Patrick Stephen
  Cardinal
FABIOLA   BL 1951
(Various)

WISTER, Owen

VIRGINIAN, THE   PAR 1929
(Various)

WODEHOUSE, Percival Grenville

DAMSEL IN DISTRESS, A   RKO 1937
(Jenkins)

GIRL ON THE BOAT, THE   UA 1962
(Jenkins)

PICCADILLY JIM   MGM 1936
(Jenkins)

SUMMER LIGHTNING   BD 1932
(Jenkins)

THANK YOU, JEEVES   FOX 1936
(Jenkins)

WOLFE, Winifred

ASK ANY GIRL   MGM 1959
(Hammond)

IF A MAN ANSWERS   RANK 1962
(Hammond)

WOLFERT, Ira

AMERICAN GUERILLA IN THE   FOX 1950
   PHILIPPINES   (*I shall return*)
(Gollancz)

TUCKER'S PEOPLE   MGM 1949
(Gollancz)   (*Force of evil*)

WOLFF, Maritta Martin

WHISTLE-STOP   UA 1946
(Constable)

WOLPERT, Stanley

NINE HOURS TO RAMA   FOX 1962
(Hamilton)

WOOD, *Mrs.* Henry

EAST LYNNE   FOX 1931
(Various)   TIFFANY 1931
                        (*Ex-flame*)

WOOD, William

MANUELA   BL 1957
(Hart-Davis)

WOODS, William Howard

EDGE OF DARKNESS   WAR 1943
(Grosset, N.Y.)

WOOLL, Edward
  LIBEL (P)   MGM 1959
  (French)

WOOLLARD, Kenneth
  MORNING DEPARTURE (P)   GFD 1950
  (French)

WOOLRICH, Cornell
  BLACK ALIBI   RKO 1943
  (Simon & Schuster, N.Y.)   (*Leopard man, The*)
  BLACK ANGEL   UN 1946
  (Doubleday, N.Y.)
  BLACK CURTAIN, THE   PAR 1942
  (Grosset, N.Y.)   (*Street of chance*)

WOOLRICH, Cornell *see also*
IRISH, William *pseud*
HOPLEY, George *pseud*

WOUK, Herman
  CAINE MUTINY, THE   COL 1954
  (Cape)
  MARJORIE MORNINGSTAR WAR 1957
  (Cape)
  YOUNGBLOOD HAWKE   WAR 1963
  (Cape)

WREN, Percival Christopher
  BEAU GESTE   PAR 1939
  (Murray)   UI 1966
  BEAU IDEAL   RKO 1931
  (Murray)
  BEAU SABREUR   PAR 1928
  (Murray)

WRIGHT, Harold Bell
  CALLING OF DAN MATTHEWS, COL 1936
    THE
  (Hodder & Stoughton)
  MINE WITH THE IRON DOOR, COL 1936
    THE
  (Appleton, N.Y.)
  SHEPHERD OF THE HILLS, THE PAR 1941
  (Grosset, N.Y.)

WRIGHT, Richard
  NATIVE SON   CLASSIC 1951
  (Gollancz)

WRIGHT, S. Fowler

  DELUGE, THE   RKO 1933
  (Allied Press)

WYLIE, Ida Alexa Ross

  KEEPER OF THE FLAME   MGM 1942
  (Cassell)

  PILGRIMAGE   FOX 1933
  (Cassell)

  YOUNG IN HEART, THE   UA 1938
  (Cassell)

WYLIE, Philip

  NIGHT UNTO NIGHT   WAR 1949
  (Farrar, N.Y.)

WYLIE, Philip *see also*
BALMER, E. *jt. author*

WYNDHAM, John

  DAY OF THE TRIFFIDS, THE   RANK 1962
  (Joseph)

  MIDWICH CUCKOOS, THE   MGM 1960
  (Joseph)   (*Village of the damned, The*)

WYNNE, Barry

  COUNT 5 AND DIE   FOX 1957
  (Souvenir Press)

WYSS, Johann David

  SWISS FAMILY ROBINSON   RKO 1940
  (Various)   DISNEY 1960

Y

YARDLEY, Herbert O.

  AMERICAN BLACK CHAMBER, MGM 1935
    THE   (*Rendezvous*)
  (Faber)

YEATS-BROWN, Francis

  BENGAL LANCER   PAR 1935
  (Gollancz)   (*Lives of a Bengal lancer, The*)

YERBY, Frank

  FOXES OF HARROW, THE   FOX 1947
  (Heinemann)

YERBY, Frank (*continued*)

GOLDEN HAWK, THE   COL 1952
(Heinemann)

SARACEN BLADE, THE   COL 1954
(Heinemann)

YORDAN, Philip

ANNA LUCASTA (P)   COL 1949
(Random House, N.Y.)

MAN OF THE WEST   MGM 1957
(Deutsch)   (*Gun glory*)

YOUNG, Desmond

ROMMEL   FOX 1951
(Collins)   (*Rommel-desert fox*)

YOUNG, Francis Brett

MAN ABOUT THE HOUSE, A   LF 1947
(Heinemann)

MAN ABOUT THE HOUSE, A (P)   LF 1947
(Sampson Low)

MY BROTHER JONATHAN   AB 1948
(Heinemann)

PORTRAIT OF CLARE   ABP 1949
(Heinemann)

YOUNG, Stark

SO RED THE ROSE   PAR 1935
(Cassell)

Z

ZETTERLING, Ma

NIGHT GAMES   GALA 1966
(Constable)

ZIEGLER, Isabelle Gibson

NINE DAYS OF FATHER SERRA   FOX 1955
(Longmans)   (*Seven cities of gold*)

ZIEMER, Geogor

EDUCATION FOR DEATH   RKO 1943
(Constable)   (*Hitler's children*)

ZOLA, Emile

KILL, THE   COL 1967
(Arrow Bks)   (*Game is over, The*)

LA BÊTE HUMAINE   COL 1954
(Various)   (*Human desire*)

NAN   MGM 1933
(Elek)   GALA 1955

ZWEIG, Arnold

    CASE OF SERGEANT GRISCHA,   RKO 1930
        THE
    (Secker)

ZWEIG, Stefan

    BEWARE OF PITY   TC 1946
    (Cassell)

    LETTER FROM AN UNKNOWN   UI 1948
        WOMAN, A
    (Cassell)

    MARIE ANTOINETTE   MGM 1938
    (Cassell)

CHANGE OF ORIGINAL TITLE INDEX

*Film companies frequently change the original title
of the book or play on screening.
This alphabetical index gives the author's original
and published title of his work, followed by the screen
title where the two differ.*

A

Original Title	Film Title
ABC MURDERS, THE Christie, A.	**ALPHABET MURDERS, THE** MGM 1966
ABE LINCOLN OF ILLINOIS (P) Sherwood, R. E.	**ABE LINCOLN IN ILLINOIS** RKO 1940
ACACIA AVENUE (P) Constanduros, M. *and* D.	**29 ACACIA AVENUE** COL 1945
ACCENT ON YOUTH (P) Raphaelson, S.	**BUT NOT FOR ME** PAR 1959
ACT OF MERCY Clifford, F.	**GUNS OF DARKNESS** WAR 1964
ACT OF PASSION Simenon, G.	**FORBIDDEN FRUIT** CP 1952
ADIOS Bartlett, L. *and* V. S.	**LASH, THE** IN 1931
ADOBE WALLS Burnett, W. R.	**ARROWHEAD** PAR 1953
ADVENTURE IN DIAMONDS Walker, D. E.	**OPERATION AMSTERDAM** RANK 1958
ADVENTURES OF HAJJI BABA OF ISPAHAN Morier, J.	**ADVENTURES OF HAJJI BABA, THE** FOX 1954
ADVENTURES OF THE FIVE ORANGE PIPS, THE Doyle, *Sir* A. C.	**HOUSE OF FEAR** UN 1945
AFRICAN BUSH ADVENTURES Hunter, J. A.	**KILLERS OF KILIMANJARO** COL 1959
AFTER ALL (P) Druten, J. van.	**NEW MORALS FOR OLD** MGM 1932
AFTER THE FUNERAL Christie, A.	**MURDER AT THE GALLOP** MGM 1963
AGONY COLUMN Biggers, E. D.	**PASSAGE FROM HONG KONG** WAR 1941
AH WILDERNESS (P) O'Neill, E. G.	**SUMMER HOLIDAY** MGM 1948
AIMEZ-VOUS BRAHMS? Sagan, F.	**GOODBYE AGAIN** UA 1961
AIRING IN A CLOSED CARRIAGE Shearing, J.	**MARK OF CAIN** TC 1948

393

ALASKA Beach, R. E.	**SPOILERS, THE** UN 1942
ALEXANDRA QUARTET Durrell, L.	**JUSTINE** FOX 1969
ALICE SIT BY THE FIRE (P) Barrie, *Sir* J. M.	**RENDEZVOUS** PAR 1950
ALL BRIDES ARE BEAUTIFUL Bell, T.	**FROM THIS DAY FORWARD** RKO 1946
ALL KNEELING Parrish, A.	**BORN TO BE BAD** RKO 1950
ALL ON A SUMMER'S DAY Garden, J.	**DOUBLE CONFESSION** ABP 1950
ALL THROUGH THE NIGHT Masterton, W.	**CRY IN THE NIGHT, A** WAR 1956
AL SCHMID, MARINE Butterfield, R. P.	**PRIDE OF THE MARINES** WAR 1945
AMAZING QUEST OF MR. ERNEST BLISS, THE Oppenheim, E. P.	**AMAZING QUEST, THE** KLEMENT 1936
AMBOY DUKES, THE Shulman, I.	**CITY ACROSS THE RIVER** UI 1949
AMERICA, AMERICA Kazan, E.	**ANATOLIAN SMILE, THE** WAR 1964
AMERICAN BLACK CHAMBER, THE Yardley, H. O.	**RENDEZVOUS** MGM 1935
AMERICAN DREAM, AN Mailer, N.	**SEE YOU IN HELL, DARLING** WAR 1966
AMERICAN GUERILLA IN THE PHILIPPINES Wolfert, I.	**I SHALL RETURN** FOX 1950
AMERICAN TRAGEDY, AN Dreiser, T.	**PLACE IN THE SUN, A** PAR 1951
ANATOMY OF A CRIME Dinneen, J. F.	**SIX BRIDGES TO CROSS** GFD 1954
ANATOMY OF ME Hurst, F.	**IMITATION OF LIFE** RANK 1959
AND RIDE A TIGER Wilder, R.	**STRANGER IN MY ARMS, A** UI 1958
AND THEY SHALL WALK Kenny, *Sister and* Ostenso, M.	**SISTER KENNY** RKO 1946

ORIGINAL TITLE	FILM TITLE
ANIMAL KINGDOM (P) Barry, P.	ONE MORE TOMORROW WAR 1948
ANNA AND THE KING OF SIAM Landon, M.	KING AND I, THE FOX 1956
ANNIVERSARY WALTZ (P) Fields, J. *and* Chodorov, J.	HAPPY ANNIVERSARY UA 1959
ANOINTED, THE Davis, C. B.	ADVENTURE MGM 1945
APACHE RISING Albert, M.	DUEL AT DIABLO UA 1966
APPLESAUCE Conners, B.	BRIDES ARE LIKE THAT IN 1936
APPOINTMENT AT THE BEACH Moravia, A.	NAKED HOURS, THE COMPTON 1965
APPOINTMENT IN ZAHREIN Barrett, M.	ESCAPE FROM ZAHREIN PAR 1962
APRON STRINGS (P) Davis, D.	VIRTUOUS HUSBAND UN 1931
AROUSE AND BEWARE Kantor, M.	MAN FROM DAKOTA, THE MGM 1940
ASHENDEN Maugham, W. S.	SECRET AGENT GB 1936
ASPERN PAPERS, THE James, H.	LOST MOMENT, THE UN 1947
ASPHALT JUNGLE, THE Burnett, W. R.	CAIRO MGM 1963
ASSIZE OF THE DYING, THE Pargeter, E.	SPANIARD'S CURSE, THE BL 1957
AUGUST 1914 Tuchman, B. W.	GUNS OF AUGUST, THE RANK 1964
AUTHENTIC DEATH OF HENDRY JONES, THE Neider, C.	ONE EYED JACKS PAR 1960
AUTUMN (P) Kennedy, M.	THAT DANGEROUS AGE LF 1949

B

BABY JANE Farrell, H.	WHATEVER HAPPENED TO BABY JANE? WAR 1962

ORIGINAL TITLE	FILM TITLE
BABYLON REVISITED Fitzgerald, F. S.	**LAST TIME I SAW PARIS, THE** MGM 1954
BACK OF SUNSET Cleary, J.	**SUNDOWNERS, THE** WAR 1960
BADMAN Huffaker, C.	**WAR WAGON** UI 1966
BALLAD OF CAT BALLOU Chanslor, R.	**CAT BALLOU** COL 1965
BALLAD OF THE RUNNING MAN, THE Smith, S.	**RUNNING MAN, THE** COL 1963
BALLERINA Smith, *Lady* E.	**MEN IN HER LIFE** COL 1941
BANNER IN THE SKY Ullman, J. R.	**THIRD MAN ON THE MOUNTAIN** DISNEY 1959
BAR SINISTER, THE Davies, R. H.	**IT'S A DOG'S LIFE** MGM 1955
BASEMENT ROOM, THE Greene, G.	**FALLEN IDOL, THE** FOX 1948
BAT, THE Rinehart, M. R.	**BAT WHISPERS, THE** UA 1931
BATTLE OF NERVES, A Simenon, G.	**MAN ON THE EIFFEL TOWER, THE** BL 1950
BATTLE OF THE VILLA FIORITA, THE Godden, R.	**AFFAIR AT THE VILLA FIORITA, THE** WAR 1964
BEACHCOMBER Maugham, W. S.	**VESSEL OF WRATH, THE** PAR 1938
BEAUTY Baldwin, F.	**BEAUTY FOR SALE** MGM 1933
BEFORE THE FACT Iles, F.	**SUSPICION** RKO 1941
BEGGAR MY NEIGHBOUR Ridley, A.	**MEET MR. LUCIFER** GFD 1953
BEGINNERS LUCK Somers, P.	**DESPERATE MAN, THE** AA 1959
BEHOLD WE LIVE (P) Druten, J. van.	**IF I WERE FREE** RKO 1933
BEL AMI Maupassant, G. de.	**PRIVATE AFFAIRS OF BEL AMI, THE** UA 1947

ORIGINAL TITLE	FILM TITLE
BELLA DONNA Hichens, R.	**TEMPTATION** COL 1930
BELVEDERE Davenport, *Mrs.* G.	**SITTING PRETTY** FOX 1948
BENGAL LANCER Yeats-Brown, F.	**LIVES OF A BENGAL LANCER, THE** PAR 1935
BENIGHTED Priestley, J. B.	**OLD DARK HOUSE, THE** BL 1963
BE PREPARED Cochran, R. E.	**MISTER SCOUTMASTER** FOX 1953
BE READY WITH BELLS AND DRUMS Kata, E.	**PATCH OF BLUE** MGM 1966
BERG, THE (P) Raymond, E.	**ATLANTIC** BI 1930
BERLIN HOTEL Baum, V.	**HOTEL BERLIN** WAR 1945
BERLIN MEMORANDUM, THE Hall, A.	**QUILLER MEMORANDUM, THE** JARFID 1966
BE STILL MY LOVE Truesdell, J.	**ACCUSED, THE** PAR 1949
BETHNAL GREEN Fisher, M.	**PLACE TO GO, A** BL 1964
BETTER THAN LIFE Bromfield, L.	**IT ALL CAME TRUE** WAR 1940
BEWARE OF CHILDREN Anderson, V.	**NO KIDDING** AA 1960
BIG BOODLE, THE Sylvester, R.	**NIGHT IN HAVANA** UA 1957
BIG GRAB, THE Trinian, J.	**BIG SNATCH, THE** GALA 1963
BIG PICK-UP Trevor, E.	**DUNKIRK** MGM 1958
BIG RANGE Schaefer, J. W.	**SILVER WHIP, THE** FOX 1953
BIG TOWN, THE Lardner, R. W.	**SO, THIS IS NEW YORK** UA 1948
BIG WAR, THE Myrer, A.	**IN LOVE AND WAR** FOX 1958

BIOGRAPHY (P)
Behrman, S. N.

BIOGRAPHY OF A BACHELOR GIRL
MGM 1934

BIRD'S NEST, THE
Jackson, S.

LIZZIE
MGM 1957

BIRTHDAY (P)
Ackland, R.

HEAVEN CAN WAIT
FOX 1943

BITTER SAGE
Gruber, F.

TENSION AT TABLE ROCK
RKO 1956

BLACK ALIBI
Woolrich, C.

LEOPARD MAN, THE
RKO 1943

BLACKBURN'S HEADHUNTERS
Harkins, P.

SURRENDER—HELL
ABP 1959

BLACK CAT, THE
Poe, E. A.

TALES OF TERROR
WAR 1963

BLACK CURTAIN, THE
Woolrich, C.

STREET OF CHANCE
PAR 1942

BLANK WALL
Holding, *Mrs.* E.

RECKLESS MOMENT, THE
COL 1949

BLESSING, THE
Mitford, N.

COUNT YOUR BLESSINGS
MGM 1959

BLESS THIS HOUSE (P)
Evans, E. E.

ROOM IN THE HOUSE
MON 1955

BLOOD BROTHER
Arnold, E.

BROKEN ARROW
FOX 1950
FOX 1958

BLOOD ON HER SHOE
Field, M.

GIRL WHO DARED, THE
REP 1944

BLUE DENIM (P)
Herlihy, J. L. *and* Noble, W.

BLUE JEANS
FOX 1959

BODIES AND SOULS
Meersch, M. van der.

DOCTOR AND THE GIRL, THE
MGM 1949

BODY SNATCHERS, THE
Finney, J.

INVASION OF THE BODY
  SNATCHERS, THE
COL 1956

BOOK OF THE MONTH (P)
Thomas, B.

PLEASE TURN OVER
AA 1959

ORIGINAL TITLE	FILM TITLE
BORDER LEGION Grey, Z.	**LAST ROUND-UP, THE** PAR 1934
BOTTLETOP AFFAIR, THE Cotler, G.	**HORIZONTAL LIEUTENANT, THE** MGM 1962
BOWERY TO BELLEVUE Barringer, E. D.	**GIRL IN WHITE** MGM 1952 **SO BRIGHT THE FLAME** MGM 1952
BRAVE COWBOY, THE Abbey, E.	**LONELY ARE THE BRAVE** UI 1962
BREATH OF SPRING (P) Coke, P.	**WE'RE IN THE MINK** RANK 1959
BREWSTER'S MILLIONS McCutcheon, G. B.	**THREE ON A SPREE** UA 1961
BRICK FOXHOLE, THE Brooks, R.	**CROSSFIRE** RKO 1947
BRIDE COMES TO YELLOW SKY, **THE** Crane, S.	**FACE TO FACE** RKO 1952
BRINGING UP THE BRASS Maher, M. *and* Campion, N. R.	**LONG GRAY LINE** COL 1954
BRIXBY GIRLS, THE Marshall, P. P.	**ALL THE FINE YOUNG CANNIBALS** MGM 1960
BROKEN DISHES (P) Flavin, M.	**TOO YOUNG TO MARRY** WAR 1931 **LOVE BEGINS AT 20** IN 1936
BRONCO APACHE Wellman, P. I.	**APACHE** UA 1954
BROTHER RAT (P) Monks, J. *and* Finklehoffe, F. F.	**ABOUT FACE** WAR 1952
BROTHER VAN Smith, A. J.	**LAWLESS EIGHTIES, THE** BL 1957
BROWN ON 'RESOLUTION' Forester, C. S.	**SINGLE HANDED** FOX 1952
BRUTE, THE Cars, G. des.	**GREEN SCARF, THE** BL 1954
BUDDWING Hunter, E.	**MISTER BUDDWING** MGM 1967

BUGLE'S WAKE
Brandon, C.

SEMINOLE UPRISING
EROS 1955

BUILD-UP BOYS, THE
Kirk, J.

MADISON AVENUE
FOX 1960

BURNING HILLS
L'Amour, L.

APACHE TERRITORY
COL 1958

BURN, WITCH, BURN
Merritt, A.

DEVIL-DOLL, THE
MGM 1936

BUSMAN'S HONEYMOON
Sayers, D. L.

BUSMAN'S HOLIDAY
MGM 1940

BUT FOR THESE MEN
Drummond, J. D.

HEROES OF THE TELEMARK
RANK 1965

**BUT GENTLEMEN MARRY
BRUNETTES**
Loos, A.

GENTLEMEN MARRY BRUNETTES
UA 1955

C

CALENDAR, THE
Wallace, E.

BACHELOR'S FOLLY
WW 1932

CALL FOR THE DEAD
Le Carré, J.

DEADLY AFFAIR, THE
BL 1966

CALL GIRL, THE
Greenwald, H.

GIRL OF THE NIGHT
WAR 1960

CALL IT TREASON
Howe, G. L.

DECISION BEFORE DAWN
FOX 1951

CAME THE DAWN
Bax, R.

NEVER LET ME GO
MGM 1953

CAPPY RICKS
Kyne, P. B.

AFFAIRS OF CAPPY RICKS, THE
REP 1937

CAPPY RICKS COMES BACK
Kyne, P. B.

CAPPY RICKS RETURNS
REP 1935

CAPTAIN BLOOD RETURNS
Sabatini, R.

CAPTAIN BLOOD, FUGITIVE
COL 1952

CAPTAIN GRANT'S CHILDREN
Verne, J.

IN SEARCH OF THE CASTAWAYS
DISNEY 1962

CAPTAIN HORNBLOWER, R.N.
Forester, C. S.

CAPTAIN HORATIO HORNBLOWER,
R.N.
WAR 1951

ORIGINAL TITLE	FILM TITLE
CAPTAIN'S DAUGHTER, THE Pushkin, A. S.	**TEMPEST** PAR 1959
CARAVAN TO CARNAL, A Clou, J.	**CONQUEROR, THE** RKO 1955
CAREFUL MAN, THE Denning, R.	**ARRIVEDERCI, BABY!** PAR 1967
CARL AND ANNA Frank, L.	**AS YOU DESIRE ME** MGM 1932
CARNIVAL Mackenzie, *Sir* C.	**DANCE PRETTY LADY** BI 1931
CARPETBAGGERS, THE Robbins, H.	**NEVADA SMITH** PAR 1963
CARRIAGE ENTRANCE Banks, P.	**MY FORBIDDEN PAST** RKO 1951
CASE FILE: F.B.I. Gordon, *Mrs*. M. *and* Gordon, G.	**DOWN 3 DARK STREETS** UA 1954
CASE OF DR. VALDEMAR, THE Poe, E. A.	**TALES OF TERROR** WAR 1963
CASE OF THE CARETAKER'S CAT, THE Gardner, E. S.	**CASE OF THE BLACK CAT** IN 1936
CASE OF THE CONSTANT GOD King, R.	**LOVE LETTERS OF A STAR** UN 1936
CASE OF THE FRIGHTENED LADY, THE Wallace, E.	**FRIGHTENED LADY, THE** BI 1941
CASTING THE RUNES James, M. R.	**NIGHT OF THE DEMON** COL 1957
CASTLE MINERVA Canning, V.	**MASQUERADE** UA 1965
CAT AND THE CANARY, THE Willard, J.	**CAT CREEPS, THE** UN 1930
CAT AND THE MICE, THE Mosley, L.	**FOXHOLE IN CAIRO** BL 1960
CELEBRATED JUMPING FROG OF CALAVERAS Twain, M.	**BEST MAN WINS, THE** COL 1948
CENTURIANS, THE Larteguy, J.	**LOST COMMAND** COL 1966

CHAIR FOR MARTIN ROME, THE
Helseth, H. E.

CRY OF THE CITY
FOX 1948

CHALLENGE, THE
'Sapper'

BULLDOG DRUMMOND IN AFRICA
PAR 1938

CHICKEN EVERY SUNDAY
Taylor, R.

HEFFERAN FAMILY, THE
FOX 1956

CHILDREN OF LIGHT
Lawrence, H. L.

DAMNED, THE
BL 1963

CHILDREN OF THE DARK
Schulman, I.

REBEL WITHOUT A CAUSE
WAR 1955

CHILDREN OF THE DARK
Shulman, I.

CRY TOUGH
UA 1959

CHILDREN'S HOUR, THE (P)
Hellman, L. F.

LOUDEST WHISPER, THE
UA 1962

CHILDREN'S HOUR, THE (P)
Hellman, L. F.

THESE THREE
UA 1936

CHINESE ROOM, THE
Connell, V.

IN THE CHINESE ROOM
FOX 1959

CHRIST IN CONCRETE
Di Donato, P.

GIVE US THIS DAY
GFD 1949

CHRISTMAS CAROL, A
Dickens, C.

SCROOGE
REN 1951

CHRISTOPHER BLAKE (P)
Hart, M.

DECISION OF CHRISTOPHER BLAKE,
THE
WAR 1948

CIRCLES ROUND THE WAGON
Gipson, F. B.

HOUND DOG MAN
FOX 1959

CLAUDELLE
Caldwell, E.

YOUNG AND EAGER
WAR 1961

CLEAN BREAK
White, L.

KILLING, THE
UA 1956

CLEMENTINE
Goodin, P.

MICKEY
ABP 1950

CODE OF THE WEST
Grey, Z.

HOME ON THE RANGE
PAR 1935

COINS IN THE FOUNTAIN
Secondari, J.

THREE COINS IN THE FOUNTAIN
FOX 1954

COLOMBA
Merimée, P.

VENDETTA
RKO 1951

COLOURS OF THE DAY, THE Gary, R.	**MAN WHO UNDERSTOOD WOMEN** FOX 1959
COLUMBUS Sabatini, R.	**CHRISTOPHER COLUMBUS** GFD 1949
COMANCHE Appel, D.	**TONKA** DISNEY 1958
COME BE MY LOVE Davis, *Mrs.* L.	**ONCE MORE MY DARLING** UI 1949
COMMANDER CRABB Pugh, M.	**SILENT ENEMY, THE** ROMULUS 1958
COMMANDOS, THE Arnold, E.	**FIRST COMES COURAGE** COL 1943
COMPANIONS OF JEHU, THE Dumas, A.	**FIGHTING GUARDSMAN** COL 1945
CONDEMNED, THE Pagano, J.	**SOUND OF FURY, THE** UA 1951
CONDEMNED TO DEVIL'S ISLAND Niles, B.	**CONDEMNED** UA 1939
CONGO LANDING Burtis, M.	**CONGO MAISIE** MGM 1940
CONVICT HAS ESCAPED, A Budd, J.	**THEY MADE ME A FUGITIVE** WAR 1947
COTTONWOOD GULCH Mulford, C. E.	**NORTH OF RIO GRANDE** PAR 1937
COURT CIRCULAR Stokes, S.	**I BELIEVE IN YOU** EALING 1953
CRAIG'S WIFE (P) Kelly, G.	**HARRIET CRAIG** COL 1950
CREAKING CHAIR, THE Meynell, L. W.	**STREET OF SHADOWS** AA 1953
CRIME OF SYLVESTRE BONNARD, THE France, A.	**CHASING YESTERDAY** RKO 1935
CROWTHERS OF BANKDAM, THE Armstrong, T.	**MASTER OF BANKDAM, THE** ALL 1947
CRUCIBLE, THE (P) Miller, A.	**WITCHES OF SALEM, THE** FILMS DE FRANCE 1957

CRY TOUGH Shulman, I.	**RING, THE** UA 1953
CUP AND THE SWORD, THE Hobart, A. T.	**THIS EARTH IS MINE** UI 1959
CURE OF THE FLESH Cozzens, J. G.	**DOCTOR BULL** FOX 1933
CURIOUS CRIME Martin, A. E.	**GLASS CAGE, THE** EXCLUSIVE 1955
CUSTARD BOYS, THE Rae, J.	**REACH FOR GLORY** GALA 1962

D

DADDY AND I Jordan, E. G.	**MAKE WAY FOR A LADY** RKO 1936
DAFFODIL MYSTERY Wallace, E.	**DEVIL'S DAFFODIL, THE** BL 1961
DAMN YANKEES (P) Adler, R. *and* Ross, J.	**WHAT LOLA WANTS** WAR 1958
DARK ANGEL Kaus, G.	**HER SISTER'S SECRET** PRC 1946
DARKEST HOUR McGivern, W. P.	**HELL ON FRISCO BAY** WAR 1955
DARK FANTASTIC Echard, M.	**LIGHTNING STRIKES TWICE** WAR 1951
DARKNESS I LEAVE YOU Hooke, N. W.	**GYPSY AND THE GENTLEMAN, THE** RANK 1957
DARLING BUDS OF MAY, THE Bates, H. E.	**MATING GAME, THE** MGM 1959
DAVID GOLDEN Nemirowsky, I.	**MY DAUGHTER JOY** BL 1950
DAWN OF RECKONING Hilton, J.	**RAGE IN HEAVEN** MGM 1941
DAY IS OURS, THE Lewis, H.	**MANDY** GFD 1952
DAY THE CENTURY ENDED, THE Gwaltney, F. I.	**BETWEEN HEAVEN AND HELL** FOX 1956
DAY WITHOUT END Praag, V. V.	**MEN IN WAR** UA 1957

ORIGINAL TITLE	FILM TITLE
DEAD DON'T CARE, THE Latimer, J.	**LAST WARNING, THE** UN 1939
DEADLIER THAN THE MALE Gunn, J. E.	**BORN TO KILL** RKO 1947
DEAR EVELYN (P) Wild, E. *and* Eunson, D.	**GUEST IN THE HOUSE** UA 1944
DEATH AND THE SKY ABOVE US Garve, A.	**TWO-LETTER ALIBI** BL 1962
DEATH AT SHINGLE-STRAND Capon, P.	**HIDDEN HOMICIDE** RANK 1958
DEATH HAS DEEP ROOTS Gilbert, M.	**GUILTY?** GN 1956
DEATH IN CAPTIVITY Gilbert, M.	**DANGER WITHIN** BL 1958
DEATH IN DEEP SOUTH Greene, M.	**THEY WON'T FORGET** WAR 1937
DEATH IN THE FAMILY, A Agee, J.	**ALL THE WAY HOME** PAR 1963
DEATH IN TIGER VALLEY Campbell, R.	**GIRL FROM MANDALAY** REP 1936
DEATH OF A COMMON MAN Holdridge, D.	**END OF THE RIVER, THE** ARCHERS 1947
DEATH OF A SNOUT Warner, D.	**INFORMERS, THE** RANK 1963
DEBT DISCHARGED, A Wallace, E.	**MAN DETAINED** AA 1961
DECAMERON, THE Boccaccio, G.	**DECAMERON NIGHTS** EROS 1953
DEEP ARE THE ROOTS (P) D'Usseau, A. *and* Gow, J.	**TOMORROW THE WORLD** UA 1944
DEL PALMA Kellino, P.	**LADY POSSESSED, A** REP 1951
DESERT GUNS Frazee, S.	**GOLD OF THE SEVEN SAINTS** WAR 1961
DESERT VOICES Perkins, K.	**DESERT PURSUIT** ABP 1952
DESTRY RIDES AGAIN Brand, M.	**DESTRY** UI 1954

DEVIL AND DANIEL WEBSTER, THE Benet, S. V.	**ALL THAT MONEY CAN BUY** RKO 1941
DEVIL'S OWN, THE Curtis, P.	**WITCHES, THE** HAMMER 1966
DEVIL'S TRIANGLE Soutar, A.	**ALMOST MARRIED** FOX 1932
DILDO CAY Hayes ,N.	**BAHAMA PASSAGE** PAR 1941
DIVING FOR ADVENTURE Hass, H.	**UNDER THE CARIBBEAN** BL 1954
DOCTORS ON HORSEBACK Flexner, J. T.	**BIG JACK** MGM 1949
DOCTOR WEARS THREE **FACES, THE** Bard, M.	**MOTHER DIDN'T TELL ME** FOX 1950
DOMBEY AND SON Dickens, C.	**RICH MAN'S FOLLY** PAR 1931
DON AMONG THE DEAD MEN Vulliamy, C. E.	**JOLLY BAD FELLOW, A** BL 1964
DON CAMILLO AND THE **PRODIGAL SON** Guareschi, G.	**RETURN OF DON CAMILLO, THE** MIRACLE FILMS 1954
DON CARELESS Beach, R. E.	**AVENGERS, THE** REP 1950
DON DESPERADO Foreman, L. L.	**SAVAGE, THE** PAR 1952
DONOVAN'S BRAIN Siodmak, C.	**VENGEANCE** BL 1963
DOUBLE DEALERS Klein, A.	**COUNTERFEIT TRAITOR, THE** PAR 1962
DOVER ROAD (P) Milne, A. A.	**WHERE SINNERS MEET** RKO 1934
DR. JEKYLL AND MR. HYDE Stevenson, R. L.	**TWO FACES OF DR. JEKYLL, THE** COL 1959
DR. KILDARE'S TRIAL Brand, M.	**PEOPLE VERSUS DR. KILDARE, THE** LOE 1941
DOUBLE TAKE Huggins, R.	**I LOVE TROUBLE** COL 1948

ORIGINAL TITLE	FILM TITLE
DREADFUL SUMMIT Ellin, S.	**BIG NIGHT, THE** UA 1951
DREAMLAND Kelland, C. B.	**STRIKE ME PINK** UA 1936
DRUM, THE Mason, A. E. W.	**DRUMS** UA 1938
DUBLIN NIGHTMARE Loraine, P.	**NIGHTMARE IN DUBLIN** RANK 1957
DUNBAR'S COVE Deal, B.	**WILD RIVER** FOX 1960
DURIAN TREE, THE Keon, M.	**7th DAWN, THE** UA 1964

E

EASTER DINNER, THE Downes, D.	**PIGEON THAT TOOK ROME, THE** PAR 1962
EAST LYNNE Wood, *Mrs.* H.	**EX-FLAME** TIFFANY 1931
EBB TIDE Stevenson, R. L.	**ADVENTURE ISLAND** PAR 1947
EDDIE CHAPMAN STORY, THE Owen, F.	**TRIPLE CROSS, THE** AA 1967
EDGE OF DOOM Brady, L.	**STRONGER THAN FEAR** RKO 1952
EDUCATION FOR DEATH Ziemer, G.	**HITLER'S CHILDREN** RKO 1943
ELEPHANT IN WHITE, THE Brahms, C. *and* Simon, S. J.	**GIVE US THE MOON** GFD 1944
ELIZABETH THE QUEEN (P) Anderson, M.	**PRIVATE LIVES OF ELIZABETH AND ESSEX, THE** WAR 1939
EMPEROR'S SNUFF BOX, THE Carr, J. D.	**THAT WOMAN OPPOSITE** MON 1957
EMPORIA Sanford, H. *and* Lamb, M.	**WACO** PAR 1967
ENTER SIR JOHN Dane, C. *and* Simpson, H. de G.	**MURDER** BI 1930

ENVY MY SIMPLICITY
Barton, R.

KILLER WALKS, A
GN 1952

EPISODE OF SPARROWS, THE
Godden, R.

INNOCENT SINNERS
RANK 1957

EPITAPH FOR AN ENEMY
Barr, G.

UP FROM THE BEACH
FOX 1964

EPITAPH FOR A SPY
Ambler, E.

HOTEL RESERVE
RKO 1944

ERASMUS WITH FRECKLES
Hasse, J.

DEAR BRIGITTE
FOX 1965

ESCAPE ALONE
Howarth, D.

WE DIE ALONE
REN 1959

ESCAPE OF THE AMETHYST, THE
Earl, L.

YANGTSE INCIDENT
BL 1957

EUNUCH OF STAMBOUL, THE
Wheatley, D.

SECRET OF STAMBOUL, THE
HOB 1939

EVIL COME, EVIL GO
Masterson, W.

YELLOW CANARY, THE
FOX 1963

EXECUTIONER, THE
Macdonald, J. D.

CAPE FEAR
UI 1962

EXPERIMENT IN SINCERITY
Erskine, J.

LADY SURRENDERS, A
UN 1930

F

FACE IN THE NIGHT
Wallace, E.

MALPAS MYSTERY, THE
AA 1960

FALSE WITNESS
Stone, I.

ARKANSAS JUDGE
REP 1941

FAMILY SKELETON
Disney, D.M.

STELLA
FOX 1950

FAMOUS
Benet, S. V.

JUST FOR YOU
PAR 1952

FAREWELL, MY LOVELY
Chandler, R.

FALCON TAKES OVER, THE
RKO 1942

FAREWELL TO WOMEN
Collinson, W.

MOGAMBO
MGM 1953

FAST COMPANY
Page, M.

FAST AND LOOSE
MGM 1939

ORIGINAL TITLE	FILM TITLE
FATHER BROWN STORIES Chesterton, G. K.	**FATHER BROWN** COL 1954
FATHER WAS A HANDFUL Williams, *Mrs.* R.	**VANISHING VIRGINIAN, THE** MGM 1941
FEATHERED SERPENT, THE Wallace, E.	**MENACE, THE** COL 1932
FEMALE OF THE SPECIES, THE 'Sapper'	**BULLDOG DRUMMOND** **COMES BACK** PAR 1937
FER DE LANCE Stout, R.	**MEET NERO WOLFE** COL 1936
FIDDLER'S GREEN Gann, E. K.	**RAGING TIDE, THE** UI 1951
FIESTA Hemingway, E.	**SUN ALSO RISES, THE** FOX 1957
FIFTYMINUTE HOUR, THE Lindner, R.	**PRESSURE POINT** UA 1963
FIGHTING CARAVANS Grey, Z.	**WAGON WHEELS** PAR 1934
FINAL DIAGNOSIS, THE Hailey, A.	**YOUNG DOCTORS, THE** UA 1961
FINAL NIGHT Gaines, R.	**FRONT PAGE STORY** BL 1953
FIREBRAND, THE (P) Mayer, E. J.	**AFFAIRS OF CELLINI** UA 1934
FIRST AND LAST, THE Galsworthy, J.	**TWENTY-ONE DAYS** LF 1940
FIRST REBEL, THE Swanson, N. H.	**ALLEGHENY UPRISING** RKO 1939
FIRST TRAIN TO BABYLON Ehrlich, M.	**NAKED EDGE, THE** UA 1961
FLAMING LANCE Huffaker, C.	**FLAMING STAR** FOX 1960
FLOTSAM Remarque, E. M.	**SO ENDS OUR NIGHT** UA 1941
FLYING SAUCERS FROM **OUTER SPACE** Keyhoe, D. E.	**EARTH VERSUS THE FLYING** **SAUCERS** COL 1956

ORIGINAL TITLE	FILM TITLE
F.O.B. DETROIT Smitter, W.	**REACHING FOR THE SUN** PAR 1941
FOG FOR A KILLER Graeme, B.	**OUT OF THE FOG** GN 1962
FOR HER TO SEE Shearing, J.	**SO EVIL MY LOVE** PAR 1948
FOR LOVE OR MONEY (P) Herbert, F. H.	**THIS HAPPY FEELING** RANK 1958
FOR OUR VINES HAVE TENDER GRAPES Martin, G. V.	**OUR VINES HAVE TENDER GRAPES** MGM 1945
FORTRESS IN THE RICE Appel, B.	**CRY OF BATTLE** WAR 1964
FORTY WHACKS Homes, G.	**CRIME BY NIGHT** WAR 1946
FOUR FEATHERS, THE Mason, A. E. W.	**STORM OVER THE NILE** GFD 1955
4.50 FROM PADDINGTON Christie, A.	**MURDER SHE SAID** MGM 1961
FOUR JUST MEN, THE Wallace, E.	**SECRET FOUR, THE** MON 1940
FOUR PUNTERS ARE MISSING Rose, A.	**WHO'S GOT THE ACTION?** PAR 1963
FRANKENSTEIN Shelley, M. W.	**CURSE OF FRANKENSTEIN, THE** WAR 1957
FRIEND IN NEED, A Coxhead, E.	**CRY FROM THE STREETS, A** EROS 1958
FRIESE-GREENE Allister, R.	**MAGIC BOX, THE** BL 1951
FROM THIS DARK STAIRWAY Eberhart, M. G.	**MURDER OF DR. HARRIGAN** IN 1936
FRONT PAGE, THE (P) Hecht, B. *and* MacArthur, G.	**HIS GIRL FRIDAY** COL 1940
FUGUE IN TIME Godden, R.	**ENCHANTMENT** RKO 1949
FURNISHED ROOM, THE Del Rivo, L.	**WEST 11** WAR 1963

G

GABRIEL HORN
Holt, F.

KENTUCKIAN, THE
UA 1955

**GAMBLER AND OTHER
STORIES, THE**
Dostoevski, F. M.

GREAT SINNER, THE
MGM 1949

GAMESMANSHIP
Potter, S.

SCHOOL FOR SCOUNDRELS
WAR 1960

GASLIGHT (P)
Hamilton, P.

MURDER IN THORNTON SQUARE
MGM 1944

GATHER YE ROSEBUDS
Nolan, J.

ISN'T IT ROMANTIC
PAR 1948

GAUCHO
Childs, H.

WAY OF A GAUCHO
FOX 1952

GAY BANDIT OF THE BORDER
Gill, T.

GAY CABALLERO
FOX 1932

GENTLE PEOPLE, THE (P)
Shaw, I.

OUT OF THE FOG
WAR 1941

GETAWAY
Charteris, L.

SAINT'S VACATION, THE
RKO 1941

GIOCONDA SMILE, THE
Huxley, A. L.

WOMAN'S VENGEANCE, A
UN 1947

**GILBERT AND SULLIVAN
BOOK, THE**
Baily, L.

**STORY OF GILBERT AND
SULLIVAN, THE**
BL 1953

GILDED ROOSTER, THE
Roberts, R. E.

LAST FRONTIER, THE
COL 1955

GIRL ON A WING
Glemser, B.

COME FLY WITH ME
MGM 1963

GIRL ON THE VIA FLAMINIA, THE
Hayes, A.

ACT OF LOVE
UA 1954

GLORY FOR ME
Kantor, M.

BEST YEARS OF OUR LIVES, THE
RKO 1946

GOD AND MY COUNTRY
Kantor, M.

FOLLOW ME, BOYS!
DISNEY 1967

GOLD BUG, THE
Poe, E. A.

CALYPSO
BL 1956

GOLDEN FLEECING, THE (P)
Semple, L.

HONEYMOON MACHINE, THE
MGM 1961

GOLDEN HERD Carroll, C.	**SAN ANTONE** REP 1952
GOLDEN PORTAGE, THE Case, R. O.	**GIRL FROM ALASKA, THE** REP 1942
GOLDEN TIDE, THE Roe, V.	**PERILOUS JOURNEY, A** REP 1953
GOLD FISH BOWL, THE McCall, M.	**IT'S TOUGH TO BE FAMOUS** IN 1932
GOLD HUNTERS, THE Curwood, J. O.	**TRAIL OF THE YUKON** MONOGRAM 1949
GOODBYE AGAIN (P) Scott, A. *and* Haight, G.	**HONEYMOON FOR THREE** WAR 1941
GOWNS BY ROBERTA Miller, A. D.	**LOVELY TO LOOK AT** MGM 1952
GOWNS BY ROBERTA Miller, A. D.	**ROBERTA** RKO 1935
GRAF SPEE Powell, M.	**BATTLE OF THE RIVER PLATE, THE** RANK 1956
GRAND DUKE AND MR. PIMM, THE Hardy, L.	**ALL THIS AND MONEY TOO** UA 1963
GREAT ADVENTURE Bennett, A.	**HIS DOUBLE LIFE** PAR 1933
GREAT CROONER, THE Kelland, C. B.	**MR. DODD TAKES THE AIR** WAR 1937
GREEN GODDESS, THE Archer, W.	**ADVENTURES IN IRAQ** WAR 1943
GREEN HAT, THE Arlen, M.	**WOMAN OF AFFAIRS, A** MGM 1929
GREEN RIBBON, THE Wallace, E.	**NEVER BACK LOSERS** AA 1962
GREYFRIAR'S BOBBY Atkinson, E.	**CHALLENGE TO LASSIE** MGM 1949
GRIMMS' FAIRY TALES Grimm, J. *and* Grimm, W.	**WONDERFUL WORLD OF THE BROTHERS GRIMM, THE** MGM 1962

GUARDSMAN, THE (P)
Molnar, F.

CHOCOLATE SOLDIER, THE
LOE 1941

GULLIVER'S TRAVELS
Swift, J.

THREE WORLDS OF GULLIVER, THE
COL 1959

GUN, THE
Forester, C. S.

PRIDE AND THE PASSION, THE
UA 1957

GUN CRAZY
Kantor, M.

DEADLY IS THE FEMALE
UA 1949

GUN FOR SALE, A
Greene, G.

SHORT CUT TO HELL
PAR 1957

GUN FOR SALE, A
Greene, G.

THIS GUN FOR HIRE
PAR 1942

GUNNER, THE
Wallace, E.

SOLO FOR SPARROW
AA 1962

GUNS OF THE RIO CONCHOS
Huffaker, C.

RIO CONCHOS
FOX 1964

GUY RENTON
Waugh, A.

CIRCLE OF DECEPTION
FOX 1960

H

HALFWAY TO HEAVEN (P)
Segall, H.

HERE COMES MR. JORDAN
COL 1941

HAMLET, THE
Faulkner, W.

LONG, HOT SUMMER, THE
FOX 1957

HAMP (P)
Wilson, J.

KING AND COUNTRY
WAR 1965

HAND AND THE FLOWER, THE
Tickell, J.

DAY TO REMEMBER, A
GFD 1953

HAPPY NOW I GO
Charles, T.

WOMAN WITH NO NAME, THE
ABP 1950

HARM'S WAY
Bassett, J.

IN HARM'S WAY
COL 1965

HARRISON HIGH
Farris, J.

BECAUSE THEY'RE YOUNG
COL 1960

HAUNTING OF HILL HOUSE, THE
Jackson, S.

HAUNTING, THE
MGM 1963

HEADED FOR A HEARSE
Latimer, J.

WESTLAND CASE, THE
UN 1937

HEARSES DON'T HURRY
Ransome, S.

WHO IS HOPE SCHUYLER?
FOX 1942

HEAT WAVE (P)
Pertwee, R.

ROAD TO SINGAPORE
WAR 1931

HE FELL DOWN DEAD
Perdue, V.

SHADOW OF A WOMAN
WAR 1946

HELLCATS OF THE SEA
Lockwood, C. A. *and* Adamson, H. C.

HELLCATS OF THE NAVY
COL 1957

HELLER WITH A GUN
L'Amour, L.

HELLER IN PINK TIGHTS
PAR 1960

HERE IS YOUR WAR
Pyle, E. T.

WAR CORRESPONDENT
INT 1951

HER FATHER'S DAUGHTER
Stratton-Porter, G.

HER FIRST ROMANCE
MON 1940

HER HEART IN HER THROAT
White, E. L.

UNSEEN, THE
PAR 1945

HERO, THE
Lampell, M.

SATURDAY'S HERO
COL 1951

HE WAS FOUND IN THE ROAD
Armstrong, A.

MAN IN THE ROAD, THE
GN 1956

HIDING PLACE, THE
Shaw, R.

SITUATION HOPELESS BUT
   NOT SERIOUS
PAR 1964

HIGH CAGE
Frazee, S.

HIGH HELL
PAR 1958

HIGH PAVEMENT
Bonett, E.

MY SISTER AND I
GFD 1948

HIGH ROAD, THE (P)
Lonsdale, F.

LADY OF SCANDAL, THE
MGM 1930

HIGH SIERRA
Burnett, W. R.

I DIED A THOUSAND TIMES
WAR 1955

HIGH WINDOW, THE
Chandler, R.

BRASHER DOUBLOON, THE
FOX 1947

HIGH WRAY
Hughes, K.

HOUSE ACROSS THE LAKE, THE
ABP 1954

HIS LAST BOW
Doyle, *Sir* A. C.

SHERLOCK HOLMES AND THE
   VOICE OF TERROR
UN 1942

HISTORY OF TOM JONES, THE Fielding, H.	**TOM JONES** UA 1962
HOLD AUTUMN IN YOUR HAND Perry, G. S.	**SOUTHERNER, THE** UA 1945
HOMECOMING GAME, THE Nemerov, H.	**TALL STORY** WAR 1960
HOMECOMING GAME, THE (P) Lindsay, H. *and* Crouse, R.	**TALL STORY** WAR 1960
HOP DOG, THE Lavin, N. *and* Thorp, M.	**ADVENTURE IN THE HOP FIELDS** ABP 1954
HORSEMAN PASS BY McMurty, L.	**HUD** PAR 1963
HOT SUMMER NIGHT (P) Willis, T.	**FLAME IN THE STREETS** RANK 1961
HOUSE OF THE SEVEN FLIES, THE Canning, V.	**HOUSE OF THE SEVEN HAWKS, THE** MGM 1959
HOW SAY YOU? (P) Brooke, H. *and* Bannerman, K.	**PAIR OF BRIEFS** RANK 1961
HUMAN KIND, THE Baron, A.	**VICTORS, THE** BL 1963
HUNDRED MILLION FRAMES, A Berna, P.	**HORSE WITHOUT A HEAD, THE** DISNEY 1963

I

I AM A FUGITIVE FROM THE CHAIN GANG Burns, R. T.	**I AM A FUGITIVE** WAR 1932
I CAN GET IT FOR YOU WHOLESALE Weidman, J.	**THIS IS MY AFFAIR** FOX 1951
I, JAMES LEWIS Gabriel, G. W.	**THIS WOMAN IS MINE** UN 1941
ILIAD Homer	**ULYSSES** ARCHWAY 1954
I MARRIED A DEAD MAN Irish, W.	**NO MAN OF HER OWN** PAR 1950
IMMORTAL WIFE Stone, I.	**PRESIDENT'S LADY, THE** FOX 1953

IMPATIENT VIRGIN Clarke, D. H.	**IMPATIENT MAIDEN** UN 1932
IMPRESSARIO Hurock, S. *and* Goode, R.	**TONIGHT WE SING** FOX 1953
IN MY SOLITUDE Leslie, D. S.	**TWO LEFT FEET** BL 1965
INTERFERENCE (P) Pertwee, R. *and* Dearden, H.	**WITH REGRET** PAR 1935
INTERRUPTION, THE Jacobs, W. W.	**FOOTSTEPS IN THE FOG** COL 1955
INTRUDER, THE Beaumont, C.	**STRANGER, THE** GN 1963
ISLAND OF DR. MOREAU, THE Wells, H. G.	**ISLAND OF LOST SOULS** EROS 1959
IT DEPENDS WHAT YOU MEAN (P) Bridie, J.	**FOLLY TO BE WISE** BL 1952
IT'S A VET'S LIFE Duncan, A.	**IN THE DOGHOUSE** RANK 1961
I'VE GOT MINE Hubler, R. G.	**BEACHHEAD** UA 1953
I WAKE UP SCREAMING Fisher, S.	**VICKI** FOX 1953

J

JACKDAWS STRUT Henry, H.	**BOUGHT** WAR 1931
JACK O'JUDGEMENT Wallace, E.	**SHARE OUT, THE** AA 1962
JEANNIE (P) Stuart, A.	**LET'S BE HAPPY** ABP 1957
JENNY ANGEL Barber, E. O.	**ANGEL BABY** CONT 1961
JEWEL OF MAHABAR Marshall, E.	**TREASURE OF THE GOLDEN CONDOR** FOX 1953
JOAN OF LORRAINE (P) Anderson, M.	**JOAN OF ARC** RKO 1948

JOANNA GODDEN
Kaye-Smith, S.

LOVES OF JOANNA GODDEN, THE
GFD 1947

JOY HOUSE
Keene, D.

LOVE CAGE, THE
MGM 1965

JUBAL TROOP
Wellman, P. I.

JUBAL
COL 1956

JUPITER LAUGHS (P)
Cronin, A. J.

SHINING VICTORY
WAR 1941

JURY, THE
Bullet, G.

LAST MAN TO HANG
COL 1956

JUSTIN BAYARD
Cleary, J.

DUST IN THE SUN
WAR 1958

K

KENNEL MURDER CASE, THE
Dine, S. S. van.

CALLING PHILO VANCE
WAR 1940

KILL, THE
Zola, E.

GAME IS OVER, THE
COL 1967

KILLING A MOUSE ON SUNDAY
Pressburger, E.

BEHOLD A PALE HORSE
COL 1964

KILLING FROST, THE
Catto, M.

TRAPEZE
UA 1956

'KIND SIR' (P)
Krasna, N.

INDISCREET
WAR 1958

KINGDOM OF JOHNNY COOL, THE
McPartland, J.

JOHNNY COOL
UA 1964

KING OF HEARTS (P)
Kerr, J. *and* Brooke, H.

THAT CERTAIN FEELING
PAR 1956

KING RELUCTANT, A
Wilkins, V.

DANGEROUS EXILE
RANK 1957

KING SOLOMON'S MINES
Haggard, *Sir* H. R.

WATUSI
MGM 1958

KISS OF DEATH
Bachmann, L.

DEVIL MAKES THREE, THE
MGM 1952

KISS THE BLOOD OFF MY HANDS
Butler, G.

BLOOD ON MY HANDS
UI 1949

KON-TIKI EXPEDITION
Heyerdahl, T.

KON-TIKI
RKO 1951

L

LA BÊTE HUMAINE
Zola, E.

HUMAN DESIRE
COL 1954

LADY OF THE CAMELLIAS, THE
Dumas, A.

CAMILLE
MGM 1936

LAFITTE, THE PIRATE
Saxon, L.

BUCCANEER, THE
PAR 1938

LAMP IS HEAVY, A
Russell, S. M.

FEMININE TOUCH, THE
RANK 1956

LAST FRONTIERS
MacLean, A.

SECRET WAYS, THE
RANK 1960

LAST HOURS OF SANDRA LEE, THE
Sansom, W.

WILD AFFAIR, THE
BL 1965

LAST OF MRS. CHEYNEY, THE (P)
Lonsdale, F.

LAW AND THE LADY, THE
MGM 1951

LAST OF THE BAD MEN
Monoghan, J.

BAD MEN OF TOMBSTONE
ABP 1949

LAST OF THE MOHICANS
Cooper, J. F.

LAST OF THE REDSKINS
COL 1949

LAWRENCEVILLE SCHOOL TALES
Johnson, O.

HAPPY YEARS, THE
MGM 1950

LEADING LADY (P)
Gordon, R.

ACTRESS, THE
MGM 1953

LEGACY OF A SPY
Maxfield, H. S.

DOUBLE MAN, THE
WAR 1966

LEATHER STOCKING TALES
Cooper, J. F.

TOMAHAWK TRAIL, THE
UA 1950

LEGEND OF THE LATIN QUARTER
Moss, A. *and* Marvel, E.

HER WONDERFUL LIE
COL 1950

LEININGEN VERSUS THE ANTS
Stephenson, C.

NAKED JUNGLE, THE
PAR 1953

LE MORTE D'ARTHUR
Malory, *Sir* T.

KNIGHTS OF THE ROUND TABLE
MGM 1954

LETTER TO FIVE WIVES, A
Klempner, J.

LETTER TO THREE WIVES, A
FOX 1948

LIFE AND DEATH OF THE
   WICKED LADY SKELTON, THE
King-Hall, M.

WICKED LADY, THE
GFD 1946

ORIGINAL TITLE	FILM TITLE
LIFEMANSHIP Potter, S.	**SCHOOL FOR SCOUNDRELS** WAR 1960
LIFE WITH MOTHER SUPERIOR Trahey, J.	**TROUBLE WITH ANGELS, THE** COL 1965
LIGHT OF DAY, THE Ambler, E.	**TOPKAPI** UA 1964
LIGHTS OUT Kendrick, B. H.	**BRIGHT VICTORY** UI 1951
LIKES OF 'ER, THE (P) McEvoy, C.	**SALLY IN OUR ALLEY** RKO 1932
LINE ON GINGER Maugham, R.	**INTRUDER, THE** BL 1953
LIONS AT THE KILL Catto, M.	**SEVEN THIEVES** FOX 1960
LISA AND DAVID Rubin, T. I.	**DAVID AND LISA** BL 1963
LITTLE LAMBS EAT IVY (P) Langley, N.	**FATHER'S DOING FINE** ABP 1952
LITTLE MR. JIM Wadelton, T. D.	**ARMY BRAT** MGM 1946
LIVING AND THE DEAD, THE Boileau, P. *and* Narcejac, T.	**VERTIGO** GALA 1958
LOBO AND OTHER STORIES Seton, E. T.	**LEGEND OF LOBO, THE** DISNEY 1962
LOCK AND THE KEY, THE Gruber, F.	**MAN IN THE VAULT** RKO 1957
LODGER, THE Lowdnes, *Mrs.* M. B.	**MAN IN THE ATTIC, THE** FOX 1953
LODGER, THE Lowndes, *Mrs.* M. B.	**PHANTOM FIEND, THE** OLY 1935
LONDON WALL (P) Druten, J. van.	**AFTER OFFICE HOURS** MGM 1935
LONE HOUSE MYSTERY, THE Wallace, E.	**ATTEMPT TO KILL** AA 1961
LONELY GIRL, THE O'Brien, E.	**GIRL WITH GREEN EYES** UA 1964
LONELY SKIER, THE Innes, H.	**SNOWBOUND** RKO 1948

419

ORIGINAL TITLE	FILM TITLE
LONG HAUL Bezzerides, A. I.	**THEY DRIVE BY NIGHT** WAR 1940
LONG NIGHT, THE Truss, S.	**LONG KNIFE, THE** AA 1958
LOOK OF EAGLES Foote, J. T.	**KENTUCKY** FOX 1938
LORD ARTHUR SAVILE'S CRIME Wilde, O.	**FLESH AND FANTASY** UN 1943
LOSER WINS (P) Sartre, J-P.	**CONDEMNED OF ALTONA, THE** FOX 1964
LOSS OF ROSES, A (P) Inge, W.	**WOMAN OF SUMMER** FOX 1963
LOST COUNTRY, THE Salamanca, J. R.	**WILD IN THE COUNTRY** FOX 1961
LOST ECSTASY Rinehart, M. R.	**I TAKE THIS WOMAN** PAR 1931
LOST IN THE STARS (P) Anderson, M.	**CRY, THE BELOVED COUNTRY** BL 1951
LOTTIE AND LISA Kastner, E.	**PARENT TRAP, THE** DISNEY 1961
LOUIS BERETTI Clarke, D. H.	**BORN RECKLESS** FOX 1930
LOVE FROM A STRANGER (P) Vosper, F.	**STRANGER WALKED IN, A** REN 1949
LOVE FROM EVERYBODY Hanley, C.	**DON'T BOTHER TO KNOCK** WAR 1961
LULLABY, THE (P) Knoblock, E.	**SIN OF MADELON CLAUDET** MGM 1931

M

McLEOD'S FOLLY Bromfield, L.	**JOHNNY VAGABOND** UA 1943
MADAME BOVARY Flaubert, G.	**UNHOLY LOVE** HP 1932
MADAM TIC-TAC (P) Cary, F. L. *and* Weathers, P.	**NO ROAD BACK** RKO 1956
MAGISTRATE, THE (P) Pinero, *Sir* A. W.	**THOSE WERE THE DAYS** PAR 1940

MAGNIFICENT DEVILS
Crockett, L. H.

PROUD AND PROFANE
PAR 1956

MAIN STREET
Lewis, S.

I MARRIED A DOCTOR
IN 1936

MAJOR THOMPSON LIVES IN
    FRANCE
Daninos, P.

FRENCH ARE A FUNNY RACE,
    THE (USA title)
CONTINENTAL 1957

MAJOR THOMPSON LIVES IN
    FRANCE
Daninos, P.

DIARY OF MAJOR THOMPSON,
    THE
GALA 1957

MAKE YOU A GOOD WIFE
Foldes, Y.

MY OWN TRUE LOVE
PAR 1948

MALE ANIMAL, THE (P)
Thurber, J. *and* Nugent, E.

SHE'S WORKING HER WAY
    THROUGH COLLEGE
WAR 1952

MAN, THE (P)
Dinelli, M.

BEWARE MY LOVELY
RKO 1952

MAN ABOUT A DOG, A
Coppel, A.

OBSESSION
GFD 1949

MAN AT THE CARLTON
Wallace, E.

MAN AT THE CARLTON TOWER
AA 1961

MAN IN CHARGE
Jessup, R.

YOUNG DON'T CRY, THE
COL 1957

MAN IN HALF MOON STREET,
    THE (P)
Lyndon, B.

MAN WHO COULD CHEAT
    DEATH, THE
PAR 1959

MAN IN POSSESSION, THE (P)
Harwood, H. M.

PERSONAL PROPERTY
MGM 1937

MAN OF PROPERTY, THE
Galsworthy, J.

FORSYTE SAGA, THE
MGM 1949

MAN OF THE WEST
Yordan, P.

GUN GLORY
MGM 1957

MAN RUNNING
Jepson, S.

STAGE FRIGHT
WAR 1949

MANTRAP
Lewis, S.

UNTAMED
PAR 1940

MAN WHO BOUGHT LONDON, THE
Wallace, E.

TIME TO REMEMBER
AA 1962

MAN WHO KNEW, THE
Wallace, E.

PARTNERS IN CRIME
AA 1960

ORIGINAL TITLE	FILM TITLE
MAN WHO ROCKED THE BOAT, THE Keating, W. J. *and* Carter, R.	SLAUGHTER ON 10th AVENUE UI 1957
MANY SPLENDOURED THING, A Han Suyin	LOVE IS A MANY SPLENDOURED THING FOX 1955
MARBLE FOREST Durrant, T.	MACABRE ABP 1957
MARIA CHAPDELAINE Hemon, L.	NAKED HEART, THE BL 1950
MARK OF DUST White, J. M. E.	MASK OF DOUBT EXCLUSIVE 1954
MARK OF ZORRO McCulley, J.	MARK OF THE RENEGADE UI 1951
MARRIAGE BED, THE Pascal, E.	HUSBAND'S HOLIDAY PAR 1931
MARTIN ARROWSMITH Lewis, S.	ARROWSMITH UA 1931
MARTIN EDEN London, J.	ADVENTURES OF MARTIN EDEN, THE COL 1942
MARY ANN Karmel, A.	SOMETHING WILD UA 1962
MARY DEARE, THE Innes, H.	WRECK OF THE MARY DEARE, THE MGM 1959
MASK, THE Wilson, J. R.	BEHIND THE MASK BL 1958
MATTER OF CONVICTION, A Hunter, E.	YOUNG SAVAGES, THE UA 1960
MAURICE GUEST Richardson, H. H.	RHAPSODY MGM 1954
MEET A BODY (P) Launder, F. *and* Gilliat, S.	GREEN MAN, THE BL 1956
MEET THE TIGER Charteris, L.	SAINT MEETS THE TIGER, THE REP 1943
MEGSTONE PLOT, THE Garve, A.	TOUCH OF LARCENY, A PAR 1959

ORIGINAL TITLE	FILM TITLE
MELVILLE GOODWIN, USA Marquand, J. P.	THEIR SECRET AFFAIR WAR 1956
MEMOIRS OF A BRITISH AGENT Lockhart, *Sir* R. H. B.	BRITISH AGENT IN 1934
MEMOIRS OF A PHYSICIAN Dumas, A.	BLACK MAGIC UA 1949
MEMORY OF LOVE Breuer, B.	IN NAME ONLY RKO 1939
MEN OF IRON Pyle, H.	BLACK SHIELD OF FALWORTH, THE UI 1954
MERRILL'S MARAUDERS Ogburn, C.	MARAUDER, THE WAR 1962
MERRY GO ROUND Schnitzler, A.	LA RONDE COMMERCIAL 1951
MERTON OF THE MOVIES Wilson, H. L.	MAKE ME A STAR PAR 1932
METHINKS THE LADY Endore, G.	WHIRLPOOL, THE FOX 1951
MEXICAN, THE London, J.	FIGHTER, THE UA 1952
MEXICAN VILLAGE, A Niggli, J.	SOMBRERO MGM 1953
MICHAELS IN AFRICA, THE Michael, G.	DRUMS OF DESTINY NEW REALM 1962
MICHAEL STROGOFF Verne, J.	SOLDIER AND THE LADY, THE RKO 1937
MIDWIFE OF PONT CLERY Sandstrom, F.	JESSICA UA 1961
MIDWICH CUCKOOS, THE Wyndham, J.	VILLAGE OF THE DAMNED, THE MGM 1960
MILK WHITE UNICORN, THE Sandstrom, F.	WHITE UNICORN, THE CORFIELD 1947
MILLS OF GOD, THE Lothar, E.	ACT OF MURDER, AN UN 1948
MIND OF MR. REEDER, THE Wallace, E.	MIND OF MR. J. G. REEDER, THE RAYMOND 1939
MIRROR IN MY HOUSE O'Casey, S.	YOUNG CASSIDY MGM 1962

MISCHIEF
Armstrong, C.

DON'T BOTHER TO KNOCK
FOX 1952

MISS BISHOP
Aldrich, *Mrs*. B.

CHEERS FOR MISS BISHOP
UA 1941

MISS LONELYHEARTS
West, N.

LONELYHEARTS
UA 1959

MISS PINKERTON
Rinehart, M. R.

NURSE'S SECRET, THE
WAR 1941

MISTER MOSES
Catto, M.

MR. MOSES
UA 1965

MISTY OF CHINCOTEAGUE
Henry, M.

MISTY
FOX 1961

MOLL FLANDERS
Defoe, D.

AMOROUS ADVENTURES OF MOLL FLANDERS, THE
PAR 1964

MONEY DOESN'T MATTER (P)
D'Alton, L. L.

TALK OF A MILLION
ABP 1951

MONSIEUR LA SOURIS
Simenon, G.

MIDNIGHT EPISODE
COL 1951

MOON OVER MULBERRY STREET (P)
Cosentino, N.

WOMAN IN THE DARK
REP 1952

MORALS OF MARCUS ORDAYNE
Locke, W. J.

MORALS OF MARCUS, THE
GB 1935

MORELLA
Poe, E. A.

TALES OF TERROR
WAR 1963

MORTGAGE ON LIFE
Baum, V.

WOMAN'S SECRET, A
RKO 1949

MOTHER CAREY'S CHICKENS
Wiggin, K. D.

SUMMER MAGIC
DISNEY 1963

MOUNTAINS ARE MY KINGDOM
Hardy, S.

FORBIDDEN VALLEY
UN 1938

MOUNTEBANK
Locke, W. J.

SIDESHOW OF LIFE
WAR 1931

MOUSE THAT ROARED, THE
Wibberly, L.

MOUSE ON THE MOON
UA 1962

MOVING TARGET, THE
Macdonald, R.

HARPER
WAR 1967

424

ORIGINAL TITLE	FILM TITLE
MR. AND MRS. CUGAT Rorick, I. S.	**ARE HUSBANDS NECESSARY?** PAR 1942
MR. AND MRS. HADDOCK ABROAD Stewart, D. O.	**FINN AND HATTIE** PAR 1931
MR. ANGELL COMES ABOARD Booth, C. G.	**JOHNNY ANGEL** RKO 1945
MR. ARKADIN Welles, O.	**CONFIDENTIAL REPORT** WAR 1955
MR. BUNTING AT WAR Greenwood, R.	**SALUTE JOHN CITIZEN** BN 1942
MR. HOBBS' HOLIDAY Streeter, E.	**MR. HOBBS TAKES A VACATION** FOX 1962
M. RIPOIS AND HIS NEMESIS Hemon, L.	**KNAVE OF HEARTS** ABP 1954
MR. ISAACS Crawford, F. M.	**SON OF INDIA** MGM 1931
MR. JUSTICE HOLMES Biddle, F.	**MAGNIFICENT YANKEE, THE** MGM 1950
MR. MIDSHIPMAN EASY Marryat, F.	**MIDSHIPMAN EASY** ATP 1935
MR. PROHACK Bennett, A.	**DEAR MR. PROHACK** GFD 1949
MRS. CHRISTOPHER Myers, E.	**BLACKMAILER** GFD 1951
MRS. McGINTY'S DEAD Christie, A.	**MURDER MOST FOUL** MGM 1963
MRS. ROSS Nicholson, R.	**WHISPERERS, THE** UA 1966
MULE FOR THE MARQUESA, A O'Rourke, F.	**PROFESSIONALS, THE** COL 1966
MURDER FOR A WANTON Chambers, W.	**SINNER TAKE ALL** MGM 1936
MURDER FOR THE MILLIONS Chapman, R.	**MURDER REPORTED** COL 1957
MURDER IN THE BUD Bottome, P.	**DANGER SIGNAL** WAR 1945
MURDER MISTAKEN (P) Green, J.	**CAST A DARK SHADOW** EROS 1955

MURDER OF STEPHEN KESTER Ashbrook, H.	**GREEN EYES** CHESTERFIELD 1934
MURDER OF THE CIRCUS QUEEN, THE Abbot, A.	**CIRCUS QUEEN MURDER** COL 1933
MURDERS IN THE RUE MORGUE Poe, E. A.	**PHANTOM OF THE RUE MORGUE** WAR 1954
MUSCLE BEACH Wallach, I.	**DON'T MAKE WAVES** MGM 1966
MUTINY Tilsley, F.	**H.M.S. DEFIANT** COL 1962
MY LIFE AND HARD TIMES Thurber, J.	**RISE AND SHINE** FOX 1941
MY OLD MAN Hemingway, E.	**UNDER MY SKIN** FOX 1950
MYSTERY IN FLORENCE Fenton, E.	**ESCAPADE IN FLORENCE** DISNEY 1963
MYSTERY OF DR. FU MANCHU Rohmer, S.	**MYSTERIOUS DR. FU MANCHU** PAR 1929
MYSTERY OF HUNTING'S END Eberhart, M. G.	**MYSTERY HOUSE** WAR 1938
MY TEN YEARS AS A COUNTERSPY Morros, B.	**CONFESSIONS OF A COUNTERSPY** RANK 1960
MY THREE ANGELS (P) Husson, A.	**WE'RE NO ANGELS** PAR 1955
MY TRUE LOVE Teilhet, D. L.	**NO ROOM FOR THE GROOM** UI 1952

N

NEPOMUK OF THE RIVER Pilkington, R.	**GOLDEN HEAD, THE** CINERAMA 1965
NEWHAVEN-DIEPPE Simenon, G.	**TEMPTATION HARBOUR** AB 1947
NIGHT BUS Adams, S. H.	**IT HAPPENED ONE NIGHT** COL 1934
NIGHT CRY Stuart, W. L.	**WHERE THE SIDEWALK ENDS** FOX 1950

NORTH WEST PASSAGE Roberts, K.	FRONTIER RANGERS MGM 1959
NORTH WEST PASSAGE Roberts, K.	MISSION OF DANGER MGM 1959
NORWICH VICTIMS, THE Beeding, F.	DEAD MEN TELL NO TALES ALL 1939
NOSE ON MY FACE, THE Payne, L.	GIRL IN THE HEADLINES BL 1963
NOTHING TO LOSE Minney, R. J.	TIME GENTLEMEN PLEASE! ABP 1952
NOT SO LONG AGO (P) Richman, A.	LET'S DO IT AGAIN COL 1953
NOT TOO NARROW, NOT TOO DEEP Sale, R.	STRANGE CARGO MGM 1940
NOW BARABBAS (P) Home, W. D.	NOW BARABBAS WAS A ROBBER WAR 1949
NURSE IS A NEIGHBOUR Jones, J.	NURSE ON WHEELS WAR 1963
NUTMEG TREE Sharp, M.	JULIA MISBEHAVES MGM 1948

O

ODOUR OF VIOLETS Kendrick, B. H.	EYES IN THE NIGHT MGM 1942
OFF-ISLANDERS, THE Benchley, N.	RUSSIANS ARE COMING – THE RUSSIANS ARE COMING, THE UA 1966
OFF THE RECORD (P) Hay, I. *and* King-Hall, S.	CARRY ON ADMIRAL REN 1957
OIL FOR THE LAMPS OF CHINA Hobart, A. T.	LAW OF THE TROPICS WAR 1941
OLDEST CONFESSION, THE Condon, R.	HAPPY THIEVES, THE UA 1961
OLD JUDGE PRIEST Cobb, I. S.	SUN SHINES BRIGHT, THE REP 1953
OLD LADY SHOWS HER MEDALS, THE (P) Barrie, *Sir* J. M.	SEVEN DAYS LEAVE PAR 1930

ORIGINAL TITLE	FILM TITLE
'OLD LADY 31' (P) Crothers, R.	**CAPTAIN IS A LADY, THE** MGM 1940
OLD MAN MINICK Ferber, E.	**EXPERT, THE** WAR 1932
OLIMPIA Cole, B.	**BOBO, THE** WAR 1967
OLYMPIA (P) Molnar, F.	**BREATH OF SCANDAL, A** PAR 1960
ONCE AND FUTURE KING, THE White, T. H.	**CAMELOT** WAR 1966
ONCE OFF GUARD Wallis, J. H.	**WOMAN IN THE WINDOW, THE** RKO 1944
ONE PAIR OF FEET Dickens, M.	**LAMP STILL BURNS, THE** TC 1943
ONE STEP FROM MURDER Meynell, L.	**PRICE OF SILENCE, THE** GN 1959
ONEUPMANSHIP Potter, S.	**SCHOOL FOR SCOUNDRELS** WAR 1960
ON MONDAY NEXT (P) King, P.	**CURTAIN UP** GFD 1952
ON THE TRAIL Harris, F.	**COWBOY** COL 1957
OPERATION CICERO Moyzisch, L. C.	**FIVE FINGERS** FOX 1952
OPERATION TERROR Gordons, The	**GRIP OF FEAR, THE** COL 1962
ORCHARD WALLS, THE (P) Delderfield, R. F.	**NOW AND FOREVER** ABP 1955
ORDEAL, THE Collins, D.	**SHIP FROM SHANGHAI** MGM 1930
ORPHEUS DESCENDING (P) Williams, T.	**FUGITIVE KIND, THE** UA 1960
OTHER MAN, THE Turney, C.	**BACK FROM THE DEAD** FOX 1957
OUR VIRGIN ISLAND White, R.	**VIRGIN ISLAND** BL 1958

ORIGINAL TITLE	FILM TITLE
OUT OF THE FRYING PAN (P) Swann, F.	**YOUNG AND WILLING** UA 1943
OX-BOW INCIDENT, THE Clark, W. van T.	**STRANGE INCIDENT** FOX 1943

P

PAID IN FULL Cronin, M.	**JOHNNY ON THE SPOT** FANCEY 1954
PAINTED VEIL, THE Maugham, W. S.	**SEVENTH SIN, THE** MGM 1957
PAIVA: QUEEN OF LOVE Schirokauer, A.	**IDOL OF PARIS, THE** GFD 1948
PARAGON, THE (P) Pertwee, R. *and* Pertwee, M.	**SILENT DUST** ABP 1952
PART-TIME WIVES Baldwin, F.	**WEEK-END MARRIAGE** IN 1932
PASO POR AQUI Rhodes, E. M.	**FOUR FACES WEST** UA 1948
PASSING OF THE BLACK EAGLE Henry, O.	**BLACK EAGLE** COL 1948
PASSPORT TO OBLIVION Leasor, J.	**WHERE THE SPIES ARE** MGM 1965
PATROL Macdonald, P.	**LOST PATROL** RKO 1934
PATTERN OF ISLANDS Grimble, *Sir* A.	**PACIFIC DESTINY** BL 1956
PEABODY'S MERMAIDS Jones, G. P. *and* Jones, C. B.	**MR. PEABODY AND THE MERMAID** UN 1948
PENROD Tarkington, B.	**BY THE LIGHT OF THE SILVERY** **MOON** WAR 1953
PENTHOUSE MYSTERY Queen, E.	**ELLERY QUEEN AND THE** **PENTHOUSE MYSTERY** COL 1941
PERFECT CRIME Queen, E.	**ELLERY QUEEN AND THE** **PERFECT CRIME** COL 1941
PERSISTENT WARRIORS, THE (P) Arundel, E.	**GREEN FINGERS** BN 1947

ORIGINAL TITLE	FILM TITLE
PERSONS IN HIDING Hoover, J. E.	**QUEEN OF THE MOB** PAR 1940
PERSONS IN HIDING Hoover, J. E.	**PAROLE FIXER** PAR 1940
PETRIFIED FOREST, THE (P) Sherwood, R. E.	**ESCAPE IN THE DESERT** WAR 1945
PHANTOM CROWN Harding, B.	**JUAREZ** WAR 1939
PHILADELPHIAN, THE Powell, R.	**CITY JUNGLE, THE** WAR 1959
PHILADELPHIA STORY, THE (P) Barry, P.	**HIGH SOCIETY** MGM 1956
PHOTO FINISH Mason, H.	**FOLLOW THAT HORSE!** WAR 1959
PIGEON FLY HOME Liggett, T.	**PIGEON THAT WORKED A MIRACLE, THE** DISNEY 1958
PILLARS OF MIDNIGHT, THE Trevor, E.	**80,000 SUSPECTS** RANK 1963
PIONEER GO HOME Powell, R.	**FOLLOW THAT DREAM** UA 1962
PITY MY SIMPLICITY Massie, C.	**LOVE LETTERS** PAR 1945
PLEASURE ISLAND Maier, W.	**GIRLS OF PLEASURE ISLAND, THE** PAR 1953
POLONAISE Leslie, D.	**SONG TO REMEMBER, A** COL 1945
POLTERGEIST, THE (P) Harvey, F.	**THINGS HAPPEN AT NIGHT** REN 1947
PORTRAIT OF A REBEL Syrett, N.	**WOMAN REBELS, A** RKO 1936
POTIPHAR'S WIFE Middleton, E.	**HER STRANGE DESIRE** POWERS 1932
POWER AND THE GLORY, THE Greene, G.	**FUGITIVE, THE** RKO 1947
PRELUDE Abrahall, C. H.	**WHEREVER SHE GOES** ABP 1950

PRELUDE TO NIGHT
Stoddart, D.

RUTHLESS
EL 1948

PRISONERS ARE PEOPLE
Scudder, K. J.

UNCHAINED
WAR 1954

PRIVATE EAR, THE (P)
Shaffer, P.

PAD, THE
UI 1967

PRIVATE LIFE
Hackney, A.

I'M ALRIGHT JACK
BL 1959

PSYCHE '63
Ligneris, F.

PSYCHE '59
BL 1964

PUNITIVE ACTION
Robb, J.

DESERT SAND
UA 1955

PUZZLE FOR FIENDS
Quentin, P.

STRANGE AWAKENING, THE
AA 1958

PUZZLE OF THE BRIAR PIPE
Palmer, S.

MURDER ON A BRIDLE PATH
RKO 1938

PUZZLE OF THE PAPER TREE
Palmer, S.

MURDER ON A HONEYMOON
RKO 1935

PYGMALION (P)
Shaw, G. B.

MY FAIR LADY
WAR 1964

PYLON
Faulkner, W.

TARNISHED ANGELS
UI 1957

Q

'Q' SHIPS AND THEIR STORY
Chatterton, E. K.

BLOCKADE
RKO 1928

QUALITY
Sumner, *Mrs.* C. R.

PINKY
FOX 1949

QUEEN IN DANGER
Trevor, E.

MANTRAP
EXCLUSIVE 1953

QUEEN'S DOCTOR, THE
Neumann, R.

KING IN SHADOW
BL 1959

QUEEN'S HUSBAND, THE (P)
Sherwood, R. E.

ROYAL BED
RKO 1931

**QUEEN WAS IN THE PARLOUR,
    THE** (P)
Coward, N.

TONIGHT IS OURS
PAR 1933

QUENTIN DURWARD
Scott, *Sir* W.

**ADVENTURES OF QUENTIN
    DURWARD, THE**
MGM 1955

R

RACER, THE Ruesch, H.	**RACERS, THE** FOX 1954
RACER, THE Ruesch, H.	**MEN AGAINST SPEED** FOX 1958
RAGE OF THE VULTURE, THE Moorehead, A.	**THUNDER IN THE EAST** PAR 1951
RAGGED MESSENGER, THE Maxwell, W. B.	**MADONNA OF THE STREETS** COL 1930
RAIN (P) Maugham, W. S.	**MISS SADIE THOMPSON** COL 1954
RAINS CAME, THE Bromfield, L.	**RAINS OF RANCHIPUR, THE** FOX 1955
RAPTURE IN MY RAGS Hastings, P.	**RAPTURE** FOX 1964
RAWHIDE JUSTICE Raine, W. M.	**MAN FROM BITTER RIDGE, THE** GFD 1955
REAR CAR (P) Rose, E. E.	**MURDER IN THE PRIVATE CAR** MGM 1934
RECOLLECTIONS OF VESTA TILLEY De Frece, *Lady*	**AFTER THE BALL** BL 1957
RELATIONS ARE BEST APART (P) Lewis, E.	**WHAT EVERY WOMAN WANTS** ADELPHI 1954
RENFREW'S LONG TRAIL Erskine, L. Y.	**DANGER AHEAD** MON 1940
RENFREW RIDES AGAIN Erskine, L. Y.	**FIGHTING MAD** MON 1939
RENFREW RIDES NORTH Erskine, L. Y.	**YUKON FLIGHT** MON 1940
RENFREW RIDES THE RANGE Erskine, L. Y.	**CRASHING THRU'** MON 1939
REQUIEM FOR A NUN Faulkner, W.	**SANCTUARY** FOX 1960
RESTLESS Macdonald, J. P.	**MAN TRAP** PAR 1961
RETRIBUTION Curwood, J. O.	**TIMBER FURY** EAGLE-LION 1950

RETURN TO WOODS
Hodson, J. L.

KING AND COUNTRY
WAR 1965

RINGER, THE (P)
Wallace, E.

PHANTOM STRIKES, THE
MON 1939

RING FOR CATTY (P)
Cargill, P. *and* Beale, J.

TWICE ROUND THE DAFFODILS
AA 1962

RIPPER FROM RAWHIDE
Cushman, D.

TIMBERJACK
REP 1954

ROAD TO ROME, THE (P)
Sherwood, R. E.

JUPITER'S DARLING
MGM 1954

ROAD TO SAN JACINTO
Foreman, L. L.

ARROW IN THE DUST
ABP 1954

ROAD TO SOCORRO, THE
Locke, C. O.

MANHUNT
FOX 1958

ROGUE MALE
Household, G.

MANHUNT
FOX 1941

ROME HAUL
Edmonds, W. D.

FARMER TAKES A WIFE, THE
FOX 1953

ROMMEL
Young, D.

ROMMEL – DESERT FOX
FOX 1951

ROOM 13
Wallace, E.

MYSTERY OF ROOM 13
ALL 1941

ROSALIND (P)
Barrie, *Sir* J. M.

FOREVER FEMALE
PAR 1953

ROSE AND THE FLAME, THE
Lauritzen, J.

KISS OF FIRE
GFD 1955

ROUND THE WORLD IN 80 DAYS
Verne, J.

AROUND . . .
UA 1957

ROUND-UP, THE
Mulford, C. E.

HILLS OF OLD WYOMING
PAR 1937

ROUGHSHOD
Fox, N. A.

GUNSMOKE
GFD 1952

ROUGH SKETCH
Sylvester, R.

WE WERE STRANGERS
COL 1949

ROYAL CANADIAN MOUNTED POLICE Fetherstonhaugh, R. C.	**NORTH WEST MOUNTED POLICE** PAR 1940
ROYAL FAMILY, THE (P) Kaufman, G. S. *and* Ferber, E.	**ROYAL FAMILY OF BROADWAY** PAR 1930

S

SACAJAWEA OF THE SHOSHONES Emmons, D. G.	**FAR HORIZONS, THE** PAR 1955
SACRED FLAME (P) Maugham, W. S.	**RIGHT TO LIVE, THE** WAR 1935
SAGA OF BILLY THE KID Burns, W. N.	**BILLY THE KID** MGM 1941
SAINT JOHNSON Burnett, W. R.	**LAW AND ORDER** UN 1932
SALUTE TO THE GODS Campbell, *Sir* M.	**BURN 'EM UP O'CONNOR** MGM 1939
SAN QUENTIN Duffy, C. *and* Jennings, D.	**MEN BEHIND BARS** ABP 1954
SAN QUENTIN Duffy, C. *and* Jennings, D.	**STEEL CAGE, THE** GN 1956
SATURDAY'S CHILDREN (P) Anderson, M.	**MAYBE IT'S LOVE** WAR 1930
SEA OF TROUBLES Duras, M.	**SEA WALL** RANK 1957
SEA WOLF, THE London, J.	**WOLF LARSEN** ABP 1959
SEA WYF AND BISCUIT Scott, J. D.	**SEA-WIFE** FOX 1957
SECOND MAN (P) Behrman, S. N.	**HE KNEW WOMEN** RKO 1930
SECRET AGENT, THE Conrad, J.	**SABOTAGE** REP 1939
SEE NAPLES AND DIE (P) Rice, E.	**OH! SAILOR, BEHAVE!** WAR 1931
SEND ANOTHER COFFIN Presnell, F. G.	**SLIGHTLY HONOURABLE** UA 1939

ORIGINAL TITLE	FILM TITLE
SENTIMENTALISTS Collins, D.	SAL OF SINGAPORE PATHE 1929 HIS WOMAN PAR 1931
SERGEANT YORK AND HIS PEOPLE Cowan, S. K.	SERGEANT YORK WAR 1941
SERVICE (P) Anthony, C. L.	LOOKING FORWARD MGM 1933
7½ CENTS Bissell, R. P.	PAJAMA GAME WAR 1957
SEVEN PILLARS OF WISDOM Lawrence, T. E.	LAWRENCE OF ARABIA BL 1962
SHADES WILL NOT VANISH Fowler, H. M.	STRANGE INTRUDER ABP 1957
SHADOW AND THE PEAK, THE Mason, R.	PASSIONATE SUMMER, THE RANK 1958
SHADOW RANGE Bishop, C.	COW COUNTRY ABP 1953
SHAPE OF THINGS TO COME Wells, H. G.	THINGS TO COME UA 1936
SHE DIED YOUNG Kennington, A.	YOU CAN'T ESCAPE ABP 1955
SHETLAND BUS, THE Howarth, D.	SUICIDE MISSION EROS 1957
SHOOTING STAR (P) Thomas, B.	GREAT GAME, THE ADELPHI 1953
SHORE LEAVE (P) Osborne, H.	HIT THE DECK MGM 1954
SHORE LEAVE Wakeman, F.	KISS THEM FOR ME FOX 1957
SHORN LAMB, THE Locke, W. J.	STRANGERS IN LOVE PAR 1932
SHOW MUST GO ON, THE Verner, G.	TREAD SOFTLY APEX 1952
SIEGE AT DANCING BIRD, THE LeMay, A.	UNFORGIVEN, THE UA 1960
SIEGE OF BATTERSEA, THE Holles, R.	GUNS AT BATASI FOX 1964

ORIGINAL TITLE	FILM TITLE
SILENT REEFS Cottrell, D.	SECRET OF THE PURPLE REEF, THE FOX 1960
SILVER ROCK Short, L.	HELL'S OUTPOST REP 1954
SING A SONG OF MURDER Langham, J. R.	NIGHT IN NEW ORLEANS, A PAR 1942
SINISTER ERRAND Cheyney, P.	DIPLOMATIC COURIER FOX 1952
SIN OF SUSAN SLADE, THE Hume, D.	SUSAN SLADE WAR 1962
SINUHE, THE EGYPTIAN Waltari, M.	EGYPTIAN, THE FOX 1954
SIRE OF MALETROIT'S DOOR, THE Stevenson, R. L.	STRANGE DOOR, THE COL 1949
SISTER CARRIE Dreiser, T.	CARRIE PAR 1950
SIXTEEN HANDS Croy, H.	I'M FROM MISSOURI PAR 1939
SIXTH OF JUNE Shapiro, L.	D-DAY THE SIXTH OF JUNE FOX 1956
SKIN DEEP Kelland, C. B.	FOR BEAUTY'S SAKE FOX 1941
SKINNER'S DRESS SUIT (P) Dodge, H. I.	SKINNER STEPS OUT UN 1929
SKYSCRAPER Baldwin, F.	SKYSCRAPER SOULS MGM 1932
SLEEP LONG, MY LOVELY Waugh, H.	JIGSAW BL 1962
SLIGHT CASE OF MURDER, A (P) Runyon, D. *and* Lindsay, H.	STOP, YOU'RE KILLING ME WAR 1952
SMALL MIRACLE, THE Gallico, P.	NEVER TAKE NO FOR AN ANSWER INDEPENDENT 1951
SMALL MIRACLE (P) Krasna, N.	FOUR HOURS TO KILL PAR 1935
SMALL WOMAN, THE Burgess, A.	INN OF THE SIXTH HAPPINESS, THE FOX 1958

ORIGINAL TITLE	FILM TITLE
SMUGGLERS CIRCUIT Roberts, D.	**LAW AND DISORDER** BL 1957
SNOW BIRCH, THE Mantley, J.	**WOMAN OBSESSED, THE** FOX 1959
SOBBIN' WOMEN, THE Benet, S. V.	**SEVEN BRIDES FOR SEVEN BROTHERS** MGM 1954
SOLID! SAID THE EARL Carstairs, J. P.	**YANK IN ERMINE, A** MON 1955
SOME FACES IN THE CROWD Schulberg, B. W.	**FACE IN THE CROWD, A** WAR 1957
SOME MUST WATCH White, E. L.	**SPIRAL STAIRCASE, THE** RKO 1946
SON OF ANY WEDNESDAY (P) Resnik, M.	**ANY WEDNESDAY** WAR 1966
SORT OF TRAITORS, A Balchin, N.	**SUSPECT** BL 1960
SOUND OF HUNTING, A (P) Brown, H.	**EIGHT IRON MEN** COL 1952
SPANISH FARM, THE Mottram, R. H.	**ROSES OF PICARDY** EXCELLENT 1930
SPHINX HAS SPOKEN, THE Dekobra, M.	**FRIENDS AND LOVERS** RKO 1931
SPINNER IN THE SUN Reed, M.	**VEILED WOMAN** FOX 1929
SPINSTER Ashton-Warner, S.	**TWO LOVES** MGM 1960
SPLENDID CRIME, THE Goodchild, G.	**PUBLIC DEFENDER** RKO 1931
SPOONHANDLE Moore, R.	**DEEP WATERS** FOX 1948
SPRING CLEANING (P) Lonsdale, F.	**WOMEN WHO PLAY** GB 1932
SQUEAKER, THE Wallace, E.	**MURDER ON DIAMOND ROW** UA 1937
STAGE TO LORDSBURGH Haycox, E.	**STAGECOACH** UA 1939
STARS IN THEIR COURSES, THE Brown, H.	**EL DORADO** PAR 1967

STATE OF THE UNION (P) Lindsay, H. *and* Crouse, R.	WORLD AND HIS WIFE MGM 1948
STELLA Hartog, J. de.	KEY, THE COL 1958
STILL LIFE (P) Coward, N.	BRIEF ENCOUNTER CINEGUILD 1946
ST. IVES Stevenson, R. L.	SECRET OF ST. IVES, THE COL 1949
STONE FOR DANNY FISHER, A Robbins, H.	KING CREOLE PAR 1958
STOP AT A WINNER Delderfield, R. F.	ON THE FIDDLE AA 1961
STORY OF IVY, THE Lowndes, *Mrs.* M. B.	IVY UI 1947
STORY OF PETER MARSHALL, THE Marshall, C.	MAN CALLED PETER, FOX 1954
STORY OF THE TRAPP FAMILY SINGERS Trapp, M. A.	SOUND OF MUSIC, THE FOX 1965
STORY OF ZARAK KHAN, THE Bevan, A. J.	ZARAK COL 1956
STRANGE BOARDERS OF PALACE CRESCENT Oppenheim, E. P.	STRANGE BOARDERS GB 1938
STRANGE ONE, THE (P) Willingham, C.	END AS A MAN COL 1957
STRANGER AT HOME Sanders, G.	STRANGER CAME HOME EXCLUSIVE 1954
SUICIDE CLUB, THE Stevenson, R. L.	TROUBLE FOR TWO MGM 1936
SUSPENSE Graeme, B.	FACE IN THE NIGHT GN 1956
SWAMP WATER Bell, V.	LURE OF THE WILDERNESS FOX 1952
SWAN, THE (P) Molnar, F.	ONE ROMANTIC NIGHT UA 1930
SWEET ALOES Mallory, J.	GIVE ME YOUR HEART WAR 1936

SWIFT WATER
Annixter, P.

THOSE GALLOWAYS
DISNEY 1965

SYLVESTER
Hyams, E.

YOU KNOW WHAT SAILORS ARE
GFD 1953

T

TRACEY CROMWELL
Richter, C.

ONE DESIRE
UI 1955

TALENTED MR. RIPLEY, THE
Highsmith, P.

PURPLE NOON
HILLCREST 1961

TALES FROM THE SOUTH PACIFIC
Michener, J. A.

SOUTH PACIFIC
TODD AO 1958

TALISMAN, THE
Scott, *Sir* W.

KING RICHARD AND THE
    CRUSADERS
WAR 1954

TAMPICO
Hergesheimer, J.

WOMAN I STOLE, THE
COL 1933

TELL-TALE HEART, THE
Poe, E. A.

CALYPSO
BL 1956

TEMPLE TOWER
'Sapper'

BULLDOG DRUMMOND'S SECRET
    POLICE
PAR 1939

TEN AGAINST CAESAR
Granger, K. R. G.

GUN FURY
COL 1954

TENTACLES
Lyon, D.

HOUSE ON TELEGRAPH HILL, THE
FOX 1951

TENTACLES OF THE NORTH
Curwood, J. O.

SNOW DOG
ABP 1951

TESHA
Barcynska, *Baroness*

WOMAN IN THE NIGHT, THE
WW 1929

**THANKS GOD, I'LL TAKE IT
FROM HERE**
Allen, J. *and* Livingstone, M.

WITHOUT RESERVATION
RKO 1946

THAT UNCERTAIN FEELING
Amis, K.

ONLY TWO CAN PLAY
BL 1961

THERE WAS A LITTLE MAN
Jones, G. P. *and* Jones, C. B.

LUCK OF THE IRISH
FOX 1948

THERE'S ALWAYS JULIET (P)
Druten, J. van.

ONE NIGHT IN LISBON
PAR 1941

THESE OUR LOVERS Fineman, I.	**LOVERS MUST LEARN** WAR 1962
THEY CAN'T HANG ME Ronald, J.	**WITNESS VANISHES, THE** UN 1939
THEY CRACKED HER GLASS SLIPPER Butler, G.	**THIRD TIME LUCKY** ANGOFILM 1948
THEY DREAM OF HOME Busch, N.	**TILL THE END OF TIME** RKO 1946
THEY KNEW WHAT THEY WANTED (P) Howard, S. C.	**LADY TO LOVE, A** MGM 1930
THEY WALK ALONE (P) Catto, M.	**DAUGHTER OF DARKNESS** PAR 1948
THEY WHO SERVE Jennings, D. K.	**MASTER SPY** GN 1962
THIEVES' MARKET Bezzerides, A. I.	**THIEVES' HIGHWAY** FOX 1949
3rd AVENUE, NEW YORK McNulty, J. L.	**EASY COME, EASY GO** PAR 1947
THIRD ROUND, THE 'Sapper'	**BULLDOG DRUMMOND'S PERIL** PAR 1938
THIS IS NEW YORK (P) Sherwood, R. E.	**TWO KINDS OF WOMEN** PAR 1932
THIS WAS MY CHOICE Gouzenko, I.	**IRON CURTAIN** FOX 1948
THIS WAY OUT Ronald, J.	**SUSPECT, THE** UN 1944
THOMASINA Gallico, P.	**THREE LIVES OF THOMASINA, THE** DISNEY 1963
THOUSAND SHALL FALL, A Habe, H.	**HANGMEN ALSO DIE** UA 1943
THREE CUPS OF COFFEE Feiner, R.	**WOMAN'S ANGLE, A** ABP 1951
THREE GODFATHERS, THE Kyne, P. B.	**HELL'S HEROES** UN 1930
THREE MEN IN THE SNOW Kastner, E.	**PARADISE FOR THREE** MGM 1938

TREE OF LIBERTY Page, E.	**HOWARDS OF VIRGINIA, THE** COL 1940
TREVE Terhune, A. P.	**MIGHTY TREVE, THE** UN 1937
TRIAL BY TERROR Gallico, P.	**ASSIGNMENT – PARIS** COL 1952
TRILBY Du Maurier, G.	**SVENGALI** WAR 1931 REN 1954
TRUMPETS OF COMPANY K Chamberlain, W.	**IMITATION GENERAL** MGM 1958
TRUTH GAME, THE (P) Novello, I.	**BUT THE FLESH IS WEAK** MGM 1932
TUCKER'S PEOPLE Wolfert, I.	**FORCE OF EVIL** MGM 1949
TURN OF THE SCREW, THE James, H.	**INNOCENTS, THE** FOX 1961
TWENTY PLUS TWO Gruber, F.	**IT STARTED IN TOKYO** WAR 1961
TWENTY THOUSAND STREETS UNDER THE SKY Hamilton, P.	**BITTER HARVEST** RANK 1962
TWILIGHT OF HONOUR Dewlen, A.	**CHARGE IS MURDER, THE** MGM 1963
TWIN SOMBREROS Grey, Z.	**GUNFIGHTERS** COL 1947

TWO HOURS TO DOOM
George, P.
	**DR. STRANGELOVE; OR HOW I
	    LEARNED TO STOP WORRYING
	    AND LOVE THE BOMB**
	COL 1963

TWO O'CLOCK COURAGE Burgess, G.	**TWO IN THE DARK** RKO 1936
TYPEE Melville, H.	**ENCHANTED ISLAND** WAR 1958

U

UNCLE HARRY (P) Job, T.	**STRANGE AFFAIR OF UNCLE HARRY, THE** UN 1945

W

WARRIOR, THE
Slaughter, F. G.

NAKED IN THE SUN
RKO 1956

**WARTIME ADVENTURES OF PRESI-
DENT JOHN F. KENNEDY, THE**
Donovan, R. J.

PT 109
WAR 1963

WASHINGTON SQUARE
James, H.

HEIRESS, THE
PAR 1949

WATERLOO BRIDGE (P)
Sherwood, R.

GABY
MGM 1955

WAY OUT, THE
Graeme, B.

DIAL 999
AA 1955

WE
Lindbergh, C. A.

SPIRIT OF ST. LOUIS, THE
WAR 1956

WE ARE SEVEN
Troy, U.

SHE DIDN'T SAY NO!
ABP 1958

WEDNESDAY'S CHILD (P)
Atlas, L.

CHILD OF DIVORCE
RKO 1946

WEEKEND AT ZUYDCOOTE
Merle, R.

WEEKEND AT DUNKIRK
FOX 1965

WEEK-END GIRL
Fabian, W.

WEEK-ENDS ONLY
FOX 1932

WEEP NO MORE
Coffee, L.

ANOTHER TIME, ANOTHER PLACE
PAR 1958

WEREWOLF OF PARIS, THE
Endore, G.

CURSE OF THE WEREWOLF, THE
RANK 1960

WHAT SAY THEY (P)
Bridie, J.

YOU'RE ONLY YOUNG TWICE
ABP 1952

WHEELER-DEALERS, THE
Goodman, G. J. W.

SEPARATE BEDS
MGM 1964

WHEEL SPINS, THE
White, E. L.

LADY VANISHES, THE
MGM 1938

**WHEN KNIGHTHOOD WAS IN
FLOWER**
Major, C.

SWORD AND THE ROSE, THE
RKO 1953

ORIGINAL TITLE	FILM TITLE
WHEN KNIGHTHOOD WAS IN FLOWER (P) Kester, P.	SWORD AND THE ROSE, THE RKO 1953
WHERE THE PAVEMENT ENDS Russell, J.	SEA GOD, THE PAR 1930
WHISPERING SMITH Spearman, F. H.	WHISPERING SMITH SPEAKS FOX 1935
WHISPERING WOMAN Merner, G.	NOOSE FOR A LADY AA 1953
WHITE COLLARS (P) Ellis, E.	IDLE RICH MGM 1929 RICH MAN, POOR GIRL MGM 1938
WHITE SOUTH, THE Innes, H.	HELL BELOW ZERO COL 1953
WHITE STALLIONS OF VIENNA, THE Podhajsky, A.	FLIGHT OF THE WHITE STALLIONS, THE DISNEY 1963
WHO COULD ASK FOR ANYTHING MORE Swift, K.	NEVER A DULL MOMENT RKO 1950
WHO GOES THERE? Campbell, J. W.	THING FROM ANOTHER WORLD, THE RKO 1951
WHO IS SYLVIA? (P) Rattigan, T.	MAN WHO LOVED REDHEADS, THE BL 1954
WHO LIE IN GAOL Henry, J.	WEAK AND THE WICKED, THE ABP 1953
WHO WAS THAT LADY I SAW YOU WITH? (P) Krasna, N.	WHO WAS THAT LADY? COL 1960
WHY I QUIT SYNDICATED CRIME Vaus, J. *Jun.*	WIRETAPPER, THE EXCLUSIVE 1955
WIDE BOYS NEVER WORK Westerby, R.	SOHO INCIDENT COL 1956
WILD BILL HICKOK Wilstach, F.	PLAINSMAN, THE PAR 1936
WILD CALENDAR Block, L.	CAUGHT MGM 1948

WILDFIRE Grey, Z.	**RED CANYON** UN 1949
WILL SUCCESS SPOIL ROCK HUNTER? (P) Axelrod, G.	**OH! FOR A MAN!** FOX 1957
WINSTON AFFAIR, THE Fast, H.	**MAN IN THE MIDDLE** FOX 1963
WINTER JOURNEY (P) Odets, C.	**COUNTRY GIRL, THE** PAR 1954
WINTER WEARS A SHROUD Chapman, R.	**DELAVINE AFFAIR, THE** MON 1954
WISDOM OF FATHER BROWN, THE Chesterton, G. K.	**FATHER BROWN, DETECTIVE** PAR 1935
WISTERIA COTTAGE Coates, R. M.	**EDGE OF FURY** UA 1958
WITHIN THE TIDES Conrad, J.	**LAUGHING ANNE** REP 1953
WOMAN IN RED, THE Gilbert, A.	**MY NAME IS JULIA ROSS** COL 1945
WOMAN WITH A SWORD Noble, H.	**DRUMS IN THE DEEP SOUTH** RKO 1952
WOMEN, THE (P) Boothe, C.	**OPPOSITE SEX, THE** MGM 1956
WORLD IN MY POCKET, THE Chase, J. H.	**ON FRIDAY AT 11** BL 1961
WRATH OF GRAPES Wibberley, L.	**MOUSE THAT ROARED, THE** COL 1959

Y

YANKEE DARED, A Nevins, F. J.	**TRANSCONTINENTAL EXPRESS** REP 1950
YANKEE FROM OLYMPUS Bowen, C. D.	**MAN WITH THIRTY SONS, THE** MGM 1952
YEA, YEA, YEA McGill, A.	**PRESS FOR TIME** JARFID 1966
YELLOW FEVER Larteguy, J.	**NOT FOR HONOUR AND GLORY** COL 1965

A SUPPLEMENTARY LIST
OF FILMS
MADE IN 1968 AND 1969
AND REVISIONS

FILM-TITLE INDEX

A

ACCIDENT
MON 1967

Mosley, N.
Hodder & Stoughton

ADVENTURERS, THE
PAR 1968

Robbins, H.
Blond

AGE OF CONSENT
COL 1968

Lindsay, N.
Laurie

AIRPORT
RANK 1969

Hailey, A.
Joseph & Souvenir

ALL NEAT IN BLACK STOCKINGS
WAR 1968

Gaskell, J.
Hodder & Stoughton

AMBUSHERS, THE
COL 1968

Hamilton, D.
Coronet Bks.

AND NOW MIGUEL
UI 1965

Krumgold, J.
Cowell-Collier, N.Y.

ANNE OF THE THOUSAND DAYS
RANK 1969

Anderson, M. (P)
(*In* Best American plays) Crown, N.Y.

ANNIVERSARY, THE
WAR 1968

MacIlwraith, W. (P)
Evans

ARRANGEMENT, THE
WAR 1969

Kazan, E.
Collins

ASSASSINATION BUREAU, THE
PAR 1969

London, J. & Fish, R.
Deutsch

ASSIGNMENT 'K'
COL 1968

Howard, H.
Collins

B

BABY LOVE
AVCO EMBASSY 1969

Christian, T. C.
Cape

BACHELOR GIRL APARTMENT
WAR 1966

Resnik, M. (*Any Wednesday*) (P)
English Theatre

BACHELOR PARTY, THE
COL 1957

Chayefsky, P. (P)
(*In* Television plays)
Simon & Schuster, N.Y.

BATTLE FOR ANZIO, THE
COL 1968

Vaughan Thomas, W. (*Anzio*)
Longmans

BATTLE OF BRITAIN, THE
UA 1969

Wood, D. & Dempster, D.
(*Narrow margin, The*)
Arrow Bks.

BELLE DE JOUR
CURZON 1967

Kessel, J.
Barker

BERKELEY SQUARE
FOX 1933

Balderston, J. L. (P)
French

BEST MAN, THE
UA 1968

Vidal, G. (P)
Little, Brown. Boston

BETWEEN TWO WORLDS
WAR 1944

Vane, S. (*Outward bound*) (P)
Boni, N.Y.

BILLION DOLLAR BRAIN
UA 1967

Deighton, L.
Cape

BIRTHDAY PARTY, THE
CINERAMA 1968

Pinter, H. (P)
Methuen *and* French

BLACKBEARD'S GHOST
DISNEY 1968

Stahl, B.
Houghton, N.Y.

BLACK CAT, THE
UN 1934

Poe, E. A. (*In* Tales, poems, essays)
Various

BOFORS GUN, THE
UI 1968

McGrath, J. (*Events whilst guarding the Bofors gun*) (P)
Methuen

BOOM
UI 1968

Williams, T. (*Milk train doesn't stop here any more*) (P)
Secker & Warburg

BOSTON STRANGLER, THE
FOX 1968

Frank, G.
Cape

BOYS IN THE BAND, THE
WAR 1969

Crowley, M. (P)
Secker & Warburg

BRIDE WORE BLACK, THE
UA 1968

Irish, W.
Sphere Bks.

BRIDGE AT REMAGEN, THE
UA 1968

Hechler, K.
Panther

BULLITT
WAR 1968

Pike, R. L. (*Mute witness*)
Deutsch

BULLWHIP GRIFFIN
DISNEY 1968

Fleischman, S.
Penguin

BUSY BODY, THE
PAR 1968

Westlake, D.
Boardman

BUTTERCUP CHAIN, THE
COL 1969

Elliot, J.
Panther

C

CACTUS FLOWER
COL 1969

Burrows, A. (P)
French, N.Y.

CANDY
CINERAMA 1968

Southern, T. & Hoffenberg, M.
Geis

CAROLINE CHERIE
WAR 1968

Saint-Laurent, C.
Pan

CASS TIMBERLANE
MGM 1947

Lewis, S.
Cape

CASTLE KEEP
COL 1969

Eastlake, W.
Joseph

CATACOMBS
BL 1964

Bennett, J.
Abelard-Schuman

CAT AND THE CANARY, THE
PAR 1939

Willard, J.
Hudson

CATCH 22
PAR 1969

Heller, J.
Cape

CHARLY
CINERAMA 1968

Keyes, D. (*Flowers for Algernon*)
Cassell

CHITTY, CHITTY BANG BANG
UA 1968

Fleming, I.
Cape

CHRISTMAS TREE, THE
FOX 1969

Bataille, M.
Murray

COAST OF SKELETONS
BL 1964

Wallace, E. (*Sanders of the river*)
Ward Lock

COLD WAR SWAP, THE
PAR 1969

Thomas, R. (*Spy in the vodka*)
Hodder & Stoughton

COLD WIND IN AUGUST
UA 1961

Wohl, B.
Mayflower

COMPANY OF COWARDS
MGM 1965

Schaefer, J.
Mayflower

CONFESSIONS OF NAT TURNER, THE
FOX 1969

Styron, W.
Cape

CONNECTION, THE
CONT 1962

Gelber, J.
Faber

COOK, THE
CINEMA CENTER 1969

Kressing, H.
Panther

COOL HAND LUKE
WAR 1968

Pearce, D.
Penguin

CORSICAN BROTHERS, THE
MGM 1942

Dumas, A. (*Deux frères*)
Macmillan

COTTON COMES TO HARLEM
UA 1969

Himes, C.
Muller

COUNTERPOINT
UI 1968

Sillitoe, A. (*General, The*)
Allen

COVENANT WITH DEATH, A
WAR 1968

Becker, S.
Hamilton

CROOKED ROAD, THE
GALA 1964

West, M. L. (*Big story, The*)
Heinemann

D

DANCE OF DEATH, THE
PAR 1969

Strindberg, A. (P)
(*In* Eight famous plays) Duckworth

DANDY IN ASPIC, A
COL 1968

Marlowe, D.
Gollancz

**DANGEROUS DAYS OF KIOWA
JONES, THE**
MGM 1966

Adams, C.
Collins

DANGER ROUTE
UA 1968

York, A. (*Eliminator, The*)
Hutchinson

DAVID COPPERFIELD
FOX 1969

Dickens, C.
Various

DAY OF THE DOLPHIN, THE
UA 1969

Merle, R.
Weidenfeld & Nicolson

DEADFALL
FOX 1968

Cory, D.
Muller

DEATH DRUMS ALONG THE RIVER
PLANET 1963

Wallace, E. (*Sanders of the river*)
Ward Lock

DEATH OF A GUNFIGHTER
UI 1969

Patten, L. B. (*Law of the guns*)
Four Square Bks.

**DECLINE AND FALL . . . OF A
BIRDWATCHER**
FOX 1968

Waugh, E. (*Decline and Fall*)
Chapman & Hall

DESPERATE ONES, THE
AMERICAN INT. 1968

Ramati, A. (*Beyond the mountains*)
Penguin

DETECTIVE, THE FOX 1968	Thorp, R. Corgi
DEVIL RIDES OUT, THE WAR 1968	Wheatley, D. Hutchinson
DEVIL'S BRIGADE, THE UA 1968	Adleman, R. H. & Walton, G. Transworld
DEVIL'S OWN, THE FOX 1968	Curtis, P. Macdonald
DOCTOR FAUSTUS COL 1968	Marlowe, C. (*Tragical history of Doctor Faustus, The*) (P) Various
DON'T DRINK THE WATER AVCO EMBASSY 1969	Allen, W. (P) Random House, N.Y.
DON'T JUST STAND THERE RANK 1969	Williams, C. Cassell
DOWNHILL RACERS, THE PAR 1969	Hall, O. Bodley Head
DREAM OF KINGS, A WAR 1969	Petrakis, H. M. Barker
DUNWICH HORROR AMERICAN INT. 1969	Lovecraft, H. P. (*Shuttered room, The*) Gollancz

E

EBB TIDE PAR 1937	Stevenson, R. L. Various
ENTERTAINING MR. SLOANE WAR 1969	Orton, J. (P) Hamilton
EYE OF THE DEVIL MGM 1968	Loraine, P. (*Day of the arrow*) Collins

F

FAMILY WAY, THE BL 1966	Naughton, B. (*All in good time*) (P) French
FAREWELL, MY LOVELY RKO 1946	Chandler, R. Hamilton
FATHOM FOX 1968	Forrester, L. (*Girl called Fathom, A*) Heinemann

FIGURES IN A LANDSCAPE
CINEMA CENTER 1969

England, B.
Cape

FITZWOLLEY STRIKES BACK
UA 1968

Tyler, P. (*Garden of cucumbers, A*)
Gollancz

FIVE HAVE A MYSTERY TO SOLVE
CFF 1964

Blyton, E.
Hodder & Stoughton

FIXER, THE
MGM 1969

Malamud, B.
Eyre & Spottiswoode

FLASH, THE OTTER
DISNEY 1968

Liers, E. (*Otter's story*)
Hodder & Stoughton

FLASH THE SHEEPDOG
CFF 1966

Fidler, K.
Lutterworth

FLEA IN HER EAR, A
FOX 1968

Feydeau, G. (P)
Methuen

FOX, THE
WAR 1968

Lawrence, D. H. (*In* Tales of D. H. Lawrence, The)
Heinemann

FRAGMENT OF FEAR
COL 1969

Bingham, J.
Panther

G

GAILY, GAILY
UA 1969

Hecht, B.
Elek

GAMES, THE
FOX 1969

Atkinson, H.
Cassell

GENERATION
AVCO EMBASSY 1969

Goodhart, W. (P)
Doubleday, N.Y.

GENTLE GIANT
PAR 1968

Morley, W. (*Gentle Ben*)
Dutton, N.Y.

GETTING STRAIGHT
COL 1969

Kolb, K.
Barrie & Rockliff

GIRL ON THE MOTORCYCLE, THE
BL 1968

Mandiargues, A. P. de
Calder

GLORY GUYS
UA 1965

Birney, H. (*Dice of God, The*)
Holt, N.Y.

GOODBYE COLUMBUS
PAR 1969

Roth, P.
Deutsch

TITLE OF FILM	AUTHOR AND PUBLISHER
GOODBYE, MR. CHIPS MGM 1969	Hilton, J. Hodder & Stoughton
GOOD FAIRY, THE UN 1934	Molnar, F. Crown, N.Y.
GRADUATE, THE UA 1968	Webb, C. Penguin
GREAT BANK ROBBERY, THE WAR 1969	O'Rourke, F. Sphere
GREAT CATHERINE WAR 1968	Shaw, G. B. (P) Various
GREEN BERETS, THE WAR 1968	Moore, R. Crown, N.Y.
GUIDE FOR THE MARRIED MAN, THE FOX 1968	Tarloff, F. Price, Sterm, Sloan, L.A.
GUNS IN THE HEATHER DISNEY 1969	Amerman, L. Harcourt Brace, N.Y.

H

HAIL, HERO CINEMA CENTER 1969	Weston, J. Mackay, N.Y.
HALL OF MIRRORS, A PAR 1969	Stone, R. Bodley Head
HAMLET COL 1969	Shakespeare, W. (P) Various
HAMMERHEAD COL 1968	Mayo, J. Heinemann
HANGED MAN, THE RANK 1964	Hughes, D. B. (*Expendable man, The*) Deutsch
HANGOVER SQUARE FOX 1945	Hamilton, P. Constable
HAPPIEST MILLIONAIRE, THE DISNEY 1968	Biddle, C. D. & Crichton, K. Sphere
HEART IS A LONELY HUNTER, THE WAR 1968	McCullers, C. Penguin
HEART KEEPER, THE FOX 1969	Sagan, F. Murray
HELLO DOLLY! FOX 1968	Stewart, M. (P) D.B.S. Pubs., N.Y.

457

HEROIN GANG, THE MGM 1968	Wilder, R. (*Fruit of the poppy*) Allen
HILL, THE MGM 1965	Rigby, K. & Allen, R. S. Mayflower
HOFFMAN WAR 1969	Gebler, E. (*Shall I eat you now*) (P) Pan
HOLY MATRIMONY PAR 1943	Bennett, A. (*Great adventure*) Methuen
HOME OF THE BRAVE UA 1949	Laurents, A. (P) Dramatists, N.Y.
HONDO AND THE APACHES MGM 1966	L'Amour, L. Jenkins
HONEY POT, THE UA 1966	Sterling, T. (*Evil of the day, The*) Penguin
HONEY POT, THE UA 1966	Jonson, B. (*Volpone*) (P) Various
HORSE IN THE GREY FLANNEL SUIT, THE DISNEY 1968	Hatch, E. (*Year of the horse, The*) Crown, N.Y.
HOSTILE WITNESS UA 1968	Roffey, J. (P) Evans
HOUSE OF CARDS RANK 1968	Ellin, S. Macdonald
HOW SWEET IT IS WAR 1968	Resnik, M. (*Turquoise bikini, The*) Transworld

I

ICE STATION ZEBRA MGM 1968	McLean, A. Collins
IF I WERE KING PAR 1938	McCarthy, J. H. Heinemann
ILLUSTRATED MAN, THE WAR 1968	Bradbury, R. Hart-Davis
INADMISSIBLE EVIDENCE PAR 1968	Osborne, J. (P) Faber
IN COLD BLOOD COL 1968	Capote, T. Hamilton
INNOCENTS OF CHICAGO BI 1934	Drawbell, J. W. Collins

ISADORA
UI 1969

Duncan, I. (*My life*)
Gollancz

ISADORA
UI 1969

Stokes, S. (*Isadora Duncan*)
Pan

I WAKE UP SCREAMING
FOX 1941

Fisher, S.
Hale

J

JOHN AND MARY
FOX 1969

Jones, M.
Cape

JOHN BROWN'S BODY
FOX 1968

Benet, S. V.
Holt, Rinehart & Winston, N.Y.

JOURNEY TO SHILOH
UI 1968

Henry, W.
Gollancz

JULIUS CAESAR
MGM 1969

Shakespeare, W. (P)
Various

K

KES
UA 1969

Hines, B. (*Kestrel for a knave, A*)
Joseph

KILLER
CINECENTA 1969

Blake, N. (*Beast must die, The*)
Collins

KILLING OF SISTER GEORGE, THE
CINERAMA 1968

Marcus, F. (P)
French

KING LEAR
COL 1969

Shakespeare, W. (P)
Various

KISS ME KATE
MGM 1953

Shakespeare, W. (*Taming of the shrew, The*) (P)
Various

KREMLIN LETTER, THE
FOX 1969

Behn, N.
Allen

L

LADY IN CEMENT
FOX 1969

Albert, M. H.
Sphere

LADY IN THE CAR, THE
COL 1969

Japrisot, S. (*Lady in the car with glasses and a gun, The*)
Souvenir

LAST BATTLE, THE MGM 1968	Ryan, C. Collins
LAST GRENADE, THE CINERAMA 1969	Sherlock, J. (*Ordeal of Major Grigsby, The*) Hutchinson
LAST MAN ON EARTH, THE GOLDEN ERA 1964	Matheson, R. (*I am legend*) Bantam
LAST SAFARI, THE PAR 1968	Hanley, G. (*Gilligan's last elephant*) Collins
LAST SHOT YOU HEAR, THE FOX 1969	Fairchild, W. (*Sound of murder, The*) (P) French
LAST SUMMER FOX 1969	Hunter, E. Constable
LAUGHTER IN THE DARK UA 1969	Nabokov, V. Weidenfeld & Nicolson
LEARNING TREE, THE WAR 1969	Parks, G. Hodder & Stoughton
LIBERATION OF LORD BYRON JONES, THE COL 1969	Ford, J. H. Bodley Head
LIMBO LINE, THE MONARCH 1968	Canning, V. Heinemann
LIONHEART CFF 1968	Fullerton, A. Hodder & Stoughton
LION IN WINTER, THE AVCO EMBASSY 1969	Goldman, J. (P) French
LITTLE BIG MAN CINEMA CENTER 1969	Bergner, T. Eyre & Spottiswoode
LOCK UP YOUR DAUGHTERS COL 1968	Miles, B. (P) French
LOCK UP YOUR DAUGHTERS COL 1968	Vanbrugh, *Sir* J. (*Relapse, The*) (P) Various
LOCK UP YOUR DAUGHTERS COL 1968	Fielding, H. (*Rape upon rape*) (P) Various
LONDON NOBODY KNOWS, THE BL 1969	Fletcher, G. Penguin
LONG DAY'S DYING, THE PAR 1968	White, A. Hodder & Stoughton
LOOKING GLASS WAR, THE COL 1969	Le Carré, J. Gollancz

LOST CONTINENT, THE WAR 1968	Wheatley, D. (*Uncharted seas*) Hutchinson
LOST MAN, THE RANK 1969	Green, F. L. Joseph
LOVE IN AMSTERDAM MONARCH 1968	Freeling, N. Penguin
LOVE STORY BI 1941	Drawbell, J. W. (*Love and forget*) Collins
LOVING COL 1969	Ryan, J. M. (*Brook Wilson Ltd.*) Hodder Fawcett

M

McCABE FOX 1969	Naughton, E. Panther
MACKENNA'S GOLD COL 1969	Henry, W. Hammond
MADIGAN UI 1968	Dougherty, R. (*Commissioner, The*) Hart-Davis
MAD ROOM, THE COL 1968	Denham, R. & Percy, E. (*Ladies in retirement*) (P) Random House, N.Y.
MAGIC CHRISTIAN, THE COMMONWEALTH 1969	Southern, T. Deutsch
MAGUS, THE FOX 1969	Fowles, J. Cape
MALE ANIMAL WAR 1942	Thurber, J. & Nugent, E. (P) Random House, N.Y.
MAN CALLED HORSE, A CINEMA CENTER 1969	Johnson, D. M. Deutsch
MAN COULD GET KILLED, A RANK 1966	Walker, D. E. (*Adventure in diamonds*) Evans
MANDARINS, THE FOX 1969	De Beauvoir, S. Fontana
MAN FOR ALL SEASONS, A COL 1968	Bolt, R. (P) French
MAN IN THE SHADOW AA 1957	Davis, S. (*One man's secret*) Boardman
MARK, THE FOX 1961	Israel, C. E. Macmillan
MARLOWE MGM 1969	Chandler, R. (*Little sister, The*) Hamilton

461

MAROONED COL 1969	Caidin, M. Hodder & Stoughton
MARTY COL 1956	Chayevsky, P. (P) Simon & Schuster, N.Y.
MARY OF SCOTLAND RKO 1936	Anderson, M. (P) Harcourt, Brace, N.Y.
M.A.S.H. FOX 1969	Hooker, R. (*Mash*) Morrow, N.Y.
MAYERLING WAR 1968	Anet, C. Frewin
MIDNIGHT COWBOY UA 1969	Herlihy, J. L. Cape
MIDSUMMER NIGHT'S DREAM, A EAGLE 1969	Shakespeare, W. (P) Various
MIND OF MR. SOAMES, THE COL 1969	Maine, C. E. Panther
MIRAGE UI 1965	Fast, H. Mayflower
MISS ROBIN CRUSOE FOX 1954	Defoe, D. (*Adventures of Robinson Crusoe, The*) Various
MISTER MOSES UA 1965	Catto, M. Heinemann
MODERATO CANTABILE R. J. LEVY 1960	Duras, M. Calder
MOLLY MAGUIRES, THE PAR 1969	Lewis, A. H. (*Lament for the Molly Maguires*) Longmans
MONKEYS, GO HOME! DISNEY 1967	Wilkinson, G. R. (*Monkeys, The*) Macdonald
MONTE WALSH CINEMA CENTER 1969	Schaefer, J. Deutsch
MOST DANGEROUS MAN IN THE WORLD, THE RANK 1969	Kennedy, J. R. Joseph
MOVING TARGET, THE WAR 1966	Macdonald, R. Fontana
MURDER AHOY MGM 1964	Christie, A. (*Miss Marple*) Collins

MURDER, MY SWEET RKO 1944	Chandler, R. (*Farewell, my lovely*) Hamilton
MY FAIR LADY WAR 1964	Lerner, A. J. (P) Constable
MYRA BRECKENRIDGE FOX 1969	Vidal, G. Blond
MY SIDE OF THE MOUNTAIN PAR 1968	George, J. Bodley Head

N

NEW INTERNS, THE COL 1964	Frede, R. (*Interns, The*) Corgi
NICE GIRL LIKE ME, A AVCO EMBASSY 1969	Piper, A. (*Sweet and plenty*) Heinemann
NIGHT OF THE BIG HEAT PLANET 1967	Lymington, J. Hodder & Stoughton
NOBODY RUNS FOREVER RANK 1968	Cleary, J. (*High Commissioner, The*) Collins
NORWOOD PAR 1969	Portis, C. Simon & Schuster, N.Y.
NO WAY TO TREAT A LADY PAR 1968	Goldman, W. Coronet

O

OBLONG BOX, THE AA 1969	Poe, E. A. Collins
OEDIPUS THE KING UI 1968	Sophocles (P) Various
OLIVER COL 1968	Dickens, C. (*Oliver Twist*) Various
100 RIFLES FOX 1969	MacLeod, R. (*Californio, The*) Coronet
ON HER MAJESTY'S SECRET SERVICE UA 1969	Fleming, I. Cape
ONLY WHEN I LARF PAR 1969	Deighton, L. Sphere

ON THE RUN CFF 1969	Bawden, N. Gollancz
OTLEY COL 1969	Waddell, M. Hodder & Stoughton
OUTCAST LADY MGM 1935	Arlen, M. (*Green hat, The*) Collins
OUTRAGE MGM 1964	Kanin, F. & Kanin, M. (*Rashomon*) (P) Random House, N.Y.
OUTSIDER, THE PAR 1968	Camus, A. Hamilton

P

PADDY FOX 1969	Dunne, L. (*Goodbye to the hill*) Hutchinson
PASSAGES FROM JAMES JOYCE'S FINNEGAN'S WAKE CONT. 1969	Joyce, J. (*Finnegan's wake*) Faber
PETULIA WAR 1968	Haase, J. (*Me and the arch kook Petulia*) Heinemann
PINK JUNGLE, THE UI 1968	Williams, A. (*Snake water*) Panther
PLANET OF THE APES FOX 1968	Boulle, P. (*Monkey planet*) Penguin
PLEASURE SEEKERS, THE FOX 1965	Secondari, J. H. (*Coins in the fountain*) Eyre & Spottiswoode
POOKIE PAR 1969	Nichols, J. (*Sterile cuckoo, The*) Pan
POOR COW WAR 1967	Dunn, N. MacGibbon & Kee
POWER, THE MGM 1968	Robinson, F. Sphere
PRESS FOR TIME RANK 1966	McGill, A. (*Yea, yea, yea*) Secker & Warburg
PRETTY POISON FOX 1968	Geller, S. (*She let him continue*) Dutton, N.Y.
PRETTY POLLY RANK 1967	Coward, N. (*Pretty Polly Barlow*) Mayflower

464

PRIME OF MISS JEAN BRODIE, THE
FOX 1969

Spark, M.
Macmillan

PROMISE AT DAWN
AVCO EMBASSY 1969

Gary, R.
Joseph

PRUDENCE AND THE PILL
FOX 1968

Mills, H.
Triton

Q

QUICK, BEFORE IT MEETS
MGM 1964

Benjamin, P.
Gollancz

R

RACHEL, RACHEL
WAR 1968

Laurence, M. (*Jest of God, A*)
Macmillan

RABBIT, RUN
WAR 1969

Updike, J.
Deutsch

RASCAL
DISNEY 1969

North, S. (*Little rascal*)
Brockhampton

RAVEN, THE
UN 1935

Poe, E. A.
Various

RECKONING, THE
COL 1969

Hall, P. (*Harp that once, The*)
Heinemann

RED DUST
MGM 1932

Collison, W.
McBride, N.Y.

REIVERS, THE
WAR 1969

Faulkner, W.
Chatto & Windus

REWARD, THE
FOX 1965

Barrett, M.
Longmans

RIDE THE HIGH WIND
BUTCHER 1965

Harding, G. (*North of Bushman's Rock*)
Hale

RING OF BRIGHT WATER
RANK 1968

Maxwell, G.
Longmans

RIOT, THE
PAR 1969

Elli, F.
Heinemann

ROMAN SPRING OF MRS. STONE,
THE
WAR 1961

Williams, T.
Ace

TITLE OF FILM	AUTHOR AND PUBLISHER
ROMEO AND JULIET RANK 1966	Shakespeare, W. (P) Various
ROMEO AND JULIET PAR 1968	Shakespeare, W. (P) Various
ROSEMARY'S BABY PAR 1968	Levin, I. Joseph
ROYAL HUNT OF THE SUN, THE RANK 1968	Shaffer, P. (P) Pan
RUDDIGORE GALA 1967	Gilbert, *Sir* W. S. (P) Macmillan

S

SATAN BUG, THE UA 1964	Stuart, I. Collins
SATAN MET A LADY FIRST NATIONAL 1937	Hammett, D. (*Maltese falcon, The*) Cassell
SATURDAY'S CHILDREN WAR 1940	Anderson, M. (P) Longmans, N.Y.
SAVAGE INNOCENTS, THE RANK 1960	Ruesch, H. (*Top of the world*) Gollancz
SCREAM AND SCREAM AGAIN AMERICAN INT. 1969	Saxon, P. (*Disorientated man, The*) Baker
SEAGULL, THE WAR 1969	Chekhov, A. (P) Various
SECRET OF SANTA VITTORIA, THE UA 1969	Crichton, R. Hodder & Stoughton
SERGEANT, THE WAR 1968	Murphy, D. Sphere
SEVERED HEAD, A COL 1969	Murdoch, I. Chatto & Windus
SHALAKO WAR 1968	L'Amour, L. Bantam
SHOES OF THE FISHERMAN, THE MGM 1969	West, M. L. Pan
SHUTTERED ROOM, THE WAR 1966	Lovecraft, H. P. & Derleth, A. Gollancz
SILVER FOX AND SAM DAVENPORT DISNEY 1962	Seton, E. T. (*Biography of a silver fox, The*) Appleton

TITLE OF FILM	AUTHOR AND PUBLISHER
SINFUL DAVEY UA 1969	Haggart, D. (*Life of David Haggart, The*) Sphere
SNOW TREASURE TIGON 1968	McSwigan, M. (*All aboard for freedom*) Dent
SOUTHERN STAR, THE COL 1969	Verne, J. (*Southern star mystery, The*) Arco
SOUTHWEST TO SONORA UI 1966	MacLeod, R. (*Appaloosa, The*) Muller
SPARROWS CAN'T SING WAR 1962	Lewis, S. (*Sparrers can't sing*) (P) Evans
SPIRIT IS WILLING, THE PAR 1968	Benchley, N. (*Visitors, The*) Hutchinson
SPLIT, THE MGM 1968	Stark, R. Hodder Fawcett
SPORTING CLUB, THE AVCO EMBASSY 1968	McGuane, T. Deutsch
SPRING AND PORT WINE AA 1969	Naughton, B. (P) French
STAIRCASE FOX 1969	Dyer, C. Allen
STAIRCASE FOX 1969	Dyer, C. (P) French
STALKING MOON, THE WAR 1968	Olsen, T. V. Sphere
STAY AWAY, JOE MGM 1969	Cushman, D. Bantam
STORY OF TEMPLE DRAKE, THE PAR 1933	Faulkner, W. (*Sanctuary*) Chatto & Windus
STRANGE AFFAIR, THE PAR 1968	Toms, B. Constable
STRAWBERRY BLONDE, THE WAR 1941	Hagan, J. (*One Sunday afternoon*) (P) French, N.Y.
SWEET LOVE, BITTER FILM 2 1969	Williams, J. (*Night song*) Collins
SWEET RIDE, THE FOX 1968	Murray, W. Allen
SYNDICATE, THE WAR 1968	Rhodes, D. Four Square Bks.

T

TAI PAN
MGM 1968

Clavell, J.
Joseph

TAKE A GIRL LIKE YOU
COL 1969

Amis, K.
Gollancz

TAKE ME WHILE I'M WARM
BORDER 1965

Sulzberger, C. L. (*My brother death*)
Hamilton

TAMING OF THE SHREW, THE
COL 1968

Shakespeare, W. (P)
Various

TASTE OF EXCITEMENT
MONARCH 1969

Healey, B. (*Waiting for a tiger*)
Hale

**TELL ME THAT YOU LOVE ME,
JUNIE MOON**
PAR 1969

Kellogg, M.
Farrar, N.Y.

TELL THEM WILLIE BOY IS HERE
RANK 1969

Lawton, H. (*Willie Boy*)
Paisano Press, Calif.

TEMPEST, THE
RAFTERS 1969

Shakespeare, W. (P)
Various

TENDERFOOT
DISNEY 1964

Tevis, J. H. (*Arizona in the '50s*)
Univ. of New Mexico Press, Albuquerque

THAT COLD DAY IN THE PARK
COMMONWEALTH 1969

Miles, R.
Souvenir

THEY FOUND A CAVE
CFF 1962

Chauncy, N.
O.U.P.

THEY SHOOT HORSES, DON'T THEY?
CINERAMA 1969

McCoy, H.
Methuen

THIN RED LINE, THE
PLANET 1964

Jones, J.
Collins

THIS PROPERTY IS CONDEMNED
PAR 1966

Williams, T. (P)
New Directions, Norfolk, Conn.

1,000 PLANE RAID, THE
UA 1968

Barker, R. (*Thousand plan, The*)
Chatto & Windus

THREE FOR THE SHOW
COL 1954

Maugham, W. S. (*Home and beauty*) (P)
Heinemann

THREE IN THE ATTIC
WAR 1968

Yafa, S.
Sphere

THREE INTO TWO WON'T GO
UI 1968

Newman, A.
Triton

TIGER MAKES OUT, THE
COL 1968

Schisgal, M. (*Typists and the tiger, The*) (P)
Cape

TOO MANY HUSBANDS
COL 1948

Maugham, W. S. (*Home and beauty*) (P)
Heinemann

TOPAZ
UI 1968

Uris, L.
Kimber

TOUCH OF EVIL
UN 1958

Masterson, W. (*Bridge of evil*)
Corgi

TOUCH OF LOVE, A
BL 1969

Drabble, M. (*Millstone, The*)
Penguin

TOWN TAMER
PAR 1965

Gruber, F.
Barker

TRAITOR'S GATE
COL 1965

Wallace, E.
Hodder & Stoughton

TROPIC OF CANCER
PAR 1969

Miller, H.
Calder

TROUBLE WITH GIRLS, THE
MGM 1969

Keene, D. & Babcock, D. (*Chautuaqua*)
Four Square Bks.

TRUE GRIT
PAR 1969

Portis, C.
Cape

TUMULT
ATHENA 1969

Allen, J.
Hogarth Press

TWIST OF SAND, A
UA 1968

Jenkins, G.
Collins

TWO GENTLEMEN SHARING
PAR 1969

Leslie, D. S.
Pan

2001, A SPACE ODYSSEY
MGM 1968

Clarke, A. C.
Hutchinson

U

UP THE JUNCTION
PAR 1968

Dunn, N.
MacGibbon & Kee

V

VALLEY OF THE DOLLS
FOX 1968

Susann, J.
Cassell

VIEW FROM THE BRIDGE, A
TRANSCONTINENTAL 1961

Miller, A.
Penguin

VIOLENT ENEMY, THE
MONARCH 1969

Marlowe, H. (*Candle for the dead, A*)
Abelard-Schuman

VIRGIN SOLDIERS, THE
COL 1969

Thomas, L.
Constable

W

WAIT UNTIL DARK
WAR 1968

Knott, F. (P)
French

WALKING STICK, THE
MGM 1969

Graham, W.
Collins

WALK WITH LOVE AND DEATH, A
FOX 1968

Koningsberger, H.
Pan

WAR LORD, THE
RANK 1965

Stevens, L. (*Lovers, The*) (P)
French

WE WERE DANCING
MGM 1942

Coward, N. (P)
French

WHATEVER HAPPENED TO AUNT
ALICE
PALOMAR 1969

Curtiss, U. (*Forbidden garden, The*)
Eyre & Spottiswoode

WHEN THE BOYS MEET THE GIRLS
MGM 1965

Bolton, G. & McGowan, J. (*Girl Crazy*) (P)
Dramatic, Chicago

WHERE EAGLES DARE
MGM 1969

MacLean, A.
Collins

WHERE THE RIVER BENDS
UI 1952

Gullick, B. (*Bend of the Snake*)
Museum Press

WHISTLE DOWN THE WIND
RANK 1961

Bell, M. H.
Boardman

WHITE COLT, THE
COL 1969

Rook, D.
Hodder & Stoughton

WHO GOES NEXT?
FOX 1938

Simpson, R. & Drawbell, J. W. (P)
French

WHO KILLED THE CAT?
GN 1966

Ridley, A. & Borer, M. C. (*Tabitha*)
French

WINTER'S TALE, A
WAR 1968

Shakespeare, W. (P)
Various

TITLE OF FILM	AUTHOR AND PUBLISHER
WITCHFINDER GENERAL TIGON 1968	Bassett, R. Jenkins
WOMAN OF THE WORLD MGM 1935	Arlen, M. (*Green hat, The*) Collins
WOMAN WITHOUT A FACE MGM 1968	Hunter, E. (*Buddwing*) Constable
WOMEN IN LOVE UA 1969	Lawrence, D. H. Heinemann
WORK IS A FOUR LETTER WORD UI 1968	Livings, H. (P) Methuen
WRECKING CREW, THE COL 1969	Hamilton, D. Coronet

Y

YOU CAN'T SEE ROUND CORNERS UI 1969	Cleary, J. Collins
YOUNG AND EAGER WAR 1961	Caldwell, E. (*Claudelle*) Pan
YOUNG BILLY YOUNG UA 1969	Henry, W. (*Who rides with Wyatt?*) Bantam
YOUNG WARRIORS RANK 1966	Matheson, R. (*Beardless warriors*) Corgi

Z

Z WAR 1969	Vassilikos, V. Macdonald

c

AUTHOR INDEX

A

ADAMS, Clifton
DANGEROUS DAYS OF KIOWA
JONES, THE   MGM 1966
(Collins)

ADLEMAN, Robert H. *and*
WALTON, George
DEVIL'S BRIGADE, THE   UA 1968
(Transworld)

ALBERT, Marvin H.
LADY IN CEMENT   FOX 1969
(Sphere)

ALLEN, Johannes
TUMULT   ATHENA 1969
(Hogarth Press)

ALLEN, R. S. *see* **RIGBY, K.** *jt. author*

ALLEN, Woody
DON'T DRINK THE WATER (P)   AVCO EMBASSY 1969
(Random House, N.Y.)

AMERMAN, Lockhart
GUNS IN THE HEATHER   DISNEY 1969
(Harcourt, Brace, N.Y.)

AMIS, Kingsley
TAKE A GIRL LIKE YOU   COL 1969
(Gollancz)

ANDERSON, Maxwell
ANNE OF THE THOUSAND DAYS   RANK 1969
(P) (*In* Best American Plays. 3rd series.
Crown, N.Y.)
MARY OF SCOTLAND (P)   RKO 1936
(*In* Four verse plays.
Harcourt, Brace, N.Y.)
SATURDAY'S CHILDREN (P)   WAR 1940
(Longmans, N.Y.)

ANET, Claude
MAYERLING   WAR 1968
(Frewin)

ARLEN, Michael
GREEN HAT, THE   MGM 1935
(Collins)   (*Woman of the world*)
GREEN HAT, THE   MGM 1935
(Collins)   (*Outcast lady*)

474

ATKINSON, Hugh
  GAMES, THE   FOX 1969
  (Cassell)

B

BABCOCK, D. *see* **KEENE, D.** *jt. author*

BALDERSTON, John Lloyd
  BERKELEY SQUARE (P)   FOX 1933
  (French)

BARKER, Ralph
  THOUSAND PLAN, THE   UA 1968
  (Chatto & Windus)   (1,000 *plane raid*)

BARRETT, Michael
  REWARD, THE   FOX 1965
  (Longmans)

BASSETT, Ronald
  WITCHFINDER GENERAL   TIGON 1968
  (Jenkins)

BATAILLE, Michel
  CHRISTMAS TREE, THE   FOX 1969
  (Murray)

BAWDEN, Nina
  ON THE RUN   CFF 1969
  (Gollancz)

BECKER, Stephen
  COVENANT WITH DEATH, A   WAR 1968
  (Hamilton)

BEHN, Noel
  KREMLIN LETTER, THE   FOX 1969
  (Allen)

BELL, Mary Hayley
  WHISTLE DOWN THE WIND RANK 1961
  (Boardman)

BENCHLEY, Nathaniel
  VISITORS, THE   PAR 1968
  (Hutchinson)   (*Spirit is willing, The*)

BENET, Stephen Vincent
  JOHN BROWN'S BODY   FOX 1968
  (Holt, Rinehart & Winston, N.Y.)

BENJAMIN, Philip
  QUICK, BEFORE IT MELTS MGM 1964
  (Gollancz)

AUTHOR AND ORIGINAL TITLE	FILM TITLE

BENNETT, Arnold
GREAT ADVENTURE — PAR 1943
(Methuen) — (*Holy matrimony*)

BENNETT, Jay
CATACOMBS — BL 1964
(Abelard-Schuman)

BERGNER, Thomas
LITTLE BIG MAN — CINEMA CENTER 1969
(Eyre & Spottiswoode)

BIDDLE, Cordelia Drexel *and*
    CRICHTON, Kyle
HAPPIEST MILLIONAIRE, THE — DISNEY 1968
(Sphere)

BINGHAM, John
FRAGMENT OF FEAR — COL 1969
(Panther)

BIRNEY, Hoffman
DICE OF GOD, THE — UA 1965
(Holt, N.Y.) — (*Glory guys*)

BLAKE, Nicholas
BEAST MUST DIE, THE — CINECENTA 1969
(Collins) — (*Killer*)

BLYTON, Enid
FIVE HAVE A MYSTERY TO — CFF 1964
SOLVE
(Hodder & Stoughton)

BOLT, Robert
MAN FOR ALL SEASONS, A (P) — COL 1968
(French)

BOLTON, Guy *and* **McGOWAN, John**
GIRL CRAZY (P) — MGM 1965
(Dramatic, Chicago) — (*When the boys meet the girls*)

BORER, M. C. *see* **RIDLEY, A.** *jt. author*

BOULLE, Pierre
MONKEY PLANET — FOX 1968
(Penguin) — (*Planet of the apes*)

BRADBURY, Ray
ILLUSTRATED MAN, THE — WAR 1968
(Hart-Davis)

BURROWS, Abe
CACTUS FLOWER (P) — COL 1969
(French, N.Y.)

476

C

CAIDIN, Martin
  MAROONED   COL 1969
  (Hodder & Stoughton)

CALDWELL, Erskine
  CLAUDELLE   WAR 1961
  (Pan)   (*Young and eager*)

CAMUS, Albert
  OUTSIDER, THE   PAR 1968
  (Hamilton)

CANNING, Victor
  LIMBO LINE, THE   MONARCH 1968
  (Heinemann)

CAPOTE, Truman
  IN COLD BLOOD   COL 1968
  (Hamilton)

CATTO, Max
  MISTER MOSES   UA 1965
  (Heinemann)

CHANDLER, Raymond
  FAREWELL, MY LOVELY   RKO 1946
  (Hamilton)   (In U.S. *Murder my sweet*)
  LITTLE SISTER, THE   MGM 1969
  (Hamilton)   (*Marlowe*)

CHAUNCY, Nan
  THEY FOUND A CAVE   CFF 1962
  (O.U.P.)

CHAYEFSKY, Paddy
  BACHELOR PARTY (P)   COL 1957
  (*In* Television plays.
  Simon & Schuster, N.Y.)
  MARTY (P)   COL 1956
  (*In* Television plays.
  Simon & Schuster, N.Y.)

CHEKHOV, Anton
  SEAGULL, THE (P)   WAR 1969
  (French)

CHRISTIAN, Tina Chad
  BABY LOVE   AVCO EMBASSY 1969
  (Cape)

CHRISTIE, Agatha
  MISS MARPLE   MGM 1964
  (Collins)   (*Murder ahoy*)

CLARKE, Arthur C.
2001, A SPACE ODYSSEY   MGM 1968
(Hutchinson)

CLAVELL, James
TAI PAN   MGM 1968
(Joseph)

CLEARY, Jon
HIGH COMMISSIONER, THE   RANK 1968
(Collins)   (*Nobody runs forever*)
YOU CAN'T SEE ROUND   UI 1969
CORNERS
(Collins)

COLLISON, W.
RED DUST   MGM 1932
(McBride, N.Y.)

CORY, Desmond
DEADFALL   FOX 1968
(Muller)

COWARD, Noel
PRETTY POLLY BARTON   RANK 1967
(Mayflower)   (*Pretty Polly*)
WE WERE DANCING (P)   MGM 1942
(French)

CRICHTON, K. *see* **BIDDLE, C. D.**
    jt. author

CRICHTON, Robert
SECRET OF SANTA VITTORIA,   UA 1969
THE
(Hodder & Stoughton)

CROWLEY, Mart
BOYS IN THE BAND, THE (P)   WAR 1969
(Secker & Warburg)

CURTIS, Peter
DEVIL'S OWN, THE   FOX 1968
(Macdonald)

CURTISS, Ursula
FORBIDDEN GARDEN, THE   PALOMAR 1969
(Eyre & Spottiswoode)   (*Whatever happened to Aunt Alice*)

CUSHMAN, Dan
STAY AWAY, JOE   MGM 1969
(Bantam)

D

DAVIS, Stratford
ONE MAN'S SECRET
(Boardman)

AA 1957
(*Man in the shadow*)

DE BEAUVOIR, Simone
MANDARINS, THE
(Fontana)

FOX 1969

DEFOE, Daniel
ADVENTURES OF ROBINSON
CRUSOE, THE
(Various)

FOX 1954
(*Miss Robin Crusoe*)

DEIGHTON, Leonard
BILLION DOLLAR BRAIN
(Cape)
ONLY WHEN I LARF
(Sphere)

UA 1967

PAR 1969

DENHAM, Reginald *and* **PERCY, Edward**
LADIES IN RETIREMENT (P)
(Random House, N.Y.)

COL 1969
(*Mad room, The*)

DERLETH, A. *see* **LOVECRAFT, H. P.**
jt. author

DICKENS, Charles
DAVID COPPERFIELD
(Various)
OLIVER TWIST
(Various)

FOX 1969

COL 1968
(*Oliver*)

DOUGHERTY, Richard
COMMISSIONER, THE
(Hart-Davis)

UI 1968
(*Madigan*)

DRABBLE, Margaret
MILLSTONE, THE
(Penguin)

BL 1969
(*Touch of love, A*)

DRAWBELL, James Wedgwood
INNOCENTS OF CHICAGO
(Collins)
LOVE AND FORGET
(Collins)

BI 1934

BI 1941
(*Love story*)

DRAWBELL, J. W. *see* **SIMPSON, R.**
jt. author

DUMAS, Alexandre (*père*)
DEUX FRERES
(Macmillan)

MGM 1942
(*Corsican brothers, The*)

DUNCAN, Isadora
MY LIFE
(Gollancz)

UI 1969
(*Isadora*)

DUNN, Nell
POOR COW   WAR 1967
(MacGibbon & Kee)
UP THE JUNCTION   PAR 1968
(MacGibbon & Kee)

DUNNE, Lee
GOODBYE TO THE HILL   FOX 1969
(Hutchinson)   *(Paddy)*

DURAS, Marguerite
MODERATO CANTABILE   R. J. LEVY 1960
(Calder)

DYER, Charles
STAIRCASE (P)   FOX 1969
(French)
STAIRCASE   FOX 1969
(Allen)

E

EASTLAKE, William
CASTLE KEEP   COL 1969
(Joseph)

ELLI, Frank
RIOT, THE   PAR 1969
(Heinemann)

ELLIN, Stanley
HOUSE OF CARDS   RANK 1968
(Macdonald)

ELLIOT, Janice
BUTTERCUP CHAIN, THE COL 1969
(Panther)

ENGLAND, Barry
FIGURES IN A LANDSCAPE CINEMA CENTER 1969
(Cape)

F

FAIRCHILD, William
SOUND OF MURDER, THE (P) FOX 1969
(French)   *(Last shot you hear, The)*

FAST, Howard
MIRAGE   UI 1965
(Mayflower)

FAULKNER, William
  REIVERS, THE   WAR 1969
  (Chatto & Windus)
  SANCTUARY   PAR 1933
  (Chatto & Windus)   (*Story of Temple Drake, The*)

FEYDEAU, G.
  FLEA IN HER EAR, A   FOX 1968
  (Methuen)

FIDLER, Kathleen
  FLASH THE SHEEP DOG   CFF 1966
  (Lutterworth Press)

FIELDING, Henry
  RAPE UPON RAPE (P)   COL 1968
  (Various)   (*Lock up your daughters*)

FISH, R. *see* **LONDON, J.** *jt. author*

FISHER, S.
  I WAKE UP SCREAMING   FOX 1941
  (Hale)

FLEISCHMAN, Sid
  BULLWHIP GRIFFIN   DISNEY 1968
  (Penguin)

FLEMING, Ian
  CHITTY, CHITTY BANG BANG UA 1968
  (Cape)
  ON HER MAJESTY'S SECRET
  SERVICE   UA 1969
  (Cape)

FLETCHER, Geoffrey
  LONDON NOBODY KNOWS, THE BL 1969
  (Penguin)

FORD, Jesse Hill
  LIBERATION OF LORD BYRON COL 1969
  JONES, THE
  (Bodley Head)

FORRESTER, Larry
  GIRL CALLED FATHOM, A   FOX 1968
  (Heinemann)   (*Fathom*)

FOWLES, John
  MAGUS, THE   FOX 1969
  (Cape)

FRANK, Gerold
  BOSTON STRANGLER, THE FOX 1968
  (Cape)

FREDE, Richard
  INTERNS, THE   COL 1964
  (Corgi)   (*New interns, The*)

FREELING, Nicolas
  LOVE IN AMSTERDAM   MONARCH 1968
  (Penguin)

FULLERTON, Alexander
  LIONHEART   CFF 1968
  (Hodder & Stoughton)

G

GARY, Romain
  PROMISE AT DAWN   AVCO EMBASSY 1969
  (Joseph)

GASKELL, Jane
  ALL NEAT IN BLACK STOCKINGS WAR 1968
  (Hodder & Stoughton)

GEBLER, Ernest
  SHALL I EAT YOU NOW (P)   WAR 1969
  (Pan)   (*Hoffman*)

GELBER, Jack
  CONNECTION, THE   CONT 1962
  (Faber)

GELLER, Stephen
  SHE LET HIM CONTINUE   FOX 1968
  (Dutton, N.Y.)   (*Pretty poison*)

GEORGE, Jean
  MY SIDE OF THE MOUNTAIN PAR 1968
  (Bodley Head)

GILBERT, *Sir* William S.
  RUDDIGORE (P)   GALA 1967
  (Macmillan)

GOLDMAN, James
  LION IN WINTER, THE (P)   AVCO EMBASSY 1969
  (French)

GOLDMAN, William
  NO WAY TO TREAT A LADY PAR 1968
  (Coronet)

GOODHART, William
  GENERATION (P)   AVCO EMBASSY 1969
  (Doubleday, N.Y.)

GRAHAM, Winston
WALKING STICK, THE   MGM 1969
(Collins)

GREEN, Frederick Laurence
LOST MAN, THE   RANK 1969
(Joseph)

GRUBER, Frank
TOWN TAMER   PAR 1965
(Barker)

GULLICK, B.
BEND OF THE SNAKE   UI 1952
(Museum Press)   (*Where the river bends*)

H

HAASE, John
ME AND THE ARCH KOOK   WAR 1968
PETULIA   (*Petulia*)
(Heinemann)

HAGAN, J.
ONE SUNDAY AFTERNOON (P)   WAR 1941
(French, N.Y.)   (*Strawberry blonde, The*)

HAGGART, David
LIFE OF DAVID HAGGART, THE   UA 1969
(Sphere)   (*Sinful Davey*)

HAILEY, Arthur
AIRPORT   RANK 1969
(Joseph & Souvenir)

HALL, Oakley
DOWNHILL RACERS, THE   PAR 1969
(Bodley Head)

HALL, Patrick
HARP THAT ONCE, THE   COL 1969
(Heinemann)   (*Reckoning, The*)

HAMILTON, Donald
AMBUSHERS, THE   COL 1968
(Coronet)
WRECKING CREW, THE   COL 1969
(Coronet)

HAMILTON, Patrick
HANGOVER SQUARE   FOX 1945
(Constable)

AUTHOR AND ORIGINAL TITLE	FILM TITLE

HAMMETT, Dashiel
MALTESE FALCON, THE   FIRST NATIONAL 1937
(Cassell)   (*Satan met a lady*)

HANLEY, Gerald
GILLIGHAN'S LAST ELEPHANT   PAR 1968
(Collins)   (*Last safari, The*)

HARDING, George
NORTH OF BUSHMAN'S ROCK   BUTCHER 1965
(Hale)   (*Ride the high wind*)

HATCH, Eric
YEAR OF THE HORSE, THE   DISNEY 1968
(Crown, N.Y.)   (*Horse in the gray flannel suit, The*)

HEALEY, Ben
WAITING FOR A TIGER   MONARCH 1969
(Hale)   (*Taste of excitement*)

HECHLER, Ken
BRIDGE AT REMAGEN, THE   UA 1968
(Panther)

HECHT, Ben
GAILY, GAILY   UA 1969
(Elek)

HELLER, Joseph
CATCH 22   PAR 1969
(Cape)
HENRY, Will
JOURNEY TO SHILOH   UI 1968
(Gollancz)
MACKENNA'S GOLD   COL 1969
(Hammond)
WHO RIDES WITH WYATT?   UA 1969
(Bantam)   (*Young Billy Young*)

HERLIHY, James Leo
MIDNIGHT COWBOY   UA 1969
(Cape)

HILTON, James
GOODBYE, MR. CHIPS   MGM 1969
(Hodder & Stoughton)

HIMES, C.
COTTON COMES TO HARLEM   UA 1969
(Muller)

HINES, Barry
KESTREL FOR A KNAVE, A   UA 1969
(Joseph)   (*Kes*)

HOFFENBERG, M. *see* **SOUTHERN, T.**
  jt. author

HOOKER, Richard
  MASH   FOX 1969
  (Morrow, N.Y.)   (*M.A.S.H.*)

HOWARD, Hartley
  DEPARTMENT K   COL 1968
  (Collins)   (*Assignment 'K'*)

HUGHES, Dorothy B.
  EXPENDABLE MAN, THE   RANK 1964
  (Deutsch)   (*Hanged man, The*)

HUNTER, Evan
  BUDDWING   MGM 1968
  (Constable)   (*Woman without a face*)
  LAST SUMMER   FOX 1969
  (Constable)

I

IRISH, William
  BRIDE WORE BLACK, THE UA 1968
  (Sphere)

ISRAEL, Charles Edward
  MARK, THE   FOX 1961
  (Macmillan)

J

JAPRISOT, Sebastien
  LADY IN THE CAR WITH   COL 1969
  GLASSES AND A GUN, THE (*Lady in the car, The*)
  (Souvenir)

JENKINS, Geoffrey
  TWIST OF SAND, A   UA 1968
  (Collins)

JOHNSON, Dorothy M.
  MAN CALLED HORSE, A   CINEMA CENTER 1969
  (Deutsch)

JONES, James
THIN RED LINE, THE   PLANET 1964
  (Collins)

JONES, Mervyn
  JOHN AND MARY   FOX 1969
  (Cape)

JOYCE, James
FINNEGAN'S WAKE
(Faber)

CONTEMPORARY FILMS 1969
(*Passages from James Joyce's Finnegan's wake*)

K

KANIN, Fay *and* **KANIN, Michael**
RASHOMON (P)
(Random House, N.Y.)

MGM 1964
(*Outrage*)

KAZAN, Elia
ARRANGEMENT, THE
(Collins)

WAR 1969

KEENE, Day *and* **BABCOCK, Dwight**
CHAUTUAQUA
(Four Square Bks.)

MGM 1969
(*Trouble with girls, The*)

KELLOGG, Marjorie
TELL ME THAT YOU LOVE ME,
JUNIE MOON
(Farrar, N.Y.)

PAR 1969

KENNEDY, Jay Richard
MOST DANGEROUS MAN IN THE
WORLD, THE
(Joseph)

RANK 1969

KEROUAC, Jack
SUBTERRANEANS, THE
(Deutsch)

MGM 1960

KESSEL, Joseph
BELLE DE JOUR
(Barker)

CURZON 1967

KEYES, Daniel
FLOWERS FOR ALGERNON
(Cassell)

CINERAMA 1968
(*Charly*)

KNOTT, Frederick
WAIT UNTIL DARK (P)
(French)

WAR 1968

KOLB, Ken
GETTING STRAIGHT
(Barrie & Rockliff)

COL 1969

KONINGSBERGER, Hans
WALK WITH LOVE AND DEATH,
A
(Penguin)

FOX 1968

486

KRESSING, Harry
  COOK, THE   CINEMA CENTER 1969
  (Panther)

KRUMGOLD, Joseph
  AND NOW MIGUEL   UI 1965
  (Cowell-Collier, N.Y.)

L

L'AMOUR, Louis
  HONDO AND THE APACHES   MGM 1966
  (Jenkins)
  SHALAKO   WAR 1968
  (Bantam)

LAURENCE, Margaret
  JEST OF GOD, A   WAR 1968
  (Macmillan)   (*Rachel, Rachel*)

LAURENTS, Arthur
  HOME OF THE BRAVE (P)   UA 1949
  (Dramatists, N.Y.)

LAWRENCE, David Herbert
  FOX, THE   WAR 1968
  (*In* Tales of D. H. Lawrence, The:
    Heinemann)
  WOMEN IN LOVE   UA 1969
  (Heinemann)

LAWTON, Harry
  WILLIE BOY   RANK 1969
  (Paisano Press, Calif.)   (*Tell them Willie Boy is here*)

LE CARRÉ, John
  LOOKING GLASS WAR, THE   COL 1969
  (Gollancz)

LERNER, Alan Jay
  MY FAIR LADY (P)   WAR 1964
  (Constable)

LESLIE, David Stuart
  TWO GENTLEMEN SHARING   PAR 1969
  (Pan)

LEVIN, Ira
  ROSEMARY'S BABY   PAR 1968
  (Joseph)

LEWIS, Arthur H.
  LAMENT FOR THE MOLLY   PAR 1969
  MAGUIRES   (*Molly Maguires, The*)
  (Longmans)

LEWIS, Sinclair
  CASS TIMBERLANE   MGM 1947
  (Cape)

LEWIS, Stephen
  SPARRERS CAN'T SING (P)   WAR 1962
  (Evans)   (*Sparrows can't sing*)

LIERS, Ernst
  OTTER'S STORY   DISNEY 1968
  (Hodder & Stoughton)   (*Flash, the otter*)

LINDSAY, Norman
  AGE OF CONSENT   COL 1968
  (Laurie)

LIVINGS, Henry
  EH? (P)   UI 1968
  (Methuen)   (*Work is a four letter word*)

LONDON, Jack *and* **FISH, Robert**
  ASSASSINATION BUREAU, THE   PAR 1969
  (Deutsch)

LORAINE, Philip
  DAY OF THE ARROW   MGM 1968
  (Collins)   (*Eye of the devil*)

LOVECRAFT, H. P.
  SHUTTERED ROOM, THE   WAR 1966
  (*In* Shadow out of time and other   AMERICAN INTERNATIONAL 1969
  tales of horror: Gollancz)   (*Dunwich horror*)

LYMINGTON, John
  NIGHT OF THE BIG HEAT   PLANET 1967
  (Hodder & Stoughton)

M

McCARTHY, Justin Huntly
  IF I WERE KING   PAR 1938
  (Heinemann)

McCOY, Horace
  THEY SHOOT HORSES DON'T   CINERAMA 1969
  THEY?
  (Methuen)

McCULLERS, Carson
  HEART IS A LONELY HUNTER,   WAR 1968
  THE
  (Penguin)

MACDONALD, Ross
  MOVING TARGET, THE   WAR 1966
  (Fontana)

McGILL, Angus
YEA, YEA, YEA
(Secker & Warburg)

RANK 1966
(*Press for time*)

McGOWAN, J. *see* **BOLTON, G.**
jt. author

McGRATH, John
EVENTS WHILST GUARDING
THE BOFORS GUN (P)
(Methuen)

UI 1968
(*Bofors gun, The*)

McGUANE, Thomas
SPORTING CLUB, THE
(Deutsch)

AVCO EMBASSY 1968

MACILWRAITH, William
ANNIVERSARY, THE (P)
(Evans)

WAR 1968

MACLEAN, Alistair
ICE STATION ZEBRA
(Collins)
WHERE EAGLES DARE
(Collins)

MGM 1968

MGM 1969

MACLEOD, Robert
APPALOOSA, THE
(Muller)
CALIFORNIO, THE
(Coronet)

RANK 1966
(*Southwest to Sonora*)
FOX 1969
(100 *rifles*)

McSWIGAN, Marie
ALL ABOARD FOR FREEDOM
(Dent)

TIGON 1968
(*Snow treasure*)

MAINE, Charles Eric
MIND OF MR. SOAMES, THE
(Panther)

COL 1969

MALAMUD, Bernard
FIXER, THE
(Eyre & Spottiswoode)

MGM 1969

MANDIARGUES, Andre Pieyre de
GIRL ON THE MOTORCYCLE,
THE
(Calder)

BL 1968

MARCUS, Frank
KILLING OF SISTER GEORGE,
THE (P)
(French)

CINERAMA 1968

MARLOWE, Christopher
TRAGICAL HISTORY OF DOCTOR FAUSTUS, THE (P)   COL 1968
(Various)   (*Doctor Faustus*)

MARLOWE, Derek
DANDY IN ASPIC, A   COL 1968
(Gollancz)

MARLOWE, Hugh
CANDLE FOR THE DEAD, A   MONARCH 1969
(Abelard-Schuman)   (*Violent enemy, The*)

MASTERSON, Whit
BRIDGE OF EVIL   UN 1959
(Corgi)   (*Touch of evil*)

MATHESON, Richard
BEARDLESS WARRIORS, THE   RANK 1966
(Corgi)   (*Young warriors*)
I AM LEGEND   GOLDEN ERA 1964
(Bantam)   (*Last man on earth, The*)

MAUGHAM, William Somerset
HOME AND BEAUTY (P)   COL 1954
(Heinemann)   (*Three for the show*)
HOME AND BEAUTY (P)   COL 1948
(Heinemann)   (*Too many husbands*)

MAXWELL, Gavin
RING OF BRIGHT WATER   RANK 1968
(Longmans)

MAYO, James
HAMMERHEAD   COL 1968
(Heinemann)

MERLE, Robert
DAY OF THE DOLPHIN, THE   UA 1969
(Weidenfeld & Nicolson)

MILES, Bernard
LOCK UP YOUR DAUGHTERS (P)   COL 1968
(French)

MILES, Richard
THAT COLD DAY IN THE PARK   COMMONWEALTH U.E. 1969
(Souvenir)

MILLER, Arthur
VIEW FROM THE BRIDGE, A   TRANSCONTINENTAL 1961
(*Poem*)
(Penguin)

MILLER, Henry
  TROPIC OF CANCER   PAR 1969
  (Calder)

MILLS, Hugh
  PRUDENCE AND THE PILL   FOX 1968
  (Triton)

MOLNAR, Ferenc
  GOOD FAIRY, THE (P)   UN 1934
  (*In* Romantic comedies: Crown, N.Y.)

MOORE, Robin
  GREEN BERETS, THE   WAR 1968
  (Crown, N.Y.)

MOREY, Walter
  GENTLE BEN   PAR 1968
  (Dutton, N.Y.)   (*Gentle giant*)

MOSLEY, Nicholas
  ACCIDENT   MONARCH 1967
  (Hodder & Stoughton)

MURDOCH, Iris
  SEVERED HEAD, A   COL 1969
  (Chatto & Windus)

MURPHY, Dennis
  SERGEANT, THE   WAR 1968
  (Sphere)

MURRAY, William
  SWEET RIDE, THE   FOX 1968
  (Allen)

N

NABOKOV, Vladimir
  LAUGHTER IN THE DARK UA 1969
  (Weidenfeld & Nicolson)

NAUGHTON, Bill
  ALL IN GOOD TIME (P)   BL 1966
  (French)   (*Family way, The*)
  SPRING AND PORT WINE (P) AA 1969
  (French)

NAUGHTON, Edmond
  McCABE   FOX 1969
  (Panther)

NEWMAN, Andrea
  THREE INTO TWO WON'T GO UI 1968
  (Triton)

NICHOLS, John
   STERILE CUCKOO, THE   PAR 1969
   (Pan)   (*Pookie*)

NORTH, Sterling
   LITTLE RASCAL   DISNEY 1969
   (Brockhampton)   (*Rascal*)

NUGENT, E. *see* **THURBER, J.** *jt. author*

O

OLSEN, Theodore V.
   STALKING MOON, THE   WAR 1968
   (Sphere)

O'ROURKE, Frank
   GREAT BANK ROBBERY, THE   WAR 1964
   (Sphere)

ORTON, Joe
   ENTERTAINING MR. SLOANE (P)   WAR 1969
   (Hamilton)

OSBORNE, John
   INADMISSIBLE EVIDENCE (P)   PAR 1968
   (Faber)

P

PARKS, Gordon
   LEARNING TREE, THE   WAR 1969
   (Hodder & Stoughton)

PATTEN, Lewis B.
   LAW OF THE GUNS   UI 1969
   (Four Square Bks.)   (*Death of a gunfighter*)

PATTERSON, H. *see* **MARLOWE, H.**
   pseud.

PEARCE, Donn.
   COOL HAND LUKE   WAR 1968
   (Penguin)

PERCY, E. *see* **DENHAM, R.** *jt. author*

PETRAKIS, Harry Mark
   DREAM OF KINGS, A   WAR 1969
   (Barker)

PIKE, Robert L.
MUTE WITNESS   WAR 1968
(Deutsch)   (*Bullitt*)

PINTER, Harold
BIRTHDAY PARTY, THE (P)   CINERAMA 1968
(Methuen *and* French)

PIPER, Anne
SWEET AND PLENTY   AVCO EMBASSY 1969
(Heinemann)   (*Nice girl like me, A*)

POE, Edgar Alan
BLACK CAT, THE   UN 1934
(Various)
OBLONG BOX, THE   AA 1969
(Various)
RAVEN, THE (*Poem*)   UN 1935
(Various)

PORTIS, Charles
NORWOOD   PAR 1969
(Simon & Schuster, N.Y.)
TRUE GRIT   PAR 1969
(Cape)

R

RAMATI, Alexander
BEYOND THE MONTAINS   AMERICAN INTERNATIONAL 1968
(Penguin)   (*Desperate ones, The*)

RESNIK, Muriel
ANY WEDNESDAY (P)   WAR 1966
(English Theatre)   (*Bachelor girl apartment*)
TURQUOISE BIKINI, THE   WAR 1968
(Transworld)   (*How sweet it is*)

RHODES, Denys
SYNDICATE, THE   WAR 1968
(Four Square Bks.)

RIDLEY, Arnold *and* BORER, Mary
   Cathcart
TABITHA (P)   GN 1966
(French)   (*Who killed the cat?*)

RIGBY, Kay *and* ALLEN, R. S.
HILL, THE   MGM 1965
(Mayflower)

ROBBINS, Harold
ADVENTURERS, THE   PAR 1968
(Blond)

ROBINSON, Frank
  POWER, THE   MGM 1968
  (Sphere)

ROFFEY, Jack
  HOSTILE WITNESS (P)   UA 1968
  (Evans)

ROOK, David
  WHITE COLT, THE   COL 1969
  (Hodder & Stoughton)

ROTH, Philip
  GOODBYE, COLUMBUS   PAR 1969
  (Deutsch)

RUESCH, Hans
  TOP OF THE WORLD   RANK 1960
  (Gollancz)   (*Savage innocents, The*)

RYAN, Cornelius
  LAST BATTLE, THE   MGM 1968
  (Collins)

RYAN, J. M.
  BROOK WILSON LTD.   COL 1969
  (Hodder Fawcett)   (*Loving*)

S

SAGAN, Françoise
  HEART KEEPER, THE   FOX 1969
  (Murray)

SAINT-LAURENT, Cecil
  CAROLINE CHERI   WAR 1968
  (Pan)

SAXON, Peter
  DISORIENTATED MAN, THE   AMERICAN INTERNATIONAL 1969
  (Baker)   (*Scream and scream again*)

SCHAEFER, Jack
  COMPANY OF COWARDS   MGM 1965
  (Mayflower)
  MONTE WALSH   CINEMA CENTER 1969
  (Deutsch)

SCHISGAL, Murray
  TYPISTS AND THE TIGER, THE   COL 1968
  (P)   (*Tiger makes out, The*)
  (Cape)

SECONDARI, John H.
COINS IN THE FOUNTAIN   FOX 1965
(Eyre & Spottiswoode)   (*Pleasure seekers, The*)

SETON, Ernest Thompson
BIOGRAPHY OF A SILVER FOX,   DISNEY 1962
THE   (*Silver Fox and Sam Davenport*)
(Appleton Century, N.Y.)

SHAFFER, Peter
ROYAL HUNT OF THE SUN, THE   RANK 1968
(P)
(Pan)

SHAKESPEARE, William
HAMLET (P)   COL 1969
(Various)
JULIUS CAESAR (P)   MGM 1969
(Various)
KING LEAR (P)   COL 1969
(Various)
MIDSUMMER NIGHT'S DREAM, A EAGLE 1969
(P)
(Various)
ROMEO AND JULIET (P)   RANK 1966
(Various)   PAR 1968
TAMING OF THE SHREW, THE (P) MGM 1953
(Various)   (*Kiss me Kate*)
                         COL 1968
TEMPEST, THE (P)   RAFTERS 1969
(Various)
WINTER'S TALE, THE (P)   WAR 1968
(Various)

SHAW, George Bernard
GREAT CATHERINE (P)   WAR 1968
(Various)

SHERLOCK, John
ORDEAL OF MAJOR GRIGSBY,   CINERAMA 1969
THE   (*Last grenade, The*)
(Hutchinson)

SILLITOE, Alan
GENERAL, THE   RANK 1968
(Allen)   (*Counterpoint*)

SIMPSON, Reginald *and* DRAWBELL,
   James Wedgwood
WHO GOES NEXT? (P)   FOX 1938
(French)

SOPHOCLES
OEDIPUS THE KING (P)   RANK 1968
(Various)

SOUTHERN, Terry
MAGIC CHRISTIAN, THE   COMMONWEALTH UNITED 1969
(Deutsch)

SOUTHERN, Terry *and* **HOFFENBERG, M.**
CANDY   CINERAMA 1968
(Geis)

SPARK, Muriel
PRIME OF MISS JEAN BRODIE,   FOX 1969
THE
(Macmillan)

STAHL, Ben
BLACKBEARD'S GHOST   DISNEY 1968
(Houghton Mifflin, N.Y.)

STARK, Richard
SPLIT, THE   MGM 1968
(Hodder Fawcett)

STEVENS, Leslie
LOVERS, THE (P)   RANK 1965
(French)   (*War lord, The*)

STEVENSON, Robert Louis
EBB TIDE   PAR 1937
(Various)

STEWART, Michael
HELLO DOLLY! (P)   FOX 1968
(D.B.S., N.Y.)

STOKES, Sewell
ISADORA DUNCAN   UI 1969
(Pan)   (*Isadora*)

STONE, Robert
HALL OF MIRRORS, A   PAR 1969
(Bodley Head)

STRINDBERG, Augustus
DANCE OF DEATH, THE (P)   PAR 1969
(*In* Eight famous plays: Duckworth)

STUART, Ian
SATAN BUG, THE   UA 1964
(Collins)

STYRON, William
CONFESSIONS OF NAT TURNER, FOX 1969
THE
(Cape)

SULZBERGER, Cyrus L.
MY BROTHER DEATH
(Hamilton)

BORDER 1965
(*Take me whilst I'm warm*)

SUSANN, Jacqueline
VALLEY OF THE DOLLS
(Cassell)

FOX 1968

T

TARLOFF, Frank
GUIDE FOR THE MARRIED
MAN, THE
(Price, Sterm, Sloan, L.A.)

FOX 1968

TEVIS, James H.
ARIZONA IN THE 50's
(University of New Mexico Press,
Albuquerque)

DISNEY 1964
(*Tenderfoot, The*)

THOMAS, Leslie
VIRGIN SOLDIERS, THE
(Constable)

COL 1969

THOMAS, Ross
SPY IN THE VODKA
(Hodder & Stoughton)

PAR 1969
Cold war swap, The)

THORP, Roderick
DETECTIVE, THE
(Corgi)

FOX 1968

THURBER, James *and* NUGENT, E.
MALE ANIMAL (P)
(Random House, N.Y.)

WAR 1942

TOMS, Bernard
STRANGE AFFAIR, THE
(Constable)

PAR 1968

TYLER, Poyntz
GARDEN OF CUCUMBERS, A
(Gollancz)

UA 1968
(*Fitzwolley strikes back*)

U

UPDIKE, John
RABBIT, RUN
(Deutsch)

WAR 1969

URIS, Leon
TOPAZ
(Kimber)

UI 1968

V

VANBRUGH, *Sir* **John**
RELAPSE, THE (P)   COL 1968
(Various)   (*Lock up your daughters*)

VANE, Stephen
OUTWARD BOUND (P)   WAR 1944
(Boni, N.Y.)   (*Between two worlds*)

VASSILIKOS, Vassili
Z   WAR 1969
(Macdonald)

VAUGHAN THOMAS, Wynford
ANZIO   COL 1968
(Longmans)   (*Battle for Anzio, The*)

VERNE, Jules
SOUTHERN STAR MYSTERY, THE   COL 1969
(Arco)   (*Southern star, The*)

VIDAL, Gore
BEST MAN, THE (P)   UA 1968
(Little, Brown, Boston)
MYRA BRECKENRIDGE   FOX 1969
(Blond)

W

WADDELL, Martin
OTLEY   COL 1969
(Hodder & Stoughton)

WALKER, David Esdaile
ADVENTURE IN DIAMONDS   RANK 1966
(Evans)   (*Man could get killed, A*)

WALLACE, Edgar
SANDERS OF THE RIVER   PLANET 1963
(Ward Lock)   (*Death drums along the river*)
        BL 1964
        (*Coast of skeletons*)
TRAITOR'S GATE   COL 1965
(Hodder & Stoughton)

WALTON, G. *see* **ADLEMAN, R. H.**
    jt. author

WAUGH, Evelyn
DECLINE AND FALL   FOX 1968
(Chapman & Hall)   (*Decline and Fall ... of a birdwatcher*)

WEBB, Charles
GRADUATE, THE   UA 1968
(Penguin)

WEST, Morris L.
BIG STORY, THE   GALA 1964
(Heinemann)   (*Crooked road, The*)
SHOES OF THE FISHERMAN, THE MGM 1969
(Pan)

WESTLAKE, Donald
BUSY BODY, THE   PAR 1968
(Boardman)

WESTON, John
HAIL, HERO   CINEMA CENTER 1969
(Mackay, N.Y.)

WHEATLEY, Dennis
DEVIL RIDES OUT, THE   WAR 1968
(Hutchinson)
UNCHARTED SEAS   WAR 1968
(Hutchinson)   (*Lost continent, The*)

WHITE, Alan
LONG DAY'S DYING, THE   PAR 1968
(Hodder & Stoughton)

WILDER, Robert
FRUIT OF THE POPPY   MGM 1968
(Allen)   (*Heroin gang, The*)

WILKINSON, G. R.
MONKEYS, THE   DISNEY 1967
(Macdonald)   (*Monkeys, go home*)

WILLARD, J.
CAT AND THE CANARY, THE   PAR 1939
(Hudson)

WILLIAMS, Alan
SNAKE WATER   UI 1968
(Panther)   (*Pink jungle, The*)

WILLIAMS, Charles
DON'T JUST STAND THERE   RANK 1969
(Cassell)

WILLIAMS, John
NIGHT SONG   FILM 2 ASSOCIATES 1969
(Collins)   (*Sweet love, bitter*)

WILLIAMS, Tennessee
MILK TRAIN DOESN'T STOP   UI 1968
HERE ANY MORE (P)   (*Boom*)
(Secker & Warburg)
ROMAN SPRING OF MRS. STONE,   WAR 1961
THE
(Ace)
THIS PROPERTY IS CONDEMNED   PAR 1966
(P)
(*In* 27 wagons full of cotton and other
  one-act plays: New Directions,
  Norfolk, Conn.)

WOHL, Burton
COLD WIND IN AUGUST   UA 1961
(Mayflower)

WOOD, Derek *and* **DEMPSTER, Derek**
NARROW MARGIN, THE   UA 1969
(Arrow)   (*Battle of Britain, The*)

Y

YAFA, Stephen
THREE IN THE ATTIC   WAR 1968
(Sphere)

YORK, Andrew
ELIMINATOR, THE   UA 1968
(Hutchinson)   (*Danger route*)

CHANGE OF ORIGINAL TITLE INDEX

A

ORIGINAL TITLE	FILM TITLE
ADVENTURE IN DIAMONDS Walker, D. E.	MAN COULD GET KILLED, A RANK 1966
ADVENTURES OF ROBINSON CRUSOE, THE Defoe, D.	MISS ROBIN CRUSOE FOX 1954
ALL ABOARD FOR FREEDOM McSwigan, M.	SNOW TREASURE TIGON 1968
ALL IN GOOD TIME (P) Naughton, B.	FAMILY WAY, THE BL 1966
ANY WEDNESDAY (P) Resnik, M.	BACHELOR GIRL APARTMENT WAR 1966
ANZIO Vaughan Thomas, W.	BATTLE FOR ANZIO, THE COL 1968
APPALOOSA, THE MacLeod, R.	SOUTHWEST TO SONORA UI 1966
ARIZONA IN THE 50's Tevis, J. H.	TENDERFOOT, THE DISNEY 1964

B

ORIGINAL TITLE	FILM TITLE
BEARDLESS WARRIORS, THE Matheson, R.	YOUNG WARRIORS RANK 1966
BEAST MUST DIE, THE Blake, N.	KILLER CINECENTA 1969
BEND OF THE SNAKE Gullick, B.	WHERE THE RIVER BENDS UI 1952
BEYOND THE MOUNTAINS Ramati, A.	DESPERATE ONES, THE AMERICAN INTERNATIONAL 1968
BIG STORY, THE West, M. L.	CROOKED ROAD, THE GALA 1964
BIOGRAPHY OF A SILVER FOX, THE Seton, E. T.	SILVER FOX AND SAM DAVENPORT DISNEY 1962
BRIDGE OF EVIL Masterson, W.	TOUCH OF EVIL UN 1958
BROOK WILSON LTD. Ryan, J. M.	LOVING COL 1969

ORIGINAL TITLE	FILM TITLE
BUDDWING Hunter, E.	**WOMAN WITHOUT A FACE** MGM 1968

C

CALIFORNIO, THE MacLeod, R.	**100 RIFLES** FOX 1969
CANDLE FOR THE DEAD, A Marlowe, H.	**VIOLENT ENEMY, THE** MONARCH 1969
CHAUTUAQUA Keene, D. *and* Babcock, D.	**TROUBLE WITH GIRLS, THE** MGM 1969
CLAUDELLE Caldwell, E.	**YOUNG AND EAGER** WAR 1961
COINS IN THE FOUNTAIN Secondari, J. H.	**PLEASURE SEEKERS, THE** FOX 1965
COMMISSIONER, THE Dougherty, R.	**MADIGAN** UI 1968

D

DAY OF THE ARROW Loraine, P.	**EYE OF THE DEVIL** MGM 1968
DEPARTMENT K Howard, H.	**ASSIGNMENT 'K'** COL 1968
DEUX FRÈRES Dumas, A.	**CORSICAN BROTHERS, THE** MGM 1942
DICE OF GOD, THE Birney, H.	**GLORY GUYS** UA 1965
DISORIENTATED MAN, THE Saxon, P.	**SCREAM AND SCREAM AGAIN** AMERICAN INTERNATIONAL 1969

E

EH? (P) Livings, H.	**WORK IS A FOUR LETTER WORD** UI 1968
ELIMINATOR, THE York, A.	**DANGER ROUTE** UA 1968
EVENTS WHILST GUARDING THE **BOFORS GUN** (P) McGrath, J.	**BOFORS GUN, THE** UI 1968
EVIL OF THE DAY, THE Sterling, T.	**HONEY POT, THE** UA 1966

ORIGINAL TITLE	FILM TITLE
EXPENDABLE MAN, THE Hughes, D. B.	**HANGED MAN, THE** RANK 1964

F

FAREWELL, MY LOVELY Chandler, R.	**MURDER, MY SWEET** RKO 1944
FINNEGAN'S WAKE Joyce, J.	**PASSAGES FROM JAMES JOYCE'S FINNEGAN'S WAKE** CONTEMPORARY FILM 1969
FLOWERS FOR ALGERNON Keyes, D.	**CHARLY** CINERAMA 1968
FORBIDDEN GARDEN, THE Curtiss, U.	**WHATEVER HAPPENED TO AUNT ALICE** PALOMAR 1969
FRUIT OF THE POPPY Wilder, R.	**HEROIN GANG, THE** MGM 1968

G

GARDEN OF CUCUMBERS, A Tyler, P.	**FITZWOLLEY STRIKES AGAIN** UA 1968
GENERAL, THE Sillitoe, A.	**COUNTERPOINT** UI 1968
GENTLE BEN Morey, W.	**GENTLE GIANT** PAR 1968
GILLIGAN'S LAST ELEPHANT Hanley, G.	**LAST SAFARI, THE** PAR 1968
GIRL CALLED FATHOM, A Forrester, L.	**FATHOM** FOX 1968
GIRL CRAZY (P) Bolton, G. *and* McGowan, J.	**WHEN THE BOYS MEET THE GIRLS** MGM 1965
GOODBYE TO THE HILL Dunne, L.	**PADDY** FOX 1969
GREAT ADVENTURE Bennett, A.	**HOLY MATRIMONY** PAR 1943
GREEN HAT, THE Arlen, M.	**OUTCAST LADY** MGM 1935
GREEN HAT, THE Arlen, M.	**WOMAN OF THE WORLD** MGM 1935

H

HARP THAT ONCE, THE
Hall, P.

RECKONING, THE
COL 1969

HIGH COMMISSIONER, THE
Cleary, J.

NOBODY RUNS FOREVER
RANK 1968

HOME AND BEAUTY (P)
Maugham, W. S.

THREE FOR THE SHOW
COL 1934

HOME AND BEAUTY (P)
Maugham, W. S.

TOO MANY HUSBANDS
COL 1948

I

I AM LEGEND
Matheson, R.

LAST MAN ON EARTH, THE
GOLDEN ERA 1964

INTERNS, THE
Frede, R.

NEW INTERNS, THE
COL 1964

ISADORA DUNCAN
Stokes, S.

ISADORA
UI 1969

J

JEST OF GOD, A
Laurence, M.

RACHEL, RACHEL
WAR 1968

K

KESTREL FOR A KNAVE, A
Hines, B.

KES
UA 1969

L

LADIES IN RETIREMENT (P)
Denham, R. *and* Percy, E.

MAD ROOM, THE
COL 1968

**LADY IN THE CAR WITH GLASSES
AND A GUN, THE**
Japrisot, S.

LADY IN THE CAR, THE
COL 1969

**LAMENT FOR THE MOLLY
MAGUIRES**
Lewis, A. H.

MOLLY MAGUIRES, THE
PAR 1969

LAW OF THE GUN
Patten, L. B.

DEATH OF A GUNFIGHTER
UI 1969

LIFE OF DAVID HAGGART, THE
Haggart, D.

SINFUL DAVEY
UA 1969

505

LITTLE RASCAL
North, S.

RASCAL
DISNEY 1969

LITTLE SISTER, THE
Chandler, R.

MARLOWE
MGM 1969

LOVERS, THE (P)
Stevens, L.

WAR LORD, THE
RANK 1965

M

MALTESE FALCON, THE
Hammett, D.

SATAN MET A LADY
FIRST NATIONAL 1937

MASH
Hooker, R.

M.A.S.H.
FOX 1969

ME AND THE ARCH KOOK
PETULIA
Haase, J.

PETULIA
WAR 1968

MILK TRAIN DOESN'T STOP HERE
ANY MORE (P)
Williams, T.

BOOM
UI 1968

MILLSTONE, THE
Drabble, M.

TOUCH OF LOVE, A
BL 1969

MISS MARPLE
Christie, A.

MURDER AHOY
MGM 1964

MONKEY PLANET
Boulle, P.

PLANET OF THE APES
FOX 1968

MONKEYS, THE
Wilkinson, G. R.

MONKEYS, GO HOME
DISNEY 1967

MUTE WITNESS
Pike, R. L.

BULLITT
WAR 1968

MY BROTHER DEATH
Sulzberger, C. L.

TAKE ME WHILST I'M WARM
BORDER 1935

MY LIFE
Duncan, I.

ISADORA
UI 1969

N

NARROW MARGIN, THE
Wood, D. *and* Dempster, D.

BATTLE OF BRITAIN, THE
UA 1969

NIGHT SONG
Williams, J.

SWEET LOVE, BITTER
FILM 2 ASSOCIATES 1969

ORIGINAL TITLE	FILM TITLE
NORTH OF BUSHMAN'S ROCK Harding, G.	RIDE THE HIGH WIND BUTCHER 1965

O

OLIVER TWIST Dickens, C.	OLIVER COL 1968
ONE MAN'S SECRET Davis, S.	MAN IN THE SHADOW AA 1957
ONE SUNDAY AFTERNOON (P) Hagan, J.	STRAWBERRY BLONDE, THE WAR 1941
ORDEAL OF MAJOR GRIGSBY, THE Sherlock, J.	LAST GRENADE, THE CINERAMA 1969
OTTER'S STORY Liers, E.	FLASH, THE OTTER DISNEY 1968
OUTWARD BOUND (P) Vane, S.	BETWEEN TWO WORLDS WAR 1944

P

PRETTY POLLY BARTON Coward, N.	PRETTY POLLY RANK 1967

R

RAPE UPON RAPE (P) Fielding, H.	LOCK UP YOUR DAUGHTERS COL 1968
RASHOMON (P) Kanin, F. *and* Kanin, M.	OUTRAGE MGM 1964
RELAPSE, THE (P) Vanbrugh, *Sir* J.	LOCK UP YOUR DAUGHTERS COL 1968

S

SANCTUARY Faulkner, W.	STORY OF TEMPLE DRAKE, THE PAR 1933
SANDERS OF THE RIVER Wallace, E.	COAST OF SKELETONS BL 1964
SANDERS OF THE RIVER Wallace, E.	DEATH DRUMS ALONG THE RIVER Planet 1963
SHALL I EAT YOU NOW (P) Gebler, E.	HOFFMAN WAR 1969
SHE LET HIM CONTINUE Geller, S.	PRETTY POISON FOX 1968

SHUTTERED ROOM, THE Lovecraft, H. P.	**DUNWICH HORROR** AMERICAN INTERNATIONAL 1969
SNAKE WATER Williams, A.	**PINK JUNGLE, THE** UI 1968
SOUND OF MURDER, THE (P) Fairchild, W.	**LAST SHOT YOU HEAR, THE** FOX 1969
SOUTHERN STAR MYSTERY, THE Verne, J.	**SOUTHERN STAR, THE** COL 1969
SPARRERS CAN'T SING (P) Lewis, S.	**SPARROWS CAN'T SING** WAR 1962
SPY IN THE VODKA Thomas, R.	**COLD WAR SWAP, THE** PAR 1969
STERILE CUCKOO, THE Nichols, J.	**POOKIE** PAR 1969
SWEET AND PLENTY Piper, A.	**NICE GIRL LIKE ME, A** AVCO EMBASSY 1969

T

TABITHA (P) Ridley, A. *and* Borer, M. C.	**WHO KILLED THE CAT?** GN 1966
TAMING OF THE SHREW, THE (P) Shakespeare, W.	**KISS ME KATE** MGM 1953
THOUSAND PLAN, THE Barker, R.	**1,000 PLANE RAID, THE** UA 1968
TOP OF THE WORLD Ruesch, H.	**SAVAGE INNOCENTS, THE** RANK 1960
TRAGICAL HISTORY OF DOCTOR FAUSTUS, THE (P) Marlowe, C.	**DOCTOR FAUSTUS** COL 1968
TURQUOISE BIKINI, THE Resnik, M.	**HOW SWEET IT IS** WAR 1968
TYPISTS AND THE TIGER, THE (P) Schisgal, M.	**TIGER MAKES OUT, THE** COL 1968

U

UNCHARTED SEAS Wheatley, D.	**LOST CONTINENT, THE** WAR 1968

V

VISITORS, THE   SPIRIT IS WILLING, THE
Benchley, N.   PAR 1968

W

WAITING FOR A TIGER   TASTE OF EXCITEMENT
Healey, B.   MONARCH 1969

WHO RIDES WITH WYATT?   YOUNG BILLY YOUNG
Henry, W.   UA 1969

WILLIE BOY   TELL THEM WILLIE BOY IS HERE
Lawton, H.   RANK 1969

Y

YEAR OF THE HORSE, THE   HORSE IN THE GRAY FLANNEL
Hatch, E.   SUIT, THE
                                 DISNEY 1968

YEA, YEA, YEA   PRESS FOR TIME
McGill, A.   RANK 1966